W9-CGT-757

# World Economic Situation and Prospects 2016

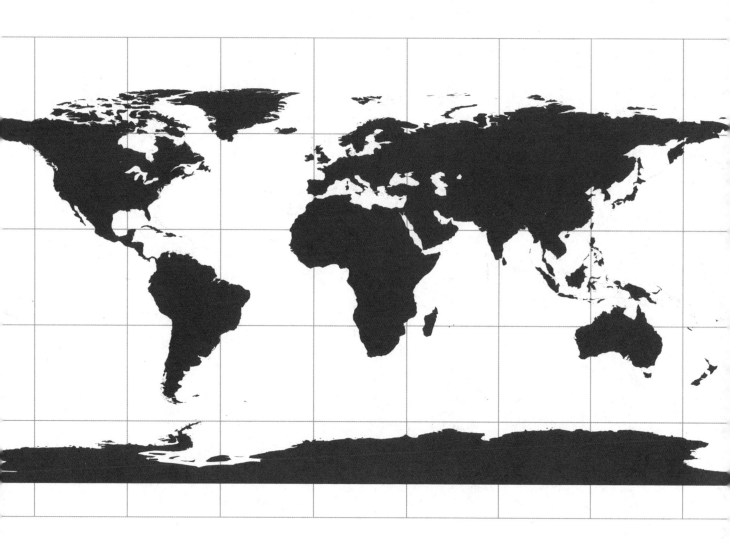

United Nations
New York, 2016

The report is a joint product of the United Nations Department of Economic and Social Affairs (UN/DESA), the United Nations Conference on Trade and Development (UNCTAD) and the five United Nations regional commissions (Economic Commission for Africa (ECA), Economic Commission for Europe (ECE), Economic Commission for Latin America and the Caribbean (ECLAC), Economic and Social Commission for Asia and the Pacific (ESCAP) and Economic and Social Commission for Western Asia (ESCWA)). The United Nations World Tourism Organization (UNWTO) also contributed to the report.

For further information, see http://www.un.org/en/development/desa/policy/wesp/index.shtml or contact:

**DESA**

Mr. Wu Hongbo, *Under-Secretary-General*

Department of Economic and Social Affairs
Room S-2922
United Nations
New York, NY 10017
USA

☎ +1-212-9635958
✉ wuh@un.org

**UNCTAD**

Dr. Mukhisa Kituyi, *Secretary-General*

United Nations Conference on Trade
    and Development
Room E-9042
Palais de Nations
1211 Geneva 10
Switzerland

☎ +41-22-9175806
✉ sgo@unctad.org

**ECA**

Dr. Carlos Lopes, *Executive Secretary*

United Nations Economic Commission for Africa
Menelik II Avenue
P.O. Box 3001
Addis Ababa
Ethiopia

☎ +251-11-5511231
✉ ecainfo@uneca.org

**ECE**

Mr. Christian Friis Bach, *Executive Secretary*

United Nations Economic Commission for Europe
Palais des Nations
CH-1211 Geneva 10
Switzerland

☎ +41-22-9174444
✉ info.ece@unece.org

**ECLAC**

Ms. Alicia Bárcena, *Executive Secretary*

Economic Commission for Latin America
    and the Caribbean
Av. Dag Hammarskjöld 3477
Vitacura
Santiago, Chile
Chile

☎ +56-2-22102000
✉ secepal@cepal.org

**ESCAP**

Dr. Shamshad Akhtar, *Executive Secretary*

Economic and Social Commission for Asia
    and the Pacific
United Nations Building
Rajadamnern Nok Avenue
Bangkok 10200
Thailand

☎ +66-2-2881234
✉ unescap@unescap.org

**ESCWA**

Ms. Rima Khalaf, *Executive Secretary*

Economic and Social Commission for Western Asia
P.O. Box 11-8575
Riad el-Solh Square, Beirut
Lebanon

☎ +961-1-981301
@ http://www.escwa.un.org/main/contact.asp

ISBN: 978-92-1-109172-4
eISBN: 978-92-1-057673-4

United Nations publication
Sales No. E.16.II.C.2

# Acknowledgements

The *World Economic Situation and Prospects 2016* is a joint product of the United Nations Department of Economic and Social Affairs (UN/DESA), the United Nations Conference on Trade and Development (UNCTAD) and the five United Nations regional commissions (Economic Commission for Africa (ECA), Economic Commission for Europe (ECE), Economic Commission for Latin America and the Caribbean (ECLAC), Economic and Social Commission for Asia and the Pacific (ESCAP) and Economic and Social Commission for Western Asia (ESCWA)). The United Nations World Tourism Organization (UNWTO) contributed to the report. The report also benefited from inputs received from the national centres of Project LINK and also from the deliberations in the Project LINK meeting held in New York on 21-23 October 2015. The forecasts presented in the report draw on the World Economic Forecasting Model (WEFM) of UN/DESA.

This publication was coordinated by Hamid Rashid, Chief, Global Economic Monitoring Unit, Development Policy and Analysis Division (DPAD), under the management of Pingfan Hong, Director, DPAD. Lenni Montiel, Assistant Secretary-General for Economic Development in UN/DESA provided general guidance.

The contributions of Grigor Agabekian, Hoi Wai Cheng, Yi Ho Chen, Anis Chowdhury, Peter Chowla, Ann D'Lima, Myriel Frische, Cordelia Gow, Tim Hilger, Dawn Holland, Jiayin Hu, Jasmine Hyman, Matthias Kempf, Leah C. Kennedy, Mary Lee Kortes, Alex Kucharski, Michael Lennard, Hung-Yi Li, Ingo Pitterle, Daniel Platz, Vladimir Popov, Hamid Rashid, Gerard F. Reyes, Ilka Ritter, Gabe Scelta, Benu Schneider, Oliver Schwank, Nancy Settecasi, Krishnan Sharma, Shari Spiegel, Alex Trepelkov, Willem Van Der Geest, Sebastian Vergara, Sergio P. Vieira, Jie Wei and Jinyang Zhang from **UN/DESA**; Bruno Antunes, Alfredo Calcagno, Pilar Fajarnes, Samuel Gayi, Ricardo Gottschalk, Mina Mashayekhi, Nicolas Maystre, Alessandro Nicita, Janvier Nkurunziza, Romain Perez, Edgardo Torija Zane and Komi Tsowou from **UNCTAD**; Yesuf Mohammednur Awel, Adam Elhiraika, Hopestone Chavula, Abbi Kedir, Heini Suominen from **ECA**; José Palacín from **ECE**; Esteban Perez Caldentey, Ramon Pineda and Daniel Titelman from **ECLAC**; Hamza Ali Malik, Shuvojit Banerjee, Daniel Jeongdae Lee, Oliver Paddison, Kiatkanid Pongpanich and Vatcharin Sirimaneetham from **ESCAP**; Mohamed El Moctar Mohamed El Hacene, Mohamed Hedi Bchir, Nathalie Khaled, Jose Antonio Pedrosa Garcia and Yasuhisa Yamamoto from **ESCWA**; Michel Julian, John Kester, and Javier Ruescas from **UNWTO** are duly acknowledged.

# Explanatory notes

The following symbols have been used in the tables throughout the report:

.. **Two dots** indicate that data are not available or are not separately reported.

– **A dash** indicates that the amount is nil or negligible.

. **A full stop** is used to indicate decimals.

- **A hyphen** indicates that the item is not applicable.

- **A minus** sign indicates deficit or decrease, except as indicated.

/ **A slash** between years indicates a crop year or financial year, for example, 2015/16.

– **Use of a hyphen between years**, for example, 2016–2017, signifies the full period involved, including the beginning and end years.

Reference to "dollars" ($) indicates United States dollars, unless otherwise stated.

Reference to "billions" indicates one thousand million.

Reference to "tons" indicates metric tons, unless otherwise stated.

**Annual rates** of growth or change, unless otherwise stated, refer to annual compound rates.

**Details and percentages** in tables do not necessarily add to totals, because of rounding.

**Project LINK** is an international collaborative research group for econometric modelling, coordinated jointly by the Development Policy and Analysis Division of UN/DESA and the University of Toronto.

For **country classifications**, see statistical annex.

**Data** presented in this publication incorporate information available as at **30 November 2015**.

The following abbreviations have been used:

| | |
|---|---|
| AAAA | Addis Ababa Action Agenda |
| ASEAN | Association of Southeast Asian Nations |
| BEPS | base erosion and profit sharing |
| BIS | Bank for International Settlements |
| bpd | barrels per day |
| BoJ | Bank of Japan |
| BRICS | Brazil, Russian Federation, India, China and South Africa |
| CIS | Commonwealth of Independent States |
| CFC | controlled foreign corporation |
| CPI | consumer price index |
| DBs | development banks |
| DFIs | development finance institutions |
| DFDQ | duty-free, quota-free market access |
| ECB | European Central Bank |
| EU | European Union |
| FDI | foreign direct investment |
| Fed | United States Federal Reserve |
| FSB | Financial Stability Board |
| G7 | Group of Seven |
| G20 | Group of Twenty |
| GATS | General Agreement on Trade in Services |
| GATT | General Agreement on Tariffs and Trade |
| GCC | Cooperation Council for the Arab States of the Gulf |
| GDP | gross domestic product |
| GVCs | global value chains |
| ICT | information and communication technology |
| IFF | illicit financial flows |
| ILO | International Labour Organization |
| IMF | International Monetary Fund |
| INDC | intended nationally determined contribution |
| LDCs | least developed countries |
| LME | London Metal Exchange |
| MDBs | multilateral development banks |
| MDGs | Millennium Development Goals |
| MFN | most favoured nation |

| | |
|---|---|
| MNEs | multinational enterprises |
| MOM | minerals, ores and metals |
| MTS | Multilateral Trade System |
| NAMA | non-agricultural market access |
| NDBs | national development banks |
| ODA | official development assistance |
| OECD | Organization for Economic Cooperation and Development |
| OPEC | Organization of the Petroleum Exporting Countries |
| pb | per barrel |
| QE | quantitative easing |
| REER | real effective exchange rate |
| RVCs | regional value chains |
| RTAs | regional trade agreements |
| SDGs | Sustainable Development Goals |
| SMEs | small and medium-sized enterprises |
| SOEs | State-owned enterprises |
| SWFs | sovereign wealth funds |
| TFA | Trade Facilitation Agreement |
| TISA | Trade in Services Agreement |
| TPP | Trans-Pacific Partnership Agreement |
| UN/DESA | Department of Economic and Social Affairs of the United Nations Secretariat |
| UN/ECA | United Nations Economic Commission for Africa |
| UN/ECE | United Nations Economic Commission for Europe |
| UN/ECLAC | United Nations Economic Commission for Latin America and the Caribbean |
| UN/ESCAP | United Nations Economic and Social Commission for Asia and the Pacific |
| UN/ESCWA | United Nations Economic and Social Commission for Western Asia |
| UNCTAD | United Nations Conference on Trade and Development |
| UNFCCC | United Nations Framework Convention on Climate Change |
| UNWTO | World Tourism Organization |
| WGP | world gross product |
| WTO | World Trade Organization |

# Executive summary

## Prospects for global macroeconomic development

### The world economy stumbled in 2015

The world gross product is projected to grow by a mere 2.4 per cent in 2015, a significant downward revision from the 2.8 per cent forecast in the *World Economic Situation and Prospects as of mid-2015*. More than seven years after the global financial crisis, policymakers around the world still face enormous challenges in stimulating investment and reviving global growth. The world economy has been held back by several major headwinds: persistent macroeconomic uncertainties and volatility; low commodity prices and declining trade flows; rising volatility in exchange rates and capital flows; stagnant investment and diminishing productivity growth; and a continued disconnect between finance and real sector activities. A modest improvement is expected to start next year, with global growth reaching 2.9 per cent and 3.2 per cent in 2016 and 2017, respectively. The anticipated timing and pace of normalization of the United States monetary policy stance is expected to reduce some policy uncertainties, while preventing excessive volatility in exchange rates and asset prices. While the normalization will eventually lead to higher borrowing costs, rising interest rates should encourage firms to increase investments in the short run. The improvement in global growth is also predicated on easing of downward pressures on commodity prices, which should encourage new investments and lift growth, particularly in commodity-dependent economies.

### The developed economies are expected to contribute more to global growth

Growth in developed economies is expected to continue gaining momentum in 2016, surpassing 2 per cent for the first time since 2010. In developing and transition economies, growth slowed in 2015 to its weakest pace since the global financial crisis amid sharply lower commodity prices, large capital outflows and increased financial market volatility. Growth is projected to reach 4.3 per cent in 2016 and 4.8 per cent in 2017, up from an estimated 3.8 per cent in 2015. Despite the slowdown in China, East and South Asia will remain the world's fastest-growing regions, with many of the region's commodity-importing economies benefiting from low prices for oil, metals and food. GDP growth in the least developed countries is expected to rebound from 4.5 per cent in 2015 to 5.6 per cent growth in 2016, but will fall short of the Sustainable Development Goal target of at least 7 per cent GDP growth per annum in the near term. While developing countries have been the locomotive of global growth since the financial crisis, the developed economies, particularly the United States of America, are expected to contribute more to global growth during the forecast period.

## Low inflation persists in developed economies, while volatility of inflation and growth remains high

Amid persistent output gaps, declining commodity prices and weak aggregate demand, global inflation is at its lowest level since 2009. In developed-market economies, annual inflation in 2015 is expected to average just 0.3 per cent. Ultra-loose monetary conditions have so far prevented deflation from becoming entrenched in the developed countries. However, low inflation has been associated with higher levels of volatility in inflation, growth, investment and consumption in a majority of large developed and developing countries and economies in transition. Significant currency depreciations have offset the disinflationary pressures in several developing economies. The Brazilian real and the Russian rouble have recorded large depreciations, and both countries remain mired in severe economic downturns, accompanied by elevated inflation.

## The economic slowdown hurts labour markets

Unemployment is on the rise in many developing and transition economies, especially in South America, while it remains stubbornly high in countries such as South Africa. At the same time, labour force participation rates, especially among women and youth, have been declining, and job insecurity has become more widespread, amid a shift from salaried work to self-employment. The declining employment intensity of growth in many countries, coupled with stagnant real wages, poses a challenge to promoting inclusive and sustainable economic growth, employment and decent work for all.

## Investment experienced sharp and broad-based deceleration

Growth rates of fixed capital formation have registered sharp declines in a majority of developed and developing economies since 2014, including negative investment growth in nine economies. The weak aggregate demand, falling commodity prices and persistent policy uncertainties constrained investment growth during 2014-2015. A modest pickup in investment is expected, provided commodity prices do not slide down further and the anticipated normalization of the United States monetary stance reduces policy uncertainties. However, coordinated efforts are still needed at national and international levels to ensure that financial sectors effectively intermediate savings and liquidity and also stimulate fixed investments.

## Reducing poverty and emission levels will require concerted policy efforts

The broad slowdown in economic growth in many developing economies and generally weak wage growth will restrain progress in poverty reduction in the near term. Further progress in poverty reduction will rely heavily on policies to reduce inequality, such as investment in education, health and infrastructure, and stronger social safety nets. Global energy-related carbon emissions experienced no growth in 2014 for the first time in 20 years, with the exception of 2009 when the global economy contracted, suggesting that a delinking of economic growth and carbon emission growth is possible with appropriate policies and adequate investment. Low-carbon energy sources now account for over 50 per cent of new energy consumption worldwide.

# International trade and financial flows

## The commodity price decline has had significant adverse effects on trade flows and public finance

The terms-of-trade of commodity exporters have deteriorated significantly, limiting their ability to demand goods and services from the rest of the world. Current-account balances of commodity exporters have deteriorated, and given the net outflow of capital from many commodity-dependent economies, countries have been forced to either draw down international reserves or cut back imports. This has had second order effects on trade in non-commodity-exporting economies, compounding longer-term trends, such as the slower expansion of global value chains and limited progress in multilateral trade negotiations, which weigh on the volume of global trade. The commodity price declines and exchange-rate realignments have also had a significant impact on fiscal balances, particularly in the commodity-dependent developing and transition economies. The sharp decline in the headline value of global trade, however, is largely attributable to the deterioration of commodity prices and appreciation of the dollar. Trade volumes have recorded a more moderate deceleration, reflecting a widening divergence between the value and volume of global trade.

## Financial market volatility has increased significantly

The steady decline in global commodity prices, including a dramatic drop in the oil price, reflects a combination of ample supply and slowing demand. Demand from China plays a key role in price swings for metals, in particular, as the country accounts for almost half of global metal consumption. The combination of commodity price adjustments and capital outflows has been associated with sharp exchange-rate realignments and heightened volatility in foreign-exchange markets.

## Strengthening the multilateral trading system will allow countries to better exploit the benefits of trade

International trade is an important determinant of global growth and development. At the global level, there remains considerable untapped potential to exploit the benefits of international trade. A universal, non-discriminatory multilateral trading system is a central element for harvesting this potential. However, the Doha Round has made limited progress in the last fifteen years. At the same time, there has been an increasing prevalence of new-generation regional trade agreements (RTAs). Mega-RTAs can diminish incentives for universal negotiations, and may have adverse effects on countries not included in the RTA, especially developing countries. The Trans-Pacific Partnership (TPP) is the first mega-RTA completed, and creates a market of 800 million people with over 40 per cent of the world gross product. Non-TPP members, however, may be impacted by diversion of trade and investment towards TPP member countries. This highlights the importance of enhancing coherence between RTAs and the multilateral trading system so they can support and sustain an enabling development environment.

## Finance for sustainable development

### Addis Ababa Action Agenda establishes a financing framework for the 2030 Agenda for Sustainable Development

A primary role of the international financial system is to channel savings to productive uses and investment in order to deliver sustainable economic growth. As such, it critically underpins the implementation of the 2030 Agenda for Sustainable Development. While the financing requirements to achieve the sustainable development agenda are extremely large, global public and private savings would be sufficient if the financial system were to effectively intermediate flows in line with sustainable development objectives. However, international finance is currently neither stable nor efficient in allocating credit where it is needed for sustained and inclusive growth, and credit is generally not channelled with social outcomes or environmental sustainability in mind. The Addis Ababa Action Agenda (AAAA) establishes a new global framework for financing sustainable development that aligns all financing flows and international and domestic policies with economic, social and environmental priorities.

### Achieving the 2030 Agenda for Sustainable Development will put significant demands on public budgets and capacities in developing countries

The mobilization and effective use of public resources will remain critical for achieving sustainable development. This will require additional and more effective international public finance, including official development assistance (ODA), South-South cooperation and other official flows. To supplement existing public funds, there is also an important role for multilateral, regional and national development banks, especially as private resources are currently not being effectively channelled in this direction. Tax evasion, tax avoidance and illicit financial flows have become a major difficulty in efficient resource mobilization. This can be improved by increased efforts towards international tax cooperation.

All stakeholders need to contribute and remain accountable for their commitments, including Member States, the private sector, civil society and other actors, in implementing the AAAA for sustainable development. The role of the annual Financing for Development Forum—the dedicated follow-up process for monitoring the implementation of the AAAA—will be crucial.

## Policy challenges and the way forward

### Policymakers need to prepare for a tightening of global financial conditions

In developed economies, central banks shouldered most of the responsibility for supporting growth during the post-crisis period, which has led to an unprecedented level of monetary accommodation in recent years. As the economic conditions in the United States have improved, the United States Federal Reserve has clearly signalled its intention to begin raising the policy rate, after seven years of near-zero interest rates. This is likely to reduce policy uncertainties on the one hand, although the pace and sequence of anticipated interest rate increases remain unknown. On the other hand, the increase in the policy rate is expected to have significant spillovers, exacerbate capital outflows from developing countries, and tighten financial conditions worldwide.

## Policy challenges are likely to intensify in the short run

Policymakers worldwide will need to make concerted efforts to reduce uncertainty and financial volatility, striking a delicate balance between their objectives for achieving sustainable economic growth and maintaining financial stability. The response to a tightening of global financial conditions will require a variety of policy tools, including macroprudential instruments, targeted monetary measures and a more accommodative fiscal stance. The challenge for developing countries is likely to be more acute, given that corporate debt in these economies—often denominated in the United States dollar—has risen sharply since the global financial crisis. These economies are thus left exposed to exchange-rate risk and rising debt-servicing costs as global financial conditions tighten. Policymakers will need to increasingly rely on macroprudential tools to prevent rapid deleveraging, redirect finance to real sector activities, and minimize financial stability risks.

## More targeted, effective and coordinated policy efforts are needed to ensure inclusive and sustainable economic growth

Stimulating inclusive growth in the near term and fostering long-term sustainable development require more effective policy coordination at the national, regional and global levels. It will be critical for policymakers to ensure that the financial sector facilitates and stimulates long-term, productive investment, breaking the vicious cycle of weak aggregate demand, under-investment, low productivity and the below-potential growth performance of the world economy. While reducing excessive reliance on monetary policy measures, policymakers will need to increasingly undertake targeted fiscal measures to stimulate aggregate demand, investment and growth. Well-designed and targeted labour market strategies can complement fiscal policies to reinvigorate productivity, employment generation and output growth. Coordinated policy efforts in economic, social and environmental dimensions will be crucial for realizing the 2030 Agenda for Sustainable Development.

# Table of contents

Acknowledgements . . . . . . . . . . . . . . . . . . . . . . . . . . . . . . . . . . . . . . . . . . . . . . . . iii

Explanatory notes . . . . . . . . . . . . . . . . . . . . . . . . . . . . . . . . . . . . . . . . . . . . . . . . iv

Executive summary . . . . . . . . . . . . . . . . . . . . . . . . . . . . . . . . . . . . . . . . . . . . . . . v

Chapter I

**Global economic outlook** . . . . . . . . . . . . . . . . . . . . . . . . . . . . . . . . . . . . . . . . 1

Prospects for the world economy in 2016–2017 . . . . . . . . . . . . . . . . . . . . . . . 1

    Global growth stumbles . . . . . . . . . . . . . . . . . . . . . . . . . . . . . . . . . . . . . . . 1

    Inflation remains benign . . . . . . . . . . . . . . . . . . . . . . . . . . . . . . . . . . . . . . 5

    Unemployment challenges persist . . . . . . . . . . . . . . . . . . . . . . . . . . . . . . 6

    Headwinds impede global growth . . . . . . . . . . . . . . . . . . . . . . . . . . . . . . 8

Persistent macroeconomic uncertainties and volatility . . . . . . . . . . . . . . . . . . 9

    Uncertainty shocks persist . . . . . . . . . . . . . . . . . . . . . . . . . . . . . . . . . . . . 9

Low commodity prices and declining trade flows . . . . . . . . . . . . . . . . . . . . . . 14

    Commodity prices have registered sharp declines. . . . . . . . . . . . . . . . . . 14

Rising volatility in exchange rates and capital flows . . . . . . . . . . . . . . . . . . . 16

    Large swings in exchange rates. . . . . . . . . . . . . . . . . . . . . . . . . . . . . . . . . 16

    Capital inflows to emerging economies decline sharply . . . . . . . . . . . . . 18

Stagnant investment and diminishing
productivity growth . . . . . . . . . . . . . . . . . . . . . . . . . . . . . . . . . . . . . . . . . . . . 19

    Diminishing productivity growth . . . . . . . . . . . . . . . . . . . . . . . . . . . . . . 19

Continued disconnect between finance
and real sector activities . . . . . . . . . . . . . . . . . . . . . . . . . . . . . . . . . . . . . . . . 23

Economic growth, poverty and carbon emissions . . . . . . . . . . . . . . . . . . . . . . 24

    Growth and poverty reduction. . . . . . . . . . . . . . . . . . . . . . . . . . . . . . . . . 26

    Growth and environmental sustainability . . . . . . . . . . . . . . . . . . . . . . . . 28

Policy stances, challenges and the way forward . . . . . . . . . . . . . . . . . . . . . . . 31

    Monetary policy. . . . . . . . . . . . . . . . . . . . . . . . . . . . . . . . . . . . . . . . . . . . 31

    Fiscal policy . . . . . . . . . . . . . . . . . . . . . . . . . . . . . . . . . . . . . . . . . . . . . . 33

    Vulnerabilities in developing economies increase . . . . . . . . . . . . . . . . . 36

    Geopolitical risks cloud regional economic prospects. . . . . . . . . . . . . . . 37

    Policy challenges are expected to intensify . . . . . . . . . . . . . . . . . . . . . . . 38

    Sustainable development will require more
        sustained policy coordination . . . . . . . . . . . . . . . . . . . . . . . . . . . . . 40

Appendix . . . . . . . . . . . . . . . . . . . . . . . . . . . . . . . . . . . . . . . . . . . . . . . . . . . . . . 43

  Baseline forecast assumptions . . . . . . . . . . . . . . . . . . . . . . . . . . . . . . . . . . . 43

    Monetary policy. . . . . . . . . . . . . . . . . . . . . . . . . . . . . . . . . . . . . . . . . . . . 43

    Fiscal policy . . . . . . . . . . . . . . . . . . . . . . . . . . . . . . . . . . . . . . . . . . . . . . 44

    Exchange rates among major currencies . . . . . . . . . . . . . . . . . . . . . . . . 45

    Oil price. . . . . . . . . . . . . . . . . . . . . . . . . . . . . . . . . . . . . . . . . . . . . . . . . . 46

    Forecast sensitivities to key assumptions. . . . . . . . . . . . . . . . . . . . . . . . . 46

*Page*

**Chapter II**
# International trade...........................................  49
**Trade flows** ..............................................  49
    Regional trends ........................................  54
    Decomposition analysis .................................  55
    Trade in services.......................................  56
**Primary commodity markets** ...............................  60
    Food and agricultural commodities .......................  62
    Minerals, ores and metals...............................  64
    Oil market prices .....................................  65
**Trade policy developments** ................................  67
    Multilateral trade negotiations ...........................  67
    Regional trade agreements .............................  73
    Future direction ......................................  76
**Appendix**.................................................  79
    **Measuring the commodity terms-of-trade effect of the commodity price drop**....  79

**Chapter III**
# International finance for sustainable development..................  81
**Trends in net resource transfers** ...........................  82
    Highly volatile private capital flows .......................  83
    Capital flows and long-term economic growth...............  86
    Pitfalls of short-term capital flows .......................  90
    Remittance flows: rising, but different ....................  91
    Global imbalances and international reserves accumulation ...............  93
**International financial stability and growth** ..................  95
    The financial sector: stability, financial depth, and access................  95
    Debt and debt sustainability ............................  98
**International cooperation and public resources for sustainable development** .......  103
    International tax cooperation and illicit capital flows ...................  103
    International public finance .............................  108
    Multilateral, regional and national development banks ...................  110
    Global architecture....................................  113

**Chapter IV**
# Regional developments and outlook...........................  117
**Developed economies** .....................................  117
    North America........................................  117
    Developed Asia and the Pacific...........................  119
    Europe ..............................................  121
**Economies in transition** ..................................  125
    South-Eastern Europe: growth recovers, but fragilities persist ..............  125
    The Commonwealth of Independent States:
        economic downturn and uncertain prospects ....................  126

*Page*

**Developing economies** . . . . . . . . . . . . . . . . . . . . . . . . . . . . . . . . . . . . . . 130

   Africa: domestic demand drives accelerating growth . . . . . . . . . . . . . . . . . . . . . 131

   East Asia: despite a weaker-than-expected performance,
      the region drives global growth. . . . . . . . . . . . . . . . . . . . . . . . . . . . . . . 135

   South Asia: growth expected to strengthen, driven by
      private consumption and investment . . . . . . . . . . . . . . . . . . . . . . . . . . . 139

   Western Asia: along with military conflicts, low oil prices weigh
      on regional GDP growth . . . . . . . . . . . . . . . . . . . . . . . . . . . . . . . . . . 144

   Latin America and the Caribbean: on a "two-track" growth path . . . . . . . . . . . 148

## Boxes

I.1    Prospects for the least developed countries . . . . . . . . . . . . . . . . . . . . . . . . 3

II.1   The current commodity price slump, terms-of-trade effects and government
         finances in commodity-dependent developing countries. . . . . . . . . . . . . . 52

II.2   Trends in international tourism . . . . . . . . . . . . . . . . . . . . . . . . . . . . . . 58

II.3   Agriculture negotiations, food security and sustainable development . . . . . 69

II.4   Sanitary and phytosanitary measures and trade distortions. . . . . . . . . . . . 75

III.1   The Addis Ababa Action Agenda . . . . . . . . . . . . . . . . . . . . . . . . . . . . 82

III.2   The "financial account", the "capital account" and twin surpluses . . . . . . . 87

III.3   Development finance in a changing climate . . . . . . . . . . . . . . . . . . . . . . 99

III.4   Data and the Addis Ababa Action Agenda . . . . . . . . . . . . . . . . . . . . . . 114

IV.1   A preliminary assessment of the macroeconomic impact of the influx of
         refugees and migrants in Germany . . . . . . . . . . . . . . . . . . . . . . . . . . . 123

IV.2   Financial dollarization in the Commonwealth of Independent States . . . . . 128

IV.3   Africa's resource exports and product imports: the untapped potential
         of value-added production . . . . . . . . . . . . . . . . . . . . . . . . . . . . . . . . . 134

IV.4   The potential impact of monetary policy normalization in the United
         States on Asia and the Pacific . . . . . . . . . . . . . . . . . . . . . . . . . . . . . . . 140

IV.5   The impact of the current oil-price shock on public finances for oil-
         exporting countries in Western Asia. . . . . . . . . . . . . . . . . . . . . . . . . . . 145

IV.6   Commodity price volatility and its impacts on Latin American and
         Caribbean economies . . . . . . . . . . . . . . . . . . . . . . . . . . . . . . . . . . . . 151

## Figures

I.1    Growth of world gross product and gross domestic product by country
       grouping, 2007–2017 . . . . . . . . . . . . . . . . . . . . . . . . . . . . . . . . . . . . . 1

I.1.1   Commodity exports as a share of GDP and share
       of the top commodity group in total commodity exports
       for the LDCs, 2014. . . . . . . . . . . . . . . . . . . . . . . . . . . . . . . . . . . . . . . 4

I.2    Contribution to global growth, 2007–2017 . . . . . . . . . . . . . . . . . . . . . . 5

I.3    Global consumer price inflation, 2006-2017 . . . . . . . . . . . . . . . . . . . . . . 6

I.4    Global employment gap, 1999–2019. . . . . . . . . . . . . . . . . . . . . . . . . . . 7

I.5    Total unemployment by regions, 2007–2019 . . . . . . . . . . . . . . . . . . . . . 7

*Page*

I.6 Excess reserves of financial institutions held with the United States Federal Reserve............................................. 11

I.7 Volatility and growth in developed economies, 2010 Q1–2015 Q2....... 13

I.8 Volatility and growth in developing economies and economies in transition, 2010 Q1–2015 Q2.................................. 13

I.9 Regional contributions to world import growth .................... 15

I.10 Price indices of selected groups of commodities, August 2013–September 2015 ............................... 15

I.11 Exchange rates of selected emerging-market currencies vis-à-vis the United States dollar, 1 September 2014–23 November 2015 ........ 16

I.12 Real effective exchange-rate volatility, January 1996–September 2015 .... 17

I.13a Developed countries' fixed investment growth: before and after the crisis . 20

I.13b Selected other countries' fixed investment growth: before and after the crisis .................................... 20

I.14a Growth accounting at the global level, 2009–2014 and 2002–2007 ..... 22

I.14b Growth accounting for developed economies, 2009–2014 and 2002–2007 22

I.15 The stock of financial assets, 2002–2013 ........................ 24

I.16 Financial sector deleveraging, 2008 Q2–2008 Q4 .................. 25

I.17 Financial sector deleveraging of securities and net contraction in GDP growth, 2008 Q2–2008 Q4.................................. 25

I.18 Relationship between poverty headcount ratio and income growth ...... 27

I.19 Emission levels and renewable energy investments .................. 30

I.20 Ten-year government bond yields in selected developed economies, October 2005–October 2015 ................................. 31

I.21 Central bank policy rates in the BRICS, October 2011–October 2015.... 32

I.22 Net external asset positions as a percentage of world gross product, 2003–2017................................................ 34

I.23 Euro area current-account balance (CAB)......................... 35

I.24 Share of exports to China ...................................... 36

I.A.1 Key policy rates.............................................. 44

I.A.2 Total assets of major central banks, December 2006–December 2017 .... 44

I.A.3 Data and assumptions on major currency exchange rates .............. 45

I.A.4 Impact of a 1 percentage point rise in United States interest rates........ 46

I.A.5 Impact of a 1 per cent of GDP increase in United States government spending ......................................... 46

I.A.6 Impact of a 5 per cent depreciation of the euro/$ rate................. 47

I.A.7 Impact of a 10 per cent rise in the oil price ....................... 47

II.1 Growth of world trade and world gross product, 2007-2017........... 49

II.2 Regional contribution to global import growth, 2011–2017 ........... 50

II.3 China's imports of selected commodities, 2014 Q1–2015 Q3 ........... 51

II.1.1 Commodity export and import price decline, April 2011–August 2015 ... 53

*Page*

II.4 World trade prices, 2006 Q1–2015 Q2 ........................... 56

II.5 Manufactured goods export price and dollar exchange rate,
2006 Q1–2015 Q1.......................................... 56

II.6 Regional shares of exports to developing and developed countries,
1995–2014 ............................................... 57

II.7 Services exports by level of development and region, 2008–2014 ........ 57

II.2.1 Countries with largest surplus on the travel balance, 2014 ............ 59

II.8 Developing economies' share in world services exports by sector,
2005 and 2014 ........................................... 60

II.9 UNCTAD non-oil commodity price index,
January 2009–September 2015 ............................... 61

II.10 Average monthly price change for selected commodities,
January 2015–September 2015 ............................... 61

II.11 Price indices of selected food and agricultural commodity groups,
January 2009–September 2015............................... 63

II.12 Price indices of selected minerals, ores and metals,
January 2009–September 2015............................... 64

II.13 Monthly Brent crude oil price average, January 1984–September 2015 ... 66

II.3.1 Food dependency index by region and development level, 2014 ......... 70

II.4.1 Exports and export loss to the European Union ..................... 76

II.A.1 Commodity export and import price decline, scaled by GDP share of
commodity export and import, April 2011–August 2015 ............. 80

III.1 Net transfer of resources to developing economies and economies in
transition, 2003–2015...................................... 83

III.2 Net financial flows to developing countries and economies in transition,
2005–2015 ............................................... 85

III.3 Year-end foreign-exchange reserves, including gold, in BRICS countries .. 86

III.2.1 Average current-account balance and capital flows, large developing
countries, 2000–2014....................................... 87

III.2.2 Current-account balance and capital flows, selected countries .......... 88

III.4 Average annual growth rates of GDP per capita and average
current-account balance, 1970–2007 ........................... 88

III.5 Portfolio flows by non-residents, selected countries, 2013 Q1–2015 Q2 ... 89

III.6 Total migrant stocks and global remittance inflows, 1990–2014 ........ 91

III.7 Selected countries' remittance inflows, 2014....................... 92

III.8 Current-account balances and remittance inflows in
selected countries, 2014 .................................... 93

III.9 Foreign-exchange reserves as a percentage of world gross product,
1980–2014 ............................................... 94

III.10 Global project finance by funding institution,
January 2012–January 2013 ................................. 96

III.11 Financial depth vs. financial access by small firms, most recent year...... 97

III.12 Global stock of debt outstanding ............................... 98
III.13 Global debt securities market, 2001–2014 ........................ 100
III.14 Emerging-market corporate debt, 2003–2014...................... 101
III.15 External debt of developing countries, 2000–2014 ................. 102
III.16 Illustrative timeline for exchange of country-by-country reports ........ 105
III.17 ODA with domestic revenue mobilization (DRM) as the core aim, 2006–2013........................................... 108
III.18 Annual disbursements of selected regional and national development banks, 2000–2014 ........................................ 111
III.19 Multilateral development bank financing, 2000–2014 ............... 112
IV.1 United States unemployment rate and wage inflation, January 1990–October 2015 .................................. 119
IV.2 Key monthly indicators for Japan, January 2010–September 2015 ....... 120
IV.3 Share of exports to the Russian Federation in total exports of goods and services, 2012.................................... 122
IV.2.1 Foreign-currency deposits and total deposits in the CIS, as of end-2014... 128
IV.2.2 Remittances and foreign-currency deposits in the CIS, as of end-2014.... 129
IV.2.3 Shares of foreign-currency deposits and loans in the CIS, 2015 ......... 130
IV.4 Africa: average budget balance as a share of GDP by subregion, 2012–2016 ........................................... 132
IV.5 Africa's exports to China, 2000–2014.......................... 133
IV.6 East Asia: contributions of expenditure components to real GDP growth, January 2014–June 2015................................. 136
IV.7 East Asia: selected vulnerability indicators ....................... 138
IV.8 South Asia: annual GDP growth and consumer price inflation rates, 2010–2017 ........................................... 143
IV.9 GDP growth by economy groups in Western Asia, 2014–2017.......... 144
IV.5.1 Western Asia: budget balance for selected oil-exporting countries, 2012–2016 ........................................... 145
IV.5.2 Top 10 countries in the world with the highest fossil-fuel subsidy per capita, 2013 ......................................... 146
IV.10 Latin America and the Caribbean: GDP growth rates, 2010–2016....... 149
IV.6.1 Average quarterly growth of commodity indices, selected periods between 2000 Q1 and 2015 Q3 ............................. 152
IV.6.2 Share of statistically significant correlations between commodity indices and equity indices (returns and volatilities), 1991–2000, 2001–2007 and 2010–2015........................................ 152
IV.6.3 Latin America (seven countries): average annual rate of investment growth in real terms, 1991–2014 .......................... 153

## Tables

I.1 Growth of world output, 2013–2017............................. 2
I.2 Key macroeconomic volatilities before and after the crisis............. 10
I.3 Growth of labour productivity, before and after the crisis.............. 21
I.4 Global debt securities outstanding ............................. 23

III.1    Net financial flows to developing countries and economies in transition, 2006–2015 . . . . . . . . . . . . . . . . . . . . . . . . . . . . . . . . . . . . . .    84

IV.1.1    Estimated macroeconomic impact of the influx of refugees and migrants in Germany . . . . . . . . . . . . . . . . . . . . . . . . . . . . . . . . . . . .    124

**Statistical annex**

## Country classifications

**Data sources, country classifications and aggregation methodology** . . . . . . . . . . . . . .    157

**Tables**

A.    Developed economies . . . . . . . . . . . . . . . . . . . . . . . . . . . . . . . . . . .    159

B.    Economies in transition . . . . . . . . . . . . . . . . . . . . . . . . . . . . . . . . .    160

C.    Developing economies by region . . . . . . . . . . . . . . . . . . . . . . . . . . . .    160

D.    Fuel-exporting countries . . . . . . . . . . . . . . . . . . . . . . . . . . . . . . . . .    161

E.    Economies by per capita GNI in 2014 . . . . . . . . . . . . . . . . . . . . . . . .    162

F.    Least developed countries (as of November 2015) . . . . . . . . . . . . . . . . . .    163

G.    Heavily indebted poor countries (as of September 2015) . . . . . . . . . . . . . .    163

H.    Small island developing States . . . . . . . . . . . . . . . . . . . . . . . . . . . . . .    164

I.    Landlocked developing countries . . . . . . . . . . . . . . . . . . . . . . . . . . . .    164

J.    International Organization for Standardization Country Codes . . . . . . . . .    165

## Annex tables

A.1    Developed economies: rates of growth of real GDP, 2007–2017 . . . . . . . .    169

A.2    Economies in transition: rates of growth of real GDP, 2007–2017 . . . . . . .    170

A.3    Developing economies: rates of growth of real GDP, 2007–2017 . . . . . . . .    171

A.4    Developed economies: consumer price inflation, 2007–2017 . . . . . . . . . .    173

A.5    Economies in transition: consumer price inflation, 2007–2017 . . . . . . . . .    174

A.6    Developing economies: consumer price inflation, 2007–2017 . . . . . . . . . .    175

A.7    Developed economies: unemployment rates, 2007–2017 . . . . . . . . . . . . .    177

A.8    Economies in transition and developing economies: unemployment rates, 2006–2015 . . . . . . . . . . . . . . . . . . . . . . . . . . . . . . . . . . . . . . . . .    178

A.9    Major developed economies: quarterly indicators of growth, unemployment and inflation, 2013–2015 . . . . . . . . . . . . . . . . . . . . . .    180

A.10    Selected economies in transition: quarterly indicators of growth and inflation, 2013–2015 . . . . . . . . . . . . . . . . . . . . . . . . . . . . . . . . . . .    181

A.11    Major developing economies: quarterly indicators of growth, unemployment and inflation, 2013–2015 . . . . . . . . . . . . . . . . . . . . . .    182

A.12    Major developed economies: financial indicators, 2006–2015 . . . . . . . . . .    184

A.13    Selected economies: real effective exchange rates, broad measurement, 2006–2015 . . . . . . . . . . . . . . . . . . . . . . . . . . . . . . . . . . . . . . . . .    185

A.14    Indices of prices of primary commodities, 2006–2015 . . . . . . . . . . . . . .    187

A.15    World oil supply and demand, 2007–2016 . . . . . . . . . . . . . . . . . . . . . .    188

A.16    World trade: changes in value and volume of exports and imports, by major country group, 2007–2017 . . . . . . . . . . . . . . . . . . . . . . . . . . . . . . . .    189

A.17    Balance of payments on current accounts, by country or country group,
        summary table, 2006–2014 .................................... 191

A.18    Balance of payments on current accounts, by country or country group,
        2006–2014 ................................................ 192

A.19    Net ODA from major sources, by type, 1993–2014 .................. 195

A.20    Total net ODA flows from OECD Development Assistance Committee
        countries, by type, 2005–2014 ................................ 196

A.21    Commitments and net flows of financial resources, by selected multilateral
        institutions, 2005–2014 ..................................... 197

**Bibliography** ...................................................... 199

# Chapter I
# Global economic outlook

## Prospects for the world economy in 2016–2017

### Global growth stumbles

The world economy stumbled in 2015, amid weak aggregate demand, falling commodity prices and increasing financial market volatility in major economies. The world gross product is projected to grow by a mere 2.4 per cent in 2015 (figure I.1 and table I.1), marking a downward revision from the 2.8 per cent forecast in the *World Economic Situation and Prospects as of mid-2015* (United Nations, 2015a). The growth rates of gross fixed capital formation and aggregate demand continue to remain subdued. The world economy is projected to grow by 2.9 per cent in 2016 and 3.2 per cent in 2017, supported by generally less restrictive fiscal and still accommodative monetary stances worldwide. The anticipated timing and pace of normalization of the United States monetary policy stance is expected to reduce policy uncertainties, while preventing excessive volatility in exchange rates and asset prices. While the normalization will eventually lead to higher borrowing costs, rising interest rates should encourage firms to front-load investments in the short run. The improvement in global growth is also predicated on easing of downward pressures on commodity prices, which should encourage new investments and lift growth, particularly in commodity-dependent economies.[1]

Figure I.1
**Growth of world gross product and gross domestic product by country grouping, 2007–2017**

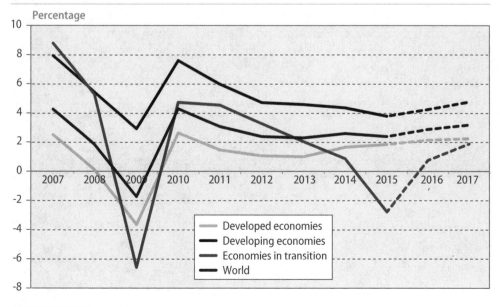

Source: UN/DESA.
Note: Data for 2015 are estimated; data for 2016 and 2017 are forecast.

---

1    The key assumptions underlying this outlook are detailed in the appendix to this chapter.

Table I.1
**Growth of world output, 2013–2017**

| Annual percentage change | 2013 | 2014 | 2015[a] | 2016[b] | 2017[b] | Change from WESP as of mid-2015 | |
|---|---|---|---|---|---|---|---|
| | | | | | | 2015 | 2016 |
| World | 2.3 | 2.6 | 2.4 | 2.9 | 3.2 | -0.4 | -0.2 |
| Developed economies | 1.0 | 1.7 | 1.9 | 2.2 | 2.3 | -0.3 | 0.0 |
| United States of America | 1.5 | 2.4 | 2.4 | 2.6 | 2.8 | -0.4 | -0.1 |
| Japan | 1.6 | -0.1 | 0.5 | 1.3 | 0.6 | -0.7 | 0.3 |
| European Union | 0.2 | 1.4 | 1.9 | 2.0 | 2.2 | 0.0 | -0.1 |
| EU-15 | 0.1 | 1.2 | 1.8 | 2.0 | 2.1 | 0.0 | 0.0 |
| New EU members | 1.2 | 2.7 | 3.2 | 3.0 | 3.2 | 0.4 | -0.2 |
| Euro area | -0.3 | 0.9 | 1.6 | 1.9 | 2.0 | 0.0 | 0.0 |
| Other European countries | 1.5 | 2.0 | 1.2 | 1.4 | 2.0 | 0.7 | 0.1 |
| Economies in transition | 2.1 | 0.9 | -2.8 | 0.8 | 1.9 | -0.8 | -0.1 |
| South-Eastern Europe | 2.4 | 0.2 | 2.1 | 2.6 | 3.0 | 0.7 | 0.1 |
| Commonwealth of Independent States and Georgia | 2.0 | 0.9 | -3.0 | 0.7 | 1.8 | -0.9 | -0.2 |
| Russian Federation | 1.3 | 0.6 | -3.8 | 0.0 | 1.2 | -0.8 | -0.1 |
| Developing economies | 4.6 | 4.3 | 3.8 | 4.3 | 4.8 | -0.6 | -0.5 |
| Africa | 3.3 | 3.4 | 3.7 | 4.4 | 4.4 | -0.3 | -0.4 |
| North Africa | 1.1 | 0.7 | 3.5 | 4.1 | 4.1 | 0.7 | 0.1 |
| East Africa | 6.9 | 7.0 | 6.2 | 6.8 | 6.6 | -0.4 | 0.1 |
| Central Africa | 0.9 | 3.7 | 3.4 | 4.3 | 4.2 | 0.0 | 0.0 |
| West Africa | 5.7 | 6.1 | 4.4 | 5.2 | 5.3 | -1.4 | -1.0 |
| Southern Africa | 3.1 | 2.5 | 2.5 | 3.0 | 3.3 | -0.4 | -0.7 |
| East and South Asia | 6.1 | 6.1 | 5.7 | 5.8 | 5.8 | -0.5 | -0.3 |
| East Asia | 6.4 | 6.1 | 5.6 | 5.6 | 5.6 | -0.4 | -0.4 |
| China | 7.7 | 7.3 | 6.8 | 6.4 | 6.5 | -0.2 | -0.4 |
| South Asia | 4.9 | 6.4 | 6.0 | 6.7 | 7.0 | -0.7 | -0.2 |
| India | 6.5 | 7.2 | 7.2 | 7.3 | 7.5 | -0.4 | -0.4 |
| Western Asia | 2.0 | 2.6 | 2.0 | 2.4 | 3.0 | -1.0 | -1.2 |
| Latin America and the Caribbean | 2.8 | 1.0 | -0.5 | 0.7 | 2.7 | -1.0 | -1.0 |
| South America | 3.1 | 0.5 | -1.6 | -0.1 | 2.4 | -1.2 | -1.2 |
| Brazil | 2.5 | 0.1 | -2.8 | -0.8 | 2.3 | -1.7 | -1.3 |
| Mexico and Central America | 1.7 | 2.5 | 2.5 | 2.9 | 3.4 | -0.5 | -0.3 |
| Caribbean | 3.1 | 3.3 | 3.4 | 3.6 | 3.3 | 0.3 | -0.1 |
| Least developed countries | 5.1 | 5.6 | 4.5 | 5.6 | 5.6 | -0.4 | 0.0 |
| *Memorandum items* | | | | | | | |
| World trade[c] | 3.1 | 3.3 | 2.7 | 4.0 | 4.7 | -1.1 | -0.8 |
| World output growth with PPP-based weights[d] | 3.2 | 3.4 | 3.0 | 3.6 | 3.9 | - | - |

Source: UN/DESA.
a Estimated.
b Forecast, based in part on Project LINK.
c Includes goods and services.
d Based on 2011 benchmark.

Since the onset of the global financial crisis, developing countries generated much of the global output growth (figure I.2). China, in particular, became the locomotive of global growth, contributing nearly one third of world output growth during 2011-2012. As the largest trading nation, China sustained the global growth momentum during the post-crisis period, maintaining strong demand for commodities and boosting export growth in the rest of the world. With a much anticipated slowdown in China and persistently weak economic performances in other large developing and transition economies—notably Brazil and the Russian Federation—the developed economies are expected to contribute more to global growth in the near term, provided they manage to mitigate deflationary risks and stimulate investment and aggregate demand. On the other hand, bottoming-out of the commodity price decline, which will contribute to reducing volatility in capital flows and exchange rates, will help reduce macroeconomic uncertainties and stimulate growth in a number of developing and emerging economies, including in the least developed countries (LDCs) (box I.1). Developing countries are expected to grow by 4.3 per cent and 4.8 per cent in 2016 and 2017, respectively.

*Developed economies are expected to contribute more to global growth*

## Box I.1
### Prospects for the least developed countries

The group of least developed countries (LDCs) is experiencing a modest slowdown of their economies, with growth rates falling from 5.1 per cent in 2014 to an estimated 4.5 per cent in 2015. Weaker export demand from emerging economies, lower commodity prices, net capital outflows, and weak investment growth—and, in some cases, military conflicts, natural disasters and adverse weather effects on agricultural output—exerted downward pressure on growth this year. A rebound to 5.6 per cent growth in both 2016 and 2017 is projected, underpinned by stronger demand from developed economies, growing domestic demand and stabilizing commodity prices. Lower commodities prices (particularly oil) have reduced the import bills of resource-importing LDCs and contributed to lower inflation, although in some countries the gains have been partially offset by depreciating exchange rates.

Bangladesh—the largest LDC in terms of both the population and size of gross domestic product (GDP)—is expected to benefit from the recovery in the developed economies, and is projected to grow by 6.5 per cent in 2016, largely driven by private consumption, investment and additional export demand from Europe and the United States of America. Government spending on power, water and transportation infrastructure projects is expected to increase significantly, supporting growth in the short term, but likely to result in a larger budget deficit. In Nepal, the economy is expected to see a gradual recovery in 2016, in part driven by reconstruction efforts after the devastating earthquake of April 2015. GDP growth is projected to strengthen from an estimated 3.3 per cent in 2015 to 4.6 per cent in 2016, but will remain below potential, partly reflecting the subpar monsoon, which is likely to result in weak agricultural output. Meanwhile, Yemen remains mired in a complex military conflict. In 2015, the United Nations declared the situation in Yemen as a high-level humanitarian emergency, with about 80 per cent of Yemen's population in need of humanitarian aid. According to the World Food Programme (WFP), the risk of famine in Yemen is now imminent, given that the country already had the highest level of poverty and malnutrition in Western Asia before the onset of the crisis. As a result of the ongoing conflict, oil and gas production have been suspended, which partly accounts for the nearly 10 per cent contraction of real GDP in 2015. Fiscal conditions, which were already challenging before the conflict, are expected to become unsustainable without external support, as public revenue becomes scarce and expenditures for repairing damage from the conflict rise.

The decline in commodity prices has had a significant impact on the terms of trade for a number of the LDCs in Africa, given their excessive dependence on commodity exports. Many LDCs remain highly dependent on the natural resource sector, with commodity exports representing, on average, 16 per cent of their GDP. Commodity exports are also highly concentrated in one or two products. LDCs that are highly dependent on fuel exports have clearly seen a pronounced decline in their commodity

*(continued)*

Box I.1 (*continued*)    Figure I.1.1
**Commodity exports as a share of GDP and share
of the top commodity group in total commodity exports for the LDCs, 2014[a]**

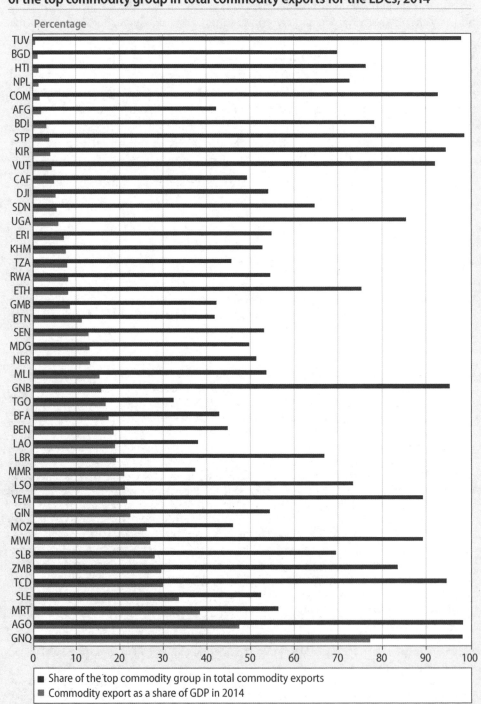

Percentage

Source: UN/DESA calculations
from UNCOMTRADE and
United Nations
Statistics Division.
a This includes all LDCs
monitored for this report.
Note: See table J in the
Statistical Annex to this
publication for definitions
of country codes.

■ Share of the top commodity group in total commodity exports
■ Commodity export as a share of GDP in 2014

(*continued*)

Box I.1 (*continued*)

terms of trade. By contrast, LDCs reliant on exports of agricultural, food and metal products registered an improvement in their terms of trade, as fuel often constitutes a major import component for these economies. Both the narrow export base, which often relies on a single commodity, and the high share of commodity trade in GDP highlight the economic vulnerabilities of LDCs and underscore the need for appropriate policies and strategies for diversification. Commodity-dependent LDCs are likely to benefit from diversification strategies that promote higher local value addition through backward and forward linkages in their resource sectors (see also chap. IV, box IV.3).

Haiti—the lone LDC in the Americas—is projected to grow by 2.4 per cent in 2015, before accelerating slightly to 2.7 per cent in 2016. The medium-term growth outlook for Haiti is rather low by the LDC benchmark. While private consumption and export growth are likely to remain resilient, difficulties regarding government spending and political uncertainties will prevent economic activity from gaining further momentum. Scaling up infrastructure investments and implementing structural reforms will remain essential to boosting growth in the medium term.

**Figure I.2**
**Contribution to global growth, 2007–2017**

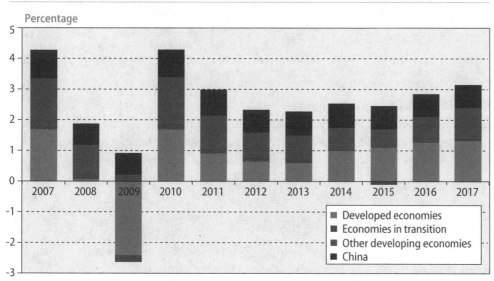

Source: UN/DESA.

## Inflation remains benign

Average global inflation continues to decline amid persistently subdued economic activity, modest wage growth and lower commodity prices. In 2015, global consumer price inflation is projected to fall to 2.6 per cent, the lowest level since 2009, owing to reduced oil and commodity prices (figure I.3).[2] Inflation in developing countries is expected to rise moderately in 2016, mainly driven by higher levels of inflation in transition economies.

Risks of deflation, however, still persist in developed countries, mainly in Japan and the euro area, and to a lesser degree in the United States, where average inflation hovered at about 0.2 per cent during the past four quarters. Across a large number of economies, low quarterly inflation has coincided with higher levels of volatility in quarterly growth in developed economies (see the section on persistent macroeconomic uncertainties and vola-

*Deflation risks linger*

---

2    Inflation figures in this section exclude the recent sharp increase in the Bolivarian Republic of Venezuela; for 2015 and 2016, inflation there is projected to rise above 150 per cent.

Figure I.3
**Global consumer price inflation, 2006-2017[a]**

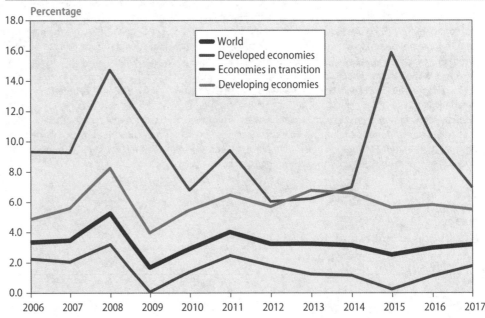

Source: UN/DESA.
[a] Figures for 2015 are partly estimated and figures for 2016 and 2017 are forecast. Figures exclude inflation figure in Venezuela (Bolivarian Republic of).

tility). This shows that price stability—which is synonymous with low levels of inflation—is neither a necessary nor a sufficient condition for reducing volatility in real activity or for stimulating economic growth. While average quarterly inflation fell relative to the pre-crisis period in almost all major economies, volatilities of both inflation and growth increased in a majority of the economies (table I.2) amid persistently weak aggregate demand.

## Unemployment challenges persist

*The employment gap widens*

The moderate pace of global growth, in an environment of weak investment growth, has failed to create a sufficient number of jobs to close the gap in the employment rate (employment-to-population ratio) that opened up during the global financial crisis. The employment gap is estimated to reach 63.2 million in 2015 (figure I.4). The average rate of job creation has slowed to about 1.4 per cent per annum since 2011, compared to an average annual growth rate of about 1.7 per cent rate in pre-crisis years. As a result, unemployment figures remain high in many regions, even though they have improved in several developed economies. Globally, the total number of unemployed is estimated to have reached 203 million, increasing by 2 million this year (figure I.5). Youth unemployment accounts for 36 per cent of all unemployed worldwide. Global employment growth is expected to continue at the relatively modest pace during the forecast period. Unemployment rates in most countries are expected to stabilize or recede only modestly in 2016 and 2017 against the backdrop of a moderate improvement in investment and growth during the forecast period.

*Long-term unemployment is on the rise in developed countries*

After some improvements in 2014, the growth rate of employment decelerated in the majority of developed economies during the first half of 2015. Consequently, unemployment in developed economies remains well above the pre-crisis level, despite recent improvements. In Organization for Economic Cooperation and Development (OECD)

Figure I.4
**Global employment gap, 1999–2019**

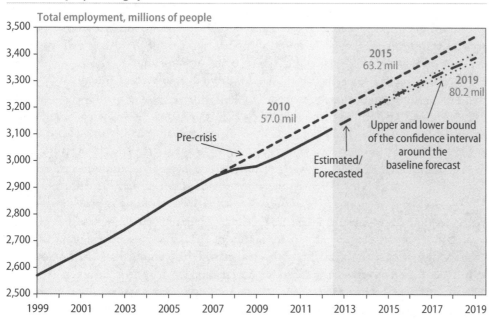

Source: International Labour Organization, Trends Econometric Models (November 2014), presented at the UN/DESA Expert Group Meeting on the World Economy, held from 21-23 October 2015 in New York.

Figure I.5
**Total unemployment by regions, 2007–2019**

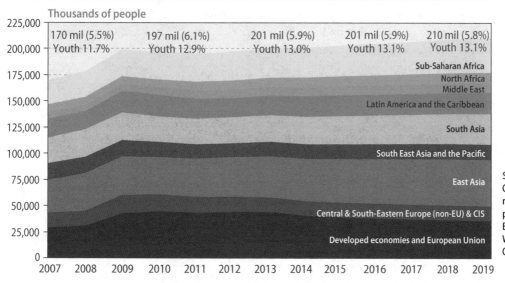

Source: International Labour Organization, Trends Econometric Models (November 2014), presented at the UN/DESA Expert Group Meeting on the World Economy, held from 21-23 October 2015 in New York.

countries, an estimated 44 million workers are unemployed in 2015, about 12 million more than in 2007. The duration of unemployment has been abnormally long in many developed economies (United Nations, 2015b), bringing long-term unemployment rates to record highs, including among youth. In OECD countries, one third of unemployed individuals were out of work for 12 months or more in the last quarter of 2014, representing a 77.2 per cent increase in the number of long-term unemployed since the financial crisis.

Despite slower employment growth, unemployment figures remained relatively stable in developing countries in 2014. In a group of large developing economies and economies in transition,[3] employment growth slowed from an average of 1.4 per cent per annum between 1999 and 2007 to 1.0 per cent between 2009 and 2014, reflecting both a slowdown in average GDP growth in these economies and a simultaneous decline in the employment intensity of growth. Demographic factors, changing economic structures, increasing automation and capital intensity also partly explain the slowdown in employment growth.

The relatively stable unemployment numbers in developing economies are also partially explained by declining labour force participation, particularly among women and youth. The real transition from employment to unemployment is not always reflected in the unemployment rate in many developing economies, because of the large informal sector in these countries. In the developing world as a whole, employment opportunities are estimated to have deteriorated in 2015, given the sharp economic slowdown in several economies.

In developed economies, the pattern of work has been shifting considerably towards more part-time employment. In the euro area, part-time employment represented 21.9 per cent of total employment in the second quarter of 2015, a 3.0 percentage point increase since the beginning of the crisis. The main concern with involuntary part-time employment is the repercussion on job security, working poverty and low long-term earnings.

In addition to slow employment growth and high unemployment rates, wages and earnings were also adversely affected by the financial crisis, signalling an overall worsening of labour market conditions worldwide. In OECD countries, the annual real wage growth was about 0.5 per cent between 2008 and 2014, significantly slower than the 1.8 per cent between 2000 and 2007. On the one hand, wage adjustments may have helped to avoid higher job losses during the financial crisis and facilitated job creation in some countries more recently. At the same time, wage adjustments, which were predicated on slowing productivity growth, increased hardship at the household level and weakened aggregate demand. Increases in part-time and temporary jobs, especially in developed economies, and a gradual shift from salaried work to self-employment in some developing regions, such as in Latin America and the Caribbean, have contributed to increasing job insecurity in many parts of the world.

### Employment growth and decent work critical for realizing the 2030 Agenda for Sustainable Development

The persistent employment gap, unemployment (particularly youth unemployment), growing prevalence of part-time employment, job insecurity, and stagnant real wages will seriously undermine the global efforts for promoting "inclusive and sustainable economic growth, employment and decent work for all", as envisaged in the 2030 Agenda for Sustainable Development (United Nations, General Assembly, 2015a, p. 4).

## Headwinds impede global growth

Global growth prospects face considerable headwinds in the near term, amid a macroeconomic environment of falling inflation and weak employment generation. Five major headwinds—both cyclical and structural—will continue to shape the near-term outlook of the global economy as well as its long-term prospects:

---

3     Argentina, Brazil, China, India, Indonesia, Russian Federation, Saudi Arabia, South Africa and Turkey.

- Persistent macroeconomic uncertainties and volatility;
- Low commodity prices and declining trade flows;
- Rising volatility in exchange rates and capital flows;
- Stagnant investment and diminishing productivity growth;
- Continued disconnect between finance and real sector activities.

# Persistent macroeconomic uncertainties and volatility

Persistent uncertainty has been a legacy of the global financial crisis that began in the third quarter of 2008. The policy deliberations in the United States Federal Reserve (Fed), for example, have repeatedly identified macroeconomic uncertainty as a key factor affecting the subdued economic performance during the post-crisis period. While lax regulations that allowed the financial sector to take excessive risks precipitated the financial crisis, persistence of macroeconomic uncertainty continues to adversely affect aggregate demand and investment in the post-crisis period.

In an economy, households and firms make decisions to consume or invest today based on the expectation of a future outcome. The change in the probability of a future economic outcome—income, profit, etc.—represents an uncertainty shock. Unlike an income or productivity shock, an uncertainty shock does not directly affect the level of income or wealth. It can, however, change the probability distribution of future income, which in turn can affect economic behaviour and the welfare of households and firms (see Knotek and Khan, 2011).

## Uncertainty shocks persist

A strand of economic research[4] generally relies on uncertainty to explain the fluctuations in real output. This research finds uncertainty to be highly countercyclical, rising during economic downturns and diminishing during financially stable times. Recessions indeed coincide with higher degrees of uncertainty (Bloom, Floetotto, and Jaimovich, 2007). When uncertainty amplifies, firms and households typically go into a "wait and see" mode, postponing costly consumption and investment decisions, especially if they are irreversible. The benefits of waiting and gathering more information about potential risks usually outweigh the cost of not doing anything when uncertainty is high. This largely explains why business activities slow down or investments freeze during economic downturns (Bernanke, 1983). In the short run, uncertainty may increase transaction costs and depress profitability. It may also induce herding behaviour among firms and depress aggregate investment.

Bloom and others (2012) shows uncertainty shocks typically induce a rapid drop and rebound in aggregate output, investment and employment, as was observed during 2009-2010 immediately after the Great Recession. An uncertainty shock also generates a negative productivity shock, as uncertainty can freeze reallocation of human and financial resources within and across firms. As such, these shocks are expected to be short-lived. Yet, seven years since the global financial crisis, uncertainties remain elevated. While the financial

*Persistent uncertainty can freeze investment and paralyze growth*

---

4    Alexopoulos and Cohen (2009), Bloom, Bond and Van Reenen (2007), Bloom (2009), and Bloom and others (2012) provide results supporting a key role for uncertainty shocks in business cycle fluctuations.

and liquidity shocks have been relatively short-lived, with equity and debt markets reaching their pre-crisis levels as early as 2010, the uncertainty shock continues to linger.

While there are compelling theoretical arguments that uncertainty can adversely affect growth, there is no consensus on how to objectively measure uncertainty. The empirical literature primarily uses proxies or indicators of uncertainty, such as the implied or realized volatility of stock market returns, the cross-sectional dispersion of firm profits or productivity, or the cross-sectional dispersion of survey-based forecasts.

The persistence of uncertainty in the global economy makes a strong case for revisiting the relationship between uncertainty and output growth in the 20 large developed and 20 large developing countries and economies in transition.[5] While the analyses presented here make no claim of a causal relationship between these variables, they provide important insights on macroeconomic volatility and the slow pace of global growth, and raise important policy questions that merit further research.

### Trends in key real and nominal variables

Both output growth and inflation have shifted downward since the global financial crisis, representing the level effects of the crisis. At the same time, volatility of output growth has increased in developed economies in the aftermath of the crisis.

As table I.2 shows, average growth rates of output, consumption and investment in the 20 large developed economies registered significant declines during the post-crisis period. The sharpest decline is observed in investment growth rates. Average inflation experienced only a slight decline in the post-crisis period, while inflation volatility experienced a sharp increase.

Surprisingly, the broad money (M2) growth also declined during the post-crisis period despite the quantitative easing (QE) policies pursued by the central banks in many developed countries. While QE injected liquidity into the financial system, a significant

Table I.2
**Key macroeconomic volatilities before and after the crisis**

|  |  | Developed 20 | | Developing 20 | |
|---|---|---|---|---|---|
|  |  | 2002 Q3: 2007 Q4 | 2010 Q1: 2015 Q2 | 2002 Q3: 2007 Q4 | 2010 Q1: 2015 Q2 |
| Output growth | Mean | 2.8 | 1.3 | 6.3 | 4.3 |
|  | Volatility | 1.2 | 1.5 | 2.9 | 2.6 |
| Consumption growth | Mean | 2.6 | 1.0 | 6.5 | 4.1 |
|  | Volatility | 1.0 | 1.4 | 2.7 | 3.7 |
| Investment growth | Mean | 4.4 | 0.9 | 10.9 | 5.6 |
|  | Volatility | 4.3 | 4.6 | 8.5 | 7.3 |
| Inflation | Mean | 1.9 | 1.6 | 6.9 | 6.6 |
|  | Volatility | 0.6 | 1.1 | 3.3 | 2.9 |
| M2 growth | Mean | 7.9 | 3.5 | 20.9 | 14.4 |
|  | Volatility | 2.9 | 2.7 | 7.8 | 5.2 |

Source: UN/DESA calculations.
Note: Volatility is measured as standard deviation.

---

5　These 40 economies accounted for more than 90 per cent of the global economy in 2014. The availability of quarterly macroeconomic data determined the selection of 20 large developing economies.

portion of that additional liquidity actually returned to central banks' balance sheets in the form of excess reserves, which possibly explains why QE has had only limited effects on boosting aggregate demand or investment rates in many developed countries. Between January 2000 and August 2008, the excess reserves of banks on the Fed's balance sheet averaged $1.8 billion. The total volume of excess reserves in the Fed reached $1 trillion by November 2009. As of October 2015, the Fed has excess reserves of $2.6 trillion (figure I.6), which represents nearly 75 per cent of total assets purchased by the Fed since the onset of the financial crisis. The ballooning of excess reserves since the crisis demonstrates that financial institutions generally chose to park their cash with the Fed instead of increasing lending to the real economy.

Figure I.6
**Excess reserves of financial institutions held with the United States Federal Reserve**

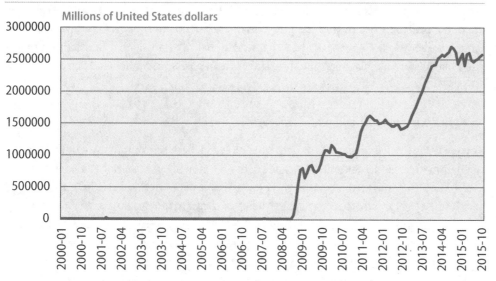

Millions of United States dollars

Source: Federal Reserve Bank of St. Louis, Excess Reserves of Depository Institutions.

The financial crisis has had similar level effects on the macroeconomic variables in 20 large developing economies, although effects have been less pronounced (table I.2). For example, average output growth declined by about 32 per cent in developing countries during the post-crisis period, relative to the 54 per cent decline in output growth in the developed countries. Investment growth also declined in developing countries, albeit at a slower pace. Several factors may explain why developing countries managed to avoid a sharper adjustment in investment, consumption and output, with one factor being that the financial crisis originated in the developed countries and has had only indirect effects through trade and capital flow channels. The relative stability of growth in developing countries is also attributable to the fact that many of them managed to implement effective countercyclical fiscal and monetary measures to sustain investment and growth during the post-crisis period.

The crisis also marks a shift in volatility trends. While volatilities increased in developed economies during the post-crisis period, volatilities in developing countries generally trended downwards. Historically, developing countries experienced higher levels of volatility in output and inflation, as documented in a number of empirical studies (see Ramey and Ramey (1995); Easterly, Islam and Stiglitz (2001); Kose, Prasad, and Terrones (2005)).

These studies cite the lack of diversification, adverse terms of trade shocks, weak financial and institutional developments, and exposure to financial shocks as reasons why developing countries generally experience more output or inflation volatility.

Developed countries
experienced sharp
increases in volatility

Volatilities sharply increased in developed countries, despite the fact that these economies are generally more diversified and have more effective institutions. Developed countries also have more open capital and financial markets, which should have allowed for international risk sharing and reduced variability in consumption. Social protection programmes, transfers and unemployment benefits—prevalent in developed countries—should have also ensured relative stability in consumption growth. Yet, during the post-crisis period, developed economies experienced significant increases in consumption volatility, reacting in a manner contrary to the findings of Bekaert, Harvey and Lundblad (2006), which claim that countries with more open capital accounts and financial liberalizations experience lower levels of consumption growth volatility. Instead, increased volatility in the developed countries during the post-crisis period tends to support the view that open capital markets do not necessarily lead to international risk sharing and that countries with more liberalized financial and capital markets often experience higher levels of volatility in growth (see Easterly, Islam and Stiglitz, 2001; Agenor, 2003).

### Output volatility and output growth

Keynes (1936) first suggested a negative relationship between output variability and average growth, arguing that businesses take into account the fluctuations in economic activity when they estimate the return on their investment. Bernanke (1983) and Ramey and Ramey (1995), also suggest the existence of a negative relationship between output volatility and growth. On the other hand, Solow (1956) suggests a positive effect of real uncertainty on output growth, arguing that output uncertainty encourages higher precautionary savings and a higher equilibrium rate of economic growth. Kose, Prasad and Terrones (2005) conclude that the relationship between growth and volatility depends on the level of economic development, where the relationship is generally positive in developed economies and negative in developing economies.

Volatility negatively affects
output growth

The data show a strong negative correlation between output volatility and output growth during the post-crisis period in developed and developing and transition economies (figures I.7 and I.8). The strong negative relationship holds even if outliers are excluded from the analysis. Growth volatility is affected by volatilities in investment, consumption, inflation and money supply, given that these variables jointly determine output growth.

Consumption, investment, inflation and their respective uncertainties and volatilities are endogenous to growth. Yet not all macroeconomic variables are endogenous. Policy choices, institutions and interventions are typically exogenous in the short run. Effective fiscal, monetary or exchange-rate policies can help reduce uncertainties and influence the behaviour of firms and households. Macroeconomic policies, as such, need to be designed and implemented more effectively to reduce uncertainties and stimulate aggregate demand and growth of the global economy.

**Figure I.7**
**Volatility and growth in developed economies, 2010 Q1–2015 Q2**

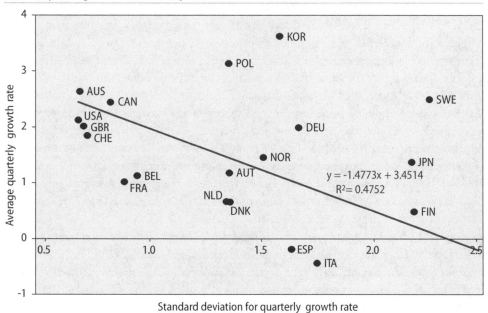

$y = -1.4773x + 3.4514$
$R^2 = 0.4752$

Source: UN/DESA.
Note: See table J in the Statistical Annex to this publication for definitions of country codes.

**Figure I.8**
**Volatility and growth in developing economies and economies in transition, 2010 Q1–2015 Q2**

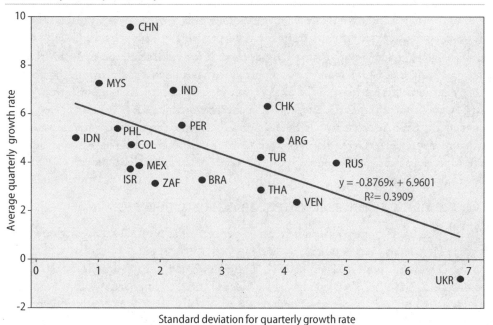

$y = -0.8769x + 6.9601$
$R^2 = 0.3909$

Source: UN/DESA.
Note: See table J in the Statistical Annex to this publication for definitions of country codes.

## Low commodity prices and declining trade flows

In the aftermath of the financial crisis, international trade, largely driven by demand from China, played a critical role in sustaining global output, particularly for developing economies. During 2009-2011, high commodity prices and early signs of recovery sustained the export income of large emerging and developing economies in Asia, Africa and Latin America. The downward trends in commodity prices since 2011 and sharp decline in oil prices since mid-2014 have altered the trade dynamics of many commodity-exporting countries. While the value of global trade has dropped sharply, trade volumes have recorded only a moderate deceleration. The decline in commodity prices largely explains the observed divergence in the value and volume of global trade flows. The commodity price declines have generally deteriorated the terms of trade of commodity exporters (see chap. II, box II.1), limiting their ability to demand goods and services from the rest of the world. This apparently has had second-order effects on non-commodity-exporting economies, unleashing a downward spiral in the value of global trade.

*The value of global trade is falling, while the volume is showing some persistence*

Global trade flows have slowed significantly in recent months, with total volumes of imports and exports projected to grow by only 2.6 per cent in 2015, the lowest rate since the Great Recession.[6] The source of the global slowdown in trade is primarily rooted in weaker demand from developing economies and a sharp decline in imports demanded by economies in transition. Global exports to the Commonwealth of Independent States (CIS) countries started to decline in 2014 and dropped sharply in 2015, as geopolitical tensions, weaker oil prices and declining remittances (see chap. III) led to large currency depreciations and erosion of real income in many of these economies. Import demand from the United States, on the other hand, accelerated, supported by the strong appreciation of the dollar since mid-2014 and relatively solid economic growth. Imports by the European Union (EU) economies have also strengthened and the EU demand is now a key impetus to the growth in world trade. On the other hand, sluggish growth, a weak yen and the slowdown in Japan's key trading partners in East Asia, particularly China, has had a dampening effect on global trade growth (figure I.9) (see chap. II for more details on trade flows).

As growth in China moderates, import growth has slowed sharply from the double-digit rates recorded for most of the last two decades. Total East Asia imports grew by an estimated 0.9 per cent in 2015, after just 3.3 per cent growth in 2014. The anticipated slowdown of the Chinese economy will have significant adverse effects on the growth prospects of many economies. A larger-than-expected slowdown in China would have further adverse effects on global trade, reducing aggregate demand and slashing global growth.

### Commodity prices have registered sharp declines

The oil price has plummeted by more than 55 per cent since mid-2014, bringing down the price of oil to levels that prevailed a decade ago. Non-oil commodity prices have continued on the downward trend initiated in 2011, with a particularly sharp drop in metals prices during 2015. The UNCTAD nominal price index of minerals, ores and metals (figure I.10) dropped 13.3 per cent in the first 9 months of 2015, and the food price index dropped by 12.2 per cent. This has led to a substantial shift in terms of trade and a sharp deterioration of GDP growth in commodity-dependent economies.

---

6     See table A.16 for detailed trade figures and projections by region.

Figure I.9
**Regional contributions to world import growth<sup>a</sup>**

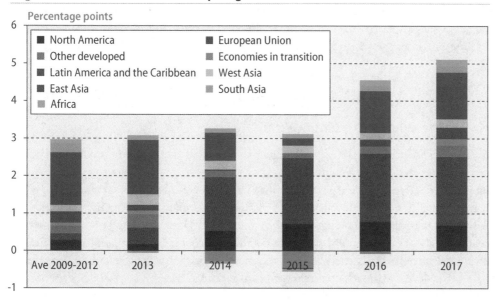

Source: UN/DESA, based on United Nations Statistics Division National Accounts Main Aggregates Database.
a 2015-2017 are forecasts.

Figure I.10
**Price indices of selected groups of commodities, August 2013–September 2015**

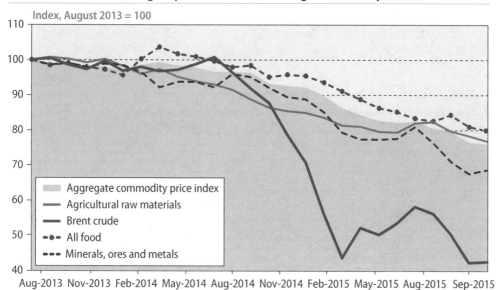

Source: UNCTADstat.

The low level of oil and non-oil primary commodity prices is projected to remain stable and extend into 2016 before seeing modest recovery for some commodities, as downward pressures recede in the later part of the forecast period (see the appendix to this chapter for the oil price assumptions underlying this forecast). The global oil market continues to remain oversupplied and demand growth is not expected to accelerate in 2016, in line with the overall weak global economic conditions, especially in China and other emerging economies that have been the main oil and metal demand drivers for the past decade.

Commodity prices are expected to remain subdued in the near term

In the outlook period, world trade is expected to grow by 4.0 per cent and 4.7 per cent in 2016 and 2017, respectively. Weak commodity prices, increased exchange-rate volatility and the slowdown in many emerging economies, including China, will continue to exert some downward pressures on trade flows, but stronger demand in the United States and Europe will offset the downward pressures and contribute to reviving global trade growth.

## Rising volatility in exchange rates and capital flows

### Large swings in exchange rates

Against the backdrop of falling commodity prices, increased capital outflows from developing countries and diverging monetary policies, exchange-rate volatilities have become more pronounced. Global exchange-rate volatility has risen considerably since mid-2014, while many emerging-market currencies have plunged amid significant capital outflows. The downward pressure on emerging-market currencies partly reflects deteriorating market expectations about these economies amid expectations of a rise in United States interest rates. As illustrated in figure I.11, the weakness of emerging-market currencies against the dollar (and other developed-market currencies) has been broad-based, but the size of the depreciations has varied substantially. The Brazilian real and the Russian rouble have recorded the largest losses, and both countries remain mired in severe economic downturns, accompanied by elevated inflation. The sharp declines of emerging-market currencies against the dollar have contributed to concerns over the high level of dollar-denominated debt of many non-financial corporations in emerging markets. In the case of a sudden currency depreciation or increase in interest rates, deleveraging pressures are likely to rise along with risks of corporate defaults in these economies (see chap. III).

**Figure I.11**
**Exchange rates of selected emerging-market currencies vis-à-vis the United States dollar, 1 September 2014–23 November 2015**

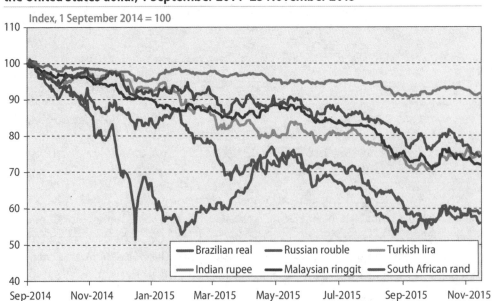

Source: UN/DESA, based on data from JPMorgan.

Between July 2014 and March 2015, the dollar index, which measures the value of the dollar against a basket of six major currencies, gained about 25 per cent. The Fed's decisions in June and September to delay its first rate hike has, at least temporarily, reduced the upward pressure on the dollar. However, a further widening of the policy gap between the Fed and other central banks, notably the European Central Bank (ECB) and the Bank of Japan, is expected to lead to a renewed strengthening of the dollar in 2016 (see the appendix to this chapter for the key exchange rate assumptions underlying this forecast).

In line with the large movements in nominal exchange rates, real effective exchange rates (REER) have changed significantly over the past year. The People's Bank of China in August adjusted the mechanism for setting the renminbi's daily reference rate—a move that resulted in a 3 per cent depreciation of the renminbi against the dollar. Despite this decline, the renminbi is still about 10 per cent stronger in real effective terms than it was in September 2014. On the other hand, the euro and the yen have depreciated by about 6 per cent, while the currencies of Brazil, Colombia and the Russian Federation have fallen by about 25 per cent in real effective terms.

These REER adjustments have been accompanied by rising exchange-rate volatility. Figure I.12 shows a measure of REER volatility for two groups of countries: 36 developed economies and 24 developing economies and economies in transition. Average exchange-rate volatility has increased significantly since mid-2014, in particular for the group of developing countries and economies in transition. While volatility is still much lower than during the global financial crisis and the emerging market crises of 1997-1998, it is relatively high for a non-crisis period.

A key question, and related policy challenge, is how the large movements in real exchange rates will impact international trade and capital flows during the forecast period. A number of recent studies (including Ahmed, Appendino and Ruta (2015) and Ollivaud, Rusticelli and Schwellnus (2015)) suggest that the rising importance of global value chains

**The dollar remains strong amid global weaknesses**

**Developing-country exchange rates are experiencing both downward pressures and increasing volatility**

**Exchange-rate volatilities coincide with large swings in capital flows**

Figure I.12
**Real effective exchange-rate volatility, January 1996–September 2015**

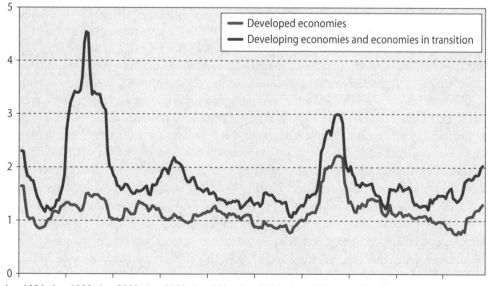

Source: UN/DESA, based on data from the Bank for International Settlements (BIS).
Note: The figure is based on monthly BIS data for real effective exchange rates for a total of 60 economies. The volatility is calculated as the standard deviation over a rolling 12-month period of the first difference of the logarithms of the monthly exchange rate. The resulting standard deviations are weighted by the respective country's 2012 share in global trade (exports + imports).

has dampened the relationship between real exchange-rate movements and trade flows. A new International Monetary Fund (IMF) (2015a) analysis, however, suggests that exchange-rate movements still tend to have strong effects on real trade volumes. This is expected to lead to a significant redistribution of real net exports from the United States to Japan and the euro area. At the same time, it provides a silver lining for some of the hard-hit emerging economies, as their exports are likely to receive a boost from depreciating emerging-market exchange rates.

## Capital inflows to emerging economies decline sharply

Sharp adjustments in commodity prices—and commensurate swings in exchanges rates, as discussed in the previous section—have led to reduced capital flows to developing countries. The prospect of an imminent increase in the United States policy rate has also affected the volume and direction of capital flows, particularly to large developing economies. Changes in the relative rates of return, heightened risk aversion, deteriorating economic prospects (especially in commodity-exporting economies), and associated sharp realignments of exchange rates leave many developing economies and economies in transition vulnerable to a sudden stop, and reversal, of capital inflows, which may adversely affect their balance of payment and put further downward pressures on their exchange rates.

*Capital inflows to developing countries experienced a sharp decline*

Capital inflows to developing countries have already slowed noticeably, as domestic vulnerabilities and the effects of lower commodity prices have impacted their medium-term investment and growth prospects. In 2015, net capital inflows to emerging economies are projected to be negative for the first time since 2008. The current retrenchment in net capital flows to emerging markets is far more severe than that experienced during the financial crisis, with net capital outflows expected to reach about $700 billion in 2015. While at the global level the bulk of the absolute deterioration in net capital flows can be attributed to China and the Russian Federation, the phenomenon is far more pervasive when considered relative to the size of individual economies. The decline in net capital inflows since 2013 has been associated with significant currency depreciations across a large number of economies, including Brazil, Indonesia, Mexico, South Africa, Thailand and Turkey. Several countries have also experienced sharp declines in equity prices and international reserves.

During the third quarter of 2015, portfolio outflows reached a record of $40 billion, the largest withdrawal since 2008. Corporate debt in emerging economies has increased more than four times faster than GDP growth over the last decade (Institute for International Finance, 2015), with much of the new debt denominated in United States dollars (World Bank, 2015a). Given the appreciation of the dollar, this will increase the debt-servicing burden for many large firms. Deleveraging and a sharp reversal of bond flows remain a risk, particularly for economies where capital inflows have been driven by global liquidity rather than by economic fundamentals (Ayala, Nedeljkovic and Saborowski, 2015). Meanwhile, cross-border lending to emerging economies, which remains highly volatile, has also shown signs of weakness. In the second quarter of 2015, cross-border lending posted an annual decline for the first time since 2012 (Bank for International Settlements, 2015), reflecting growing weaknesses in emerging economies in Asia and Latin America.

*Capital outflows may further impede investment and growth in developing economies*

The risks of more pronounced capital outflows from developing economies and economies in transition are substantial. In the short term, portfolio liquidity could dry up and financing costs might rise abruptly in response to the anticipated interest rate rises of the Fed, putting pressure on exchange rates, equity prices and international reserves.

Such a scenario would exacerbate the difficulties that many economies face in reinvigorating investment, as volatile capital flows tend to amplify financial and real business cycles (Claessens and Ghosh, 2013). In the medium term, the adjustment in emerging economies to the new global conditions, including lower financial market liquidity and commodity prices and higher levels of risk aversion, will pose new challenges for monetary, fiscal and exchange-rate policies.

# Stagnant investment and diminishing productivity growth

The global financial crisis has had the most pronounced negative effect on investment rates. Notwithstanding the debates as to whether the lack of aggregate demand or the absence of structural reforms and improved business environment inhibit new investments, it remains clear that global investment rates have sharply declined since the onset of the financial crisis (figures I.13a and I.13b). After an early recovery in 2010-2011, the growth rates of fixed capital formation have sharply slowed down since 2012, exerting downward pressure on productivity, employment and growth. The growth rates of fixed capital formation nearly collapsed since 2014, registering negative quarterly growth in as many as 9 large developed and developing countries and economies in transition. Only a few economies, notably Finland, France, and Greece, saw acceleration in investment rates between 2014 Q1 and 2015 Q2.

*Investment growth nearly collapsed in both developed and developing economies during the post-crisis period...*

Investment in productive capital has been even weaker than the total investment figures suggest, as dwelling and intangible assets account for the majority of investment in developed economies. According to OECD data on fixed capital formation, investments in intangible and intellectual property assets together represent the largest share of fixed capital formation in a number of developed economies in 2014, including in Germany (47.2 per cent) and the United States (42.3 per cent). Acquisition of intangible assets, such as trademarks, copyrights and patents, may increase financial returns to firms without necessarily increasing labour productivity or productive capacity. Fixed capital formation is, however, likely to witness a moderate increase during the forecast period, supported by less restrictive fiscal positions, an accommodative monetary policy stance and also by reduced macroeconomic uncertainty and stabilization of commodity prices. Low (but stable and predictable) commodity prices are likely to attract new investments in the sector.

*...and investment in productive capacities has been even weaker*

## Diminishing productivity growth

Alongside declines in investment rates, productivity growth has also slowed down significantly in recent years across a large set of economies (table I.3). During the pre-crisis period, the United States and the euro area countries registered healthy growth in labour productivity, averaging 1.5-2.0 per cent per year. Productivity growth has also slowed down in developing economies, which underscores the need for improving infrastructure, investing in human capital and implementing structural reforms (i.e., improving corporate governance, the business environment and competitiveness). In addition, decent work, job security and employment benefits can also contribute to boosting productivity growth in developing countries.

Figure I.13a
**Developed countries' fixed investment growth: before and after the crisis**

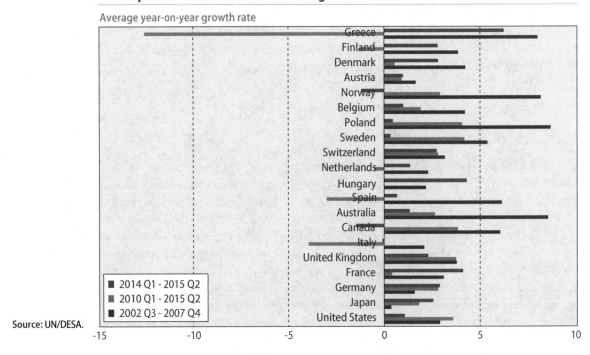

Source: UN/DESA.

Figure I.13b
**Selected other countries' fixed investment growth: before and after the crisis**

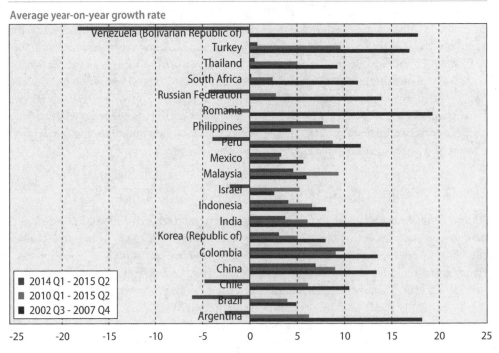

Source: UN/DESA.

Table I.3
**Growth of labour productivity, before and after the crisis**

| | Average percentage change per year | |
| --- | --- | --- |
| | 2001–2007 | 2009–2014 |
| France | 1.5 | 0.9 |
| Germany | 1.3 | 1.2 |
| Japan | 1.6 | 1.2 |
| United Kingdom | 2.2 | 0.3 |
| United States | 2.0 | 0.9 |
| China | 9.5 | 7.4 |
| India | 4.4 | 7.0 |
| Russian Federation | 5.4 | 2.0 |
| South Africa | 3.1 | 1.5 |

Source: UN/DESA, based on data from OECD and Asian Productivity Organization.
Note: Measured as real GDP per hour worked.

A composite growth accounting for 128 economies (representing over 95 per cent of the world economy) shows that the combined contribution of labour quality, labour quantity and total factor productivity to total global growth declined from 52.5 per cent during the period 2002-2007 to 16.8 per cent during 2009-2014, marking a commensurate sharp increase in capital intensity of growth (figure I.14a). In 26 developed economies, the contribution of these three factors declined from 44.9 per cent to 10.8 per cent, with the quantity of labour contributing negatively (-9.2 per cent) to output growth in these economies during the post-crisis period (figure I.14b).

*Labour productivity growth has been stunted in recent years*

While investment growth remained stagnant or fell in many economies, the contribution of capital to total growth increased worldwide during the post-crisis period, which presents a growth accounting puzzle. In a growth accounting framework, the contribution of capital to total output includes capital services rendered by existing capital stocks—in the form of depreciation and depletion—and also new capital investments. With both labour inputs and investment growth falling since the global financial crisis, capital services from existing capital stock accounted for most of the growth during the post-crisis period.

The slowdown in productivity growth is closely linked to the near collapse in investment rates. However, Gordon (2012) argues that the productivity slowdown is inevitable, given that new innovations have been less effective in generating large-scale productivity growth compared to innovations in earlier generations. According to Gordon (ibid.), demography, education, inequality, globalization, energy and environment, and the overhang of consumer and government debt will put downward pressure on productivity growth in developed economies. On the other hand, Bloom and others (2012) argue that increased uncertainty also reduces productivity growth because it reduces the degree and pace of reallocation in the economy, which is usually one of the key drivers of productivity growth.[7] However, Bloom and others (ibid.) caution that the productivity slowdown did not cause the recession. Instead, it was a by-product of the Great Recession.

Reversing the trends in productivity growth will be critical for putting the world economy on a trajectory of sustained, inclusive and sustainable growth, as envisaged in the

---

[7] Foster, Haltiwanger, and Krizan (2000; 2006) show that reallocation, mainly entry and exit of firms, accounts for about 50 per cent of manufacturing and 80 per cent of retail productivity growth in the United States.

Figure I.14a
**Growth accounting at the global level, 2009–2014 and 2002–2007**

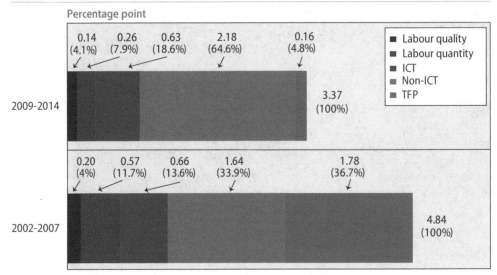

Source: UN/DESA, based on
the productivity data from the
Conference Board *Total
Economy Database*.
Note: The composite
contribution to world
output is weighted by each
country's share of GDP in the
world economy. The data in
parenthesis show the absolute
contribution (%) to global
growth during the period.

Figure I.14b
**Growth accounting for developed economies, 2009–2014 and 2002–2007**

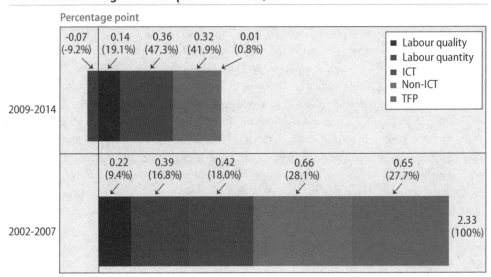

Source: UN/DESA, based on
the productivity data from the
Conference Board *Total Economy
Database*.
Note: The composite
contribution to output is
weighted by each country's
share of GDP. The data in
parenthesis show the absolute
contribution (%) to growth
during the period.

2030 Agenda for Sustainable Development. This will require extensive policy efforts and coordination among fiscal, monetary and development policies to increase investments in physical infrastructure and human capital. This will also require alignment of policies and effective regulations to ensure that the financial sector facilitates and stimulates long-term and productive investment. There also needs to be greater international policy coordination and support to facilitate transfer and exchange of technologies, which can also help stimulate productivity growth.

# Continued disconnect between finance and real sector activities

A growing disconnect between finance and real sector activities is evident in the data: fixed investment growth nearly collapsed (figures I.13a and I.13b), while debt securities (a financial instrument to raise capital) issued by non-financial corporations increased by more than 55 per cent between 2008 and 2014, representing a nearly 8 per cent increase per year (table I.4). One plausible explanation is the weak aggregate demand in developed economies, which has discouraged new investment. Policy uncertainties and the risk of deflation also partly explain the collapse in investment. On the other hand, the structural transformation of economies, with most of the growth coming from the service sector, provides another explanation. Service sectors typically require less capital inputs to produce outputs. Frey (2015), for example, has argued that digital technologies are much less capital-absorbing, creating little new investment demand relative to other revolutionary technologies. But there has been little or no structural transformation in the developed economies since the financial crisis to support this argument. The share of service sectors, including ICT sectors, has remained reasonably constant during the post-crisis period. Summers (2014) blames low real interest rates for the growing disconnect between finance and real sector activities, which, according to him, encourages excessive risk-taking by the financial sector and "greater reliance on Ponzi finance and increased financial instability" (ibid., p. 69). While the low real interest rates since the financial crisis partly explain the rapid build-up of the stock of financial assets—including the build-up of debt-securities and equity prices—it does not explain why this did not lead to investment booms in the developed countries.

The total stock of financial assets worldwide is estimated at $256 trillion at the end of 2014 (figure I.15), increasing from $184 trillion at the end of 2008. Total financial assets in the world—measured in terms of all debt securities outstanding, equities and the stock of bank credit—exceeded the pre-crisis level as early as 2010. Given the rapid build-up of financial assets and the decoupling of finance and real sector activities, the world economy again faces the risk of rapid financial deleveraging, as observed at the onset of the financial crisis between the second and fourth quarters of 2008. In G7 economies, the financial sector deleveraging of securities averaged 6.1 per cent of GDP during those periods (figure I.16). In the United Kingdom of Great Britain and Northern Ireland, total deleveraging was as high as 18.3 per cent of GDP in 2008. The data also show a strong correlation between financial sector deleveraging and GDP contraction during the last two quarters of 2008. During the years leading up to the crisis, the financial sectors rapidly increased their

*Financial sector recovery has been swift and has outpaced real sector recovery*

Table I.4
**Global debt securities outstanding**

| Billions of United States dollars | 2002 Q4 | 2008 Q4 | 2014 Q4 |
|---|---|---|---|
| Total debt securities | 42,426 | 76,532 | 92,867 |
| *issued by*: | | | |
| Financial corporations | 19,664 | 38,998 | 36,629 |
| Non-financial corporations | 5,585 | 7,226 | 11,211 |
| General government | 17,001 | 29,950 | 44,743 |
| *of which*:<br>International debt securities | 7,374 | 17,648 | 19,763 |

Source: UN/DESA, based on the BIS debt securities data.

Note: The different types of securities do not add up to the total because of some over-laps of securities issued by financial and non-financial corporations.

leverages to finance activities, including the risky activities by non-bank financial sectors (shadow banks). With the collapse of Lehman Brothers in September 2008, many financial firms were forced to rapidly deleverage as their equity prices collapsed and debt-to-equity ratios skyrocketed. Preliminary UN/DESA estimates suggest that 1 per cent deleveraging is associated with a 0.1 per cent contraction in GDP growth in 16 developed economies, while controlling for changes in credit flows and market capitalization (figure I.17). On the other hand, the correlation between the net change in market capitalization and the net contraction in GDP is very weak, controlling for net changes in leverage and credit stock. One possible explanation is that the fall in market capitalization affects GDP only through indirect channels—mostly wealth effects—and those, too, with a lag.

*Deleveraging pressure is on the rise*

A similar deleveraging pressure may rise—particularly in developing countries—with increases in the United States policy rates, which may increase the debt-servicing cost and the counter-party risks of borrowing firms. A sudden and disorderly adjustment in equity prices could increase the debt to equity ratio of highly leveraged firms and force them to reduce their debt level to avoid defaults. The deleveraging may increase financial market volatility and have significant negative wealth effects on households and corporations, reducing investment and aggregate demand and possibly pushing the world economy towards an even weaker growth trajectory than currently anticipated.

Figure I.15
**The stock of financial assets, 2002–2013**

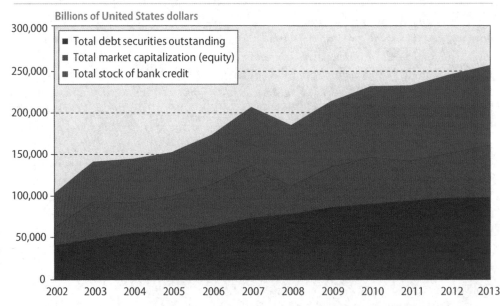

Billions of United States dollars

- Total debt securities outstanding
- Total market capitalization (equity)
- Total stock of bank credit

Source: UN/DESA, based on estimates, using the BIS data on debt securities, World Federation of Exchanges data on market capitalization and the Bankscope data on the stock of bank credit.

# Economic growth, poverty and carbon emission

The 2030 Agenda for Sustainable Development underscores the imperative of achieving inclusive and sustainable economic growth. On the one hand, this will require a recoupling of growth and poverty reduction, and on the other, a decoupling of growth and emission

Figure I.16
## Financial sector deleveraging, 2008 Q2–2008 Q4

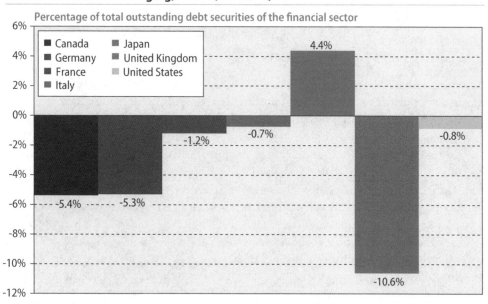

Source: UN/DESA, based on the
BIS debt securities data.

Figure I.17
## Financial sector deleveraging of securities and net contraction in GDP growth, 2008 Q2–2008 Q4

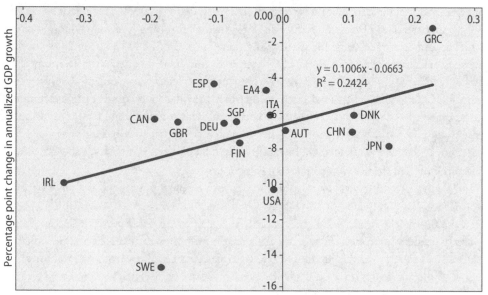

Source: UN/DESA, based on the
BIS debt securities data.

Notes: EA4 refers to Belgium,
France, the Netherlands
and Portugal. See table J in the
Statistical Annex to this
publication for definitions
of country codes.

levels to ensure that economic growth is sufficiently inclusive and sustainable. Given the imperative of sustainable development, the following section presents an analysis of the recent trends in growth, poverty reduction and environmental sustainability.

## Growth and poverty reduction

According to the *Millennium Development Goals Report 2015* (United Nations, 2015c), the proportion of people living in extreme poverty in developing countries declined by 50 per cent between 1999 and 2011. Nonetheless, one in five people in developing regions still live below the international poverty line of $1.90 a day and the improvements have been unevenly spread across regions. In sub-Saharan Africa, for instance, extreme poverty declined by just 21 per cent, while in East Asia it declined by 82 per cent. In order to progress further with the goal of poverty reduction, the Sustainable Development Goals (SDGs) provide a number of targets to support economic growth including economic diversification, technological upgrades and innovation, development of high value added and labour-intensive sectors; while targets to reduce economic inequality include implementing social protection systems and achieving gender equality and equal pay for work of equal value. Both stronger growth and redistribution may be addressed by such targets as broadening access to finance and economic resources, achieving universal health care, ensuring inclusive and equitable education and building resilient infrastructures.[8]

Reduction in inequality can have lasting, positive effects on poverty reduction

The relationships between growth, poverty and inequality are complex, as highlighted by Kanbur (2004). One generally finds a negative correlation between growth in per capita income and poverty. A decline in inequality is also generally associated with declining rates of poverty. These relationships follow from the interlinkages between poverty, average income and income distribution, as shown by Bourguignon (2003). This relationship also shows that the pace of poverty reduction is related to prevailing levels of economic development and relative income inequality. The percentage decline in the poverty headcount ratio associated with a rise in income will accelerate as average income in the economy rises, while reduction in inequality can also permanently accelerate the speed of poverty reduction (ibid.), allowing a virtuous circle to develop, provided both targets can be achieved simultaneously. However, the relationship between income growth and inequality is much less straightforward. Growth in GDP per capita can only necessarily reduce poverty if it does not at the same time increase inequality; the data on this relationship show considerable variation and the academic literature is inconclusive.

Figure I.18 illustrates the relationship between income growth and the poverty headcount ratio for a sample of 90 developing economies and economies in transition. On average, a 1.0 per cent rise in GDP per capita is associated with a 1.5 per cent decline in the poverty headcount ratio in this sample. This relationship is often referred to as the "income elasticity of poverty" and is broadly in line with elasticity estimates from other studies.

While different rates of GDP growth per capita can clearly explain some of the observed heterogeneity in poverty reduction across countries, the observed correlation is relatively loose, reflecting differences in the levels of development, the level of income inequality, and the change in income inequality over the sample period. The relationship between the income elasticity of poverty and the level of development, measured as the distance between the poverty line and average income, is intuitively straightforward. Where the poverty gap

---

8   See https://sustainabledevelopment.un.org/topics.

is high, for a given path of economic growth the decline in poverty in percentage terms will be smaller than in countries with a lower incidence of extreme poverty. In the figure, it is clear that the majority of low-income countries have seen relatively slower rates of poverty reduction, while upper-middle-income countries have generally seen faster rates. Fragile and conflict-affected countries are particularly vulnerable to high poverty rates, with little prospect for either economic growth or income redistribution. For example, Burundi falls within the quadrant of low growth and slow poverty reduction in figure I.18 reflecting the fact that the sample period falls within the period of the Burundian Civil War.

The income elasticity of poverty has been strong in many Latin American economies. While these countries had relatively lower levels of extreme poverty at the onset compared to the low-income countries in the sample, the implementation of more redistributive policies has also been a crucial factor that allowed poverty to recede rapidly. Redistributive policies or other fiscal or employment policies that prevent inequalities from rising can, thus, significantly accelerate poverty reduction for a given rate of economic growth.

*Redistribution can positively affect both growth and poverty reduction*

The sectoral composition of production also has implications for income distribution and the evolution of relative income inequality, and, consequently, poverty. When economic growth is led by sectors that are labour intensive, such as agriculture, construction and manufacturing, the impact of GDP growth on poverty reduction tends to be stronger (Loayza and Raddatz, 2006). This reflects the impact on income distribution: a closer relationship between production and employment growth in these sectors allows more inclusive growth, with greater potential to create jobs and support wages of the lowest-income groups. Labour-intensive growth has been an important factor behind declining inequality

**Figure I.18**
**Relationship between poverty headcount ratio and income growth**

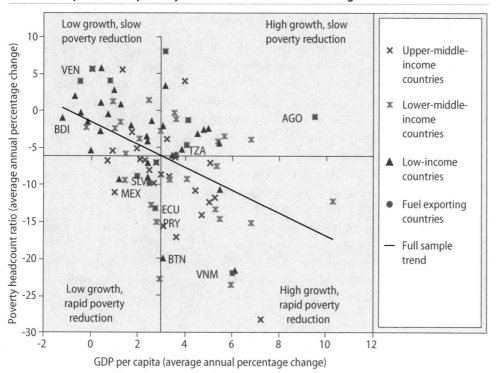

Source: UN/DESA based on United Nations Statistics Division National Accounts, United Nations population statistics, World Bank Poverty and Equity Database.
Note: The sample includes 90 developing economies and economies in transition. High-income countries are excluded. Time periods differ across countries owing to data available, but extend 5-15 years to the most recent available observation. Axes cross at the mean growth rates for each series, so that the quadrants include observations above or below these means. See table J in the Statistical Annex to this publication for definitions of country codes.

in several economies located in East and South Asia. In Viet Nam, for example, agriculture, construction and manufacturing sectors together accounted for nearly 50 per cent of production in 2000. This, together with important progress in providing universal education, may help to explain the impressive decline in extreme poverty in Vietnam over the last 15 years. Conversely, resource-rich economies that have a dominant energy or mining sector, which are highly capital intensive, tend to have a weaker relationship between GDP growth and poverty reduction (Christiaensen, Chuhan-Pole and Sanoh, 2013). While per capita GDP growth in resource-rich countries in Africa was measurably higher than in resource-poor countries in the past decade, poverty reduction registered a faster pace largely because of higher employment intensity of growth in the resource-poor economies.

Growth slowdown will impede global poverty reduction efforts

Looking forward, the broad slowdown in economic growth in many developing economies can be expected to restrain progress in poverty reduction in the near term. Poverty rates remain high in many parts of the world, most notably in sub-Saharan Africa, where in many countries more than 50 per cent of the population still lives below the poverty line of $1.90 per day. While GDP growth per capita is expected to hold up moderately well in this region, achieving the SDG target of achieving at least 7 per cent GDP growth per annum in the LDCs is most likely unattainable in the near term. Recent experiences with poverty reduction show that strong economic growth in itself is not sufficient to maintain and accelerate the momentum of poverty alleviation, but must be accompanied by some form of redistribution. Policies aimed at reducing inequality, such as investment in education, health and infrastructure, and building stronger social safety nets, can play a crucial role. The promotion of labour-intensive industries can also be an effective policy for poverty reduction, so long as this is not achieved at the expense of productivity growth, which is essential for real wage growth and decent work as envisaged in the 2030 Agenda for Sustainable Development.

## Growth and environmental sustainability

Global energy-related carbon emissions experienced no growth in 2014 for the first time since 1990 (except for 2009, when the global economy contracted, and 1992, the year after the dissolution of the Soviet Union (figure I.19a)).[9] The latest evidence shows signs that the world might start to see some delinking between economic growth and carbon emissions. While still accounting for only about 13 per cent of the world's total energy consumption, low-carbon energy sources accounted for over 50 per cent of the new energy consumption in 2014—the first time in 20 years.[10]

As an example, China saw a net decline of 1.5 per cent in its carbon emissions in 2014. It follows a decade of continuous improvement in carbon intensity (i.e., carbon emissions per unit of GDP) and reflects the gradual shift in energy structure from a heavy reliance on fossil fuel, particularly coal, to renewable energy sources. The expected continuing expansion of the service sector and the declining growth of investment (particularly in heavy industries) in the context of structural transformation should further weaken the link between economic growth and carbon emissions. Despite the stall of global carbon emission growth in 2014, it is not certain that the stabilization trend continued into 2015 and the rest of the forecast

---

9    Unless otherwise specified, carbon emissions in this section refer to energy-related carbon emissions. See International Energy Agency (2015).

10   Low-carbon energy sources include hydro, wind, geothermal, solar, non-traditional biomass and nuclear. See BP Global (2015).

period. Some of the weather factors that contributed to the 2014 emissions decline in certain regions might weaken. China, for example, experienced significant growth in hydropower generation in 2014 largely due to above-trend rainfall; also, its carbon emissions level is not expected to peak until between 2020s and early 2030s.[11] Additionally, low oil prices will hamper emissions mitigation efforts should the oil prices remain subdued.

In 2014, renewable energy investment reversed its two-year downward trend and reached $270.2 billion, up 17 per cent from 2013 levels (United Nations Environment Programme, 2015). It reflects strong policy support and a growing realization among institutional investors that renewable energy is a stable and relatively low-risk investment. The rise in renewable energy investment in 2014 contrasts the sharp slowdown of overall fixed investment growth since 2012. Considering the significant decline in capital cost in renewable energy sources over the past several years—wind and solar in particular—the investment increase is even more impressive, as each dollar of investment is translated into more renewable power capacity than previous years. At the global level, it is estimated that about 103 gigawatts (GW) of renewable power capacity (excluding large hydro) was installed in 2014. Wind and solar photovoltaics alone accounted for 95 GW of newly installed capacity in 2014, surpassing the total renewable power capacity of 86 GW installed in 2013. It is estimated that renewable energy accounted for 48 per cent of the net power capacity installed in 2014 and its share of total global electricity generation reached 9.1 per cent, up from 8.5 per cent in 2013. Developing countries witnessed $131 billion of renewable energy investment in 2014 and have been quickly catching up with the developed countries, which saw a total investment of $139 billion in the same year (figure I.19b). Among all economies, China led renewable energy investment with $83.3 billion in 2014.

*Investment in renewable energy is on the rise*

Despite the low oil prices, renewable energy investments remained strong in the first three quarters of 2015, at roughly an equal level as the same period in 2014. A possible explanation is that oil and renewable energy are largely used for different purposes: the former is mainly used in the transportation sector, whereas the latter for electricity generation. At the global level, only about 4 per cent of electricity is generated from oil. However, since gas and oil prices are linked in many markets and gas is more commonly used for generating electricity, the impact of low oil prices on renewable energy investment could start to pass through, should oil prices remain low. Even in that case, oil prices would need to plunge considerably further to have a strong impact. It is estimated that the outlook of mature renewable energy sources such as wind and solar would be only significantly affected if the oil prices drop to about $20-30 per barrel (Goossens, 2015).[12]

*Investments in renewable energy remain strong despite subdued oil price*

The latest available cross-country data in 2012 show an inverted U-shaped relationship between per capita GDP and per capita carbon emission (figure I.19c). Rather than implying countries will automatically witness a fall in per capita emissions after reaching certain income levels,[13] it reflects the combined effects of the various factors in determining emissions trajectory. These factors include the changes in energy prices and energy structure, economic

11 As part of its intended nationally determined contribution communicated to the United Nations Framework Convention on Climate Change Secretariat, China has committed to reach carbon emission peak by about 2030.

12 For example, Deutsche Bank estimates that electricity generated from oil would cost about $0.08/kWh at the oil price level of $40 per barrel. Given that unsubsidized rooftop solar electricity typically costs between $0.08-$0.13/kWh, oil prices would have to drop below $40 to make electricity generated from solar power uncompetitive when compared to that generated from oil. See Deutsche Bank (2015).

13 In the literature, there is no clear consensus on the existence of the inverted U-shaped relationship between emissions and growth—the so-called Environmental Kuznets Curve—when other control variables are being taken into account.

structural transformation, and emission mitigation policies adopted by the Government, among others. On the other hand, global warming resulting from high atmospheric concentration of greenhouse gas emissions also has economic consequences. Immediate impacts can be transmitted through extreme weather events that affect agriculture, displace populations, bring damages to infrastructures, etc. Climate change is also posing increasing risks to global financial stability: for example, insurance companies are facing a rising number of claims

**Figure I.19**

**Emission levels and renewable energy investments**

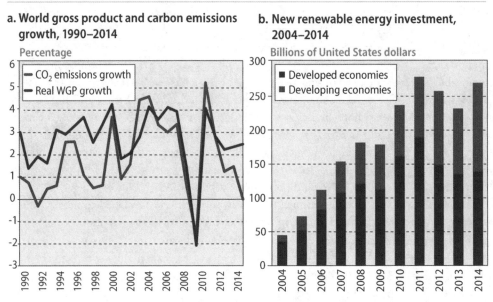

a. World gross product and carbon emissions growth, 1990–2014

b. New renewable energy investment, 2004–2014

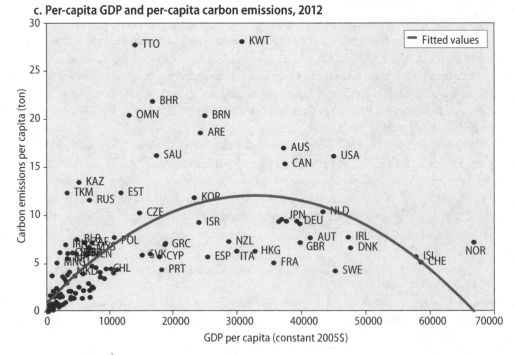

c. Per-capita GDP and per-capita carbon emissions, 2012

Source: a. World Bank (2015b); International Energy Agency (2014a; 2015); b. United Nations Environment Programme (2015); c. World Bank (2015b); International Energy Agency (2014a). Note: See table J in the Statistical Annex to this publication for definitions of country codes.

associated with large-scale, costly natural disasters caused by extreme weather.[14] Structural transformations that shift the economy towards a low-carbon path and impose stringent restrictions on carbon emissions could also lead to a repricing of assets—particularly those related to natural resources and extraction sectors—and change the incentive structures to minimize carbon footprints and promote sustainable development.

## Policy stances, challenges and the way forward

### Monetary policy

Global monetary policy has remained generally accommodative in the face of weakening growth and subdued inflationary pressures in many parts of the world. In 2015, developed economies continued to rely on accommodative monetary policy—such as asset purchases in the euro area and Japan and near-zero (or negative) policy rates—to deliver growth. There is, however, a growing understanding among policymakers that monetary easing is not sufficient for stimulating real economic activity. While accommodative monetary policy stances helped avert a financial sector meltdown and prevent a prolonged recession, they have not been as effective as expected in stimulating investment and growth. The key monetary policy assumptions underlying the central forecast, and forecast sensitivities to these assumptions, are reported in the appendix to this chapter.

Monetary policy stances during the post-crisis period clearly kept the cost of borrowing at historically low levels. From a historical perspective, both short- and long-term interest rates in developed economies are still very low. Figure I.20 shows ten-year govern-

*Monetary easing prevented further worsening of the economic slowdown*

Figure I.20
**Ten-year government bond yields in selected developed economies, October 2005–October 2015**

Source: UN/DESA, based on data from JPMorgan.

---

14    For example, it is estimated that, while holding other factors constant, the 20cm of sea level rise at the southern tip of Manhattan since the 1950s has increased insured losses from 2012 Hurricane Sandy by 30 per cent in New York. See Lloyd's (2014).

Monetary policy stances of
developed economies are
expected to diverge

ment bond yields since October 2005 for France, Germany, Japan, the United States and
the United Kingdom.

While monetary conditions in most developed economies remain loose, the policy
stances of the Fed and other major central banks have diverged over the past year. The Fed
has moved closer to its first interest-rate hike since 2006 as the labour market in the United
States has continued to improve gradually. However, amid concerns over the impact of global economic weakness on domestic activity and inflation, the Fed rate rise is now expected
to occur in December 2015, but could be pushed into 2016 in the case of a weaker-than-
expected global economic outlook. After the initial lift-off, the pace of interest-rate
normalization by the hike is likely to be slow and highly sensitive to inflation and job
market developments.

Unlike the Fed, other developed-country central banks, including the ECB and
the Bank of Japan, are still easing monetary policy. The ECB continues to implement its
expanded asset purchase programme, which was launched in March 2015 in an attempt to
steer inflation closer to the 2 per cent target. The monthly asset purchases of public and private sector securities amount to an average of €60 billion and are expected to be carried out
through the end of March 2017. While the programme has supported the recovery of the
euro area, a downgrading of the inflation forecast has opened the door for further stimulus.
A first interest-rate increase by the ECB is not expected until late 2017 or 2018. The Bank
of Japan has maintained the pace of asset purchases under its quantitative and qualitative
monetary easing programme (QQME), targeting an increase in the monetary base at an
annual pace of about 80 trillion yen. The authorities have not specified an end date for the
programme, indicating that it will continue until inflation is stable at 2 per cent. The like-
lihood of a further expansion of the programme has increased in recent months as headline
and core inflation once again declined and economic activity weakened.

Against the backdrop of weakening growth, rising financial market volatility, sharp
exchange-rate depreciations and increasing portfolio capital outflows, monetary policies
in developing and transition economies have shown some divergence in 2015 (figure I.21).

**Figure I.21**
**Central bank policy rates in the BRICS, October 2011–October 2015**

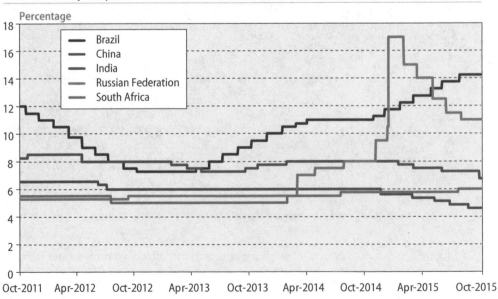

Source: UN/DESA, based on data
from various National
central banks.

Many Asian central banks cut their policy rates in 2015, responding to declining inflation and seeking to support growth.

The People's Bank of China has reduced its one-year benchmark lending rate six times since November 2014, lowering the rate from 6 per cent to 4.35 per cent. The authorities have also used other measures, such as reserve requirement cuts and targeted lending facilities, to inject liquidity into the economy. The Reserve Bank of India cut its main policy rate four times in 2015, by a total of 125 basis points. For many developing economies, especially those with open capital accounts, the monetary policy stance over the next two years will not only depend on growth and inflation trends, but also on potential spillover effects of policy changes in the United States.

In several South American and African countries, including Brazil, Colombia, Kenya and South Africa, monetary policy has recently been tightened in a bid to halt rising inflation, significant capital outflows and large currency depreciations. For most of these countries, the monetary tightening is expected to further lower growth prospects, which have already been hit by the drop in commodity prices and a range of domestic factors.

## Fiscal policy

Most of the developed economies—whose fiscal deficits and public debt levels are averaging about 3 per cent and 100 per cent of GDP, respectively—have gradually transitioned since 2013 from post-crisis consolidation of public finances to a more neutral fiscal stance. With few exceptions, no significant fiscal drag is expected in 2015-2016 in developed countries. The key fiscal policy assumptions underlying the central forecast, and forecast sensitivities to these assumptions, are reported in the appendix to this chapter.

In the United States, the federal budget deficit has improved by 7 percentage points of GDP since 2009, supported by stronger economic growth in 2014-2015. Following several years of austerity, the fiscal policy stance has become more neutral, and this is expected to continue in the near term. Real federal government consumption expenditure is expected to remain at 2015 levels in both 2016 and 2017, but given the moderate improvement in the state and local government fiscal positions, real government expenditure at this level will grow by about 1 per cent in both 2016 and 2017.

Among the countries of the EU, fiscal policy stances diverge. Several EU members, including France, are running budget deficits exceeding 3 per cent of GDP and have to consolidate their public finances, complying with the Excessive Deficit Procedure of the EU. In Japan, the Government conducts a flexible fiscal policy, but is pursuing medium-term fiscal consolidation, aiming to achieve a primary budget surplus by 2020. However, the Government decided to postpone the planned consumption tax increase from October 2015 to April 2017 and to implement additional stimulus measures. The Government also intends to reduce the corporate tax rate in April 2016. The country's public debt-to-GDP ratio stands at over 220 per cent and may become unsustainable in the long run, but as most of this debt is held domestically, default risks are relatively small compared to countries that face large external and foreign-currency-denominated debt burdens.

Among the major developing countries, fiscal policy in China is expected to be moderately expansionary in the medium-term and the consolidated government deficit may reach historically high levels, mostly because of large and growing indebtedness of the regional governments. The central Government's support to the regions may increase in order to prevent the excessive reliance of local governments on commercial borrowing. The ongoing debt-restructuring programme is expected to reduce financial risks at the local level. In Brazil, by contrast, the Government is tightening its fiscal stance, in part by curbing subsidized public lending, in order to reduce public debt and to restore the country's investment grade.

Fiscal tightening is likely
in commodity-exporting
economies

Among the economies in transition, the Government of the Russian Federation had to revise its 2015 budget against the backdrop of the fall in oil prices and weaker economy, and foresee a wider than initially anticipated budget deficit. However, fiscal tightening in the near-term will be somewhat mitigated by drawing from the Reserve Fund and expanding the tax base. Other commodity-exporting economies are also bracing for fiscal tightening during the forecast period.

Global imbalances continue
to pose a potential risk to
global financial stability

While the dispersion of global current-account deficits and surpluses has narrowed somewhat from the peaks leading up to the global financial crisis, a significant degree of imbalance still persists, posing a potential risk to global financial stability. Global imbalances in net external debt holdings have continued to widen since 2011, as illustrated in figure I.22. High levels of gross external debt leave a country exposed to a sudden withdrawal of foreign capital, and pose additional risks linked to exchange-rate fluctuations if the external debt is denominated in foreign currency. Without any additional narrowing of the global current-account imbalance, global imbalances in net external debt can be expected to continue to widen beyond the end of this decade, and global vulnerabilities related to external debt are unlikely to recede.

A strong dollar may
reverse the trend in
global imbalances, which
have improved since the
financial crisis

Two key factors interacting with the recent evolution and outlook for global imbalances are the sharp exchange-rate realignments and the deterioration of commodity prices, especially the oil price. The pace of global net debt accumulation has moderated signif-

Figure I.22
**Net external asset positions as a percentage of world gross product, 2003–2017[a]**

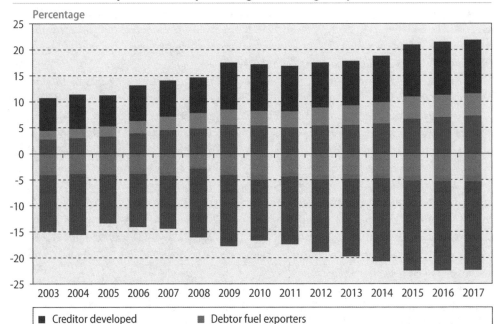

Source: UN/DESA, based on
United Nations Statistics Division
National Accounts Main Aggregates Database, International
Monetary Fund, International
Financial Statistics and updated
and extended version of dataset
constructed by Lane and
Milesi-Ferretti (2007).
a Data for 2015-2017
are projections.

icantly in recent years, largely associated with the United States current-account deficit narrowing from 5.8 per cent of GDP in 2006 to 2.2 per cent in 2014, matched by a decline in China's current-account surplus from 8.5 per cent of GDP to 2.1 per cent over the same period. The real appreciation of the dollar highlighted above can be expected to unwind some of this improvement, although at the global level this deterioration may be partially offset by narrowing surpluses in creditor countries with currencies that are closely tied to the dollar, as well as the impact of commodity price declines on imbalances.

IMF (2006, chap. II) highlighted the role that rising oil prices played in exacerbating global imbalances in the lead-up to the financial crisis. By contrast, the recent drop in oil prices should help to improve imbalances at the global level. The vast majority of net debtor countries are fuel importers, while the majority of fuel exporters have historically run persistent current-account surpluses. The sharp deterioration of current-account balances in fuel-exporting economies will be partially financed by drawing down reserves in countries that have normally run large current-account surpluses.

As China's current-account surplus has narrowed, Germany is now the largest surplus country in the world. Germany's intra-euro area trade surplus has narrowed sharply since 2007, but its extra-euro area surplus has continued to widen, as illustrated in figure I.23. The growing external surplus of Germany partly explains the widening current-account surplus of the euro area as a whole, which also reflects the rapid adjustment of the external positions of Greece, Ireland, Italy, Portugal and Spain (figure I.23). Please see Chapter III for more details on global imbalances and reserves accumulation.

**Figure I.23**
**Euro area current-account balance** (*CAB*)

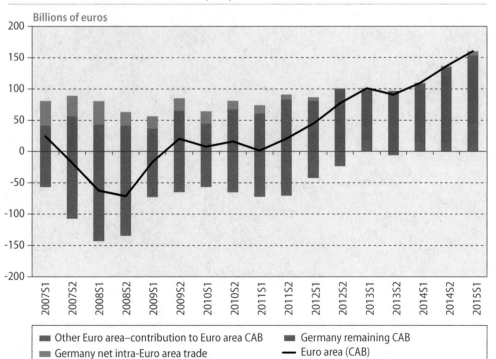

Source: UN/DESA, based on data from Eurostat and ECB databases.

## Vulnerabilities in developing economies increase

A number of economies
are likely to be hard hit by
a sharper-than-expected
slowdown of the Chinese
economy

A larger-than-expected slowdown in China, the second largest economy in the world, is likely to have substantial ripple effects on the rest of the global economy. The hardest hit would be China's immediate neighbours (Mongolia, Lao People's Democratic Republic, the Republic of Korea) who have strong trade ties with China. Figure I.24 highlights 29 countries that are particularly exposed, as China is the number one export destination for these economies.[15] These include both commodity-exporting economies—such as Angola, Brazil, Chile, Mongolia—as well as a few high-income economies, including Australia, New Zealand and the Republic of Korea. Exports to China account for more than 25 per cent of total exports in the case of 11 of these economies, making them particularly vulnerable to the slowdown of the Chinese economy.

Lower commodity prices have already significantly worsened the fiscal position of many commodity-dependent developing economies and exacerbated their external debt burden. The risk of debt default, although still relatively low for small commodity-exporting economies, can intensify if commodity prices decline further. The increased risk of debt unsustainability may compel investors to move both their equity and debt capital to a relatively safer investment environment, exacerbating capital outflows and further undermining the economic health of commodity-exporting economies. The vicious cycle of low growth, depressed revenue prospects, increased risk perceptions, capital outflows, reduced liquidity and increased borrowing costs may become mutually reinforcing, restraining growth further. This may have a cascading, contagious effect on a range of developing

**Figure I.24**
**Share of exports to China**

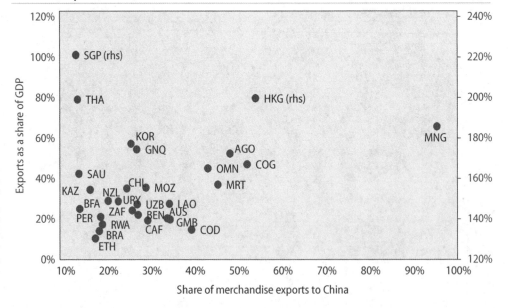

Source: UN/DESA, based on
United Nations Statistics Division
National Accounts
Main Aggregates Database
and IMF Direction of
Trade Statistics.
Note: See table J in the
Statistical Annex to this
publication for definitions
of country codes.

15    Angola, Australia, Benin, Brazil, Burkina Faso, Central African Republic, Chile, Congo, Democratic Republic of the Congo, Equatorial Guinea, Ethiopia, Gambia, Hong Kong Special Administrative Region of China, Kazakhstan, Lao People's Democratic Republic, Mauritania, Mongolia, Mozambique, New Zealand, Oman, Peru, Republic of Korea, Rwanda, Saudi Arabia, South Africa, Thailand, Uruguay and Uzbekistan.

economies, both commodity exporters and others, leading to a broader debt crisis reminiscent of the debt crisis in the late 1980s.

Developing economies in general would need to find new sources of growth domestically or regionally to escape the potential downward spiral emanating from commodity-price- and exchange-rate-related shocks. This would require Governments to pursue comprehensive structural transformation and industrial policies that would mobilize domestic savings and investment, improve institutions and corporate governance and reduce transaction costs and increase competitiveness. Sustained and sustainable improvement in labour productivity would allow many developing countries to create more decent jobs, increase the labour share of income and reduce income inequality both within and between countries.

## Geopolitical risks cloud regional economic prospects

The near-term global economic forecast remains susceptible to a number of geopolitical tensions and risks. These include the situations in Afghanistan, Iraq, the Syrian Arab Republic, Ukraine and Yemen and the refugee crisis that has engulfed various neighbouring countries of some of these crisis spots, as well as Europe.

The intermittent geopolitical crisis around Ukraine presents a risk to the economic outlook, at least at the regional level. Despite the ceasefire agreement reached in February 2015, the conflict in the East of Ukraine is not yet resolved. The mutual economic sanctions between the Russian Federation and many OECD economies, including the United States and the EU, were extended in July 2015. As a result, many leading Russian companies and banks remain cut off from the major international capital markets, and cooperation with a number of Russian enterprises is under embargo. The Government of the Russian Federation, on its side, implemented a one-year extension of the ban on imports of food products from those countries that are participating in the sanctions. Together with the fall in oil prices, the sanctions have taken a toll on the Russian economy, leading to outflows of capital and a contraction in investment. As many of the smaller CIS economies significantly depend on remittance inflows from the Russian Federation, the downturn in the Russian economy has had a negative spillover effect on the region, which is set to continue in 2016. The weaker Russian import demand also had a knock-on effect on some countries in the EU-15, while the food import ban has had a sectoral impact on some of the new EU member States, in particular on the Baltic States, Hungary and Poland, and also has affected transit trade revenues for these economies. The sanctions were only one of the factors leading to the drastic depreciation of the Russian currency in 2014. A further escalation of the conflict may lead to interruption of the Russian natural gas flow through Ukraine, which would be especially damaging for Eastern Europe, while the increased defence expenditure in the EU-15 may weigh on the public finances.

Violent conflicts continue in Afghanistan, Iraq, Libya, the Syrian Arab Republic and Yemen, with significant spill over effects on the regional economies. The prolonged conflicts, particularly in the Syrian Arab Republic, aggravated the problem of refugees who already numbered in the millions in neighbouring countries. An increasing number of citizens have been fleeing from these countries, and also from North Africa, towards Europe. The presence of a large number of refugees is likely to increase political and financial strains in the host economies, with the potential for contagion of conflict spreading beyond the

*Further spread of conflict would depress growth in some regions*

Syrian Arab Republic and reaching the door-step of Europe. There is also mounting pressure from refugees trying to enter Western Europe in search of a better livelihood. This has added new challenges for a number of transit and destination countries, both in logistical and financial terms. In addition, in a number of destination countries, issues regarding the integration of refugees into society and the labour market are likely to create additional policy challenges.

## Policy challenges are expected to intensify

More than seven years after the global financial crisis, policymakers around the world still face enormous difficulties in restoring robust and balanced global growth. In developed countries, most of the burden of promoting growth has fallen on central banks, which have used a wide range of conventional and unconventional policy tools, including various large-scale QE programmes, forward guidance and negative nominal interest rates. These measures have led to an unprecedented degree of monetary accommodation in recent years, with monetary bases soaring and short- and long-term interest rates falling to historically low levels.

Accommodative monetary conditions and abundant supply of global liquidity have also given rise to wide swings in capital flows to emerging markets. Financial stability risks have increased amid concerns over the excessive build-up of financial assets, commensurate asset price bubbles and balance-sheet vulnerabilities, especially in emerging markets. Volatility in commodity, currency, bond and stock markets has moved up since mid-2014, partly as a result of monetary policy adjustments and uncertainties over future policy moves.

Against this backdrop, the monetary authorities in developed countries face the task of balancing the need for continued monetary accommodation with the goal of limiting real and nominal volatilities and minimize the risks to global financial stability. In this context, macroprudential policies have become increasingly important since the global financial crisis. The ultimate goal of macroprudential tools—such as capital requirements for banks and other financial institutions, limits on loan-to-value and debt-to-income ratios, and limits on banks' foreign-exchange exposure—is to temper the financial cycle and contain systemic risks (see Constâncio, 2015). Macroprudential policies, when designed and applied effectively, can help mitigate financial sector volatility and redirect financial resources to more productive sectors of the economy.

*Monetary policy normalization will need to strike a balance between sustaining growth and managing financial stability risks*

For developed-country central banks, the main challenge over the coming years is how to normalize monetary policy without crushing asset prices, causing major financial volatility and potentially threatening the expected recovery. At present, the international focus is on the Fed, which is the first major central bank to start the monetary tightening cycle. While the Fed's decision-making is guided by its dual mandate—promoting maximum stable employment and price stability—it is taking into account the potential spill-over effects of its policies on the world economy. By keeping the Fed fund rate at the zero lower bound, the Fed has also temporarily prevented a widening of the monetary policy gap with other central banks and a further strengthening of the dollar. Going forward, the challenge for the Fed is not only to get the timing of interest-rate hikes right, but also to adequately prepare financial markets for the moves via effective communication of its plans.

While the normalization of United States interest rates is expected in late 2015, some uncertainties remain regarding both the anticipated path of interest rates and the reaction of global financial markets and the real economy to the shift in policy rates. A rise in debt-servicing costs will necessarily be associated with the United States interest-rate normalization, both domestically and in the many developing economies and economies in transition that hold debt denominated in United States dollars. In addition, as the rates of return on United States assets normalize, a sudden change in risk appetite could trigger a collapse of capital flows to developing economies and economies in transition, or sharp exchange-rate realignments as experienced following the Fed's announcement in 2013 that it would soon begin tapering its QE programme. Significant levels of net capital outflows have already occurred in many developing economies in anticipation of the normalization of United States policy rates (for more discussion, see the section on rising volatility in exchange rates and capital flows), and there is a risk that these withdrawals could increase further, drying up liquidity in many developing economies. This may lead to a depreciation of many developing-country exchange rates, or pressure them to raise interest rates to prevent capital outflows. Countries that hold a large stock of net external debt are particularly exposed to the associated rising costs of debt servicing. As a downside risk to the outlook, financial markets could overreact and overshoot the adjustment, or exhibit a sudden change in risk appetite, leading to heightened financial market volatility, an even sharper withdrawal of capital from developing markets, and a more significant slowdown in global growth.

In developing countries and economies in transition, the current global economic and financial environment poses major challenges for monetary and exchange-rate policies. Economic growth in most countries has slowed significantly over the past few years amid declining commodity prices and domestic weaknesses.[16] Although potential growth is likely to be lower than before the global financial crisis, sizeable negative output gaps have opened up in many countries. These gaps would call for considerable monetary loosening. However, the room for monetary easing is constrained for a number of developing-country and economies in transition central banks in the CIS and South America that have encountered high inflationary pressures. Furthermore, in several cases, policy rates have not returned to pre-financial crisis levels, which limit the scope for interest rate cuts. These constraints are accompanied by concerns that rising United States interest rates and a further strengthening of the dollar could trigger a wave of emerging-market corporate defaults over the coming years.

Given that monetary policies have done most of the heavy lifting for supporting growth during the post-crisis period, both developed and developing countries will need to rely more on fiscal policy instruments to stimulate growth in the near term. Fiscal policies will need to primarily focus on boosting investment and productivity growth. Most of the EU countries enjoy low sovereign borrowing costs, supported by the ongoing sovereign bond purchases by the ECB. While this mitigates the costs of financing deficits, policymakers will continue to struggle to find a balance between supporting growth and employment and adhering to their commitments under the Stability and Growth Pact. This may become more challenging if deflation in the euro area persists, which may inflate fiscal deficits and public debt-to-GDP ratios.

> Going forward, fiscal policy will need to do the heavy lifting to stimulate investment and growth

Compared with the developed economies, developing countries and economies in transition generally have smaller budget deficits and public debt levels. This should encourage developing countries to pursue expansionary fiscal policies, including well-timed and

---

16    Average growth in developing countries for 2015 is estimated at 3.8 per cent. In the past 25 years, average annual growth has been lower only during acute crisis episodes: the Asian crisis in 1998, the financial crises in Argentina and Turkey in 2001 and the global financial crisis in 2009. Economies in transition are estimated to contract by an average rate of 2.8 per cent in 2015.

targeted fiscal stimuli, to boost domestic demand and growth. In oil-exporting economies, persistently low oil prices should eventually encourage public finance reforms, including discretionary spending, and support policies targeting economic diversification. Oil-importing developing countries, on the other hand, should take advantage of low oil prices to redirect their fiscal savings to productive investments.

Well-designed fiscal policies can play a central role in fostering employment creation and reducing both unemployment and underemployment. Furthermore, current income disparities and low wage growth can be addressed with social transfers as well as with effective training policies to advance workers' employability, and through stronger collective bargaining mechanisms that can improve income distribution. Additionally, considering that labour force participation is low and long-term unemployment extremely high, more active labour market policies may be considered as a complement to unemployment benefits to make labour markets more inclusive. Efforts to enhance access to credit for small and medium-sized enterprises can also play a significant role in investment recovery and job creation.

Progressive tax structures, including income tax relief for lower-income groups, are also effective in addressing working poverty and income inequalities, with potential benefits for growth and employment creation. Particularly in developing economies, where the informal sector is larger, well-designed tax systems can encourage formal employment creation in general, but they can also support more disadvantaged social groups and improve government revenue. In addition, since working poverty is also often associated with low-skilled labour, training policies targeting low-skilled workers may play a critical role in enhancing employment, productivity and output growth. They can help address income disparities between groups of workers, by increasing labour productivity and reducing working poverty. According to OECD (2015a), wage inequality is lower in countries where skills are more equally distributed. At the same time, training programmes for low-skilled workers can also stimulate discouraged workers to re-enter the labour market and reduce long-term unemployment.

Increasing labour's share of income can help boost aggregate demand and revive global growth

Labour's declining share of total income has been identified as a key underlying factor limiting aggregate demand and, ultimately, output growth. This is in part the result of a long-term trend, which has led to a widening gap between wage growth and productivity growth (see United Nations, 2015a). In addition, as has been underscored by several international organizations (OECD, the International Labour Organization (ILO), IMF, UNCTAD, UN/DESA), the weakening of workers' bargaining power is another important factor underpinning the declining labour share of total income. Mandatory minimum wages, where they do not exist, can directly help those at the bottom of the income distribution, but they can also secure fair pay and increase tax revenues. As a complementary policy, collective bargaining mechanisms can be designed to realign wage growth with productivity growth, rendering economic growth more inclusive and equitable. Evidence shows that Governments that have introduced new measures to increase minimum wages, as well as collective bargaining, were able to curb working poverty and income inequality, while boosting aggregate demand.

## Sustainable development will require more sustained policy coordination

Effective policy coordination is needed to boost investment, employment, productivity and growth

Stimulating inclusive growth in the near term and fostering long-term sustainable development will require more effective policy coordination—between monetary, exchange-rate and fiscal policies—to break the vicious cycle of weak aggregate demand, under-investment, low productivity and low growth performance in the global economy. Equally critical is the coordination of monetary and macroprudential policies to align the objectives of financial stability and growth, and to ensure that finance indeed supports the real economy and that the world economy does not lapse into yet another financial crisis. This would also be critical to ensuring a smooth adjustment in asset prices to minimize the negative spillover effects of the normalization of monetary policy stances worldwide. Furthermore, economic, social and environmental policies need to be coordinated to realize the comprehensive and universal 2030 Agenda for Sustainable Development. There also needs to be stronger international coordination of various domestic-level policies, taking into account the possible spillover effects on the rest of the economy.

Policy coordination, however, has become increasingly difficult against the backdrop of ever greater complexity in the financial market, persistent and growing disconnect between finance and the real economy, and the chronic misalignment and incentive incompatibility of various policy objectives pursued by different stakeholders at both national and international levels. At the domestic level, policies are often designed and implemented in compartments, with little integration and coordination of different policy objectives.

In the aftermath of the global financial crisis, the G20 undertook concrete measures to improve policy coordination at the global level. However, a quick but shallow recovery of global growth in 2011-2012 rendered the measures less of an imperative. Against the backdrop of a prolonged period of slow growth combined with the global commitment to the 2030 Agenda for Sustainable Development, the international community needs to renew its efforts to improve policy coordination at national, regional and international levels.

International policy coordination is critically important for realizing the ambitious, comprehensive and universal 2030 Agenda for Sustainable Development and achieving its associated goals and targets. First and foremost, policy coordination is needed to revive global growth and put the world economy on a new path of equitable, sustained and sustainable growth. The Addis Ababa Action Agenda, agreed at the Third International Conference on Financing for Development in July 2015, provides the framework for policies and actions to align all financing flows and international and domestic policies with economic, social and environmental priorities (see chap. III, box III.1). A successful conclusion of the multilateral trade negotiations (i.e., reducing barriers to market access, especially for developing economies) will provide a much-needed impetus to investment, stimulate productivity growth and output, facilitate redistribution of global income, reduce global imbalances and address both within- and between-country income inequalities. The imperative of international policy coordination is also most evident in the area of climate change and environment. The successful conclusion of the 2015 United Nations Climate Change Conference in Paris, leading to binding commitments to reduce emission levels, is expected to pave the way for more effective international policy coordination for sustainable development in all three dimensions: economic, social and environmental.

*Policy coordination will continue to face daunting challenges*

*Agreements on trade and climate change will provide a much-needed impetus to stimulate sustainable growth*

# Baseline forecast assumptions

This appendix summarizes the key assumptions underlying the baseline forecast, including monetary and fiscal policies for major economies, exchange rates for major currencies and the international prices of oil. It also assesses the sensitivity of the baseline forecast to these assumptions, using the World Economic Forecasting Model (WEFM) of UN/DESA. WEFM is a large-scale global macroeconomic model, covering 160 countries, which ensures the global consistency of the forecasts presented in this report.

## Monetary policy

The United States Federal Reserve Board (Fed) is expected to raise its key policy rate by 25 basis points by the end of 2015. The target for the federal funds rate will then increase gradually, by 50 basis points and 100 basis points in 2016 and 2017, respectively (figure I.A.1). The Fed terminated its asset purchase programme in October 2014, which has so far not driven a strong rebound of long-term government bond yields in the United States of America. Until the end of 2017, the Fed is expected to maintain its policy of reinvesting principal payments from its holdings of agency debt and agency mortgage-backed securities in agency mortgage-backed securities and of rolling over maturing Treasury securities at auction, broadly maintaining the size of its balance sheet (figure I.A.2).

The European Central Bank (ECB) significantly loosened its monetary stance in 2015, introducing an expanded asset purchase programme, with monthly purchases of public and private sector securities amounting to €60 billion. This policy is expected to continue until the end of March 2017, bringing the size of the ECB balance sheet close to its level in 2012. After cutting interest rates twice in 2014, the ECB is expected to maintain policy interest rates at current levels for one year following the termination of the asset purchase programme, and raise interest rates by 50 basis points by end-2017.

The Bank of Japan (BoJ) increased the scale of its asset purchase programme in October 2014 from 60-70 trillion to 80 trillion yen per annum. The BoJ is expected to keep the scale of asset purchases at this level until at least the end of 2017, and to maintain its policy interest rate at current levels of 0-10 basis points.

The People's Bank of China (PBOC) is expected to continue to carry out targeted measures, including further cuts to the reserve requirement ratio and targeted lending facilities, to inject liquidity into the economy. These measures will roughly offset the decline of foreign-exchange deposits—a major source of liquidity—and the overall monetary condition will remain neutral during the forecast period.

Figure I.A.1
**Key policy rates**

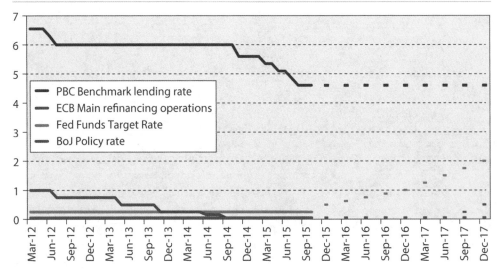

Source: UN/DESA, based on data
from relevant central banks.

Figure I.A.2
**Total assets of major central banks, December 2006–December 2017**

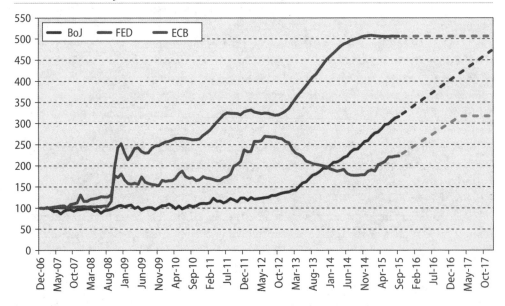

Source: UN/DESA, based on
data from Bank of Japan, United
States Federal Reserve and
European Central Bank.

## Fiscal policy

Fiscal policy in the United States is expected to become marginally expansive. Real government consumption expenditure is expected to expand by 0.9 per cent in both 2016 and 2017, and there will be no major change in the tax system. The accord reached between the legislative and executive branches of the United States Government in October 2015 suspended the debt ceiling until March 2017, and it is assumed that an appropriate debt ceiling beyond March 2017 will be set in a timely manner.

In aggregate, the fiscal stance in the EU is neutral in 2015, and is expected to be broadly neutral or marginally expansionary in 2016. A slightly tighter stance is expected for 2017. Excessive Deficit Procedures remain ongoing in 9 EU countries, which will entail tightening measures of at least 0.5 per cent of GDP per annum.

In Japan, the scheduled date for the second increase in the consumption tax rate was delayed from October 2015 to April 2017, and it is assumed that the increase will come into effect as currently scheduled. The corporation tax rate will be cut in April 2016 from 32.1 per cent to 31.3 per cent. Government outlays are expected to increase during the fiscal year beginning in April 2016.

In China, the fiscal policy stance will remain mildly expansionary during the forecast period. The ratio of local government debt to total fiscal capacity is expected to reach about 86 per cent by end-2015, but will remain below the 100 per cent ceiling over the forecast period.

## Exchange rates among major currencies

The dollar/euro exchange rate is assumed to average 1.117 in 2015, and to depreciate in line with the widening differential between ECB and Fed interest rates to 1.094 in 2016 and 1.042 in 2017.

The yen/dollar exchange rate is assumed to average 120.75 in 2015, 122.98 in 2016 and 124.80 in 2017.

The renminbi/dollar exchange rate is assumed to average 6.225 CNY/dollar in 2015 and 6.53 in 2016 and 6.47 in 2017.

Figure I.A.3
**Data and assumptions on major currency exchange rates**

Source: UN/DESA, based on data from JPMorgan and WEFM working assumption.

## Oil price

The price of Brent oil is expected to average $53 per barrel in 2015, $51 per barrel in 2016 and $62 per barrel in 2017.

## Forecast sensitivities to key assumptions

Below are illustrative sensitivities of forecasts for the major global regions to some of the key underlying assumptions of the forecast, based on simulations using WEFM.

Figure I.A.4
**Impact of a 1 percentage point rise in United States interest rates**

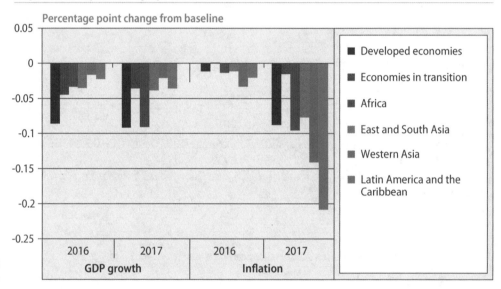

Source: UN/DESA-WEFM
simulation.

Figure I.A.5
**Impact of a 1 per cent of GDP increase in United States government spending**

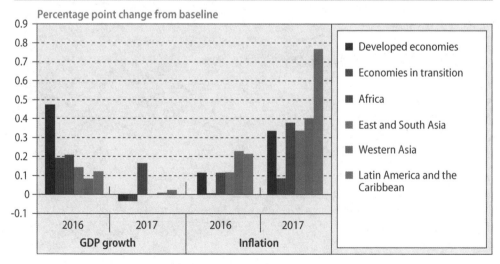

Source: UN/DESA-WEFM
simulation.

Figure I.A.6
## Impact of a 5 per cent depreciation of the euro/$ rate

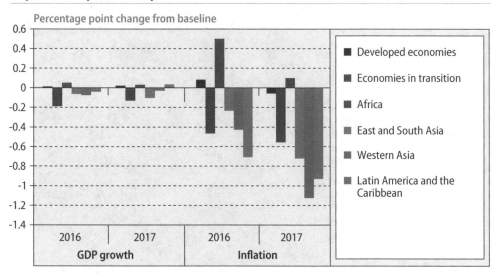

Source: UN/DESA-WEFM
simulation.

Figure I.A.7
## Impact of a 10 per cent rise in the oil price

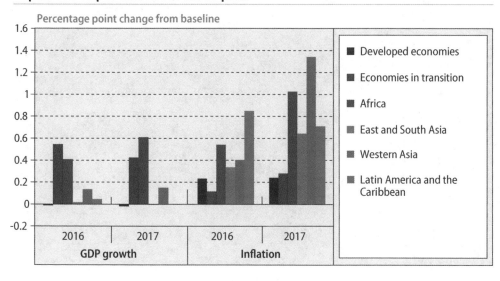

Source: UN/DESA-WEFM
simulation.

# Chapter II
# International trade

## Trade flows

The subdued performance of world trade flows persisted into 2015, with the volume of world trade projected to increase by only 2.7 per cent for the year, the lowest rate since the global financial crisis and approximately the same rate as the estimated world gross product growth for 2015 (figure II.1). For the second consecutive year, developed economies played the leading role in driving global trade. Among all regions, the developed economies in Europe contributed most significantly to global import growth in 2015, accounting for 70.3 per cent of the growth (figure II.2). On the other hand, the contribution from developing East Asia dropped sharply. The region is projected to be responsible for just 8.4 per cent of global import growth in 2015, after accounting for 27 per cent on average in the previous decade. In the outlook, global trade growth is expected to pick up to a moderate pace of 4.0 per cent in 2016 and 4.7 per cent in 2017, outpacing real world gross product growth, but still considerably below the rates witnessed during the pre-crisis period.

The subdued performance of world trade reflects a combination of cyclical and structural factors. On the cyclical side, weak aggregate demand—initially emanating from the slow recovery in the euro area and more recently the slowdown of large emerging economies—has restricted global trade. In the first half of 2015, the volume of imports into the Russian Federation dropped by more than 25 per cent, while in Brazil and India imports declined by 8-9 per cent, and China's import demand also slowed sharply.

China's slowdown in import demand in particular has significant spillovers to the rest of the world. As of 2014, China accounts for more than 12 per cent of global mer-

> World trade growth remained weak in 2015, but is expected to rise moderately in the forecast period

> Subdued global trade reflects both cyclical and structural factors

Figure II.1
**Growth of world trade and world gross product, 2007-2017**[a]

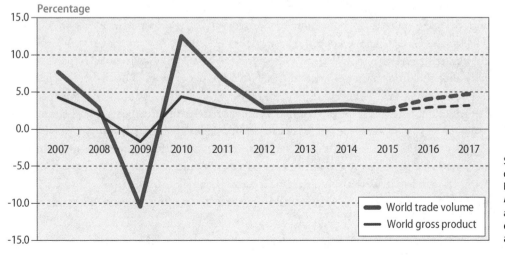

Source: UN/DESA, based on United Nations Statistics Division National Accounts Main Aggregates Database.
a Growth rate for 2015 is partially estimated; growth rates for 2016 and 2017 are forecast.

**Figure II.2**
**Regional contribution to global import growth, 2011–2017[a]**

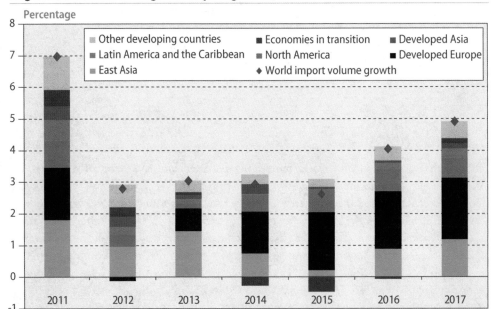

Source: UN/DESA, based
on United Nations Statistics
Division National Accounts Main
Aggregates Database.
Note: The "Other developing"
countries includes Africa,
Western Asia and South Asia.
a Figures for 2015 are partially
estimated; figures for 2016 and
2017 are forecast.

chandise exports and about 10 per cent of total merchandise imports. In addition, China is the top shipment destination for about 29 economies, which include many countries of the Asia Pacific region and commodity-exporting economies. Slowing demand from China has had an important impact on the global demand for certain commodities, contributing to the downward trend in commodity prices. In the first three quarters of 2015, China's imports of coal and steel (in volume terms) recorded a dramatic year-over-year decline, which reflects the slowdown in fixed investment (figure II.3). Imports of copper ores continued to rise, but the growth rate dropped by 10 percentage points compared to the first three quarters of 2014. By contrast, growth of crude oil imports have remained steady, which could reflect a strategy of increasing inventories while the price is low (see section on oil market prices). Overall, it is estimated that China accounted for about 20 per cent of the slowdown in import growth of developing economies and economies in transition between 2014 and 2015.

The slowdown in world trade also reflects a structural shift in the relationship between trade and gross domestic product (GDP) growth since the mid-2000s (Hoekman, 2015). The composition of global demand may be one factor explaining the shift. At the global level, the share of capital goods in total imports gradually dropped from 35.0 per cent in 2000 to 30.1 per cent in 2014, whereas consumer goods maintained their share of about 30 per cent throughout the same period.[1] Consumption tends to have a lower import content relative to investment, and the extended period of weak global investment (as discussed in chapter 1) has partly changed the import intensity of GDP growth. Given the continued uncertainty of the global economy, investment growth is expected to remain weak, and a significant rebound in the share of capital goods in world trade is unlikely in the near term. The lack of trade finance has also been attributed as a factor for the slowdown in world trade since the financial crisis. However,

---

1    World Integrated Trade Solution, available from http://wits.worldbank.org/.

Figure II.3
**China's imports of selected commodities, 2014 Q1–2015 Q3**

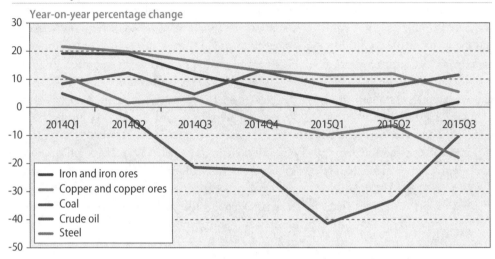

Source: UN/DESA calculation, based on data from China Customs Statistics.

this is not supported by cross-country data from bank surveys (International Chamber of Commerce, 2015).

The slower expansion of global value chains (GVCs) in recent years also partly explains the reduced trade intensity of global growth. Rapid expansion of the GVCs played a key role in accelerating global trade growth in the 1990s and early 2000s. This acceleration was also driven by a period of rapid integration of China and countries in Central and Eastern Europe into global markets. There is, however, a natural limit to the international fragmentation of production, and these factors have made a more limited contribution to world trade growth since the mid-2000s. In particular, China has been increasingly relying on domestic inputs for intermediate goods. Its share of intermediate goods in total imports dropped from almost 33 per cent in 2001 (when China joined the World Trade Organization (WTO)) to about 18 per cent in 2013, partly explaining the diminished importance of GVCs in trade flows. Further integration of other large emerging economies such as Brazil, India and South Africa into global markets, and a more prominent role for Africa, have the potential to accelerate global trade growth in the medium term. This will, however, require policy initiatives to reduce trade costs and barriers, and deepen regional integration; it remains to be seen to what extent these potential actors can provide a new impetus to global trade.

> The slower expansion of global value chains has weighed on global trade

The WTO Doha Round of multilateral trade negotiations has made little progress in providing an additional push to global trade in the last fifteen years. There has been a rise in regional trade agreements (RTAs) around the world, which have the potential to generate significant new trade flows. But RTAs can also have trade-diversion effects, with trade growing within a RTA, thereby adversely affecting trade flows with and among non-RTA members. The recent conclusion of the Trans-Pacific Partnership (TPP) Agreement, which involved twelve countries and over 40 per cent of the world gross product, could expand trade opportunities for certain countries. Nonetheless, the proliferation of the RTAs cannot replace the role of the multilateral trading system (see section on trade policy), and can only partially offset the negative effects of restrictive trade measures, which continue to rise but at a slower pace than in previous years. Between October 2014 and May 2015, the Group of Twenty (G20), for example, adopted 119 new trade-restrictive measures (World Trade Organization, 2015a).

> Multilateral trade negotiations have made little progress in boosting trade

In recent years, large swings in exchange rates and the steep decline in commodity prices have had adverse effects on world trade. Currencies of many emerging markets and some developed economies have depreciated significantly against the dollar. While the associated competitiveness gains have supported exports in some countries—in Western Europe and South Asia, for instance—the sharp rise in import prices has cut back import demand significantly in many developing economies and economies in transition. A growing disconnect between exchange-rate swings and export performance has been argued in some empirical studies, owing to the greater relevance of GVCs in international trade (Ahmed, Appendino and Ruta, 2015). Backward and forward production linkages may make exchange-rate depreciations less effective in boosting exports. However, conventional trade that does not involve the GVCs still contributes a considerable amount of global trade, with the foreign content of exports averaging only about 25 per cent across economies (Leigh and others, 2015). While exports may have become less responsive to exchange-rate fluctuations in economies that are deeply integrated in GVCs, recent evidence also suggests that exchange-rate swings continue to have significant implications for the volume of exports (International Monetary Fund, 2015a, chap. 3).

The decline in commodity prices has also affected the volume, value and composition of trade flows (see section on the decomposition analysis). The collapse in the oil price in particular has led to a significant worsening of commodity terms of trade and of public finances for fuel-exporting economies, whereas other economies have largely seen an improvement in commodity terms of trade (box II.1). The oil price drop has signifi-

---

**Box II.1**

## The current commodity price slump, terms-of-trade effects and government finances in commodity-dependent developing countries

Given the decline in commodity prices since 2011, commodity-dependent developing countries (CDDCs) —defined by UNCTAD as developing countries deriving at least 60 per cent of their export revenues from commodity exports[a]—have experienced a deterioration of public finances. For example, public revenues of African CDDCs dropped from an average of 26.1 per cent of GDP between 2004 and 2007, to 21.2 per cent of GDP between 2011 and 2014. This partly explains the deterioration of these countries' average primary budget balances from a surplus of 3.6 per cent of GDP to a deficit of 1.8 per cent of GDP between the two periods. Many CDDCs have increased or are contemplating an increase in borrowing in order to shore up their finances.

Falling commodity-related revenues, depreciation in exchange rates and adverse terms of trade effects explain the deterioration in fiscal balance. Figure II.1.1 shows the declines in the commodity export and import price indices for 81 commodity-dependent countries between April 2011 and August 2015. Countries close to the 45-degree line have experienced similar declines in their export and import price indices, with minimal impact on their terms of trade. The further away a country is from the 45-degree line, the more asymmetric the impact has been. Economies above the 45-degree line have experienced an improvement in the commodity terms of trade, and those below the line experienced deterioration. As expected, most fuel exporters have seen a negative net price effect, with the commodity terms-of-trade worsening on average by 16.2 per cent (for more details on methodology of the estimates of the terms-of-trade effects, see the appendix to this chapter).

The commodity price slump has had the most adverse effect in countries where a high threshold oil price defined the overall fiscal envelope. In Algeria and Saudi Arabia, for example, fiscal breakeven oil prices were $129.80 per barrel (pb) and $111.30 pb, respectively, in 2014 (International Monetary Fund, 2015b). These were already too high, and the margin between actual and breakeven prices widened further in 2015. Oil prices averaged $62 pb in December 2014 and $47 pb in August 2015. As a result, many of the oil-exporting economies (Algeria, Angola, Iraq, Nigeria, Saudi Arabia and Venezuela (Bolivarian

*(continued)*

Republic of) have been forced to cut spending and government investment. Saudi Arabia, which had built large foreign-currency reserves during the commodity boom, has drawn down its reserves to cover last year's shortfall in oil revenue.[b] Other oil exporters are also experiencing downward pressure on their international reserves.

The commodity price collapse has also had similar fiscal effects on non-oil commodity exporters. In July 2015, Chile, the world's biggest copper producer, halved the growth rate of its projected fiscal revenue from the original estimate of 5.0 per cent to 2.4 per cent. The revision reflects the continued deterioration in copper price from $3.12 to $2.75 per pound.[c] In Zambia, where copper exports represent more than two thirds of total export earnings and account for 25-30 per cent of government revenue, the decline in copper prices will also contribute to the widening of the budget deficit. The International Monetary Fund (2015c) has revised the country's 2015 projected budget deficit from 4.6 per cent to 7.8 per cent of GDP.

The decline in commodity prices has been associated with significant currency depreciations in a number of CDDCs. In 2015, currencies in many CDDCs, including the Zambian kwacha, the Angolan kwanza, and the Nigerian naira, recorded some of their strongest depreciations against the United States dollar in several years. This has pushed up the prices of non-commodity imports, further amplifying the sharp deterioration in their terms of trade. Given the limited capacity to substitute imports with domestic goods, this suggests that many CDDCs will experience a deterioration of both their current-account and government budget balances in the short to medium term. Countries where budget deficits are being financed through external borrowing are exposed to currency risks, which may, in turn, adversely affect their debt sustainability. In the short term, the prospect of a twin deficit is likely to negatively affect these countries' standing in terms of sovereign risk and credit worthiness.

The current pressure on CDDCs' government budgets calls for strong policy actions to improve the governance of the commodity sector. The need to adopt countercyclical fiscal rules that require CDDCs to save during price booms and draw on the savings when prices collapse cannot be overemphasized. The current experience also highlights the importance of economic and fiscal diversification to reduce countries' exposure to the vagaries of commodity market cycles. Furthermore, current CDDCs difficulties suggest that, to the extent possible, the international community should adopt appropriate measures to reduce excessive price volatility in commodity markets. The Agricultural Market Information System (AMIS)—an initiative of the Group of Twenty established in the aftermath of the 2007-2008 food crisis—presents a good example of an international measure.

Box II.1 (*continued*)

Source: UNCTAD, Special Unit on Commodities and UN/DESA.

a In 2014, out of 146 developing countries for which data was available, 94, or about two thirds, were CDDCs.

b From April to September 2015, the country's central bank withdrew about $70 billion from global asset managers (*Financial Times*, 28 September 2015).

c The data is from Chile's Minister of Finance (Quiroga, 2015).

Figure II.1.1

**Commodity export and import price decline, April 2011–August 2015**

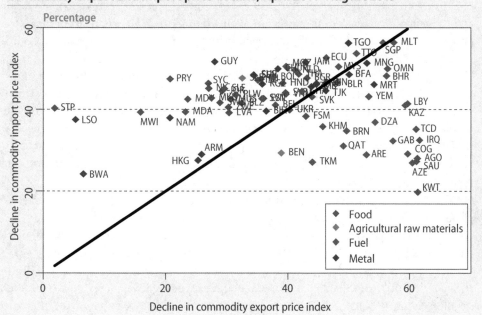

Source: UNCTAD, Special Unit on Commodities and UN/DESA.

Note: See table J in the Statistical Annex to this publication for definitions of country codes.

cantly limited fuel-exporting countries' demand for goods and services from the rest of the world, with knock-on effects in non-fuel-exporting countries. UN/DESA estimates suggest that only 39 out of a sample of 178 economies have experienced a deterioration in their commodity terms of trade since 2011. Collectively, these 39 economies accounted for approximately 16 per cent of the global merchandise imports in 2014. As the positive terms-of-trade shock in other countries is absorbed, this may support somewhat stronger world trade growth next year.

Overall, global trade continues to be subdued and is expected to pick up only moderately during the forecast period. This underscores the need for renewed efforts for strengthening the multilateral trading system, as well as for reducing trade-restrictive measures, to fully exploit the potential gains from global trade and facilitate the realization of the Sustainable Development Goals (SDGs).

## Regional trends

**Western Europe is expected to drive the recovery of global trade**

Western European economies will continue to be the main drivers of global trade growth in the outlook period, averaging more than 5 per cent growth per annum in imports during 2016-2017. The region's exports will continue to be supported by a high level of intraregional trade and competitiveness gains, via depreciation of the euro relative to the United States dollar. The United States of America will also see an improvement in export growth in 2016 and 2017, provided the dollar does not experience a further sharp appreciation in the near term. Import growth is projected to remain higher than export growth, reflecting the positive terms-of-trade effect of the strong United States dollar and some revival of private fixed investment.

The economies in transition experienced a sharp drop in the volume of trade in 2015. The Commonwealth of Independent States (CIS) is projected to register a fall of 3.1 per cent in export volumes and 15.6 per cent in import volumes, following sharp currency depreciations and weaker domestic demand. Exports from Ukraine saw the steepest decline amidst ongoing conflicts in the East of the country. The trade prospects of CIS economies remain affected by the economic difficulties faced by the Russian Federation and Ukraine and the geopolitical tensions in the region. Going into 2016-2017, exports from the CIS are projected to grow by only 0.7 per cent, whereas imports are forecast to expand by about 1.4 per cent per annum.

Exports from Africa expanded by an estimated 4.5 per cent in 2015, while imports grew by about 3.5 per cent. The slowdown in China—Africa's biggest trading partner—weighed on the trade performance of the continent. However, exports to India and trade within Africa have been robust, providing some support to total export volumes. Low commodity prices have nevertheless driven a decline in the region's export values of about 21.3 per cent in 2015. In the outlook, annual growth of export and import volumes is expected to average about 4.6 per cent.

**Trade growth in East and South Asia is expected to recover in the near term**

Trade growth in East Asia was unusually tepid in 2015. East Asian currencies displayed resilience in the beginning of 2015, but downward pressures increased and several currencies depreciated to multi-year lows against the dollar by the end of the third quarter, partly reflecting interventions in the currency markets. Both export and import growth in the region is expected to rebound—to 3.4 and 3.9 per cent, respectively—reflecting stronger demand from developed economies and expanding investment growth in several major economies. South Asia's merchandise exports have also been weak in 2015, partly reflecting some country-specific factors. Similar to East Asia, merchandise export growth from South Asia is also expected to recover to 5.4 per cent, on average, during 2016-2017, due to a pickup in external demand and currency depreciations. In value terms, Western Asia's exports faced a sharp decline of 20 per cent in 2015. This sudden drop was driven by the collapse in the oil price, although export volumes grew by 7.9 per cent. As oil prices are expected to remain low, oil-exporting economies will continue to suffer declining exports in value terms in 2016 before seeing a return to growth in 2017. Real import growth into the region is projected to remain stable at about 3.8 per cent per annum during 2016-2017, supported by the growing non-oil sector.

In Latin American and Caribbean economies, export volume growth is projected to improve by 2.8 per cent in 2015, whereas import volumes will contract by 0.3 per cent. In value terms, exports are expected to experience a sharp decline on account of the lower commodity prices. However, trade performance has been divergent within the region. Trade flows from Mexico and Central America continue to improve, partly explained by the recovery of the economy of the United States, while commodity-exporting economies in South America have been significantly affected by the slowdown in China's demand for metals and by the lower mineral and metal prices. Overall, regional annual average export and import growth are projected to improve to 4.2 per cent in 2016-2017.

*Trade performance in Latin America remains divergent across subregions*

## Decomposition analysis[2]

The total value of world merchandise trade started to contract rapidly in late 2014. In addition to the weak growth in the volume of trade, as discussed in the previous sections, a key factor explaining this contraction was the sharp decline of dollar-denominated prices for traded merchandise. Aggregate world trade prices declined by more than 14 per cent over this period, including the sharp plunge in the price of oil, more moderate but widely spread declines in non-oil commodities prices (see section on primary commodity markets), and a decline in export prices for manufactured goods[3] (figure II.4). Most major exporters of manufactured goods saw the price of their exports decline in United States dollar terms because of the strong appreciation of the dollar, although when measured in national currencies, those prices were stable or increasing mildly (figure II.5).[4]

*World trade prices declined across the board in 2015*

The decline of trade prices has temporarily suspended the shift in trade patterns that were observed in recent decades.[5] As developing countries were the major commodity exporters, reduced commodity prices have slowed down the expansion of developing countries' nominal market share in world trade (figure II.6). On the other hand, developing countries' share in developed countries' imports of manufactured goods increased from 31.7 per cent to 32.3 per cent between 2013 and 2014. For developing countries' import of

---

2   This section only discusses international trade in merchandise.

3   The decline in export prices for manufactured goods was noticeably lower than the plunge in oil and non-oil commodities. Nevertheless, statistical analysis shows that its contribution to the change in the total trade price was similar, reflecting the magnitude of manufacturing trade relative to commodities.

4   According to the Bank of International Settlements, the United States dollar effectively appreciated by 12 per cent against a basket of 60 currencies during the first half of 2015.

5   See United Nations (2015b, chap. 2), section on trade decomposition.

Figure II.4
**World trade prices, 2006 Q1–2015 Q2**

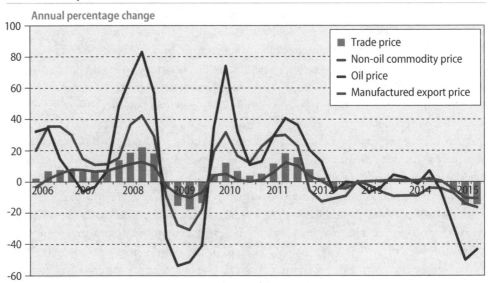

Source: UN/DESA, based on data
from WTO and UNCTAD.

Figure II.5
**Manufactured goods export price and dollar exchange rate, 2006 Q1–2015 Q1**

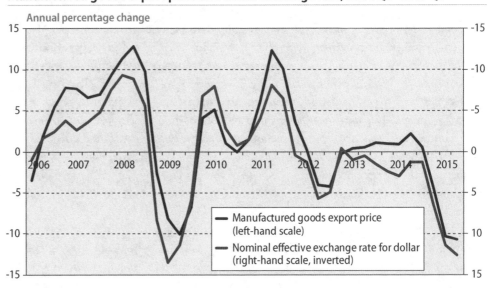

Source: UN/DESA, based on data
from WTO and UNCTAD.

manufactured goods, this share increased from 60.3 per cent to 60.9 per cent, which was much slower than the average speed for the past two decades.

## Trade in services

**World services trade continues to expand robustly, especially in developing countries**

Trade in services is providing the much-needed support to the feeble performance of global trade. More dynamic than merchandise trade, global services exports grew at an average annual rate of 3.6 per cent—faster than merchandise exports, which grew at an average rate of 3 per cent annually during 2008-2014. Services exports were also more resilient through

Figure II.6
**Regional shares of exports to developing and developed countries, 1995–2014**

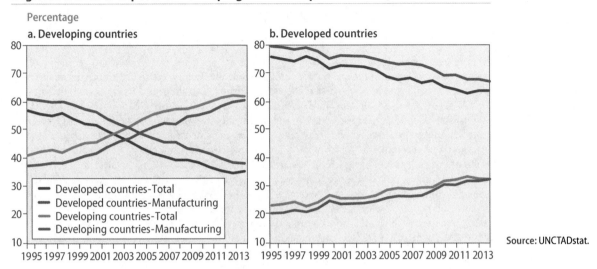

Source: UNCTADstat.

Figure II.7
**Services exports by level of development and region, 2008–2014**

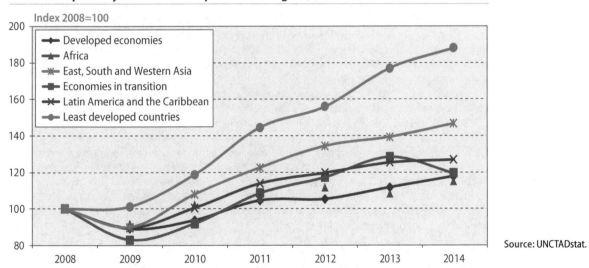

Source: UNCTADstat.

the global financial crisis, highlighting the importance of services as an option for export diversification. In fact, the fragmentation of production through GVCs—which has been rising during the past decade—requires efficient professional, business and infrastructure services such as energy, transport, information and communications technology and financial services. It also requires value-added services, including research and development, product design and marketing.

Most of the growth in services exports has been driven by developing countries—in Asia and Latin America and the Caribbean, for example—while least developed countries (LDCs) have also continued to register impressive growth (figure II.7). This dynamism is mostly due to travel (box II.2), financial services, telecommunications, computer and

Box II.2
**Trends in international tourism**

### Tourism and the Sustainable Development Goals

Over the past decades, tourism has grown into a major economic sector and an important source of foreign-currency revenue for many countries around the world. Tourism is also increasingly recognized as a powerful tool for addressing global challenges including job creation, poverty eradication and sustainable development. The United Nations World Tourism Organization (UNWTO), together with United Nations sister agencies, is committed to the advancement of the 2030 Agenda for Sustainable Development, in which sustainable tourism is firmly positioned. In particular, UNWTO promotes tourism as a direct and indirect contributor to each of the 17 Sustainable Development Goals (SDGs) recently adopted by the United Nations General Assembly. In particular, tourism is featured in three goals (8, 12 and 14), focusing on sustainable and inclusive economic growth, job creation, and sustainable consumption and production. The Sustainable Tourism Programme (STP) of the 10-Year Framework of Programmes on Sustainable Consumption and Production Patterns (10YFP) aims at accelerating the shift towards sustainable consumption and production in both developed and developing countries.[a] Led by UNWTO, the vision of 10YFP STP is for a tourism sector that has globally adopted sustainable consumption and production practices, enabling enhanced environmental and social outcomes and improved economic performance.

### Tourism as a source of job creation

Tourism is a relatively labour-intensive sector and it has become a major source for job creation at all skill levels. In particular, tourism accounts for one in eleven jobs worldwide, including direct, indirect and induced jobs. Tourism has a significant multiplier effect, creating employment in related sectors such as agriculture, construction, maintenance, retail, handicrafts or financial services. In addition, in times of economic difficulties, employment in tourism tends to be less affected and to recover more quickly than other economic sectors (United Nations World Tourism Organization and International Labour Organization, 2011). The key challenge is to establish sustainable policies that enhance both the quantity and quality of employment in the tourism sector.

In September 2015, the G20 Ministers of Tourism (T20) met in Turkey to discuss how tourism can create more and better jobs as a means to reduce inequalities at national and international levels. Recalling that tourism is one of the most dynamic and resilient economic sectors, the T20 committed in their Declaration[b] to maximize the potential of tourism to generate jobs, particularly for women and youth, as well as to enhance the role of small and medium-sized enterprises in the tourism value chain. Importantly, tourism has a higher share of women employees and entrepreneurs than the economy as a whole and creates significant employment opportunities for young people, thus firmly contributing to reducing youth unemployment. For instance, research by UNWTO and UN Women (2011) shows that the percentage of women entrepreneurs in hotels and restaurants is significantly higher than in other activities in several developing countries.

### International tourism maintains sustained growth

Tourism continues to grow robustly despite the weak economic conditions at the global level. In 2014, international tourist arrivals (overnight visitors) increased by 4 per cent, reaching a total of 1,133 million worldwide, up from 1,087 million in 2013. The positive trend continued in the first half of 2015, with international arrivals growing by 4 per cent compared to the same period last year. However, tourism flows have been shifted somewhat by currency fluctuations and lower oil prices in 2015. Many destinations are benefitting from more favourable exchange rates, while the stronger United States dollar is fuelling outbound demand from the United States. The decline in oil prices has lowered transport costs, but at the same time it has weakened outbound demand from oil-exporting economies such as Brazil, Nigeria, the Russian Federation and Saudi Arabia. According to projections by UNWTO, international tourist arriv-

*(continued)*

Box II.2 (*continued*)

als are expected to increase by 3 to 4 per cent worldwide in 2015, in line with the long-term forecast of 3.8 per cent a year for the period between 2010 and 2020 (United Nations World Tourism Organization, 2015a and 2015b).

### International tourism is the fourth largest export category

Receipts earned by destinations from international visitors grew by 4 per cent in real terms, to $1,248 billion, while an additional $222 billion were generated by international passenger transport (rendered to non-residents). Hence, international tourism generated total export earnings of $1.5 trillion in 2014. Tourism is a major international trade category at the sectoral level, ranking fourth after fuels, chemicals and food. In fact, international tourism (travel and passenger transport) accounts for 6 per cent of total exports of goods and services, and for 30 per cent of services exports alone. As a result, earnings from tourism contribute substantially to the improvement of the balance of payments of many emerging and advanced economies, offsetting a deficit in their trade balance or adding to an already positive balance.

International tourism can generate a tourism trade surplus (when receipts exceed expenditure) or a deficit (vice versa) in the national account of a country. The United States of America has the world's largest travel surplus of $66 billion, resulting from tourism receipts of $177 billion and expenditure of $111 billion. Among emerging economies, Thailand and Turkey boast the largest travel surpluses, while Malaysia, Croatia, Mexico, South Africa, Morocco, Dominican Republic, Viet Nam, India, Egypt, Hungary and Jordan all recorded a surplus between $3 billion and $10 billion (figure II.2.1). For many small developing countries, including most small island States, tourism is a major source of foreign-currency income as well. On the opposite side of the spectrum, some key source markets record a deficit in their tourism trade balance. China has the largest deficit of $108 billion. China earned a substantial $57 billion in 2014, but, as the world's top tourism outbound market, it spent $165 billion.

Source: United Nations World Tourism Organization (UNWTO).

a More information on 10YFP is available from http://sdt.unwto.org/sustainable-tourism-10yfp.

b G20 Tourism Ministers Declaration, available from https://g20.org/wp-content/uploads/2015/09/T.20Declaration.pdf.

### Figure II.2.1
### Countries with largest surplus on the travel balance, 2014

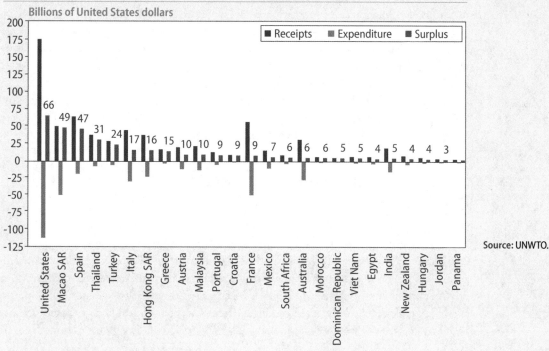

Billions of United States dollars

Source: UNWTO.

**Figure II.8**
**Developing economies' share in world services exports by sector, 2005 and 2014**

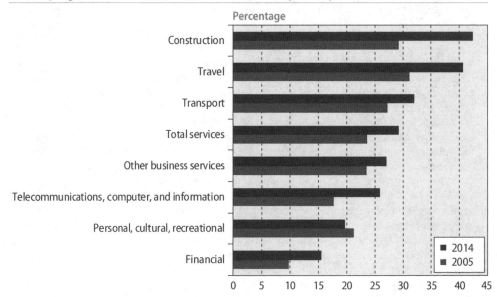

Source: UNCTADstat.

information services, and other business services. Developing countries have increased their participation in global services exports from 24 per cent in 2005 to 29 per cent in 2014. This increased participation was more pronounced in construction, travel, and telecommunications, computer and information services (figure II.8).

The actual magnitude and importance of services trade is not fully captured by most statistics, as they rely mainly on cross-border services trade data. Services trade increasingly occurs through foreign direct investment and the movement of natural persons. Services sales by affiliates could be estimated to be in the order of $18 trillion in 2014, nearly four times greater than global cross-border services exports (United Nations, General Assembly, 2015b). Trade through the movement of natural persons has also risen significantly, given the growth in global remittance flows (see chap. III).

## Primary commodity markets

**Most commodities continue with a downward trend in prices**

In 2015, commodity prices continued their slump that began in 2011. The United Nations Conference on Trade and Development (UNCTAD) Non-oil Nominal Commodity Price Index averaged 193 points in September 2015, nearly 41 per cent lower than its peak of 329.5 points in February 2011 (figure II.9).[6] Almost all commodity prices have fallen across the board since the beginning of the year, and this trend is expected to continue into 2016 if current conditions persist. Out of 24 commodities which are major components of the index considered, only three products, namely cocoa, cotton and tea, recorded price increases between September and January 2015 (figure II.10). The global commodities rout

---

6    The United Nations Conference on Trade and Development (UNCTAD) Non-oil Nominal Commodity Price Index covers these subgroups of commodities: All food (Food, Tropical beverages, Vegetable oilseeds and oils), Agricultural raw materials; and Minerals, ores and metals.

Figure II.9
**UNCTAD non-oil commodity price index, January 2009–September 2015**

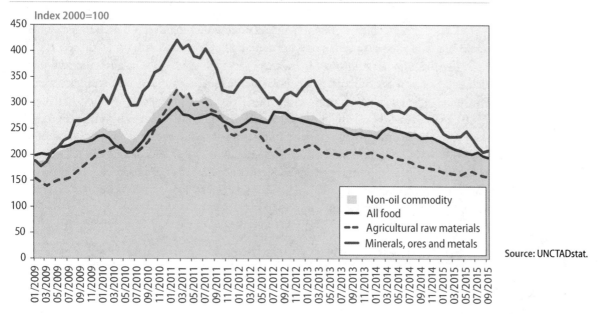

Source: UNCTADstat.

Figure II.10
**Average monthly price change for selected commodities,
January 2015–September 2015**

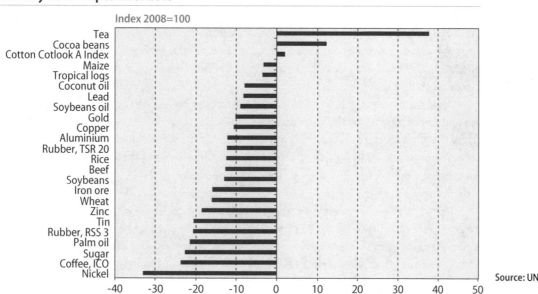

Source: UNCTADstat.

is negatively impacting the macroeconomic performance of commodity-dependent developing countries and economies in transition, as evidenced by their deteriorating terms of trade, international reserves and public finances (box II.1).

**Ample supply and slowing demand are contributing to the decline in commodity prices**

The continuing bearish mood in global commodity markets is driven by a number of factors including ample supplies; slowing demand in China and other emerging economies, especially for minerals and metals;[7] faltering economic recovery in advanced economies such as Japan; and a strong dollar. In addition, the ongoing commodity slump is associated with increasing outflows of commodity-based financial investments, which has in turn further exacerbated the slump in prices.[8] Ample supplies and a sluggish world economy are likely to continue through 2016, maintaining the downward pressure on most commodities prices. However, some potential risk factors, including the unfolding El Niño phenomenon for agricultural commodities prices and significant cutbacks in production by miners, as well as delays in new projects for minerals and metals, may partly offset the downward pressures on commodity prices.

## Food and agricultural commodities

**Market fundamentals maintain low prices for most agricultural commodities...**

In agricultural food markets, prices generally trended downward during the first nine months of 2015, thanks to good harvests (figure II.11). For instance, the average price of wheat (*Hard Red Winter No.2*) and maize (*Yellow Maize No. 3*) dropped respectively by 23 and 17 per cent in the period from January to September 2015 compared with the same period last year. These drops are mainly driven by ample supplies, thanks to record production, which should exceed 700 and 1000 million tons in 2014/15 for wheat and maize, respectively. With respect to rice, prices continue to soften as a result of good production and the release from Thai government stockpiles. The average price of Thai rice dropped below $400 per ton in April 2015 for the first time since 2008, reaching $356 in September 2015. Looking ahead, grain markets should remain calm, at least throughout 2016, underscored by high levels of stocks, unless the developing El Niño phenomenon severely impacts major producing regions.

**...but the El Niño phenomenon remains a major risk factor**

In sugar markets, prices continued to collapse owing to good harvests that prolonged the glut and, recently, by the weakening of the Brazilian real which boosted exports from Brazil. In September 2015, the FOB price of sugar at Caribbean ports averaged $11.86 per pound, almost a third of its record price of 30 cents reached in January 2011. In 2016, the effects of the developing El Niño on sugarcane production is likely to put an upward pressure on sugar prices.

For vegetable oilseed and oils, good supply conditions for products such as soybeans, soybean oil and palm oil in major exporting countries including the United States, Brazil, Indonesia and Malaysia exerted downward pressure on prices. The situation was exacerbated by the slump in crude oil prices that reduced interest in biofuel production, for which

---

7   For example, China's merchandise imports decreased by 2.2 per cent in the second quarter of 2015 year on year. This was partly driven by drops in quantities of metals such iron and steel (-10.0 per cent) and copper (-6.0 per cent). See World Trade Organization (2015b).

8   According to data from Hedge Fund Research Ltd, cited by Bloomberg, the amount of money under management by hedge funds specializing in commodities stood at $24 billion in 2014, 15 per cent below the peak of 2012. See Blas (2015).

vegetable oils are inputs. In September 2015, the UNCTAD Vegetable Oilseeds and Oils Price Index halved from its peak in 2011.

The prices of tropical beverages followed divergent paths. Coffee prices remained relatively high in 2014, driven primarily by drought in Brazil, but subsequently weakened as a result of improved weather conditions; strong exports, boosted by the weakening of major producing countries' currencies, such as the Brazilian real and Colombian peso; and only moderate growth in global demand. In September 2015, the Composite Indicator Price of the International Coffee Organization (ICO) averaged $1.13 per pound, 35 per cent down compared to a peak of $1.73 in October 2014. The price of cocoa beans trended up from $1.32 per pound in January to $1.49 in September 2015. The increase was driven mainly by supply disruptions in Ghana following disappointing harvests caused by problems in the application of pesticides and fungicides. In tea markets, the Mombasa tea price averaged $3.71 per kilogram in September 2015 compared to the relatively low prices of less than $2.65 per kilogram in 2014. The price surge was largely driven by reduced output in Kenya, the world's biggest exporter of the black variety of tea, following dry weather.

Raw material prices have generally been declining from their peaks in 2011 owing to a fragile recovery in the global economy in a context of abundant supplies. In September 2015, the price of natural rubber (RSS 3) averaged $1.31 per kilogram, well below the peak of $6.26 in February 2011. In the case of cotton, the A Index, a proxy for world cotton markets, moved up from an average of 67 cents per pound in January to nearly 73 cents in May 2015 and retreated afterwards, reaching 69 cents in September 2015. Relative to their levels in 2011, cotton prices have declined significantly, owing to good harvests which helped to build stocks and, more recently, to the release of stockpiles from China.[9]

**Figure II.11**
**Price indices of selected food and agricultural commodity groups, January 2009–September 2015**

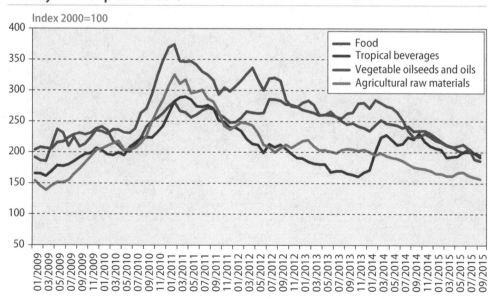

Source: UNCTADstat.

---

9    Cotton stocks are estimated at nearly 22 million tons for the 2014-2015 season, with China accounting for half of this quantity.

## Minerals, ores and metals

China plays a key role on
price swings for metals

Minerals, ores and metals (MOM) prices are sensitive to two main factors: global supplies and macroeconomic trends in industrialized and emerging economies. More specifically, MOM markets are particularly sensitive to developments in China, as the country accounts for almost half of the global metal consumption. MOM prices peaked in 2011, but have generally trended down since (figure II.12). The bearish markets have been underpinned by decelerating demand from China and other large emerging economies; the fragile recovery in developed economies; low energy prices; and the appreciated dollar. In addition, structural changes occurring in China, including the country's objective to achieve a more environmentally sustainable economic model, have put downward pressure on some base minerals and metals such as iron ores and steel. Furthermore, a number of specific markets such as iron ore and copper are well supplied, due to large investments made during the commodity boom period.

During the first nine months of 2015, prices for minerals and metals rebounded slightly between February and May but trended down afterwards. The UNCTAD Minerals, Ores and Metals Price Index[10] gained a modest 5 points between January and May 2015. Thereafter, with continued strong supply combined with low energy prices and weak global economic growth, metal prices retreated. In September 2015, the Index averaged 207 points, well below its peak of 418 points in February 2011. Meanwhile, iron ore prices

**Figure II.12**
**Price indices of selected minerals, ores and metals, January 2009–September 2015**

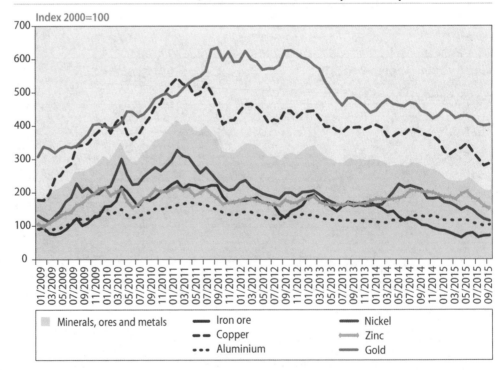

Source: UNCTADstat.

---

10    The UNCTAD Minerals, Ores and Metals Price Index covers copper, aluminium, iron ore, nickel, lead, zinc, tin, phosphate rock, manganese ore, and tungsten ore. Gold is not included in the price index.

rebounded briefly between April and June 2015 before receding afterwards. In September 2015, the iron ore price at the Chinese port of Tianjin averaged $57 per ton, almost a third of its peak in February 2011. Low iron ore prices are underscored by a global glut exacerbated by low-cost mining from big producers such as Rio Tinto, BHP Billiton and Vale SA, combined with weak growth in steel production, especially in China.

The London Metal Exchange (LME) price of copper increased from $5,701 to $6,296 per ton between February and May 2015. Thereafter the price dropped as a result of weak demand, notably from construction activity and infrastructure investments in China. In September 2015, the LME copper price averaged $5,203 per ton. Moreover, demand for substitutes such as aluminium, which averaged $1,588 per ton in September 2015 from a peak of $2,662 in April 2011, exerted downward pressure on copper prices. In nickel markets, prices were relatively strong in the first part of 2014, driven by the enforcement of an export ban on unprocessed ores by Indonesia, the world's leading nickel producer. However, from July 2014, nickel prices have been generally falling, as China has been able to partly replace imports from Indonesia with those from the Philippines. In September 2015, the LME nickel price averaged $9,895 per ton, a significant drop from a peak of $19,434 in May 2014. The capacity of exporting countries such as the Philippines to supply international markets will play a key role in determining the price fluctuations for nickel in 2016.

**Slowing construction and infrastructure in China weighed on prices for copper**

In precious metals markets, the gold price over the first nine months of 2015 was much lower than its levels in 2011 and 2012. In September 2015, it averaged $1,125 per troy ounce compared with prices of over $1,500 between May 2011 and March 2013. The key driving factors of the bearish trend include sizeable outflows from gold exchange-traded funds due to the strengthening dollar and improved economic prospects in the United States. Looking ahead, by mid-2016, gold prices will be sensitive to market fundamentals, to the possibility of a rise in the policy rate in the United States, to geopolitical tensions and to uncertainty over the global economic recovery. Overall, metals, ores and mineral prices are likely to remain low throughout 2016 if current global economic conditions continue. However, significant production cutbacks by big miners remain an important upward risk factor in these markets.

**Prices for metals, ores and minerals are likely to remain relatively low**

## Oil market prices

The global oil market remains oversupplied, as changes on demand and supply dynamics have not derailed the overall unbalanced market. Consequently, prices have been low in 2015 and will continue so during the forecast period, as there is no indication that production will stop outpacing demand in the near future. Thus, considering that the gap between oil demand growth and oil supply growth will continue in 2016, the average Brent oil price is expected to remain subdued next year, before recovering to a higher equilibrium price in 2017 (figure II.13).

**Oil prices are expected to remain low in 2015 and 2016**

Oil demand spikes were observed at the beginning of 2015, following an extremely cold winter in the Northern Hemisphere. In addition, demand from China remained unexpectedly strong during the first half of 2015, indicating that the country has been building stocks. Nevertheless, for the year as a whole, demand growth has been moderate. After growing by 1.1 million barrels per day (bpd) in 2014 to 92.4 million bpd, global demand is expected to grow by 1.3 million bpd in 2015, mainly driven by non-Organization for Economic Cooperation and Development (OECD) economies, China in particular. In 2016, demand growth is expected to remain subdued, in line with overall global economic con-

**Growth of oil supply outpaced that of oil demand in 2015**

**Figure II.13**
**Monthly Brent crude oil price average, January 1984–September 2015**

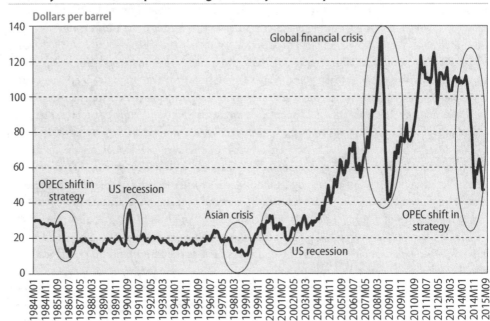

Source: UN/DESA, based on data from the World Bank.

ditions, especially in emerging economies. In particular, weaker GDP growth projections for the Chinese economy are expected to weigh on oil demand. Even if the United States partially offsets the weaker demand from other regions, global demand growth for crude oil should remain moderate and is not expected to exceed 1.2 million bpd.

On the supply side, oil production remained much stronger than originally anticipated. In 2014, global supply grew by 2.4 million bpd to 93.4, with the bulk of the increase originating from non-Organization of the Petroleum Exporting Countries (OPEC) oil producers, the United States in particular. In 2015, despite an over-supplied market and lower oil prices, non-OPEC supply continued to increase, albeit at a slower pace than in the previous year. So far, United States oil production has been extremely resilient, but growing financial pressure on shale operators and a sharp fall in the number of active rigs will have their toll on production. At the same time, OPEC producers, Saudi Arabia in particular, have continued to increase production, letting oil prices fall. Thus, in 2015, global supply is expected to grow by 2.2 million bpd to 95.6 million bpd.

In 2016, total global supply will remain similar to the 2015 level, as different forces are expected to offset each other. On the one hand, North American production is expected to decline, particularly in the United States where oil production is projected to fall by about 400,000 bpd. On the other hand, Iran's production will contribute to global supply—especially in the second half of 2016, given the delay in lifting the sanctions—as a deal was reached with the P5+1 nations. At the same time, despite internal pressures from several members, OPEC as a group is not expected to cut production, keeping downward pressure on prices. Inventories have also been growing fast and reaching unprecedented levels. In OECD countries, inventories reached almost 2.7 billion barrels at the end of 2014 and are expected to increase further in both 2015 and 2016, remaining at record highs.

In 2015, the Brent oil price started the year on an upward trend following a demand revival, mainly due to the cold winter in the Northern Hemisphere. However, the oil price rebound was short-lived, as concerns over global demand growth started to emerge soon afterwards, owing to the anticipated slowdown in China and other emerging economies, which have been the main oil demand drivers in the past decade. As a result, by the end of the second quarter and throughout the third quarter of 2015, the Brent oil price dropped significantly again, reaching as low as $41.76 per barrel (pb) on 26 August. Thus, the average Brent oil price for 2015 is expected to be $53 pb. In 2016, considering that the gap between oil demand growth and oil supply growth will continue, the average price is expected to be $51 pb, before recovering to a higher equilibrium price of $62 pb in 2017.

These price assumptions face a number of downside risks. A sharper economic slowdown in the global economy, especially in emerging economies and China, would weaken demand and put further downward pressure on oil prices. Another downside risk is related to Iran's production. The market price has already adjusted to some extent to the fact that Iran's production will enter the global market. However, the pace and volume at which this will happen is unclear, which could lead to further downward price adjustments.

There are also upside risks to these assumptions. Non-OPEC production may decline more than anticipated, as the low oil price squeezes new entrants out of the market. OPEC may decide to cut production in order to sustain prices, as fiscal pressures are mounting in several OPEC economies. Furthermore, if internal conflicts escalate or political instability surges—in Africa or Western Asia, for instance—oil production could be disrupted and oil prices pushed higher. It is nevertheless assumed that the overall supply would grow more slowly and prices would be expected to rise relative to current assumptions.

## Trade policy developments

### Multilateral trade negotiations

Global trade is an important determinant of strong growth and development. It provides the means to access larger external markets, as well as skills, technology and capital, which in turn allow for specialization, a better use of productive resources and economies of scale to catalyse a desired structural transformation. At the global level, there remains considerable untapped potential to exploit the benefits of international trade. A set of coherent and integrated policies is required to tap the potential. At the heart of such a policy mix are trade policy and a multilateral trading system that promotes trade performance without discrimination.

A universal, rules-based, non-discriminatory and equitable multilateral trading system is a central element for harvesting the development potential of trade, also recognized in goal 17 of the SDGs. Existing WTO norms and disciplines constitute the cornerstone of a rules-based multilateral trading system, serving as a guarantee against discrimination. In fact, the WTO dispute settlement mechanism is widely regarded as a success and has handled disputes covering over $1 trillion (United Nations, General Assembly, 2015b). This is important, as the effectiveness of the rules-based trading system hinges upon the actual enforcement of its rules. The universality of the multilateral system, also envisaged in the SDGs, is pursued through accession processes. Since 1995, 34 protocols were signed, bringing membership to 161 countries. Kazakhstan joined the WTO as its 162nd member in November 2015, and the accessions of Afghanistan and Liberia are in sight. Those countries undertook important policy reforms to make their trade regime WTO-compatible,

*Strengthening the multilateral trading system will allow countries to better exploit the benefits from trade...*

facing the challenge of negotiating balanced terms of accession consistent with their development needs.

...but the Doha Round has made little progress in the last fifteen years

Importantly, to harvest the benefits of the multilateral trading system, it is necessary to find a way forward when negotiations hit an impasse. The Doha Round was launched in 2001 and negotiations were to give priority attention to developing countries' implementation difficulties with a view to redressing existing imbalances and enhancing openness. However, progress remains limited, affecting the credibility of the system. Meanwhile, plurilateral and regional agreements outside the WTO have increased, affecting its centrality.

In this regard, different views on how to face evolving economic realities continue to pose a stumbling block to progress in multilateral negotiations. For instance, developed countries maintain that higher commodity prices and policy reforms in previous years had led to a substantial reduction in their use of trade-distorting agricultural support, while there was an increased use of such measures by developing countries, including for food security purposes. Meanwhile, many developing countries have stressed that persistent development challenges, such as pervasive poverty, food insecurity and a nascent industrial base, call for flexibilities and special and differential treatment.

Interlinkages across issues have become a stumbling block for the Doha Round

Another main bottleneck that shapes the contours of the post-Bali work programme is the interlinkage across different topics of the negotiations. For many developing members, this calls for "sequencing"—that is, an early harvest in terms of concrete results in reducing domestic support as a pre-requisite for providing concessions in other areas of the negotiations. For several developed countries, "parallelism" is essential to advancing negotiations, meaning that concrete results in domestic support are subject to parallel advancements in the market access package comprising agriculture, non-agricultural market access (NAMA) and services.

Several recent developments suggest no major breakthrough is expected from the Tenth WTO Ministerial Conference (MC10) in Nairobi in December 2015. A group of 50 developing and developed members submitted a communication stating their strong support to the multilateral trading system and determination to continue intensive efforts to develop a comprehensive package of credible outcomes that allows the conclusion of the Doha Round. In particular, these countries have called on all of the largest of the WTO members to work together and show the leadership necessary to make MC10 a success. The group underscores that a success would highlight the unique capacity of the WTO to deliver meaningful improvements in global trade rules and bring development benefits that cannot be matched through trade negotiations conducted outside the WTO.

The WTO Director-General confirmed that a work programme would not be delivered as it had been mandated, but that members had identified a road to success in Nairobi. Although several views will be difficult to reconcile, important commonalities can yield results in Nairobi. These would include development issues, particularly on LDCs, export competition on agriculture, and improved transparency in several areas. Regardless of the outcome of MC10, it will remain an imperative to pursue and promote the development dimension of the multilateral trading system, whether under the current framework or under a reformulated architecture. In any case, it is necessary to ensure that there is coherence between the multilateral trading system and the SDGs.

## Agriculture and non-agriculture market access

In agriculture, the market pillar is still looking for a common strategy to reduce tariffs and increase market access. In these discussions, the Group of 33—a group of developing countries concerned about food security issues—stressed the continued need for special products and special safeguard mechanisms to afford these countries with some flexibility to address, inter alia, the challenges related to higher and more volatile food prices affecting the food supply and the livelihood of subsistence and small-scale farmers. Also, the ongoing negotiations on domestic support aim to reduce trade-distorting agricultural subsidies in line with target 2.b of the SDGs. Countries that have traditionally used trade-distorting support have reduced it, while increasing non-trade distorting green box support, thus meeting technical commitments without reducing actual spending (box II.3). This has promoted the discussion on how limits for support should be applied and if the de minimis support for developing countries should be granted with special and differential treatment. In addition, the search for a permanent solution to the issue of public stockholding for food security in developing countries continues. Possible options include raising the limit of support for developing countries or redefining the method for calculating the subsidy.

**Reductions in tariffs and increased market access remain central in agricultural negotiations**

---

Box II.3
### Agriculture negotiations, food security and sustainable development

The demand on world food is rising and projected to increase by 20 per cent by 2030. At the same time, hunger remains a challenge for almost 795 million people worldwide in 2014-2016—most of them from developing regions, representing 13 per cent of those regions' populations (Food and Agriculture Organization of the United Nations, 2015). The challenge of eliminating hunger and ensuring food security (i.e., the physical, social and economic access of all people, at all times, to sufficient, safe and nutritious food which meets dietary needs and food preferences for an active and healthy life) is duly recognized in the 2030 Agenda for Sustainable Development (target 2.1). The Agenda also aims to ensure sustainable food production (2.4) and double agricultural productivity, including through access to productive resources and inputs, knowledge, financial services, markets and opportunities for value addition (2.3) by 2030.

Many countries pursue policies and strategies for ensuring food security, which include subsidies for the production of staple food. Nevertheless, beyond environmental and geographical challenges, these strategies may not be economically viable or optimal as they may affect diversification and structural transformation. As such, several countries rely on foreign markets to meet their food demands, linking food security strategies to international trade. According to the food dependency index of the United Nations Conference on Trade and Development (UNCTAD), many countries in East Africa, Latin America and South Asia tend to be net food exporters while the remaining African and Asian countries are net food importers (figure II.3.1). Furthermore, many African and Asian economies have increased their dependence on imported food since 2008 (United Nations Conference on Trade and Development, 2015a).

Consequently, fair and predictable international agricultural markets are necessary for contributing to food availability and affordability for many food-importing economies. The multilateral trading system needs to ensure access to staple food while encouraging more investment in food production and promoting sustainable agriculture. In multilateral trade negotiations, the market access pillar seeks to ensure the availability of food through tariff reduction, while the domestic support pillar aims to ensure stable prices and access to food by eliminating distortions in agricultural markets. Arguably, reducing subsidies will increase food prices and hence a balance must be reached by limiting trade-distorting support.

In the market access pillar, discussions revolve around tariff cuts and how these can be applied. An UNCTAD analysis (Vanzetti, 2015b) compared the impact on the African, Caribbean and Pacific Group of States (ACP) of different formulas regarding tariff cuts. It found that the different scenarios produce

*(continued)*

Source: UNCTADstat.
a Food dependence is estimated as exports minus imports of agricultural products, divided by agricultural trade (imports plus exports). The index varies between -1 (more dependent) and 1 (less dependent).

**Box II.3** (*continued*)

**Figure II.3.1**

**Food dependency index by region and development level, 2014[a]**

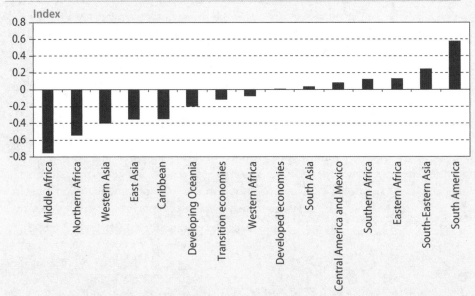

modest and somewhat similar results in tariff reduction. For ACP imports, the impact of the formulas on applied tariffs is small, since there is an important difference between bound and applied rates. On exports, there is also a limited reduction in tariffs. This is due both to increased trade with other developing countries that are not making considerable tariff cuts and to little improvement in market access in the European Union, where preferential treatment is already applied. In addition, the ACP would not benefit from market access improvements because of preference erosion. ACP countries presented a proposal insisting on the need for flexibilities for developing countries in agriculture, even in the event of changes in the tariff reduction approach. These include special products, for which developing countries are to be given extra flexibility in market access for food and livelihood security and rural development. They also comprise a special safeguard mechanism to allow developing countries to raise tariffs temporarily to deal with import surges or price falls. Other big coalitions of developing countries in the World Trade Organization (WTO), including the Group of Thirty Three, have also insisted on flexibilities (United Nations Conference on Trade and Development, 2015b). Discussions are still ongoing on the options for cutting tariffs and related issues. In agriculture, tariffs are more important than domestic support or export subsidies.

Target 2.b of the Sustainable Development Goals provides a context for domestic support negotiations. It confirms that correcting and preventing trade distortions in agricultural markets, including through the elimination of all forms of export subsidies and all export measures with equivalent effect, in accordance with the Doha mandate, contributes to the objective of ending hunger, achieving food security and promoting sustainable agriculture. Disciplining the "Overall Trade-Distorting Domestic Support", a category of support comprising all subcategories of trade-distorting support, was foreseen in the 2008 modalities. This envisaged limiting the possibility of eluding reduction commitments by changing the nature of support measures or targeted products. Still, some economies shifted trade-distorting support to "green box" support, meeting reduction commitments without reducing actual spending levels. This led to recent discussions focusing on whether numerical limits should apply to all countries and on whether the de minimis support for developing countries of 5.0 per cent of domestic production should be changed or granted with special and differential treatment. A permanent solution on public stockholding, still to be found, should contribute to food security.

The outcome of these negotiations is linked to results in other negotiating areas, placing agricultural issues as key points influencing the overall outcome of the Tenth Ministerial Conference of the WTO and perhaps of the Doha Round. The success of multilateralism therefore remains critical for eliminating hunger and promoting food security as underscored in the 2030 Agenda for Sustainable Development.

Source: UNCTAD, Division on International Trade in Goods and Services, and Commodities.

Increased industrial trade opportunities for developing countries, under the auspices of NAMA, are in line with targets 17.11 and 8.2 of the SDGs, contributing to diversification, technological upgrading and innovation. The key issue in negotiations has been how to ensure real market access while fulfilling the "less than full reciprocity" principle for developing countries. The issue of non-tariff barriers is not yet addressed but its use is on the rise. Possible outcomes in this area may be influenced by ongoing plurilateral negotiations, namely the Information Technology Agreement and the Environmental Goods Agreement. Increased market access in these areas would be relevant in terms of meeting certain targets and goals of the SDGs.

### Services

With the focus on agricultural negotiations, there has been limited engagement on services negotiations. Members agree that the focus should be on areas of market access and domestic regulation, and that a strong development dimension with flexibilities for developing countries should be part of the negotiations. Still, some members consider that the negotiations on the General Agreement on Trade in Services (GATS) rules on government procurement, subsidies and emergency safeguard measures have not advanced enough to become part of the work programme. Furthermore, discussions since the Bali Ministerial Conference have not narrowed the divergent positions on the level of ambition for the services negotiations, including whether certain sectors or modes should be given a greater focus, and whether to move forward with the services component of the post-Bali work programme or to wait until it is clearer what the work programme will contain for agriculture and industrial goods.

*Several countries are engaged in plurilateral negotiations on services outside the Doha Round*

Furthermore, several major players are engaged in the plurilateral negotiations for the Trade in Services Agreement (TISA) outside the Doha Round, which has diverted attention from multilateral negotiations on services in the WTO. These negotiations involve 25 WTO members representing at least 70 per cent of global services trade, and negotiations are aiming for comprehensive and ambitious services liberalization with substantial sectoral coverage that attracts broad participation and that could be multilateralized. It is notable that some major developing countries are not part of this process, and the TISA compatibility with the WTO and GATS is questionable. In the absence of a critical mass, the future agreement would take the form of a preferential services agreement in the sense of GATS Article V. The negotiations are based on the GATS positive list approach while national treatment commitments would be applied horizontally. The negotiations also address regulatory disciplines such as licensing, financial services, telecommunications, e-commerce, and movement of professionals. The existence of multiple services RTAs among TISA participants implies that the effect of TISA on intragroup services trade may be limited. TISA participants' overall export interests may primarily rest with non-TISA participants.

One important development objective in multilateral services negotiations, in line with target 17.11, is achieving preferential market access for LDCs. In this regard, a services waiver allows non-LDCs to deviate from market access and national treatment obligations relating to the most favoured nation (MFN) principle under the GATS. Although the waiver aimed at allowing non-LDCs to deviate from market access and national treatment obligations relating to MFNs under the GATS was adopted in 2011, WTO members had not introduced preferential access in services for LDCs. The Bali decision provided a road map for the operationalization of LDC services waivers, resting largely on the formulation by LDCs of a collective request identifying the sectors and modes of their export interest.

UNCTAD assisted LDCs in their collective request and in evaluating preferential treatment intentions and notifications. The LDCs collective request, submitted in July 2014, addressed horizontal and sectoral market access and national treatment restrictions in many sectors, including travel, tourism, banking, transport, logistics, education, information and communications technology, business process outsourcing and creative industry. The barriers affecting mode 4 (the movement of natural persons) were given particular attention, such as those relating to the recognition of educational and professional qualifications, and to costly application fees and burdensome documentation for visas, licences and work permits.

In the context of this waiver, 17 notifications expressing preferential treatment for LDCs services and services suppliers had been received by 2 November 2015, which was fewer than expected. Of these, several notifications address only parts of the collective request that had been presented by LDCs, and at least one notification is perceived as backtracking with regard to intentions that had been previously expressed. In general, the notifications addressed modes 1, 2 and 3 of trade in services. Some notifications include good examples of preferential treatment, including extending periods of entry and stay and waiving economic needs tests, visa fees and work permits. Some notifications also detail measures to enhance LDCs supply capacity, including by facilitating temporary movement for study and capacity-building and assistance in relation to the construction of infrastructures for tourism, education, medical, cultural and sporting services. Nonetheless, a commercially meaningful outcome will require more waivers for LDCs. Furthermore, the notifications did not adequately address trade through mode 4, which is important for many LDCs.

### Trade facilitation

**The Agreement on Trade Facilitation is still in the process of ratification**

Implementation of trade facilitation measures is expected to reduce overall trade costs and contribute to developing countries' exports in line with target 17.11 of the SDGs. It is also projected to promote economic diversification, technological upgrading and innovation in line with target 8.2 of the SDGs. The Agreement on Trade Facilitation, an outcome of the Ninth Ministerial Conference (MC9) of the WTO in 2013 in Bali, was the first binding multilateral agreement since the Uruguay Round. When two thirds of the WTO members ratify, it will enter into force. As of August 2015, twelve countries had completed ratification, and 73 countries, including four LDCs, notified the WTO of their "Category A" commitments (the self-designated provisions for immediate implementation). Depending on the progress in the ratification process, the Agreement could be a concrete outcome at MC10. Several developing countries, however, remain concerned regarding the cost and complexity of implementing some of the measures. Special and differential treatment in this agreement links the level and timing of commitments to implementation capacity, the provision of capacity-building, and acquisition of capacity. In this context, the WTO launched a Trade Facilitation Agreement Facility in 2015 in order to help developing countries build implementation capacity.

### Development issues

The duty-free and quota-free (DFQF) market access for LDCs, addressed by target 17.12 of the SDGs, is supported by a WTO ministerial decision. Almost all developed countries have implemented it and several developing countries have also extended it. Simpler and more transparent rules of origin are important for LDCs to use DFQF preferences. The new European Union (EU) Generalized System of Preferences, where third-party certification by public authorities will change to self-certification by registered exporters, is a relevant example of how to simplify and facilitate the rules of origin administration. In addition, provisions related to special and differential treatment should be precise, effective and operational to ensure that they are meaningful for LDCs.

## Regional trade agreements

The developments in the multilateral trading system, or the lack thereof, have been impacted by the increased prevalence of RTAs. As of April 2015, the WTO received notification of 612 RTAs, of which 406 were in force, including South-South, twenty-first century and mega-RTAs. The twenty-first century RTAs aim for full market opening and "behind-the-border" measures, pursuing regulatory coherence, overcoming non-tariff barriers and creating a platform for GVCs. These measures focus on services, investment, competition, capital movement, intellectual property and government procurement. Regulatory coherence is sought through harmonization, mutual recognition or mechanisms such as prior comments on regulatory initiatives. Mega-RTAs are the likely game changers. For instance, the Transatlantic Trade and Investment Partnership between the United States and the EU would cover half of global output and a third of global trade. The Regional Comprehensive Economic Partnership would create a free trade area between the Association of Southeast Asian Nations and its six external partners, covering half of the world's population.

The Trans-Pacific Partnership (TPP) Agreement among Australia, Brunei Darussalam, Canada, Chile, Japan, Malaysia, Mexico, New Zealand, Peru, Singapore, the United States and Viet Nam was concluded in October 2015. It is the first case of a completed new-generation mega-RTA, which has a significant bearing on the future evolution of the international trading system and could give further impetus to negotiations of other mega-RTAs. The TPP creates a market of 800 million people with a GDP of $28 trillion, over 40 per cent of the world gross product. Comprehensive in scope, the TPP covers goods, services, investment, e-commerce, intellectual property, government procurement, competition, labour protection, environment, regulatory harmonization, small and medium-sized enterprises (SMEs) and state-owned enterprises (SOEs). Driven also by geopolitical considerations, it is principally aimed at facilitating trade and investment among TPP parties, including through regulatory harmonization. The agreement sets a high-standard "template" for trade agreements in the twenty-first century and may attract new members, such as Indonesia, the Republic of Korea and Thailand.

The TPP is projected to yield annual global income gains of $223 billion by 2025 pushing up world gross product by 1.0 per cent, and generating an estimated $305 billion in additional world exports per year (United Nations Conference on Trade and Development, forthcoming). The bulk of the gains are estimated to arise from regulatory harmonization and mutual recognition, which will reduce trade costs. TPP members are the major beneficiaries of trade creation and diversion, but with asymmetries. For instance, exports from New Zealand and Viet Nam to the United States are estimated to increase by 13 per cent. Their high initial tariffs imply an important increase in market access, especially in meat for New Zealand and clothing for Viet Nam.

Non-TPP members, on the other hand, can be impacted by trade and investment diversion that is induced by preferential liberalization, and by adjustment costs derived from regulatory harmonization. The trade effects can be significant for some undiversified economies dependent on a few products and markets for exports, particularly certain

**RTAs cannot replace the role of the multilateral trading system**

**The Trans-Pacific Partnership is the first mega-RTA completed**

**Most of the gains from the Trans-Pacific Partnership are related to the reduction of trade costs...**

**...but other countries can also be affected by trade and investment diversion**

LDCs. Some TPP members, such as Canada, Mexico, Peru and Singapore that already benefit from pre-existing RTAs may also experience some trade diversion, as their relative preference margins diminish in favour of other TPP partners. These trade effects could be amplified if these immediate trade shocks lead to durable changes in investment, competition, technology and employment levels.

A computable general equilibrium analysis conducted by UNCTAD confirms that trade liberalization is generally beneficial in terms of income gains.[11] Still, these income effects are very modest globally, especially when compared with underlying growth. This is because tariff cuts are not very deep, due to already liberalized markets and to the abundance of persistent exemptions. Because of trade-diversion-related losses for non-members, the global gains in mega-RTAs are much lower than those of a potential Doha Round (Vanzetti, 2015a). Positive outcomes from the Doha Round, particularly on MFN tariff reduction and the effective implementation of DFQF market access for LDCs, could also serve for attenuating the possible adverse effect of mega-RTAs on non-members. Multilateral negotiations could also lead to generalized preference erosion with an impact for preference-dependent countries.

Efforts are warranted at the national and international levels to enhance productive capacities and export competitiveness, particularly in countries facing the adverse effects of trade diversion and preference erosion. Such efforts include assistance in meeting regulatory standards, as well as promoting diversification for greater resilience, and supporting adjustment processes through the implementation of social safety nets and active labour market policies such as labour reskilling. The RTAs have other potential development benefits: Many South-South trade agreements intensify and deepen regional integration, and contribute to productive capacity and regional infrastructure networks. Substantial income gains are expected from the volume of trade covered in new RTAs, and even larger gains from the strong regulatory focus aiming to reduce regulatory barriers. Non-trade measures, comprising sanitary and phytosanitary and technical barriers, affect over 50 per cent of exports from developing countries, 90 per cent of trade in natural resources, and 80 per cent of trade in manufacturing. They represent about 14 per cent of tariff equivalents on average, and even higher on agriculture.

*The increasing prevalence of RTAs affects the credibility of the multilateral trading system*

These transformational shifts have implications for developing countries. Regulatory harmonization can raise costs of adjustment. Such costs should be minimized through the use of less stringent standards, mutual recognition and international standards. Stronger regulatory disciplines limit regulatory autonomy and thus may limit the scope of proactive development plans and industrial policies. Discipline on government procurement, SOEs and export taxes could limit support to domestic industries and to SMEs. For example, some RTAs aim for competitive neutrality but developing countries stress the importance of SOEs in delivering public policy goals. Also, investor-State disputes may lead to regulatory freezes, created by fear of legal challenge and compensation claims from investors. There

---

11      This analysis uses a multi-regional Computable General Equilibrium (CGE) model GTAP, capturing linkages between countries and inter-sectoral effects. Five scenarios are modelled: baseline from 2011 to 2025, Doha Round of multilateral negotiations, RCEP, TPP and TTIP. For more information, see Vanzetti (2015a).

## Box II.4
## Sanitary and phytosanitary measures and trade distortions

Valued at about $1.5 trillion annually, the international trade in agricultural products offers great op-
portunities to farmers from developing countries. Yet it is a challenging task for them to access the international agricultural market. Recent years have brought a significant shift in the trade policy of many
countries, which is increasingly focused on "behind-the-border" measures. Consequently, for exporting
farmers, market access is now more about fulfilling quality and safety criteria rather than dealing with
quotas and border protection. Indeed, the commerce of agricultural products is heavily and increasingly
determined by compliance issues, involving a wide array of regulatory measures. Many of these measures fall in the category of sanitary and phytosanitary (SPS) measures and include diverse conditions
such as import licenses, inspection requirements, testing and certification requirements, labelling and
packaging requirements, and quarantines. Many of these measures, although necessary to address quality, safety and environmental concerns as well as the needs of agrifood businesses to streamline food
production chains, do ultimately add to production and transaction costs.

One of the most relevant aspects of SPS measures is their potential distorting effect on international trade. For exporters, the main concern is how well they can compete for market shares in highly
regulated markets where costs of compliance are not trivial. Importantly, the cost of compliance with
regulatory measures is often asymmetric across exporters, as the cost depends on infrastructure, technical know-how and the availability of production facilities. These aspects are usually available to larger
firms based in developed and emerging markets and to firms integrated in global value chains, but they
are generally less available—often not available at all—to smaller firms in many developing countries.
Any proliferation and increased stringency of SPS measures therefore can induce shifts to exporters with
stronger capacities for SPS compliance.

A recent UNCTAD study by Murina and Nicita (2014) examines the European Union (EU) framework
of SPS measures and investigates the extent to which these measures affect export to the EU from low-
income countries.[a] The study argues that the comprehensiveness of the EU regulatory framework, as well
as its higher stringency vis-à-vis frameworks implemented by trading partners, act as an important market-
access barrier for low-income countries. In quantitative terms, the study finds that the distorting effects
of the EU SPS measures vary across product groups and result in a total loss of about $3 billion, or about
15 per cent of exports, from low-income countries (figure II.4.1).

The UNCTAD study also finds that low-income countries which have deep preferential trade
agreements with the EU (i.e., an agreement that goes beyond simple preferential access to cover be-
yond-the-border issues) can more effectively comply with SPS measures. This finding is important, as it
suggests that some of the costs associated with SPS compliance can be reduced through well-targeted
technical assistance programmes incorporated in trade agreements. Technical assistance programmes
can help in meeting some of the fixed costs of compliance, such as those related to lack of infrastructure,
quality control mechanisms and certification agencies, making low-income countries more competitive.
Indeed, the disproportionate effect of the EU regulations on the exports of agricultural products from
developing countries is recognized even within the EU regulatory framework.[b]

Going forward, developing countries will confront the challenges of adapting to the high levels
of regulatory standards that regional trade agreements such as the Trans-Pacific Partnership Agreement
are expected to enforce. Whether in terms of mutual recognition or harmonization, regulatory measures are likely to take a central role in many trade agreements in the future. In this regard, low-income
countries would need to make sure that the sharing of costs related to compliance with the regulatory
framework is addressed within the agreement, and possibly facilitated by targeted technical assistance.
In addition, multilateral cooperation through an improved trade facilitation agenda, paired with existing
initiatives such as Aid for Trade and the Enhanced Integrated Framework, should surely help developing
countries cope with the challenges of meeting SPS and other regulatory standards.

Source: UNCTAD, Division
on International Trade in
Goods and Services, and
Commodities.

a Using the UNCTAD TRAINS
database on non-tariff
measures, this paper utilizes a
gravity model of bilateral trade
to investigate the effect of the
EU sanitary and phytosanitary
measures for 125 exporting
countries and covering about
700 different products in 21
agricultural sectors.

b For example, EU Regulation
No. 882/2004 acknowledges
the special needs of
developing countries, in
particular of the least
developed countries, for
technical assistance to comply
with EU regulations.

*(continued)*

Box II.4 *(continued)*

Figure II.4.1
**Exports and export loss to the European Union**

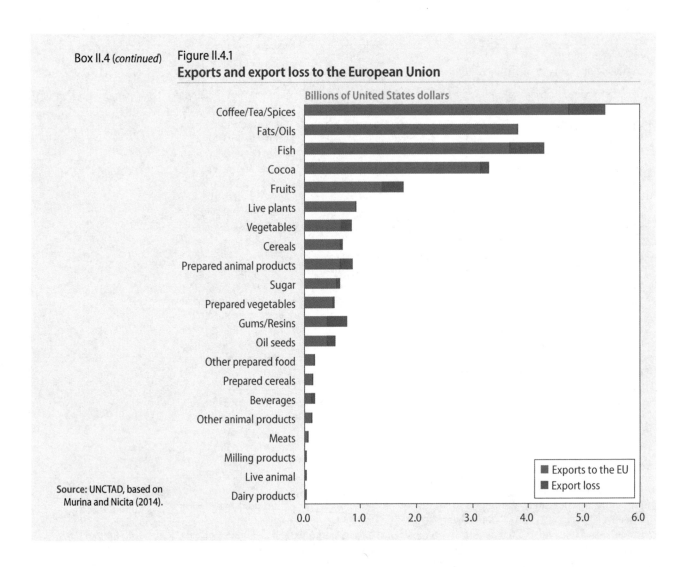

Source: UNCTAD, based on
Murina and Nicita (2014).

are also systemic implications for the multilateral trading system. For instance, mega-RTAs can affect incentives for multilateralism and the regulatory templates of RTAs might be used as a basis for future multilateral negotiations. Most significantly, proliferation of RTAs may lead to a two-tiered trading system which would differentiate countries and affect the relevance and centrality of the multilateral trading system.

## Future direction

**Further coherence is needed between the multilateral trading system and the RTAs**

The multilateral trading system is a global public good with a universal, rules-based, non-discriminatory and equitable nature that can maximize the development potential of international trade. This is especially important as the potential of trade is not automatically translated into development benefits. The fact that the 20 largest exporters in 2014 (mainly developed and Asian economies) represented 71 per cent of world trade reminds us that inequality between and within countries—a concern explicitly stated in SDGs—remains a persistent development challenge requiring policy attention.

Furthermore, the importance of multilateralism is matched by its challenges. Limited progress in the Doha Round, together with an increasing prevalence of new-generation RTAs, affects the credibility and centrality of the multilateral system. Mega-RTAs in particular can diminish incentives for multilateral negotiations with potential implications for outsiders, especially for developing countries. This highlights the importance of enhancing coherence between RTAs and the multilateral trading system so they can support and sustain an enabling development environment. It also underscores the need to review the institutional adaptations that the multilateral trading system requires for enhancing its relevance and effectiveness as it faces the reality of multiple parallel processes.

Global trade and its governance should be consistent with sustainable development goals, and the multilateral trading system has to be revitalized, with improved credibility and relevance. This will require a fair, equitable and open trading environment and coherence among multilateralism, RTAs and policy space, including through special and differential treatment, so that trade can contribute to broad-based sustainable development and reduce inequalities among and within economies. Furthermore, the potential of large benefits from productivity gains underlines the importance of developing a best-fit policy mix that includes trade policy, regulatory and institutional frameworks, and a new generation of industrial policies focused on enhancing competitiveness and value addition through technology, innovation and structural change.

# Measuring the commodity terms-of-trade effect of the commodity price drop

In an attempt to measure the net commodity terms-of-trade[1] effect of the global commodity price changes at the country level, monthly commodity export and import price indices for a total of 178 economies have been created. For each economy, the indices are constructed by weighing the monthly spot price of a commodity by its share in the economy's commodity export or import basket.[2] A total of 41 international commodity prices have been considered, with the indices covering, on average, 90 per cent of commodity export values and 86 per cent of commodity import values in 2014. The construction of these monthly indices allows examination of the country-specific impact of the commodity price shocks on the commodity terms of trade. Focus is primarily on commodity-dependent countries, defined here as countries for which the sum of commodity exports and imports accounts for over 30 per cent of GDP. These countries are classified into four groups, based on their main export commodity: fuel, food, metals and agricultural raw materials.

Figure II.1.1 in box II.1 shows the declines in the commodity export and import price indices for 81 commodity-dependent countries over the period April 2011-August 2015. In a second step, indices are scaled by the respective share of commodity exports and imports in GDP in order to take into account differences in the importance of commodity trade across countries. This provides a first indication of how the commodity terms of trade shock affects gross domestic income and domestic demand.[3] Figure II.A.1 depicts the adjusted declines in the export and import price indices. The adjustment tends to reinforce the negative price effects for fuel exporters as indicated by the significant distance from the 45-degree line. Many fuel exporters have not only seen sharp price declines on the export side and very limited price declines on the import side, but the share of fuel exports in GDP is also large. As a result, the negative impact of the commodity terms-of-trade shock on these countries is expected to be large.

---

1 Commodity terms-of-trade is defined here as the price of a country's commodity exports in terms of its commodity imports.

2 Commodity price data were retrieved from UNCTADstat, IMF Primary Commodity Price data and the World Bank Commodity Price Data (The Pink Sheet). Commodity trade data were retrieved from UNCTADstat.

3 A comprehensive assessment of the country-level impact of the commodity price shocks would require a more complex and dynamic framework that takes into account the changes in inflation, exchange rates, fiscal balances and other macroeconomic variables.

Figure II.A.1

**Commodity export and import price decline, scaled by GDP share of commodity export and import, April 2011–August 2015**

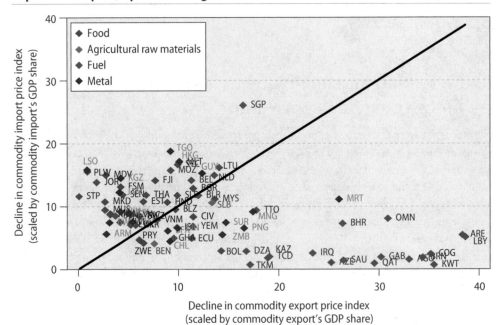

Source: UN/DESA.

Note: See table J in the Statistical Annex to this publication for definitions of country codes.

## Chapter III
# International finance for sustainable development

The year 2015 has been a significant one for global cooperation in development. In September, world leaders adopted a new set of Sustainable Development Goals (SDGs) and targets as part of the 2030 Agenda for Sustainable Development. They also agreed in July on a new financing framework for achieving sustainable development, embodied in the Addis Ababa Action Agenda (AAAA) (box III.1). Earlier in March, Governments adopted a post-2015 framework on disaster risk reduction. Taken together, these new global agreements provide a comprehensive framework within which international finance should flow.

Although the amount of financing needed to achieve the SDGs is vast, global public and private savings would be sufficient—if the financial system were to effectively intermediate savings and investments in line with sustainable development objectives. This is not currently the case: the international finance system is neither stable nor efficient in allocating finance where it is needed for sustained and inclusive growth. Additionally, finance is not generally channelled with social outcomes or environmental sustainability in mind.

These are very large challenges. The world requires action at both the national and international levels to simultaneously finance sustainable development and to develop sustainable finance.[1] Nationally, countries need to craft sustainable development financing strategies, based on their national developmental models. These strategies should seek to unlock the potential of people and the private sector, and incentivize changes in consumption, production and investment patterns to support sustainable development. At the international level, there is a need for a coherent set of rules and policies that can channel finance to support sustainable development, leaving sufficient policy space for countries to pursue their chosen development model.

These issues are at the core of the new international agreement on financing for development. The AAAA provides the guidance needed, covering domestic and international public finance, private finance, and cross-cutting and systemic issues. Member States need to implement the commitments contained in the AAAA, including forging a true global partnership in support of sustainable development. That partnership of nations, supported by other stakeholders, should shape a supportive international environment and provide the basis for further progress towards sustainable development. Achieving the SDGs and transforming the world depend on this.

The Addis Ababa Action Agenda establishes a framework to realign the international financial system with the sustainable development agenda

---

[1] Sustainable finance is defined as finance that is long-term oriented and aligned with economic, environmental and social values through products and markets that balance inclusion with stability.

Box III.1
## The Addis Ababa Action Agenda

At the Third International Conference on Financing for Development, held in Addis Ababa, Ethiopia, from 13 to 16 July 2015, United Nations Member States adopted the Addis Ababa Action Agenda (AAAA). The Agenda provides

- A new global framework for financing sustainable development that aligns all financing flows and international and domestic policies with economic, social and environmental priorities.
- A comprehensive set of policy actions by Member States, with a package of over 100 concrete measures that draw upon all sources of finance, promote technology and innovation, reform trade, harness data, and address systemic issues to transform the global economy and achieve the Sustainable Development Goals (SDGs).

The AAAA serves as a guide for actions by Governments, international organizations, businesses, civil society and philanthropists. The Agenda reiterates that countries have primary responsibility for their economic and social development, while committing the international community to creating an enabling environment. Together, these positions support a revitalized and strengthened global partnership for sustainable development that can end extreme poverty and deliver sustainable development for all.

The policy framework presented in the AAAA seeks to realign financial flows with public goals, underpinned by country-led development models that reflect the diverse stages of a country's development and its specific circumstances and financing needs. Official development assistance remains crucial, particularly for countries most in need. But aid alone will not be sufficient. As in the Monterrey Consensus, the AAAA recognizes that finance is not just about financing flows; it depends on public policies that strengthen the national and international enabling environments and seek to align private behaviour with public goals. The AAAA offers a nuanced understanding of the benefits and risks associated with different types of finance: It stresses the importance of long-term investment and the need for all financing to be aligned with sustainable development. It puts forward specific public policies and regulatory frameworks to encourage private investment to support the SDGs. It spells out the potential contributions of public finance, highlighting the growing role of national, regional and multilateral development banks.

But the AAAA goes beyond the Monterrey Consensus to fully take into account the regulatory and other policy requirements for realizing all three dimensions of sustainable development—economic, social and environmental—in an integrated manner. It emphasizes that trade, development and dissemination of technology, as well as capacity-building, are key means of implementation for the 2030 Agenda for Sustainable Development.

The AAAA is an integral part of the 2030 Agenda for Sustainable Development. To ensure adequate implementation and follow-up, the AAAA establishes an annual Financing for Development Forum, with intergovernmentally agreed conclusions and recommendations that will inform the review of the 2030 Agenda for Sustainable Development.

Source: UN/DESA.

## Trends in net resource transfers

As articulated in the AAAA, the new financing framework for sustainable development incorporates all sources of financing, including the transfer of resources to developing countries in the form of foreign private capital inflows, official development assistance (ODA) and other forms of international cooperation. As can be seen in figure III.1, net resource transfers[2] to developing countries as a whole have been negative, implying that resources are flowing from developing to developed countries. Least developed countries (LDCs), where resource shortfalls have been most acute, have been receiving almost no resources in net terms.

---

2     Net transfer of resources refers to the net flow of capital and capital servicing, the net foreign earnings of labour, plus the net change in reserves. Cf. United Nations (1990), box IV.1.

Figure III.1
**Net transfer of resources to developing economies and economies in transition, 2003–2015**

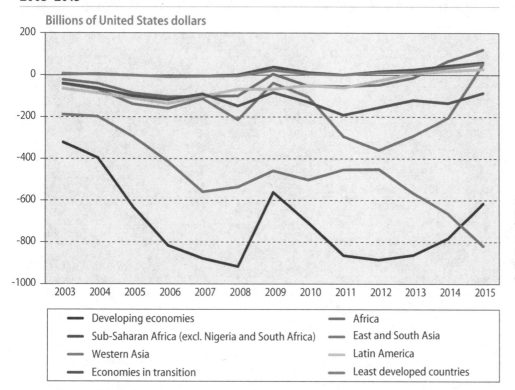

Billions of United States dollars

| | |
|---|---|
| ▬ Developing economies | ▬ Africa |
| ▬ Sub-Saharan Africa (excl. Nigeria and South Africa) | ▬ East and South Asia |
| ▬ Western Asia | ▬ Latin America |
| ▬ Economies in transition | ▬ Least developed countries |

## Highly volatile private capital flows

Table III.1 and figure III.2 show the recent trends in capital flows to developing countries and economies in transition. While most forms of capital inflows initially rebounded following the 2008 crisis, they began to slow after 2010, with total net capital flows to developing countries and transition economies turning negative in 2014, driven by large net outflows from transition economies, particularly the Russian Federation. In 2015, it is estimated that over $700 billion of capital left developing and transition economies, greatly exceeding the magnitude of net outflows during the Great Recession. It is estimated that foreign direct investment (FDI) fell by $145 billion, driven by large declines in East and South Asia, and that portfolio flows, which tend to be more volatile, turned negative. The greatest decline, however, was in "other" investment (mostly interbank loans and currency/deposits, trade credits and other equity), which has historically been the most volatile form of capital flow (table III.1). This decline partly reflects a continuation of commercial banks reducing their exposures to higher risk economies (including emerging markets) and could potentially be further impacted going forward by the introduction of Basel III capital adequacy standards for banks.

Foreign direct investment, especially greenfield direct investment, typically has longer-term investment horizons and is generally attracted by factors such as high growth rates, lower factor costs (including labour costs), rule of law and strong macroeconomic fundamentals. This, to a large extent, explains the lower volatility of FDI relative to portfolio investment and cross-border interbank lending, which are typically driven by short-term

In 2015, net capital outflows from developing and transition countries exceeded the magnitude of net outflows that occurred during the Great Recession

Table III.1

**Net financial flows to developing countries and economies in transition, 2006–2015**

| Billions of United States dollars | | | | | | | | | | |
|---|---|---|---|---|---|---|---|---|---|---|
| | 2006 | 2007 | 2008 | 2009 | 2010 | 2011 | 2012 | 2013 | 2014 | 2015[a] |
| **Developing countries** | | | | | | | | | | |
| Total net flows | -24.5 | 292.3 | 20.5 | 496.5 | 614.6 | 421.4 | 177.1 | 379.2 | 104.3 | -614.9 |
| Direct investment | 241.1 | 344.8 | 368.4 | 270.8 | 371.6 | 454.0 | 415.8 | 474.9 | 404.3 | 259.7 |
| Portfolio investment[b] | -187.5 | -81.6 | -129.6 | 29.7 | 153.1 | 102.6 | 119.6 | -13.1 | 48.3 | -47.7 |
| Other investment[c] | -78.2 | 29.1 | -218.3 | 196.0 | 89.9 | -135.2 | -358.3 | -82.6 | -348.2 | -826.9 |
| Change in reserves[d] | -669.4 | -1058.4 | -745.3 | -711.6 | -884.5 | -756.2 | -477.9 | -643.0 | -285.9 | 395.2 |
| **Africa** | | | | | | | | | | |
| Total net flows | -33.2 | 27.0 | 18.1 | 54.3 | 12.0 | 29.8 | 47.1 | 62.3 | 80.2 | 91.9 |
| Direct investment | 23.5 | 40.9 | 55.4 | 46.3 | 46.2 | 40.6 | 39.2 | 34.4 | 33.1 | 42.8 |
| Portfolio investment[b] | 16.8 | 4.7 | -36.9 | -5.3 | 4.3 | 12.8 | 21.5 | 17.9 | 17.9 | 8.2 |
| Other investment[c] | -73.5 | -18.6 | -0.4 | 13.2 | -38.4 | -23.6 | -13.5 | 10.0 | 29.3 | 40.9 |
| Change in reserves[d] | -78.1 | -85.4 | -74.7 | 5.4 | -20.0 | -29.4 | -25.9 | 9.6 | 30.7 | 59.7 |
| **East and South Asia** | | | | | | | | | | |
| Total net flows | 53.9 | 109.6 | -39.5 | 349.7 | 382.0 | 276.3 | 15.7 | 238.2 | -44.7 | -795.4 |
| Direct investment | 139.9 | 162.9 | 155.7 | 99.6 | 199.3 | 259.9 | 212.9 | 270.6 | 229.2 | 87.2 |
| Portfolio investment[b] | -128.2 | -55.4 | -45.3 | 38.0 | 35.2 | 24.7 | 2.8 | -85.4 | 48.7 | -104.5 |
| Other investment[c] | 42.2 | 2.1 | -150.0 | 212.2 | 147.5 | -8.2 | -199.9 | 53.1 | -322.6 | -778.1 |
| Change in reserves[d] | -433.1 | -675.2 | -490.8 | -667.6 | -684.9 | -505.3 | -219.6 | -515.1 | -264.1 | 214.3 |
| **West Asia** | | | | | | | | | | |
| Total net flows | -48.5 | 43.4 | -35.3 | 14.3 | 14.6 | -110.2 | -106.6 | -138.7 | -170.4 | -60.2 |
| Direct investment | 44.3 | 48.1 | 57.7 | 54.4 | 35.4 | 22.7 | 26.0 | 6.0 | 5.8 | 17.0 |
| Portfolio investment[b] | -71.3 | -75.4 | -54.1 | -26.8 | -17.7 | -53.3 | -19.2 | -50.6 | -130.0 | -21.1 |
| Other investment[c] | -21.4 | 70.7 | -38.8 | -13.4 | -3.1 | -79.6 | -113.4 | -94.1 | -46.2 | -56.2 |
| Change in reserves[d] | -105.2 | -167.3 | -138.8 | 5.7 | -89.1 | -110.7 | -173.2 | -131.2 | -15.1 | 99.1 |
| **Latin America and the Caribbean** | | | | | | | | | | |
| Total net flows | 3.2 | 112.3 | 77.3 | 78.2 | 206.0 | 225.4 | 220.8 | 217.4 | 239.2 | 148.8 |
| Direct investment | 33.4 | 92.9 | 99.6 | 70.5 | 90.7 | 130.8 | 137.8 | 164.0 | 136.3 | 112.6 |
| Portfolio investment[b] | -4.7 | 44.5 | 6.7 | 23.8 | 131.3 | 118.4 | 114.6 | 105.0 | 111.7 | 69.8 |
| Other investment[c] | -25.5 | -25.1 | -29.1 | -16.0 | -16.0 | -23.8 | -31.5 | -51.6 | -8.8 | -33.5 |
| Change in reserves[d] | -53.0 | -130.5 | -40.9 | -55.1 | -90.5 | -110.8 | -59.2 | -6.3 | -37.3 | 22.2 |
| **Economies in transition** | | | | | | | | | | |
| Total net flows | 32.5 | 132.1 | -102.4 | -2.6 | -6.9 | -56.7 | -14.1 | -15.4 | -122.7 | -87.5 |
| Direct investment | 28.4 | 34.8 | 55.4 | 22.0 | 12.9 | 21.0 | 30.6 | 8.8 | -14.2 | 20.0 |
| Portfolio investment[b] | 7.5 | -2.7 | -36.0 | 6.1 | 14.3 | -15.8 | -1.3 | 2.3 | -26.5 | -19.5 |
| Other investment[c] | -3.3 | 100.1 | -121.8 | -30.7 | -34.1 | -61.9 | -43.4 | -26.5 | -82.0 | -88.0 |
| Change in reserves[d] | -134.5 | -170.2 | 29.6 | -10.5 | -51.5 | -26.6 | -25.6 | 22.3 | 114.1 | 43.5 |

Source: UN/DESA, based on IMF World Economic Outlook database, October 2015.
Note: WEO has adopted the sixth edition of the Balance of Payments Manual (BPM6). The composition of developing countries above is based on the country classification located in the statistical annex, which differs from the classification used in the World Economic Outlook.
a Preliminary.
b Including portfolio debt and equity investment.
c Including short- and long-term bank lending.
d Negative values denote increases in reserves.

interest-rate differentials and/or the expectation of short-term returns. However, there is also evidence of recent increasing financialization of FDI, with cross-border merger and acquisition sales in developing countries surpassing pre-crisis peaks to hit an historic high of $120 billion in 2014 (United Nations Conference on Trade and Development, 2015c, annex table 9). FDI also remains concentrated in a few regions (mostly Asia and Latin America), countries (mostly middle-income and upper-middle-income) and sectors (e.g., a significant portion of the investment in LDCs is geared towards resource-rich countries).

Overall, the largest net capital outflows in 2015 were from East and South Asia and Commonwealth of Independent States (CIS) countries. Similar trends were observed in virtually all major emerging economies, particularly those that received large inflows of capital during 2009-2013, such as Brazil and Turkey. Capital outflows from China were the major driver of the trend, which could intensify further in the medium term as the country moves to a slower growth path.

**Figure III.2**
**Net financial flows to developing countries and economies in transition, 2005–2015**

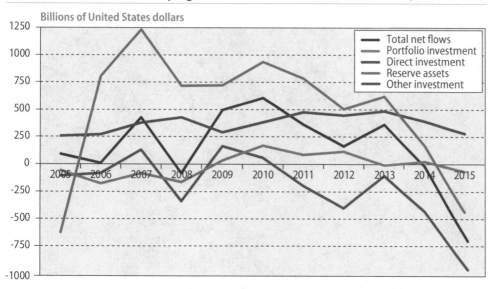

Source: Table III.1 of this publication.
Note: A positive value means inflow of capital and increase in reserves.

As discussed in Chapter I, declines in commodity prices, the slowdown in China and other emerging economies, and the prospects of higher interest rates in the United States of America all contributed to the reduction in inflows and acceleration of capital outflows from developing economies. In the past, Governments facing large net capital outflows typically responded by raising interest rates and/or letting their currencies devalue. These types of measures often failed to stem outflows and/or had negative repercussions on the domestic economy, often adversely affecting growth because of the higher costs of capital for domestic borrowers. Recently, many Governments have used foreign-exchange reserves to support their currency. Some have also implemented other forms of direct or indirect capital-account management (e.g., macroprudential regulations and/or direct capital controls). The choice of policy option is often predicated on the exchange-rate regime as well as the monetary policy framework. In practice, countries generally combine these policy options. For example, China spent a significant amount of its reserves to counteract

Declining commodity prices, the slowdown in many emerging economies, and the prospects of higher interest rates in the United States have all contributed to net capital outflows from developing economies

the downward pressure on the currency, which partly contributed to the decline in total reserves from nearly $4 trillion in mid-2014 to $3.65 trillion in mid-2015 (figure III.3). To discourage currency speculation, China also mandated a deposit of 20 per cent of sale on currency forwards. At the same time, in one of the most visible events that marked the reversal of the trend in global capital flows, China adjusted its mechanism to determine the daily reference rate of the renminbi yuan against the dollar on 11 August 2015, which was followed by the increase of the reference rate by 4.4 per cent over the ensuing three days. A drop in reserves combined with currency depreciation was also observed in most other emerging economies, with the Russian Federation hit particularly hard by the oil price decline, sanctions and geopolitical uncertainties. Russian reserves declined from over $500 billion in early 2014 to $370 billion in early October 2015 (figure III.3), while the Russian rouble lost over 50 per cent of its value in the same period. The changes in foreign-exchange reserves virtually coincide with the recent decline in net capital flows (figure III.2).

**Figure III.3**
**Year-end foreign-exchange reserves, including gold, in BRICS countries**

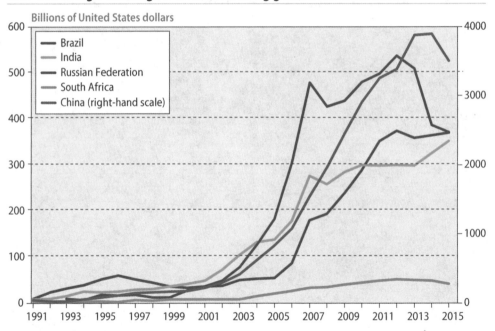

Source: IMF, International Financial Statistics.
Notes: For China, use right-hand scale; for all other countries, left-hand scale. Figures for 2015 are as of end-September.

## Capital flows and long-term economic growth

In the 1990s, a common argument advanced in favour of capital-account liberalization was that capital would flow from industrialized countries, where capital has low marginal returns, to developing countries, where its relative scarcity implies high marginal returns. This phenomenon should help relax the foreign-exchange constraint of developing countries that run large current-account deficits. In other words, capital-account liberalization was expected to delink investment from domestic savings, allowing developing countries' investment rates to exceed their savings rates and lead to increased growth. However, empirical studies have found that most if not all countries that managed to achieve high growth rates were net creditors, not net borrowers—meaning that they were saving more

Box III.2

## The "financial account", the "capital account" and twin surpluses

The balance of payments generally refers to the current account plus the capital account plus the inverse of the change in international reserves. A positive current account is usually associated with a negative capital account (or capital outflows), although the question of causality between the current and capital account is complex, and depends on country circumstances.

In economic literature, the "capital account" generally refers to the portion of the balance of payments that includes both financial flows and capital transfers. However, since 1993, the International Monetary Fund (IMF) balance-of-payment statistics have used the term "capital account" to only include capital transactions (e.g., capital transfers and acquisition or disposal of non-produced, non-financial assets), while using the term "financial account" to denote all financial flows classified according to type of investment (i.e., direct investment, portfolio investment, derivatives and other investment) as well as the change in reserve assets.[a] The IMF financial and capital accounts together are, therefore, roughly equivalent to the traditional capital account in the economic literature plus the change in international reserves. This chapter uses the term "capital account" to refer to four types of capital flows: direct investment, portfolio investment, derivatives and other investment.

The relationship between current and capital account is not straightforward. In some countries, a trade deficit (negative current account) is financed by foreign capital inflows, while in other countries a surge in capital inflows can lead to an overvalued exchange rate, which will drive down demand for the country's exports and increase imports, leading to a negative current account.

In the early 2000s, however, several emerging-market countries maintained both positive current and capital accounts, running what is called "twin surpluses". Central banks intervened in the foreign-exchange market, keeping exchange rates from appreciating while also building international reserves. China is the most often cited case, but a number of countries witnessed this phenomenon in some years (figure III.2.2), although only four large developing countries (with a population of more than 50 mil-

a  In many ways, the IMF balance-of-payments statistics' "financial account" plus "capital account" is similar to the United Nations concept of net resource transfer, as presented at the beginning of this chapter, as it includes both capital flows and reserve accumulation. The main difference is that the net resource transfer also addresses capital servicing (such as income from direct investment) and the net foreign earnings of labour, both of which are recorded on the current account.

Figure III.2.1

## Average current-account balance and capital flows, large developing countries, 2000–2014

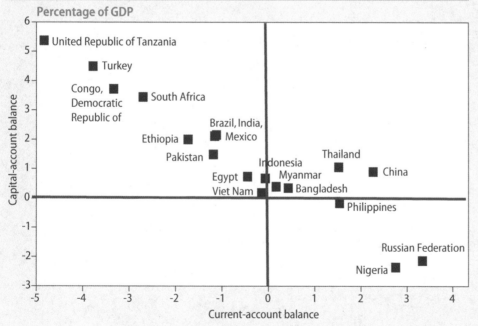

Source: IMF Balance of Payments.

(*continued*)

Box III.2 (*continued*)

Source: UN/DESA.

lion) did so over a 15 year period (figure III.2.1). As the balance of payments must be equal to zero, twin surpluses generally reflect a build-up in international reserves, while twin deficits generally reflect the opposite. The build-up of reserves usually entails opportunity costs in terms of missed investment or consumption opportunities, but it may also help to reduce exchange-rate volatility.

**Figure III.2.2**
**Current-account balance and capital flows, selected countries**

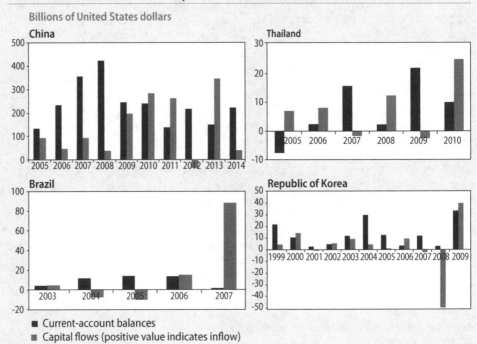

Billions of United States dollars

Source: IMF Balance of Payments.

■ Current-account balances
■ Capital flows (positive value indicates inflow)

**Figure III.4**
**Average annual growth rates of GDP per capita and average current-account balance, 1970–2007**

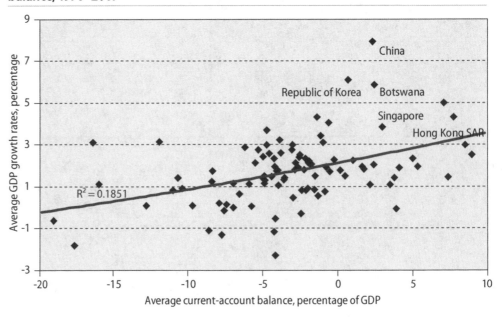

Source: UN/DESA calculations, based on World Bank World Development Indicators and IMF Balance of Payments.

than investing domestically—and that their current accounts were in surplus.[3] As shown in figure III.4 the relationship between the current-account surplus and growth rates has been positive.[4]

More broadly, there has been a high correlation between investment and domestic savings, even among countries with relatively open capital accounts, a phenomenon also known as the Feldstein-Horioka puzzle (Feldstein and Horioka, 1980). Three factors explain the puzzle. First, in some developing countries with open capital accounts, there has been a lower absolute level of foreign capital inflows than would have been predicted by theory. Second, in countries with large capital inflows, a significant portion of the inflows facilitated by an open capital account have tended to be based on a short-term investment horizon and, by definition, have been volatile in nature (figure III.5). Third, countries with high domestic savings rates generally intervened in the foreign-exchange market to maintain their competitiveness as an integral part of their export-oriented industrialization strategy, and managed their foreign-exchange inflows, including by building foreign-exchange reserves, which explains the strong correlation between investment and domestic

**There is a high correlation between investment and domestic savings, even in countries with open capital accounts**

Figure III.5
**Portfolio flows by non-residents, selected countries, 2013 Q1–2015 Q2**

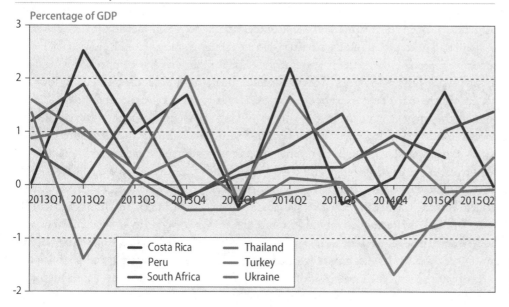

Source: UN/DESA calculations, based on IMF Balance of Payments.

---

3    The investment rate can be held back despite high saving rates when countries face a binding foreign-exchange constraint. The savings rate eventually falls to equate with the investment rate. See literature survey by Thirwal (2011).

4    The relationship is significant, even after controlling for the level of development:
$$y = 0.85\ Ycap + 0.08\ CA + 1.06,$$
$$\quad\ (3.07) \qquad (2.19)$$
N=91,   $R^2$ = 0.23, robust standard errors, T-statistics in brackets below, where
y – annual average growth rates of per capita GDP in 1970-2013, %,
Ycap – logarithm of per capita PPP GDP in 2000,
CA – average current-account balance to GDP ratio in 1970-2013, %.
This regression does not imply causality, but shows that growth and current-account surpluses more often than not go hand in hand.

savings. The growth of exports stimulates the economy, creating a virtuous circle of high saving and investment rates (see the section on global imbalances). A few countries thus enjoyed surpluses on both current and capital accounts (box III.2). This is associated with an accumulation of reserve assets, part of which are essentially recycled back into developed countries as capital and typically held in developed-country government bonds. This phenomenon runs contrary to the objectives of capital-account liberalization.

## Pitfalls of short-term capital flows

Since the early 1980s there have been several waves of large short-term capital flows to developing countries, but not one of them resulted in a growth miracle. On the contrary, large waves of short-term capital inflows often ended in financial crises (Krugman, 2009). This was largely owing to procyclical capital flows—induced by irrational exuberance and herding behaviour—as well as the short-term nature of many of these flows, which often induced currency and maturity mismatches, leading to sudden reversals of capital flow.

The impact of sudden surges or exits of short-term capital flows can seriously undermine sustainable development, as was seen in past financial crises in the Russian Federation, East Asia and Latin America.[5] For example, a sudden surge in outflows generally causes large exchange-rate depreciation, which raises the costs of servicing foreign-currency denominated debt. This can force firms into bankruptcy, destroy jobs and increase macroeconomic instability. Bankruptcies among exporters can also result from surges in inflows, which can suddenly appreciate the exchange rate, thereby making exports less competitive. Contrary to the claim by the proponents of capital-account liberalization, short-term capital flows do not contribute to the deepening of the domestic financial sector (Stiglitz and others, 2006). Instead, they may increase the fragility of the domestic financial sector and increase the risk of financial and banking crises as observed in South-East Asia during 1997-1998. In sum, short-term capital flows cannot be regarded as part of sustainable finance. Additionally, one recent International Monetary Fund (IMF) study finds that capital-account liberalization has contributed to a rise in inequality, arguing that foreign capital is more complementary to skilled workers, which can increase wage gaps and inequality (Furceri and Loungani, 2013).

The link between open capital accounts and increased volatility is now relatively well understood. In 2012, the IMF developed an institutional view which recognized that capital flows "carry risks, which can be magnified by gaps in countries' financial and institutional infrastructure" (International Monetary Fund, 2012, p. 1). Nonetheless, capital-account liberalization continued to be encouraged in practice; they are frequently included in bilateral and regional trade agreements between developed and developing countries, even for countries such as Chile, which had previously used capital-account restrictions effectively.[6] The AAAA thus includes an agreement for countries to use necessary macroeconomic policy adjustment, supported by macroprudential regulations and, as appropriate, capital flow management measures when dealing with risks from large and volatile capital flows. The AAAA also contains a pledge that trade and investment agreements would have appropriate

The impact of sudden surges or exits of short-term capital flows can seriously undermine sustainable development

---

5    For more on these crises, see Muchhala, ed. (2007); Dasgupta, Uzan and Wilson, eds. (2001); and De Paula and Alves (2000).

6    See Article 9.8 and Annex 9-E of the Trans-Pacific Partnership (TPP) Agreement. Chile negotiated a special clause to the TPP, which allows it to maintain reserve requirements on capital transfers, but the clause limits these in size and duration.

safeguards that protect the public interest by preventing a constraint in domestic policies and regulation.

## Remittance flows: rising, but different

While more stable than most private capital flows, personal remittances have also been affected by the weakened global economy (figure III.6). The World Bank expects the growth rate of remittance flows to developing countries and economies in transition to decline in 2015 because of subdued growth in Europe and the Russian Federation. This follows the enormous growth of remittances over the last 15 years, to reach more than $580 billion in 2014 (with $436 billion to developing countries).[7] Remittances are resource transfers between resident and non-resident households (generally in the form of wages transferred from migrant workers to their families) reported in a country's current account, which includes the balance of trade, net income from abroad and net current transfers.

Some countries are highly dependent on remittance flows as indicated by the remittance share in their gross domestic product (GDP) (figure III.7). For example, remittances account for over 40 per cent of Tajikistan's GDP, even though in volume terms, it is not one of the large remittance-recipient countries. On the other hand, India, which receives the highest amount of remittances, has a flow accounting for less than 5 per cent of its GDP. Obviously, the size of remittances in relation to a country's GDP has important implications for its economy, even though the impact of remittances on economic growth and development in recipient countries depends on a variety of factors. In many ways, remittances have a similar effect on the economy as wages earned domestically. Similar to domestic wages, remittances increase the disposable income of households, stimulating consumption with a multiplier effect on the economy. Their impact on savings and investment, and hence on growth, will depend, to a large extent, on financial inclusion.

Remittance flows to developing countries have been restrained by the global slowdown

Figure III.6
**Total migrant stocks and global remittance inflows, 1990–2014**

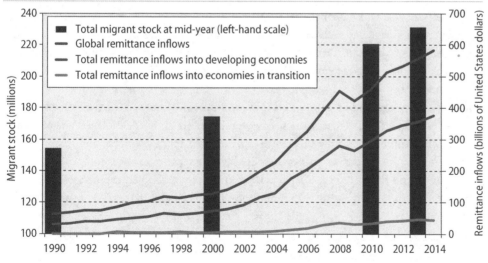

Source: World Bank.

---

7    Overall remittance flows from World Bank; additional figures from World Bank (2015c).

## Figure III.7
### Selected countries' remittance inflows, 2014

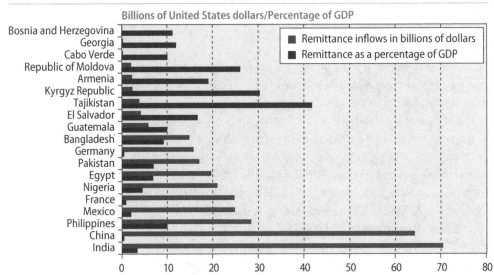

Source: World Bank/World
Development Indicators.

**Remittances are predominantly spent on smoothing consumption and on human capital**

Unlike domestic wages, remittances have cross-border and balance-of-payments effects. For example, remittances can support the balance of payments (figure III.8) and help cover a country's trade deficit or foreign-exchange shortfall. However, large-scale inflows of foreign exchange also strengthen the exchange rate, which can erode domestic competitiveness—a phenomenon known as Dutch disease. The impacts on the balance of payments and the exchange rate will depend on how the incoming funds are ultimately used. Existing data indicate that remittances are predominantly spent in smoothing consumption and on human capital, such as expenditure on education and health care, although there is some evidence of increased direct investment of remittances into small and medium-sized enterprises (SMEs) and real estate in some countries.[8] When primarily used for consumption, remittances are more likely to cause inflationary pressure and appreciation of the exchange rate (Narayan, Narayan and Mishra, 2011).[9] On the other hand, the use of remittances in productive investment, such as in SMEs, should help prevent inflationary pressure and consequent loss of competitiveness. Access to the formal financial system can help remittance-recipient households to save and facilitate investments.

Remittances are also directly linked to economic cycles in both the host and home countries, and some studies have found that remittances demonstrate countercyclical tendencies (Frankel, 2010). Other studies, however, have found that remittances are procyclical in most countries, especially those with less financial depth (Giuliano and Ruiz-Arranz, 2009). There is evidence that remittances regularly increase after natural disasters (Mohapatra, Joseph and Ratha, 2009). Nepal is the most recent example, where shortly after the devastating earthquake in April 2015 remittance inflows increased by 26.3 per cent.[10] High

---

8    See, for example, Yang (2008).

9    For Bangladesh, one study found that a 1 per cent increase in remittance inflows will raise inflation by 0.72 per cent, while food inflation would rise by 1.91 per cent. See Roy and Rahman (2014).

10   See http://kathmandupost.ekantipur.com/news/2015-10-03/remittance-jumps-to-rs53b-in-first-month.html.

Figure III.8
**Current-account balances and remittance inflows in selected countries, 2014**

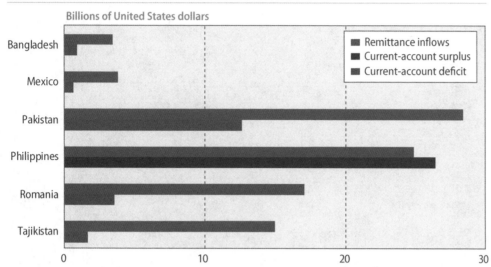

Source: World Bank.

levels of remittances might be an indicator that insufficient domestic investment in productive enterprises is serving as a push factor for emigration.[11]

Better access to financial services can lower the high remittance transaction costs in underserved areas, as called for in the AAAA. Combining remittance receipts with broader access to other financial services can increase the impact of remittances on growth by facilitating savings and investments. If a portion of earnings is saved in the financial system, financial institutions can turn such savings into productive investments, even if the household ultimately uses the earning for consumption. Pools of small savings in rural areas can allow an expansion of support to agribusiness and SMEs. Indeed, one study estimates that if the predominantly informal savings of remittance receivers in four Central American countries could be mobilized, formal savings would increase by $2 billion, representing about 1.7 per cent of GDP (Orozco and Yansura, 2015). The AAAA stresses the need to protect labour rights in accordance with International Labour Organization core labour standards and that destination countries should promote and effectively protect the human rights of all migrants.

## Global imbalances and international reserves accumulation

International reserve accumulation by monetary authorities constituted the most prominent macroeconomic policy shift of the late 1990s. Accumulated reserves increased from 5.9 per cent of world gross product, or $1.9 trillion in 2000, to 14.4 per cent or $9.3 trillion in 2010 (figure III.9). However, since 2014, the process of accelerated reserve accumulation stopped, mirroring the decline in capital inflows (figure III.2). Reserves in developing and transition economies increased by only $172 billion in 2014 (table III.1). In 2015, reserves in developing and transition countries are expected to decline by nearly $440 billion in

Since 2014, the rapid accumulation of reserve assets in developing and transition economies has halted

---

11 Economic theory describes push and pull factors in migration decisions as being equally important, however recent evidence on migration to OECD countries finds that origin country unemployment rates are not significantly correlated with migration. See Mayda (2010).

Figure III.9
**Foreign-exchange reserves as a percentage of world gross product, 1980–2014**

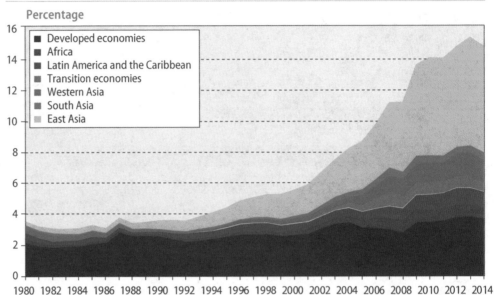

Source: IMF International
Financial Statistics.
Note: Excludes the value of gold
held as official reserves.

aggregate. It remains to be seen whether this is a temporary interruption of the trend or a permanent change.

Countries accumulate reserves as "self-insurance" against potential external shocks in the current account (often due to fluctuations in commodity prices) and in the capital account (often due to volatility of capital flows). Reserve accumulation also allows countries to better manage and smooth capital flow cycles, and can also be a by-product of export-led growth strategies that maintain an undervalued currency through interventions in the currency market (Griffith-Jones and Ocampo, 2010). The level of development, investment climate, the accumulated level of reserves and the level and dynamics of foreign trade can also explain reserve accumulation by a country. Empirical research indicates that there is no single explanation for reserves accumulation that applies to all countries at all times (International Monetary Fund, 2010). One study finds that deliberate policy-induced foreign-exchange reserve accumulation is an important explanatory variable in growth regressions, implying that development models involving accumulation of reserves may help spur long-term growth in developing countries (Polterovich and Popov, 2004).

Countries can also accumulate reserves to prevent asset price bubbles in the short run, and to prevent the overvaluation of the currency in the long run, both of which can have significant adverse consequences on macroeconomic stability and long-term growth. Consequently, reserve accumulation can have positive externalities on the production and export of tradables and industrial development and can thus be a feature of the country's development model. Undervaluation of the exchange rate can increase the competitiveness of exports, without the need for sector- or firm-specific subsidies or interventions.

Reserve accumulation can, however, be costly, particularly in terms of the opportunity cost of forgone domestic investment. While it may ease upward pressure on the exchange rate, it also maintains upward pressure on the costs of capital for domestic borrowers. Furthermore, the strategy of reserve accumulation by all countries might not be sustainable because it suffers from a fallacy of composition. To be sustainable, there must be at least one country—as has been the case with the United States—that is large enough and willing to run consistent and ever larger current-account deficits and provide reserve assets to the rest of the world. The mechanism facilitates an almost unlimited supply of credit from reserve-accumulating countries, resulting in increased global liquidity. This, in turn, has to be intermediated by the financial system, which, as discussed, has not been effective in allocating resources to support investment growth and sustainable development.

## International financial stability and growth

A primary role of the international financial system is to channel savings to productive uses and support investment necessary for inclusive and sustainable economic growth. The existing system does not adequately allocate resources for long-term sustainable development needs (box III.3). Furthermore, vulnerabilities and instability in the financial system pose risks to the real economy and sustainable development, as demonstrated by the global financial crisis. Vulnerabilities include volatile capital flows (discussed above) and additional risks generated by the financial sector, as well as risks posed by debt overhangs and debt distress. Ultimately, stability and sustainability should be mutually reinforcing: stable markets encourage greater investment, while long-term investment can play a stabilizing, countercyclical role. There are, however, trade-offs between stability and enhancing access to credit necessary for achieving sustainable development, particularly in higher risk areas. The balance between stability and access is at the crux of the AAAA, which emphasizes the importance of policy and regulatory environments that support both financial market stability and access to credit and financial services in a balanced manner. In its strategy for implementing the 2030 Agenda for Sustainable Development, the IMF also prioritized "policy analysis and capacity building to balance financial market deepening with financial stability" and promoting "a stable and inclusive financial system that mitigates the trade-offs between financial deepening and financial stability" (International Monetary Fund, 2015d, p. 2).

The existing international financial system does not adequately allocate resources for long-term sustainable development needs

### The financial sector: stability, financial depth, and access

The current international financial regulatory standards have focused on stability and, in particular, ensuring the safety and soundness of financial institutions, as well as reducing systemic risks. There is, however, growing recognition of the effect of regulations on incentives for investment, and on what have come to be known as the "unintended consequences" of the impact of financial regulations on access to credit.

Concerns have been expressed about the potential but unintended negative impact of Basel III regulations on long-term financing, trade finance, SMEs and other areas of importance for achieving sustainable development (Financial Stability Board, 2012). For example, international banks had been major providers of project finance for infrastructure (figure III.10). However, there are concerns that Basel III's treatment of risk weights for long-term finance in developing countries may constrain infrastructure lending by commercial banks going forward. The Financial Stability Board (FSB) has started surveying its members about unintended consequences of Basel III. As of their last survey, FSB members did not report any empirical evidence or data suggesting that internationally agreed regulatory reforms have had material adverse effects on the provision of long-term finance in their jurisdictions (Financial Stability Board, 2014). However, it was emphasized that it is too

Figure III.10
**Global project finance by funding institution, January 2012–January 2013**

Percentage

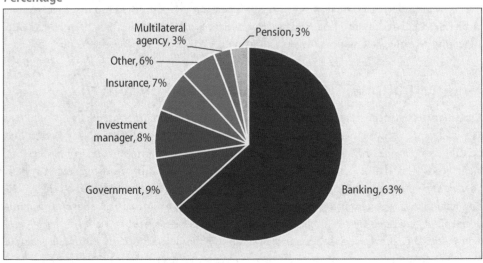

Source: World Economic Forum (2014); Standard & Poor's Rating Services (2013).

early to fully assess the effect of regulatory reforms, since many of them are still in the early stages of implementation and some are still in the process of being developed.

On the other hand, there has been an emphasis on increasing access to credit and on developing and deepening financial and capital markets—often without sufficient concern for issues of stability and sustainability (UN System Task Team, 2013). A common argument is that the deepening of financial sectors is associated with greater investment and stronger economic performance (Levine, 2005). However, preliminary research indicates that for countries with shallow financial markets, a larger financial system is associated with greater productivity growth (Cecchetti and Kharroubi, 2012; Cottarelli and Jaramillo, 2012), but in more developed markets this relationship is unclear, with financial instability increasing with financial sector depth (Sahay and others, 2015).  One possible explanation is that credit growth is not directed towards productive investments. Excess market liquidity can increase financial market volatility and risk, particularly when markets are short-term oriented.

**Policy intervention can contribute to increasing access to finance for small enterprises**

Furthermore, the correlation between financial depth—measured by domestic credit to the private sector as a percentage of GDP—and access to banking-sector financing by small enterprises is low in a large number of countries (figure III.11). The large differences in small firm access to credit among economies with similar levels of financial depth suggests that there exists a space for policy interventions that can contribute to increasing access to finance for small enterprises.

In developed countries, much of the growth in financial depth has been through shadow banking, which includes financial intermediation that is often outside of the regulatory framework.[12] Shadow banking entities can create leverage or engage in maturity and liquidity transformation. Its growth has been driven by a multitude of country-spe-

---

12    The term "shadow banking" is sometimes used to refer to unregulated financial intermediation that facilitates the creation of credit; however, the FSB defines shadow banking as credit intermediation involving entities and activities outside of the regular banking system.

Figure III.11
**Financial depth vs. financial access by small firms, most recent year**

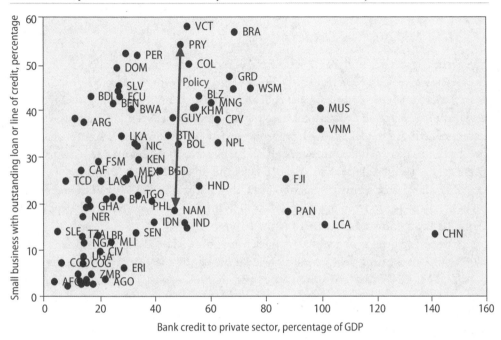

Source: World Bank Enterprise Surveys, World Bank World Development Indicators.

Notes: Most recent data for 80 developing countries from Asia, Latin America and sub-Saharan Africa with data from 2009 or later. See table J in the Statistical Annex of this publication for a definition of country codes.

cific factors, including hedging activity, financial innovation, regulatory or tax arbitrage, efforts to increase leverage cheaply and reap high returns, and efforts to take advantage of information asymmetries, as well as means to increase financial inclusion.[13] According to FSB data, shadow banking grew by $5 trillion during 2013-2014, to about $75 trillion worldwide. The 2008 crisis exposed risks associated with unregulated shadow banking, which dramatically increased leverage in the system, with a lack of transparency regarding counterparty exposures, insufficient collateralization, uncoordinated default management, and concerns about market misconduct. There is a need to continue to enhance central counterparties' resilience, as well as recovery planning and resolvability. The FSB has spearheaded the process of designing a framework for managing systemic risks in the shadow banking system with the goal of preventing impacts on the regulated banking sector.

While shadow banking in emerging markets is experiencing the fastest growth, the sector has a different profile in these economies than in developed countries. In some countries, it includes elements of inclusive finance (i.e., non-bank financial intermediaries that fill an important credit gap, such as unregulated microfinance institutions). However, the growth of for-profit microfinance, along with recent crises in some microfinance institutions, confirms the importance of including all forms of financial intermediation in a robust regulatory framework that balances safety and soundness with access, as highlighted in the AAAA.

In view of the 2030 Agenda for Sustainable Development, the international community may wish to explore new methods for regularly assessing the impact of international financial regulatory reforms on access to long-term and sustainable finance in developing

**It is important to include all forms of financial intermediation in a robust regulatory framework that balances safety and soundness with access**

---

**13**    For a fuller discussion, see United Nations (2013), box III.1.

countries. This will support the goal of reaching the SDGs, particularly for countries that are not members of the FSB.[14]

## Debt and debt sustainability

One of the triggers of the global financial and economic crisis in 2007-2008 was the build-up of excessive debt and leverage in the private financial sector in many advanced economies. The risks emanating from global debt and leveraging continue in the global economy as global debt is reported to have increased by $57 trillion between 2007 and the second quarter of 2014 (figure III.12), with government debt accounting for the fastest growth.[15] Developing-country debt accounts for half of that growth, with China alone accounting for 37 per cent of the global growth in debt (Dobbs and others, 2015, p. 16).

The global debt securities market—meaning debt that is publicly traded and excluding bank loans—grew from just over $60 trillion in 2007 to about $100 trillion by 2013 (figure III.13) (Gitlin and House, 2015, p. 5).

Overall, traded corporate debt has been roughly stable since the financial crisis in 2008, with government debt accounting for most of the increase. However, emerging-market corporate debt has risen from $4 trillion in 2004 to well over $16 trillion in 2014

Figure III.12
**Global stock of debt outstanding**

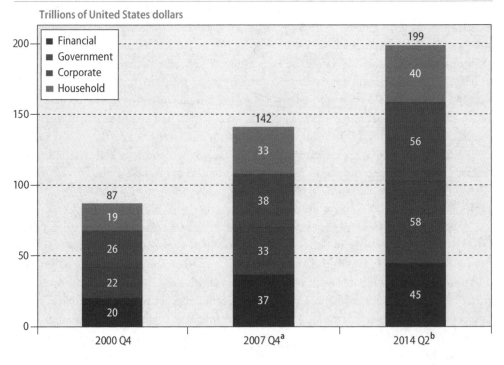

Sources: Bank for International Settlements; Haver Analytics; IMF World Economic Outlook; national sources; McKinsey Global Institute analysis.
Note: Constant 2013 exchange rates.
a Figures do not sum to total, because of rounding.
b 2014 Q2 data for advanced economies and China; 2013 Q4 data for other developing countries and economies in transition.

14    See, for example, United Nations Conference on Trade Development (2015d, chap. IV), for further discussion.

15    Total debt is defined as household, corporate, government and financial sector debt and stood at 286 per cent of GDP in 2014 Q2.

Box III.3
## Development finance in a changing climate

The year 2015 is projected to be the hottest since recordkeeping began; the global temperature is now 0.85 degrees higher than pre-industrial levels (National Oceanic and Atmospheric Administration, 2015). As the costs related to climate change intensify, impacts on public finance, financial institutions and businesses, not to mention human life, will become more profound. However, the current incentives structure is such that corporate management at publicly listed companies is incentivized to focus on short-term equity prices rather than longer-term risks to businesses. In addition, the full cost of climate change will not be borne by any one company, making it a classic externality. The Addis Ababa Action Agenda (AAAA) includes commitments to increasing regulations, designing incentives to change production and consumption patterns, and aligning private and public behaviour with a low-emissions and climate-resilient economy.

Amidst entrenched policies that perversely support an unsustainable energy economy, 2015 signalled renewed momentum for nations to review and reform their ecological footprint in the lead-up to the twenty-first climate change conference in Paris in December 2015. In all, 119 intended nationally determined contributions (INDCs), or national climate plans, were submitted prior to the conference, covering 80 per cent of global emissions (United Nations Framework Convention on Climate Change, 2015a), and have the capability of limiting the forecast temperature rise to about 2.7 degrees Celsius by 2100 (United Nations Framework Convention on Climate Change, 2015b). This could be achieved either through direct regulation of emissions or by having private actors internalize the cost of emitting greenhouse gases into the atmosphere. Efforts at the latter are proliferating by pricing carbon through taxation or through emissions trading systems under cap-and-trade (CAT) markets.[a]

Globally, a lack of coherence characterizes carbon market policy and other initiatives to price pollution more generally. The spread on carbon pricing is significant, ranging from the Swedish valuation of carbon at $130 per ton to the Mexican carbon tax at less than $1 per ton (World Bank and Ecofys, 2015, fig. 6). The INDC system also adheres to a pledge and review framework for climate action, which is a fragmented, bottom-up model for global climate action. The lack of coordinated environmental policies poses two major information gaps for private actors to effectively internalize the cost of emitting greenhouse gases and encourage more effective financial intermediation: (i) the economic value of potential damages arising from climate change is uncertain and variable, and (ii) there is a lack of reliable information on the cost of mitigating greenhouse gas emissions. Furthermore, there is a risk of "carbon leakage", as firms and industries may respond to robust carbon mitigation regimes by migrating to jurisdictions where emissions costs are lowest. The World Bank's review of the carbon market suggests that leakage has not yet significantly materialized, perhaps owing to the predominance of other investment factors shaping the location decisions of emissions-intensive industries. The AAAA stresses the need for regulations and policies that shift incentives and realign financing with low-carbon investments.

At the same time, developed countries have committed to deliver $100 billion annually for climate finance by 2020. According to the United Nations Climate Tracker, in 2013-2014, donor countries pledged $62 billion towards climate mitigation and adaption activities and multilateral development banks offered $15 billion (Organization for Economic Cooperation and Development, 2015b). However, it remains unclear how these figures are calculated, how much is double-counted as official development assistance (ODA), and whether it will be annually recurring. According to the most recent (2013) project-level data from the Organization for Economic Development and Cooperation Development Assistance Committee, only $13 billion of climate finance was administered as a grant. While this number may be incomplete, it points to a credible assumption that the bulk of climate finance is private finance or loans (concessional and non-concessional). In addition, it remains unclear how the funds will be allocated between climate change mitigation—which contributes to a global public good and is generally geared towards middle-income countries—and adaptation—which is generally geared towards more vulnerable countries and for which there is a higher overlap with development impact. In addition, there is no international system for defining and tracking climate finance, which gives rise to the possibility of double counting of ODA and climate commitments. The Green Climate Fund, which was established under the Copenhagen Accord in 2009 to support climate financing goals, currently has pledges of only $10 billion. There is also concern that there are insufficient incentives to guarantee that the pool of climate finance flows to those hardest hit and least able to respond to climate impacts, such as the LDCs and small island developing States. The AAAA underscores the need for transparent methodologies for reporting climate finance.

a CAT market is a system whereby a regulatory entity sets a limit (a cap) on total pollution units, or "emissions rights" within a boundary, but allows firms the ability to sell their emissions rights (or trade) among each other. The result is that emissions occur at locations where it would be costliest to avoid them, while firms that can increase their emissions efficiency are rewarded with revenue from the sale of their emissions rights.

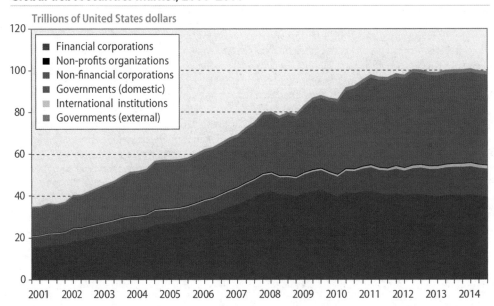

Figure III.13
**Global debt securities market, 2001–2014**

Trillions of United States dollars

Legend:
- Financial corporations
- Non-profits organizations
- Non-financial corporations
- Governments (domestic)
- International institutions
- Governments (external)

Source: Gitlin and House
(2015), p.5.

(figure III.14) (International Monetary Fund, 2015e, chap.3). Many emerging-market firms have borrowed in foreign currency to take advantage of low international interest rates, with 45 per cent of emerging-market corporate debt (excluding Chinese firms) since 2010 being denominated in foreign currencies, compared to 40 per cent before 2007 (ibid., p. 97). A recent study has found that a significant portion of the proceeds of borrowing in Latin America are being held in cash deposits, rather than being invested in corporate expansion (Inter-American Development Bank, 2014). Analysis at the level of global firms suggests that such borrowing by non-financial corporates has, in part, been driven by interest-rate differentials. This may indicate that they are participating in carry trade activities by keeping United States dollar-denominated bond issuance on their balance sheets in cash and liquid assets (Bruno and Shin, 2015). These partly explain the growing disconnect between the growth in finance and real sector activities, as discussed above, as well as in chapter I.

**Some debtors will have problems refinancing their foreign-currency-denominated debt when United States interest rates rise**

There is a growing risk that some debtors, public or private, will have problems refinancing their foreign-currency-denominated debt when United States interest rates rise, as discussed in chapter I. While many countries have strengthened bank balance sheets and reduced currency mismatches through macroprudential regulations—to the extent that currency mismatches remain on non-financial firms' balance sheets—currency depreciations can still have systemic implications, including through a rise in non-performing loans (Acharya and others, 2015). The risks arising from non-financial corporate issuance of foreign currency-denominated bonds are compounded when corporate debt is backed by sovereign guarantees. Even when the debt is not formally backed by the sovereign, corporate bailouts, particularly in the financial sector, exacerbate the risk of sovereign debt problems.

Sharp depreciations combined with interest rate increases may overwhelm the ability of companies to repay debt and prohibit new borrowing, particularly for corporations that have not used financial instruments to mitigate these risks, or that do not have sufficient foreign-currency earnings to cover their foreign-currency debt exposures. Bankruptcies may follow, as happened in the context of the Asian financial crisis in 1997-1998.

Figure III.14
**Emerging-market corporate debt, 2003–2014**

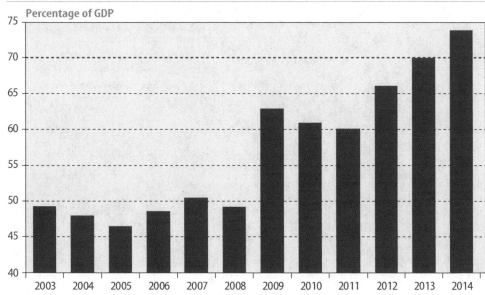

Source: International
Monetary Fund (2015e).

Despite the increased foreign-exchange borrowing by non-financial corporates, aggregate (public and private) external debt of developing countries, which measured 23.2 per cent of their GDP in 2014 (figure III.15), appears moderate. Nonetheless, the aggregate masks the rapid build-up of debt in some countries. Some low-income countries issued bonds on international capital markets during the period of low interest rates. Rwanda's ten-year bond was priced with a yield of 6.875 per cent in April 2013, a time of high market liquidity. However, subsequent issuances from African countries have all yielded above 8 per cent, with some as high as 10 per cent. There is a risk that some countries will have difficulties servicing these debts when interest rates rise, potentially leading to new sovereign debt crises. Among low-income countries, many are caught in debt difficulties and exhibiting persistently high external debt-to-GDP ratios. Using a broader set of indicators and analysing both external and public sector debt, as of April 2015, 3 low-income countries are in debt distress, 13 are at high risk, 32 are at moderate risk, and only 22 low-income countries are at low risk of debt distress.[16] The environment of moderated global growth described in chapter I will make it more difficult for countries with high debt burdens to grow quickly enough to reduce their risks of debt distress.

To help attenuate the risks, Governments can take a number of actions at the domestic level, including enacting macroprudential policies and reforming domestic corporate insolvency procedures, as endorsed in the AAAA. Sovereign debt issuers can also explore GDP-linked bonds, commodity-linked bonds, or other warrants that can help attenuate the macroeconomic risks. While financial market participants have thus far not been willing to buy these at reasonable prices, official lenders should consider these risk sharing instruments as ways to reduce the risks of default for borrowing countries. At the same time, the international community needs to put in place an effective and credible framework to ensure that creditors and debtors are taking appropriate responsibility for borrowing. In the

---

16    See https://www.imf.org/external/Pubs/ft/dsa/DSAlist.pdf.

**Figure III.15**
**External debt of developing countries, 2000–2014**

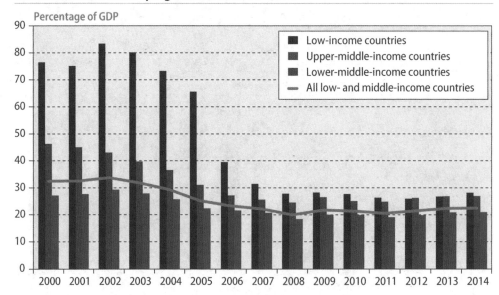

Source: IMF, World Economic
Outlook database.
Note: Percentage of GDP
calculated by taking total gross
external debt in US dollars
(consisting of public and publicly
guaranteed long-term debt, private nonguaranteed long-term
debt, the use of IMF credit, short-
term debt, and arrears) divided
by nominal GDP in US dollars.

case of sovereign borrowing, the current incentives reward creditors with risk premiums for higher risk credits, yet strongly discourage that losses be imposed on creditors in the case of debt distress. Once a country is in debt distress, its options are more limited. While some countries, such as Ecuador, have had success with buybacks, these are difficult to do because of the need for finance and the rapid response of market prices to such market activity. There is, thus, a new urgency to promote responsible borrowing and lending, as Member States committed to doing in the AAAA.[17]

**Improvement is needed in the process for resolving sovereign debt crises**

The process for sovereign debt restructuring remains fragmented, ad hoc, and uncertain, carrying high costs for debtors and, in the case of systemically important countries, a threat to financial stability. Although sovereign debt restructurings do take place, these are often "too little too late". The most recent example is Greece, which also illustrates how the official sector often pays for the exit of private capital from countries in debt crisis. The cases of Argentina and the Democratic Republic of the Congo have illustrated the problems in creditor coordination, hold-outs and the costs of litigation by hold-out creditors (Schumacher, Trebesch and Enderlein, 2014).

Following the 2014 United States court judgement against Argentina and in favour of hold-out creditors (United Nations, 2015b, box III.I), the International Capital Markets Association and the IMF endorsed reforms to contractual clauses in sovereign bonds, including enhancing collective action clauses (International Monetary Fund, 2015f). Since then, a number of countries have adopted key features of these recommendations in their new international sovereign bond issuances, although this still leaves out the outstanding stock of bonds estimated to be approximately $915 billion (International Monetary Fund,

---

[17]    In September 2015, the United Nations General Assembly adopted a resolution specifying a set of nine basic principles to guide how a government and its creditors should go about reducing repayment obligations when they become unpayable (United Nations, General Assembly, 2015c). See http://www.un.org/ga/search/view_doc.asp?symbol=A/RES/69/319&Lang=E.

2015g). Correspondingly, the AAAA affirms the need to further improve the processes for the resolution of sovereign debt crises and emphasizes the need for mechanisms to deal with hold-outs in a debt restructuring.[18]

# International cooperation and public resources for sustainable development

As reiterated in the AAAA, the mobilization and effective use of public resources is central to the pursuit of sustainable development. The AAAA stresses the importance of ODA, but also brings fresh thinking to the challenges of international public finance. It emphasizes the importance of international tax cooperation in boosting efficient resource mobilization and the possibility of public development banking serving as a complement to the private financial system.

## International tax cooperation and illicit capital flows

Tax evasion, tax avoidance and illicit financial flows have become a major difficulty in efficient resource mobilization.[19] The ability to raise revenue domestically is not only a function of domestic policies and institutions but is also strongly affected by international tax norms, the policy environment, and the prevalence of international tax avoidance and evasion.[20] Indeed, in an interdependent world with high levels of capital mobility, international tax norms function as a global public good. International rules have important distributional implications, as the structure of tax agreements affects the distribution of resources between corporations and Governments, as well as among Governments.

In October 2015, the Organization for Economic Cooperation and Development (OECD) provided a glimpse of the extent of tax avoidance and evasion by multinational enterprises (MNEs). Its report "confirms that profit shifting is occurring, is significant in scale and likely to be increasing, and creates adverse economic distortions" (Organization for Economic Cooperation and Development, 2015c, p. 16). Their conservative estimate is that between 4 and 10 per cent of corporate income tax is evaded, meaning between $100 billion and $240 billion annually.

### Setting tax norms

The global response to illicit financial flows will need to include reforms to international tax norms. MNEs often transact across borders through multiple branches or subsidiaries, but for purposes of taxation, operations in each branch or subsidiary are generally treat-

> Tax evasion, tax avoidance and illicit financial flows have become a major difficulty in efficient resource mobilization

---

18    On 12 July 2015, Belgium became the first country to pass a comprehensive law to deal with this problem. Under the new Act, any creditor which is determined by a Belgian judge to be acting as a "vulture" (i.e., one who pursues an "unfair benefit" by purchasing government bonds/receivables) cannot claim more than the discounted price paid for the bonds/receivables. See http://www.stibbe.com/en/news/2015/september/bru-fin-act-introducing-measures-to-restrict-vulture-fund-activities.

19    There is no agreed definition of the concept of illicit financial flows (IFFs), but it is generally used to convey three different sources of IFFs: the proceeds of commercial tax evasion, revenues from criminal activities, and public corruption.

20    See African Union Commission and United Nations Economic Commission for Africa (2015); Kar and Spanjers (2015); United Nations Conference on Trade and Development (2014).

ed separately. When two related companies trade with each other, implicit prices (called transfer prices) are used to attribute profits. The United Nations Conference on Trade and Development (UNCTAD) estimates that about 30 per cent of all international trade is intra-firm trade, which must be accounted for with transfer pricing, valued at over $6 trillion in 2010 (United Nations Conference on Trade and Development, 2013, p.136).

**Transfer mispricing should be addressed through international tax cooperation**

Transfer mispricing is one of the most-often-used techniques of MNEs to shift profits to low- or no-tax jurisdictions, irrespective of the actual location of economic activities, and thus reduce their total tax burden. This can frequently be accomplished through the prices applied to intangible goods or services, such as intellectual property, where no clear market price exists. Through such techniques, MNEs can avoid paying taxes in both the MNE home (residence) country and in the country that hosts the economic activity of the MNE (source country). This double non-taxation is a key problem to be addressed through international tax cooperation.

Both the United Nations Committee of Experts on International Cooperation in Tax Matters and the OECD have chosen to use the arm's-length principle enshrined in most bilateral tax treaties. According to the arm's-length principle, transfer prices charged between associated enterprises reflect market prices (i.e., prices charged between independent entities at arm's length), taking into account the circumstances specific to the transaction. However, questions have been raised about the efficacy of this principle, particularly with difficult-to-price assets, such as intellectual property. Alternative approaches would treat profit-maximization as occurring at the level of the MNE itself (unitary taxation), with mechanisms to allocate group profit internationally; for example, allocation could follow a fixed formula agreed in advance and intended as a proxy for the level of economic activity in each jurisdiction (formulary apportionment) (Independent Commission for the Reform of International Corporate Taxation, 2015). In turn, questions have been raised about how effective and beneficial a unitary approach—particularly a global one—would be for developing countries, and whether an agreed formula is even possible.[21]

**How taxation is divided between the source and resident country can be critically important to helping developing countries finance sustainable development**

To realign taxation with economic substance and value creation, the OECD and Group of Twenty (G20) launched a base erosion and profit shifting (BEPS) project in 2013. A BEPS Action Plan, including 15 action items, was published in October 2015, and endorsed by G20 leaders at their November 2015 summit. The BEPS package includes guidance in eleven substantive areas, including on how MNEs may allocate profits derived from intellectual property, on the use of management fees, and on other intra-group service provision charges, which have been used to shift profits to shell companies in low-tax or no-tax jurisdictions. While the outcome was welcomed by some developing-country Governments and civil society organizations, the initial BEPS focal areas were made without participation of developing countries and did not address the issue of ensuring adequate source-country taxation. The division of taxation rights between source countries, which are frequently developing countries, and residence countries, which are frequently developed countries, is embedded in international tax norms and constrains the ability of developing countries to realize greater resource mobilization from cross-border economic activity, including FDI. How taxation is divided between the source and resident country can be critically important to helping developing countries finance sustainable development.

Furthermore, the complex set of rules developed under the BEPS project will be difficult to implement, even for developed countries with high capacity tax administra-

---

21    See, for example, Spencer (2014).

tions. Effective application of the new rules will require extensive knowledge and information on the internal structure of an MNE. While the MNE transfer pricing documentation may include some of the relevant information, full knowledge may require access to country-by-country reports by the MNEs.

The OECD endorsed an implementation package for country-by-country reporting of MNEs in May 2015, whereby the ultimate parent entity of an MNE group would file a country-by-country financial report in its jurisdiction of residence (figure III.16). There are template agreements to facilitate the exchange of such reports, but no central registry exists. Furthermore, the exchange of information will be subject to the existence of bilateral tax agreements and information technology, all of which disadvantage developing countries. The exclusion from country-by-country reporting of MNEs with total consolidated group revenue of less than 750 million euros further limits the policy's benefits. There is also no provision for public transparency on the number of such reports filed or the number exchanged among tax authorities. The inability of developing countries to effectively access such reports will hamper their ability to properly audit the activities of MNEs within their borders, and is likely to widen the gap further between the taxation capacity of developed and developing countries.

Another area of transfer pricing development under the BEPS project has been interest deductibility. Intra-MNE group loans from related parties in low-tax jurisdictions to related parties in high-tax jurisdictions allow companies to transfer profits through interest payments. The BEPS package includes the provision for countries to set limits on interest deductibility of 10-30 per cent of income, but does not link the interest deductions to actual third-party interest costs of the MNE as a whole, making it possible to shift some profit through this channel. Additional provisions that indicate that interest payments should be

**Tax authorities, especially in developing countries, may lack the capacity to apportion tax burdens across different arms of an MNE group**

Figure III.16
**Illustrative timeline for exchange of country-by-country reports**

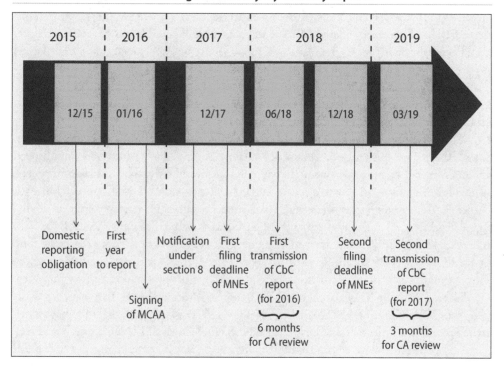

Source: OECD.

based on the actual risks taken by different parts of the MNE will be very hard to implement in practice. Such risk weighting is difficult for bank regulators, even in the most advanced financial markets, as evidenced by the bank solvency problems experienced in the 2008 financial crisis. Again, tax authorities, especially in developing countries, may not have capacity, expertise, or information to correctly judge the financial risk-bearing capacity of different arms of an MNE group.

The BEPS project also included recommendations, but not minimum standards, on the formulation of controlled foreign corporation (CFC) rules. CFC legislation seeks to combat the sheltering of profits for companies residing in low- or no-tax jurisdictions, but the rules are complicated and difficult to implement; countries need help to develop and apply these effectively. Greater beneficial ownership information can improve the operation of CFC rules. While there has been no agreement that all countries should pursue the creation of centralized, public beneficial ownership registries, which require full disclosure of corporate control structures, some countries are proceeding unilaterally. The United Kingdom of Great Britain and Northern Ireland has already legislated to implement a centralized, public beneficial ownership registry, which will be fully operational by April 2016. Norway and Denmark also committed to operate such registries, while in May 2015, the European Union (EU) promulgated rules stipulating that all EU member States must have centralized registries available to country authorities, although it did not require them to be public. United Kingdom dependencies, such as the Cayman Islands, have not yet decided how they will respond to the United Kingdom's policy that they must maintain beneficial ownership registries.

### Tax norm implementation

**A multilateral instrument to implement new tax norms is needed**

The mechanism of implementation of tax norms also has implications regarding which countries gain and which lose. Action 15 of the OECD BEPS package is the development of a multilateral instrument to implement the treaty-related new tax norms that have been agreed by the OECD/G20 countries. Because of the existence of over 3,000 tax treaties, implementation of the treaty-related BEPS outcomes through amendment of existing treaties would be a laborious process. Instead, a BEPS project report concluded that a multilateral instrument would be desirable, and that negotiations for the instrument should be convened quickly (Organization for Economic Cooperation and Development 2015d; 2015e). As of September 2015, 89 countries, including the United States, had indicated their participation in the negotiations for a multilateral instrument.

Some Member States are interested in including binding arbitration for tax disputes, though there is no consensus on the scope of its application. Such arbitration would speed resolution of tax disputes when source countries and resident countries have unresolved differences of opinion on how to allocate the profit of a particular MNE operating in both countries. Yet, sovereignty is often raised as a concern with third party arbitration of disputes, including possible biases towards taxpayers and away from Governments. Overall, many developing countries are wary of being obliged to implement the tax norms that were set in the OECD/G20 forum, as they have not participated equally in the setting of the norms. Progress is also expected in automatic exchange of information for tax purposes. The Global Forum on Transparency and Exchange of Information for Tax Purposes, hosted by the OECD, now has 127 full members. The G20 member States agreed to have automatic exchange of information fully functional by the end of 2017, while other members of the Global Forum have committed to implementing automatic exchange by the end of

2018. However, the majority of developing countries are not ready or able to take advantage of automatic exchange. In particular, they do not have sufficient capacity, including information technology, to fully analyse the large volume of information that would become available through automatic exchange. This would be especially complicated by the need to dedicate human resources to production and dissemination of information on actors from their own jurisdiction.

### Capacity-building and accountability

It is clear that capacity in tax administration is important both for improving the effectiveness and efficiency of domestic revenue mobilization as well as in implementation of international tax norms. Currently, many developing countries lack the resources, information technology or human capacity to participate effectively in international tax co-operation. One important first step is using international finance, usually in the form of ODA, to build the capacity of developing countries' tax administration. Estimates of the proportion of ODA devoted to projects that are primarily aimed at tax capacity-building or domestic resource mobilization stood at 0.06 per cent of ODA in 2013, or just $93 million (figure III.17).[22]

*Many developing countries lack the resources, information technology or human capacity to participate effectively in international tax cooperation*

A number of important initiatives in this regard were announced in Addis Ababa, including the Addis Tax Initiative, a commitment for developed-country participants to at least double the amount of ODA they give for tax capacity-building. The Addis Tax Initiative includes, among others, Canada, Germany, the Netherlands, the United Kingdom and the United States. The initiative and other commitments made during the Addis Ababa Conference in 2015 are welcome first steps towards the investment needed in domestic resource mobilization and tax capacity and administration. Such initiatives, however, do not replace the need for inclusive norm setting. The most effective capacity development will be related to norms over which developing countries feel ownership, and thus are more likely to implement rigorously.

In the AAAA, Member States agreed that "efforts in international tax cooperation should be universal in approach and scope and should fully take into account the different needs and capacities of all countries, in particular least developed countries". This implies that norm setting should be done in an inclusive, universal forum. There is thus an ongoing debate as to whether the OECD is the appropriate forum for discussions on global taxation norms, or whether a more universal forum situated at the United Nations would be more appropriate.

Transparency about implementation of international tax norms will be critical, especially to facilitate monitoring and accountability of implementation of the AAAA. Follow-up and accountability require public information about the status of international norm implementation (at least in the aggregate)— a report of volume of transactions on which tax information has been exchanged, for example. The follow-up process of the AAAA should give an opportunity for stakeholders and peers to discuss success and areas for further work. However, such a discussion will be frustrated by a lack of empirical evidence and data (box III.4), especially when it comes to global data on international tax cooperation.

*Transparency about implementation of international tax norms will be critical*

---

22    Development Initiatives (forthcoming), based on an assessment of the OECD Creditor Reporting System database.

Figure III.17

**ODA with domestic revenue mobilization (*DRM*) as the core aim, 2006–2013**

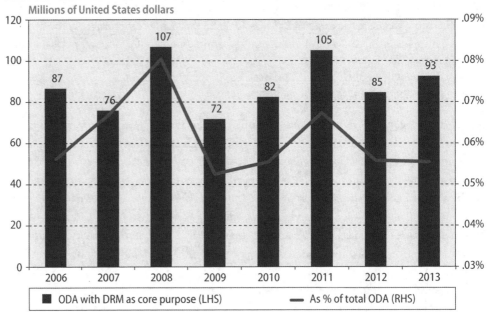

Source: Strawson and Ifan
(2014); Development Initiatives
(forthcoming).

## International public finance

ODA will continue to play
a key role in the poorest
countries and in those
areas and sectors where
risks and returns are not
attractive for private
investment

Achieving the 2030 Agenda for Sustainable Development will put significant demands on public budgets and capacities in developing countries. This will require additional and more effective international public finance, including ODA, South-South cooperation and other official flows. ODA will continue to play a key role in the poorest countries and in those areas and sectors where risks and returns are not attractive for private investments such as health and education. In Addis Ababa, ODA providers reaffirmed their respective ODA commitments, including the commitment by many to provide 0.7 per cent of their gross national income (GNI) in ODA to developing countries.

ODA flows reached $135.2 billion in 2014, according to preliminary estimates by OECD (2015f). However, as a group, developed countries continue to fall short of their commitments, with DAC donors providing 0.29 per cent of their GNI as ODA in aggregate as compared to the 0.7 per cent commitment (United Nations, 2015d). ODA to LDCs has also been far below target, at less than 0.10 per cent of GNI (the target is 0.15–0.2 per cent of GNI). Preliminary 2014 data indicate a fall of 16 per cent in bilateral ODA to LDCs in real terms.

South-South
development
cooperation is
increasingly important

South-South development cooperation is playing an increasingly important role. Estimates based on available data show that South-South development cooperation may have reached $20 billion in 2013 as a result of a major increase in contributions from a few Arab countries.[23] Southern partners have further committed to increasing their cooperation in

---

23   Many partners participating in South-South development cooperation do not publish data on a yearly basis. Figures are based on data collected in preparation for the forthcoming second International Development Cooperation Forum Report (UN/DESA).

the context of the 2030 Agenda for Sustainable Development, with China committing to set up a fund with an initial contribution of $2 billion to support South-South cooperation.

Given the large financing needs associated with implementing the 2030 Agenda for Sustainable Development, particularly for sustainable, resilient and green infrastructure, existing public funds will not be sufficient. For this reason, the potential of ODA and South-South cooperation flows to catalyse additional resources for sustainable development has come into sharper focus. Highly effective aid should help build institutions, human and productive capital in recipient countries, improving the enabling environment and laying the foundations for greater sustainable-development-oriented investment, both public and private.

In recent years, donor countries have increasingly looked towards using ODA in specific market-like instruments that crowd-in (or leverage) private financing and other public financing flows. Generally used by development banks and development finance institutions (DFIs), such instruments include blending of grants with private flows, equity investments and guarantees. It is difficult to estimate the amount of ODA used to leverage private flows, but all evidence points to a steady increase in recent years, albeit from a low base. Market-like instruments are less suitable in sectors and areas where private returns are limited—such as social spending—and in the poorest countries.[24] They should not come at the expense of traditional ODA, with its focus on social issues. ODA equity flows amounted to $1.8 billion and ODA that was channelled via a limited number of formally recognized public-private partnerships amounted to $669 million in 2013.[25] Southern partners have also set up new institutions (i.e., funds and development banks) that leverage public contributions to mobilize additional private finance (see the section on multilateral, regional and national development banks).

A core appeal of these new instruments is financial additionality, whereby the public component of the package facilitates a private contribution that would not have otherwise been made. Public involvement can also have impacts on project design to improve its development impact, and can have positive demonstration effects. However, financial additionality is difficult and costly to determine. Instead of catalysing additional private resources, the public finance contribution could also subsidize private investments that would have been undertaken anyway. The results of a review of additionality for infrastructure projects of five major DFIs were mixed. It found that a majority of projects had financial additionality, but that more than a third of the projects would have gone ahead without DFI involvement. Relatedly, there are concerns over the development impact of blending and other market-like instruments, particularly if there are trade-offs between commercial and sustainable development objectives. The same review found that DFI involvement tends to enhance growth effects of projects, but does little to increase their direct poverty impacts (Spratt and Ryan-Collins, 2012). The technical capacity needed to implement such instruments effectively points to development banks as the most suitable institutions to put them in place.

Donor countries have increasingly looked towards using ODA in specific market-like instruments that crowd-in private financing and other public financing flows

---

24 For example, guarantees for development have mobilized $15.3 billion from the private sector for development purposes from 2009 to 2011, but have benefited upper-middle-income countries disproportionally, see Mirabile, Benn and Sangaré (2013).

25 Based on OECD/DAC Stats. The PPP component includes ODA channelled through a limited number of formally established and DAC-recognized PPPs such as GAIN, the Global Water Partnership and others. See also Martin, 2015.

## Multilateral, regional and national development banks

**Multilateral, regional and national development banks are integral to financing sustainable development**

As existing public funds remain inadequate and private resources are also currently not being effectively channelled into sustainable development investments, the AAAA underscores the role of alternative mechanisms, and, in particular, multilateral, regional and national development banks (DBs). DBs are integral to financing infrastructure, agriculture, SMEs, capital market development, and stimulating sustainable private finance. DBs have a long-term developmental perspective, can provide affordable long-term financing, and should play a vital role in supporting sustainable development strategies. In general, DBs operate by borrowing from the private sector at low interest rates through quasi-sovereign bonds, and then lend or invest in areas of public need.[26]

Overall, DBs play three valuable functions: (i) mobilizing financial resources to support development, for example by leveraging private sector resources; (ii) intervening in cases of market failure and in areas where there is a dearth of private long-term financing, such as investments with positive social and environmental externalities; and (iii) providing countercyclical finance.

DBs complement and provide an alternative to the private financial sector, particularly in those credit market segments in which private financial institutions and channels are inadequate or ineffective. An additional contribution by DBs can be bridging the so-called missing middle for development finance. As countries transition from low-income to middle-income status, the decline in grants and concessional finance comes much more quickly than countries can compensate for, either by raising financing from other sources or by increasing domestic revenue mobilization (Kharas, Prizzon and Rogerson, 2014). While some countries may prefer bond issuance to multilateral development bank (MDB) borrowing because there are no policy strings attached to the funds, financing from DBs is generally at lower interest rates than that offered by the private sector through sovereign bond issuance, and generally longer term. For example, the most recent sovereign bonds of Ghana (a lower-middle-income country) were floated with a coupon rate of 8.25 per cent in September 2014, whereas World Bank ten-year loans would have carried interest rates of about 1.3 per cent plus origination fees of about 0.5 per cent. In the AAAA, Member States encourage shareholders of MDBs to develop graduation policies that are sequenced, phased and gradual, facilitating smoother transitions from MDB grant windows to their ordinary lending windows, and using more blending of terms and fewer cut-offs and thresholds.

Recent studies have also shown that DBs have played a valuable countercyclical role, especially in cases of crisis when private sector entities become highly risk averse (Brei and Schclarek, 2013). This was particularly salient during the financial crisis, when the MDBs increased lending, as did many national development banks (NDBs) in both developed and developing countries.

### Recent developments

Figures III.18 and III.19 show recent trends in regional and national development bank and MDB lending, respectively. Annual commitments of non-grant subsidized finance from seven MDBs reached $71.1 billion in 2014-2015. In July 2015, a set of six MDBs and the

---

26  As a matter of fact, development banks are not new. They have been one of the main vehicles for industrial policy, but were largely dismantled during the era of financial sector deregulation in the 1980s.

IMF signalled plans to extend more than $400 billion in financing over the subsequent three years (World Bank, 2015d).

There are more than 40 NDBs, and an additional 40 export credit agencies, based in all regions of the world. The term "NDB" generally denotes the ownership structure rather than the sphere of operation; a majority of NDBs are state-owned, but within public ownership models the structure varies. Some banks have mixed federal and state ownerships, such as the German Kreditanstalt für Wiederaufbau (KfW) Development Bank, which operates as part of the KfW Group. In addition, a number of NDBs in developing countries are starting to operate internationally, joining KfW and similar NDBs that operate overseas in traditional donor countries such as Japan and the Netherlands. For example the Brazilian Development Bank (BNDES), one of the largest lenders in the world by exposure, has begun international operations alongside their national development lending, much as KfW began channelling international development finance in the 1960s along with its own work on German economic development.

Figure III.18
**Annual disbursements of selected regional and national development banks, 2000–2014**

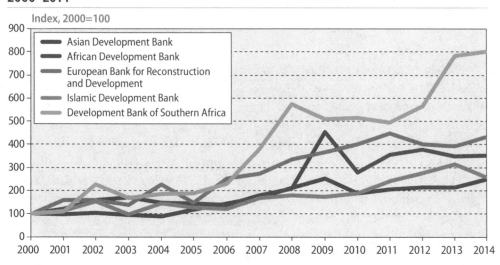

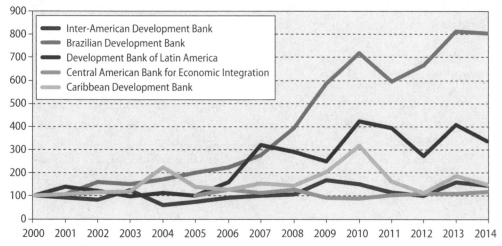

Source: UN/DESA, based on data from annual reports from relevant organizations.

Figure III.19
**Multilateral development bank financing, 2000–2014**

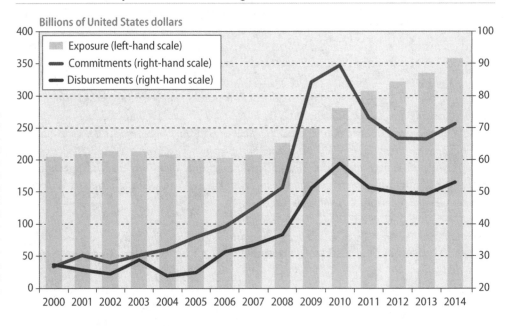

Source: UN/DESA calculations, based on annual reports from relevant organizations. Note: Includes non-grant subsidized finance from Asian Development Bank, African Development Bank, European Bank for Reconstruction and Development, Inter-American Development Bank, Inter-American Investment Corporation, International Bank for Reconstruction and Development, and International Finance Corporation.

**Newly established development banks have the potential to significantly contribute to the SDGs**

Newly established development banks have the potential to significantly contribute to the SDGs. After the formal establishment of the New Development Bank with a $50 billion subscribed capital base, and the signing of a Memorandum of Understanding on the Asian Infrastructure Investment Bank (AIIB) with a $100 billion subscribed capital base, estimates of their lending capacity of $30 billion each per year were made (United Nations, 2015b). In June 2015, the AIIB was formally established and the Articles of Agreement adopted by 50 founding members, including 33 countries from the Asia-Pacific region,[27] 15 European countries, 1 African country and 1 Latin American country. In July 2015, the New Development Bank was inaugurated in Shanghai and its president-designate Kundapur Vaman Kamath indicated that the Bank would approve financing for its first infrastructure projects in April 2016. During the Addis Ababa conference, Canada and Italy also announced that they would set up new development banks, while the United Kingdom promised a capital increase for its DFI, the CDC Group.

### Key issues for the future

Existing MDBs greatly stepped up cooperation in the last few years to more effectively contribute to the 2030 Agenda for Sustainable Development, including coordination in the context of preparing the AAAA. MDBs have also been more conservative than private banks in the amount of risk they will take in leveraging their paid-in capital. Many of the MDBs have announced plans to optimize their balance sheets in order to take on more risk and increase lending (Group of Twenty, 2015). This is supported in the AAAA with the proviso that the DBs should maintain financial integrity.

---

27    Includes Western Asia.

An equally important question is how all DBs—multilateral or national, existing or new—modify their business practices to ensure coherence with the new sustainable development agenda. To align with the SDGs, the DBs need both "do no harm" as well as promote positive social, environmental and economic outcomes while respecting human rights. For the "do-no-harm" and human rights agendas, safeguards are critical. The AAAA calls for all the banks to move towards operations that are coherent with all the SDGs in an integrated manner, and suggests that the DBs establish processes to examine their own role, scale and functioning.

The AIIB issued new draft safeguards in early September. The World Bank is in the final phase of a safeguards review, which began in 2012. The AAAA calls for safeguard policies that are timely and efficient, as well as effective. At the same time, DBs can actively support projects that are mostly closely aligned with all the multiple sustainable development goals as an integrated whole, rather than those projects that might align with just one goal—on economic growth, for example.

## Global architecture

The 2030 Agenda and the AAAA contain an ambitious set of goals and a new vision for the global economy. To achieve these aims, a more inclusive form of global coordination, which better reflects the ideal of the global partnership set out in both agendas, is strongly needed. The close interlinkages among the economic, social and environmental systems are now recognized. Still, the rules and institutions that govern these systems have not yet adapted. Ineffective intermediation and existing deficiencies in the international financial system can be further exacerbated by failures of international cooperation in promoting coherence and a robust implementation of the new agenda.

The AAAA recognizes the need for strengthening the permanent international financial safety net, and for enhancing cooperation between the IMF and regional financial initiatives. Despite progress, most of the regional safety net mechanisms are still insufficient to offer an adequate safeguard in times of emergency. The fact that some of these arrangements have not been used undermines their ability to work as deterrents to financial speculation. The largest element of the global safety net—$1.25 trillion—is provided by the IMF, but portions of these funds are not permanent. Making them permanent requires the approval of the IMF governance reforms agreed in 2010, reforms that remain unimplemented in late 2015 and are seen as only a step towards a more representative, responsive and accountable governance structure, not as the final result. The United States, which maintains veto power over governance changes at the IMF due to its 17 per cent voting share, is yet to have the reforms ratified by the United States Congress. The failure to implement the 2010 reforms has delayed the next round of reforms, which were to be completed by January 2014. Also in 2010, at the World Bank, member States agreed to move towards equitable voting power between developed and developing countries. Yet, its 2010 reforms only marginally changed voting rights, with the shares of high-income OECD countries declining from 60.7 per cent in 2008 to just 58.8 per cent in July 2015. Taking all countries currently classified as "high-income" as a group, they still wield 69.3 per cent of voting rights at the World Bank. The World Bank members agreed to review shareholding every five years, but in the first such regular review in 2015, the members were unable to agree on a concrete set of reforms, and instead pushed the deadline by an additional two years (World Bank,

*To align with the SDGs, the DBs need to both "do no harm" as well as promote positive social, environmental and economic outcomes—all within the context of continuing respect for human rights*

*Most of the regional safety net mechanisms are still insufficient to offer an adequate safeguard in times of emergency*

Box III.4
## Data and the Addis Ababa Action Agenda

The final section of the Addis Ababa Action Agenda (AAAA) considers how the international community should monitor implementation of the agreed actions. It emphasizes the importance of high quality disaggregated data for policymaking and for monitoring progress of implementation of the AAAA and the 2030 Agenda for Sustainable Development, and also prioritizes capacity-building in this area.

Hard data on international financial flows is a key component of efforts to track implementation and to better understand the risks and possibilities for sustainable development. However, despite strengthened technical capacities, high-quality data on financial flows can be scarce, delayed and insufficiently detailed for policymakers to manage risks and fine-tune their development models and strategies.

There is, for example, no accurate, comprehensive and robust data on private portfolio investments. Data presented in table III.1 are based on balance-of-payments data collated by national authorities such as central banks. However, this data is neither disaggregated by source nor by fine-grained destination. Only a handful of countries maintain robust data on the maturities of these flows. It is difficult to examine—let alone mitigate—the risk that short-term private sector portfolio investment will experience a sudden stop when it is not possible to know the volume of such flows. While the International Monetary Fund had previously produced estimates that separated private and non-private portfolio flows, these estimates are no longer being made.

This is but one example of the many areas where financing data is lacking. Data on economic activity is notoriously inaccurate and subject to revision. Even databases on sovereign debt levels are not comparable across institutions. Data on tax-to-GDP ratios are not comparable across official institutions. Data on cross-border capital flows are not tracked on the source side, let alone matched to recipient side data, providing scope for misreporting or illicit conduct. Ultimately, a to-whom-from-whom framework for all financial flows would be important for monitoring implementation and tracking risks. Such a framework has become commonplace for flows of official development assistance. It would have many applications relevant to financing sustainable development: monitoring financial stability, resolving bankrupt financial institutions, implementing innovative financing mechanisms, countering money laundering and preventing the financing of terrorism, enforcing financial regulation, as well as eliminating other types of illicit financial flows and facilitating the return of stolen assets.

The technologies to track such data are available and being implemented. The global legal entity identifier system being implemented to help resolve insolvent financial institutions is a relevant model for beginning to build such a framework. Some countries are already experimenting with to-whom-from-whom information in some sectors, such as extractive industries. Global data on a to-whom-from-whom basis can be a long-term goal that will further efforts towards achieving the 2030 Agenda for Sustainable Development as well as monitoring the implementation of the AAAA. The capacities needed to monitor financial flows are different than the statistical capacities needed to track achievement of most of the SDGs. Monitoring the outcomes in terms of health, education or the environment can often be done by line ministries in conjunction with national statistical offices. Tracking financial flows will involve investing in central banks, tax authorities, and financial regulators, among others. As countries move to invest in sustainable development data, it is vital that some investment is directed to improvements in the tracking of financial flows.

Source: UN/DESA.

2015e). This unresolved imbalance in the governance of the main international financial institutions has undermined their credibility and encouraged proliferation of new development banks and regional financial safety nets described earlier in this chapter.

*Achieving the Addis Ababa Action Agenda will require concerted political will*

The outcomes sought in Addis Ababa and the 2030 Agenda for Sustainable Development can be achieved through concerted political will. All stakeholders need to contribute and be accountable for their commitments, including Member States, the private sector, civil society, and other actors. The role of the annual Financing for Development Forum, the dedicated follow-up process for monitoring the implementation of the AAAA, will be crucial. Good faith efforts by all actors to assess their progress and take further steps will be vital. Financing the transformation of our world requires the commitment of high-level political actors and leaders of all types.

# Chapter IV

# Regional developments and outlook

## Developed economies

The developed economies, particularly the United States of America, are expected to contribute more to global growth in the near term than they did in 2011-2014. Economic growth in developed economies as a whole accelerated from 1.7 per cent in 2014 to an estimated 1.9 per cent in 2015, and growth is expected to strengthen further to 2.2 per cent in 2016 (see annex table A.1). The expected acceleration in 2016 is partly attributable to a stronger outlook for Japan, which is expected to be cut short by a planned increase in the consumption tax in April 2017. The developed economies continued to rely on accommodative monetary policy to deliver growth in 2015. Over the forecast period, the majority of central banks in developed countries, with the exception of the United States Federal Reserve (Fed) and the Bank of England, are expected to maintain their highly accommodative monetary policies. This divergence in monetary stance has been associated with a strong appreciation of the United States dollar relative to other developed-economy currencies, and is expected to lead to a significant redistribution of real net exports from the United States to Japan and Europe.

Low commodity prices have generally supported the outlook in developed economies. The exceptions are the commodity-reliant economies of Australia, Canada and Norway, where investment in the commodity sectors has stalled and economic prospects have deteriorated significantly. Low commodity prices have introduced deflationary pressures in many developed economies, with annual inflation in 2015 expected to average just 0.3 per cent in the developed-market economies. While the highly accommodative monetary policy stances in developed economies have prevented deflation from becoming entrenched in expectations, the persistent near-zero inflation will do little to boost consumer spending or ease the debt burden that remains a legacy of the financial crisis.

### North America

#### *The United States: monetary policy stance is shifting*

Economic conditions in the United States have strengthened sufficiently for the Fed to signal its intention to raise its policy rates. As monetary accommodation is withdrawn, the fiscal stance will become slightly less restrictive, signalling a gradual shift towards a more balanced policy mix. Gross domestic product (GDP) growth in the United States is expected to be 2.4 per cent in 2015, the same rate as in 2014. However, the contribution of the external sector has shifted, as export growth is expected to have decelerated from 3.4 per cent in 2014 to 2.7 per cent in 2015, while import growth accelerated from 3.8 per cent to 5.5 per cent over the same period. This shift reflects both the appreciation of the United States dollar and the deteriorating demand from major emerging economies. The shift in net trade is offset by a less restrictive fiscal position.

**Less restrictive fiscal stance supports GDP growth**

In the outlook period, GDP is expected to grow by 2.6 per cent and 2.8 per cent in 2016 and 2017, respectively (see annex table A.1). This modest improvement will be supported by somewhat stronger expansions in private fixed investment and in government spending. Following several years of austerity, the stance of fiscal policy has become marginally expansionary and this is expected to continue in the near term. The accord reached between the legislative and executive branches of the United States Government in October 2015 made this possible. The expected increase in government consumption is concentrated at the state and local level, reflecting an improvement in their fiscal balance. In total, real government consumption is assumed to increase by 0.9 per cent in both 2016 and 2017. At the federal level, government consumption growth will remain tepid, allowing the federal deficit to stabilize relative to GDP. Publicly held federal debt is expected to remain at about 74 per cent of GDP over the outlook period.

**Dollar appreciation and low commodity prices stabilize external balance**

The sharp appreciation of the United States dollar (vis-à-vis almost all major currencies) that started in mid-2014 has stabilized in recent quarters; no significant reversal of the appreciation is expected for the outlook period. As a consequence, growth of real imports is projected to remain higher than real export growth. Meanwhile, the appreciation of the United States dollar has led to a significant drop in the dollar value of non-oil merchandise goods; the non-oil import price declined year on year by more than 2.5 per cent in the first nine months of 2015. At the same time, the lower oil price has pushed down the value of crude oil imports, which have also fallen in volume terms. As a result, the trade deficit is expected to stabilize at about 2.5 per cent of GDP through 2017.

**Low wage growth complicates monetary policymaking**

By late 2015, the unemployment rate had declined to about 5 per cent, close to the pre-crisis level. However, nominal wage growth actually slowed marginally in 2015, posing a challenge to the Fed regarding the speed and timing of interest-rate normalization. The belief that reduced slack in the economy (including the labour market) would cause higher inflation has served as a key foundation for monetary policy decisions. However, statistics for 2015 do not fully support this relationship (figure IV.1), contributing to uncertainty about the anticipated path of interest-rate increases. In the outlook period, the labour force participation ratio is expected to stabilize, and the unemployment rate is expected to remain broadly stable in 2016 and 2017.

**Deflationary risks have receded**

Inflation has been weak in 2015 as a result of the decline in the prices for oil and imported goods. However, with the relative stabilization of both the oil price and the dollar exchange rate, year-over-year inflation became slightly positive again in the second quarter of 2015, and risks of deflation had receded. Average consumer price inflation is expected to accelerate to 1.6 per cent and 2.3 per cent in 2016 and 2017, respectively.

### Canada: lower oil price hampers GDP growth

The sudden drop in the crude oil price has been associated with a sharp decline in private fixed capital formation in the oil production sector in Canada. As a result, growth in the Canadian economy slowed to an estimated 1.2 per cent in 2015, the lowest growth rate since the Great Recession. This reflects an expected decline in total private fixed investment of 3.5 per cent in 2015, despite the continuous growth in residential investment. As commodity prices stabilize and the economy of the United States strengthens, GDP growth is expected to recover to 2.2 per cent and 2.9 per cent in 2016 and 2017, respectively.

Figure IV.1
**United States unemployment rate and wage inflation, January 1990–October 2015**

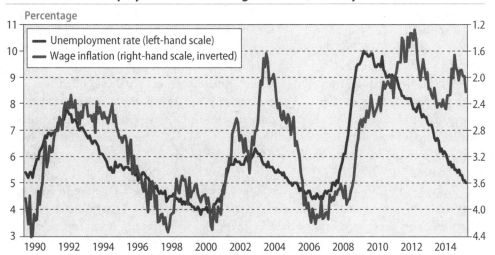

Source: UN/DESA, based on data from the United States Bureau of Labor Statistics.

The recovery in 2016 and 2017 is expected to be broad-based. Private consumption will expand by about 1.9 per cent on average in 2016 and 2017. The drag from non-residential investment on growth is expected to fade out in 2016. Export growth is expected to increase from the estimated 3.0 per cent growth in 2015, supported by the sharp depreciation of the Canadian dollar vis-à-vis the United States dollar and sustained growth in the United States. A new Government was formed in late 2015, which plans to reduce the income tax rate for middle-income bands, financed by increasing the rate for higher income bands. It is expected that growth in government consumption and investment will increase to 1.7 per cent in 2017. Employment growth is predicted to outpace the labour force growth, leading to a slight reduction in the unemployment rate from 6.8 per cent in 2015. The wage rate is expected to increase by close to 3 per cent per year during the outlook period, maintaining upward pressure on inflation.

**More accommodative fiscal policy stance lifts the prospects for growth**

## Developed Asia and the Pacific

### Japan: policy-induced downturn anticipated in 2017

The Japanese economy slumped immediately after the introduction of a higher consumption tax rate in April 2014. Recovery since then has been sluggish; GDP declined again in mid-2015 as both private consumption and exports fell sharply. The growth rate for 2015 as a whole is expected to be only 0.5 per cent, increasing to 1.3 per cent in 2016 before dropping again to 0.6 per cent in 2017, reflecting the planned tax hike in April 2017.

The most important factor impeding growth of the Japanese economy is the feeble private consumption expansion. Growth in household employment income has been slow, although the general situation in the labour market has been relatively solid. Employment has been growing at a slow but persistent pace since 2013, allowing the unemployment rate to recede gradually to 3.4 per cent in 2015. Nevertheless, low wage growth has held back household buying power.

**Low wage inflation restrains consumption growth**

**Erosion of production capacity restrains export growth**

Japanese merchandise export volumes have yet to recover their pre-crisis levels (figure IV.2). A short-lived expansion in exports started in early 2014, but lost its momentum in early 2015, as a result of a slowdown in many of Japan's export markets, including China. At the annual level, export growth is expected to be only 1.8 per cent in 2015, in contrast to 8.4 per cent in 2014. For the outlook, exports are expected to grow by 3.3 per cent in both 2016 and 2017.

**Production facilities expand overseas, limiting domestic investment growth**

Private fixed capital formation has been expanding since 2011, although the pace has diminished over time. While corporate profits remain strong, actual investment in the expansion of domestic production capacities has been relatively mild. Instead, large Japanese corporations have been expanding their production facilities overseas since 2011. Domestic fixed capital formation is expected to grow by about 1.5 per cent per annum on average during 2015-2017.

**Primary balance improved**

Although the 2014 hike in consumption tax caused extreme disruption to economic activity, it also increased government revenue. This has allowed the primary balance to improve, and the government to increase spending, while issuing much less debt. It is assumed that real government consumption will grow slightly faster than GDP in the period of 2015-2017.

The accommodative monetary policy of the Bank of Japan and the increase in consumption tax helped the headline consumer price index (CPI) reach 2.7 per cent. However, inflation is predicted to be 0.7 per cent in 2015 and will decline marginally to 0.5 per cent for 2016.

### Australia: lower commodity prices impede investment and income growth

In Australia, GDP growth decelerated to an estimated 2.3 per cent in 2015, mainly owing to the continuous decline in fixed investment in the natural resource sectors and weaker export growth. Although export growth is expected to recover by 2017, the sustained low prices for major commodities in Australia's export basket will continue to hold back invest-

Figure IV.2
**Key monthly indicators for Japan, January 2010–September 2015**

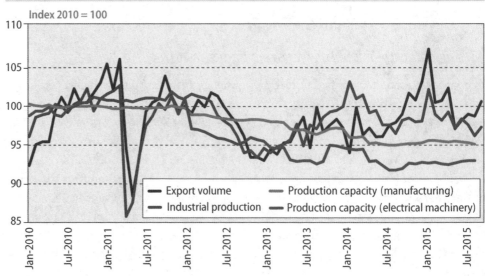

**Source:** UN/DESA, based on data from the Bank of Japan and the Ministry of Economic, Trade and Industry.

ment and will dent the growth of household income and private consumption. Government consumption is expected to increase by less than 2 per cent per annum, owing to efforts to balance the budget. For 2016 and 2017, GDP growth is expected to be 2.5 per cent and 2.2 per cent, respectively. During 2015-2017, employment is expected to remain stable. As the economy will not be in a position to absorb the total expansion of the labour force, the unemployment rate is predicted to remain above 6 per cent in both 2016 and 2017.

## Europe

### Western Europe: economic prospects improving despite global slowdown

Despite a broad deterioration in global economic activity, economic prospects in Western Europe have generally improved. The European Union (EU) is one of the few major global regions, where the forecast for 2015 GDP growth has not been downgraded from the growth rate projected in 2014. The European policy environment has become more supportive, with expansive monetary stimulus programmes and some easing of the pressure for fiscal consolidation. Meanwhile, the unexpected drop in energy prices has boosted household spending and reduced production costs. This has supported solid retail sales and rising confidence indicators. The EU is now the driving force behind world trade growth, supported by the high level of intraregional trade and also by competitiveness gains relative to the United States. Bank lending conditions have softened and the demand for new loans is rising. While the crisis in Greece overshadowed the broad-based improvement during the first three quarters of 2015, an agreement reached in August on a third bailout programme has dispelled the risk of a Greek withdrawal from the European Monetary Union, removing an important source of uncertainty.

Against this backdrop, GDP growth in the EU-15 is expected to accelerate from 1.8 per cent in 2015 to 2.0 per cent in 2016 and 2.1 per cent in 2017. The growth has been fairly broad-based across countries. While Germany and the United Kingdom of Great Britain and Northern Ireland were at the forefront of the recovery, there has also been a strong rebound in Denmark, Ireland, the Netherlands, Spain and Sweden. Even the beleaguered Greek economy expanded at an annualized rate of 3.2 per cent in the second quarter of 2015. However, given the severe political and economic turmoil that ensued, including a three-week closure of Greek banks and the imposition of stringent capital controls, much of this apparent revival was reversed in the third quarter of the year.

**Recovery is fairly broad-based across countries…**

The economic performance of Austria, Finland, France and Italy has lagged behind other EU-15 members, partly reflecting the overhang of bank fragility related to the financial crisis. Existing fragilities have been accentuated by exposure to the Russian Federation. Austrian banks have the highest relative level of exposure, while French and Italian banks are also relatively exposed compared to banks from other developed economies (International Monetary Fund, 2014a); Finland's exposure is instead through the trade channel, with more than 10 per cent of Finnish exports destined for the Russian Federation (figure IV.3).

**… exposure to the Russian Federation is restraining growth in Austria, Finland, France and Italy**

Outside the EU, Norway and Switzerland have experienced a sharp slowdown in economic activity. In Switzerland, the decision in January 2015 to delink the Swiss franc from the euro led to a shock appreciation of 16 per cent against the United States dollar and 18 per cent against the euro over a two-day period. While much of the sudden adjustment was subsequently corrected, the Swiss franc remains nearly 10 per cent stronger against the euro, which is its biggest trading currency, and net trade impeded growth in 2015. In

Figure IV.3
**Share of exports to the Russian Federation in total exports of goods and services, 2012**

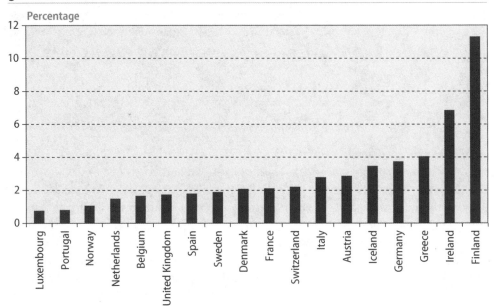

Source: UN/DESA, based on data
from UNCTAD and Eurostat.

Norway, the slowdown reflects the low oil price, which has hit export revenues and stalled investment in the oil sector.

**Labour market recovery remains very uneven across countries**

While GDP growth is recovering in many European countries, the unemployment rate in the EU-15 stood at 10 per cent in mid-2015, compared to an average of 7.1 per cent in 2007. The aggregate figures mask stark differences across countries, with double-digit unemployment rates in France, Greece, Italy, Portugal and Spain, compared to just 4.5 per cent in Germany. The economic rebound in Spain has allowed the unemployment rate to recede by more than 2 percentage points relative to a year ago, although more than 22 per cent of the labour force still remains unemployed. France, on the other hand, has seen the unemployment rate edge up in recent months. The job vacancy rate in the EU is at its highest level since 2008, pointing to improving labour market opportunities going forward. However, opportunities remain uneven across countries, with job openings concentrated in Belgium, Germany and the United Kingdom. For the EU-15 as a whole, the unemployment rate is expected to fall to 9.2 per cent as GDP growth accelerates in 2016 and 2017, but will remain uncomfortably high in many parts of Europe.

**Risks of prolonged deflation have receded**

While euro area inflation dipped below zero again in September, core inflation has edged up to 1 per cent, and labour cost inflation has accelerated relative to 2014. If global oil prices do not fall further, the impact of low energy prices on inflation will become more muted by early 2016, and deflation is unlikely to become entrenched in expectations. Nonetheless, inflation of just 0.9 per cent in the euro area is forecast for 2016, well below the European Central Bank (ECB) inflation target.

**Monetary stance has eased across Western Europe**

Responding to prolonged economic weaknesses and deflation risks, the ECB announced a significant loosening of the monetary stance in January 2015. The latest Bank Lending Survey by the ECB suggests that there has been some pass-through from the quantitative easing programme to easier bank lending conditions and an increasing demand for new loans from both enterprises and households. The central bank of Switzerland has set the lowest interest rates in the world in response to the appreciation of the Swiss franc, at -0.75 per cent. The central banks of Norway and Sweden have cut interest rates three times since December 2014. All of these measures provide a more accommodative policy environment to sustain the recovery, and have put downward pressure on exchange rates.

The euro began depreciating against the United States dollar in June 2014, following the introduction of a negative interest rate target by the ECB. The associated gains in competitiveness, coupled with the drop in commodity-related import values, have allowed the current-account balance to continue to widen, reaching 3 per cent of GDP in mid-2015. This is largely attributable to Germany, which is running the largest current-account surplus in the world. Germany's widening trade surplus outside the euro area may suggest that the euro is undervalued from the perspective of the German economy.

**Germany's trade surplus continues to widen**

Government investment remains restrained in many European economies, due to commitments under the Stability and Growth Pact to balance public finances. However, the pressure to consolidate has eased significantly in most countries, and in aggregate the fiscal stance in the EU is expected to be broadly neutral in 2015 and 2016, with additional corrective measures postponed until 2017. However, the Excessive Deficit Procedures (EDP) will remain ongoing in France, Greece, Spain and the United Kingdom next year. These economies remain under pressure to cut spending, which will hold back prospects of revival of the French economy, in particular. In Greece, the net impact of the economic adjustment programme attached to the third bailout, in conjunction with targeted funding mobilized by the European Commission to support investment, is expected to be broadly neutral in 2016.

**The Excessive Deficit Procedure remains ongoing in France, Greece, Spain and United Kingdom**

Box IV.1

### A preliminary assessment of the macroeconomic impact of the influx of refugees and migrants in Germany

During the first 10 months of 2015, more than 800,000 refugees and migrants arrived in the European Union (EU), nearly 82 per cent via Greece and nearly 18 per cent via Italy, with the remaining 0.8 per cent via Spain and Malta. At least 3,455 refugees and migrants lost their lives in tragic circumstances in the Mediterranean Sea during their journeys. The main country of origin is the Syrian Arab Republic (35 per cent), with Afghanistan, Eritrea and Iraq accounting for at least another 17 per cent.

During the last quarter of 2015, arrivals accelerated sharply, with the total number of refugees and migrants entering the EU in 2015 estimated to exceed 1 million persons—a dramatic increase over the 5 preceding years, during which the EU-28 countries received a total of 1.8 million asylum applications. Between 2010 and 2014, Germany received nearly a quarter of all asylum applications in the EU-28, with France and Italy together receiving another quarter of these applications. However, in response to decisions taken by the German Government on humanitarian grounds, it is expected that the number of persons seeking asylum in Germany by the end of 2015 will have risen to approximately one million.

In 2014, some 362,850 persons received asylum in Germany with a total public expenditure outlay of €2.4 billion. The increased asylum support will lead to additional public expenditure in Germany to the tune of €20 billion during 2015-17, and possibly even more, taking into account indirect expenditures on education, security and accommodation.

Using the United Nations World Economic Forecasting Model, preliminary simulations indicate that the macroeconomic impact of this sizable additional outlay of €20 billion is relatively modest. The

(continued)

Box IV.1 (*continued*)    additional public expenditure is likely to reduce the budget surplus by 0.1 to 0.2 per cent of GDP, while the current-account surplus would decline by 0.2 per cent of GDP. The projected impact on the GDP growth of Germany would be small but positive at close to 0.1 percentage points during 2016 and 2017, reflecting that the increased expenditure primarily stimulates aggregate domestic demand.

The simulations also indicate that real wage growth would slow down in response to the increased labour supply, assuming that about half of the asylum applications will be granted and that a sizeable share of these will meet the challenges of social integration and entering the labour market. These results are similar to those published by the European Commission (2015, box I.1).

According to the baseline forecast, government debt in Germany was due to fall by 8.4 per cent of GDP between 2014 and 2017. But because of the influx of refugees and migrants, it is more likely to fall by 8.0 per cent, as Germany may pay off a smaller share of its debt than it might have done without the influx.

Table IV.1.1
**Estimated macroeconomic impact of the influx of refugees and migrants in Germany***

|  | 2015 | 2016 | 2017 |
|---|---|---|---|
| Extra-government spending (billions of euros) | 7.60 | 7.80 | 4.60 |
| GDP growth (percentage point) | 0.07 | 0.08 | 0.10 |
| Government budget balance (percentage of GDP) | -0.12 | -0.23 | -0.11 |
| Current account (percentage of GDP) | -0.10 | -0.22 | -0.24 |

Source: UN/DESA.    * Changes relative to the WESP 2016 Baseline scenario.

## *The new EU members: recovery is more solid, but still facing challenges*

All of the new EU members are expected to register positive GDP growth rates in 2015. The Czech Republic is expected to record an impressive economic upturn at 4 per cent; Poland and Romania may also approach that benchmark. In the outlook, growth in some of the new EU members may ease in 2016 owing to moderation in investment.

**Growth is driven by domestic demand**

In 2015, growing real wages, bolstered by low or negative inflation and improving labour market conditions, expedited a recovery in private consumption. At the same time, low government bond yields, supported by the quantitative easing by the ECB and the revival of cross-border capital flows, mitigated the pressure on public finances. This has supported fiscal spending. Investment remained robust as the countries absorbed EU funds. In some countries, foreign-currency-denominated debt of households still remains a problem, aggravated by the strengthening of the Swiss franc in 2015. Croatia and Hungary adopted measures to convert most of the loans into domestic currency. A similar action is under consideration in Poland, which would pass the costs to the banks, and spread them over time.

**Inflation remains low or negative**

The Russian food import ban has led to an oversupply in domestic markets of some new EU members, putting downward pressure on food prices. In conjunction with the lower energy prices, this drove annual inflation into a negative territory in several countries of the region and to near-zero figures in the others. The deflation in parts of the region have so far not had an adverse impact on consumer purchases, thanks to the rising real incomes and the moderation in household deleveraging. However, its long-run risks, including the impact on servicing the debt burden, cannot be discounted.

Monetary conditions among the new EU members remain accommodative, while stable growth, supported by the low oil price, has provided many countries with additional fiscal space. However, several countries in the region still remain subject to the excessive deficit procedure of the EU and have to reduce their budget deficit to a level below 3 per cent of GDP. Even in those countries a serious fiscal drag is unlikely in the near term and public investment programmes should continue.

Despite the positive outlook, the region faces several risks. Although the new EU members' direct exposure to trade with China is limited, the cooling of the Chinese economy may influence them through EU-15 industries. The prospective monetary tightening by the Fed may inflate the dollar-denominated share of public debt, but should not significantly alter capital flows to the region, which predominantly come from Europe. On the other hand, a serious unfolding of the political conflict between the Russian Federation and Ukraine may have negative spillovers for the region. Europe's migrant crisis has created additional challenges. Spending by migrants passing through the new EU members may somewhat strengthen aggregate demand and stimulate output, but increased domestic security-related expenditures may divert funds from social programmes. As the new EU members significantly depend on intra-industry trade, any disruptions in the free flow of goods between them and their European partners can curb growth prospects.

## Economies in transition

Aggregate GDP of the Commonwealth of Independent States (CIS) and South-Eastern Europe contracted by 2.8 per cent in 2015 (see annex table A.2) and is forecast to expand by only 0.8 per cent in 2016 and 1.9 per cent in 2017. The decline in output in 2015 is exclusively attributed to the downturn in the CIS, driven by lower energy prices, geopolitical tensions and precarious access to external finance. South-Eastern Europe, in contrast, saw a pickup in growth in 2015, benefitting from the recovery in the European Union and stronger domestic demand. In 2016, the upturn in South-Eastern Europe is expected to strengthen, while the CIS is projected to see a return to mildly positive growth. Both regions nevertheless face significant downside risks and economic policy challenges.

### South-Eastern Europe: growth recovers, but fragilities persist

Economic activity in South-Eastern Europe picked up in 2015 and is expected to accelerate further to 2.6 per cent in 2016 and 3.0 per cent in 2017. The region has benefited from a favourable external environment, including low energy prices and accelerating growth in the EU. Domestic demand has provided a major impulse for the recovery. There are, however, significant differences across countries; Serbia, the largest economy in the region, has seen more subdued growth, constrained by fiscal austerity.

The economic recovery supported job creation, although unemployment levels remain very high. In Bosnia and Herzegovina and the former Yugoslav Republic of Macedonia, the unemployment rate is over 25 per cent. Unemployment is also above the levels observed before the 2008 crisis, except in Montenegro and the former Yugoslav Republic of Macedonia. The possible repatriation of asylum seekers from the EU may increase domestic labour market tensions, in particular in Albania. Youth employment is a particularly acute problem. High unemployment is accompanied by low activity rates, which limits growth potential.

**Large external imbalances remain**

The EU recovery has facilitated growth in exports, which have expanded faster than imports. The region's import bill has also benefited from low oil prices, while rising inflows of remittances have supported net factor income. However, with the exception of Serbia, these influences have been insufficient to make an impact on the large current-account deficits in the region. Albania and Montenegro, which have the largest deficits, have even seen a further deterioration. While strong foreign direct investment (FDI) inflows helped finance the deficits, foreign debt has also grown in recent years.

**Fragilities and downside risks remain**

The region will mostly continue to benefit from low oil prices but, given its reliance on external financing, could suffer from a tightening of global financial conditions. The high levels of non-performing loans need to be addressed to reduce financial fragility and facilitate credit growth. Europe's migrant crisis poses additional challenges for the region, by raising fiscal expenditures and threatening to disrupt trade with the EU.

## The Commonwealth of Independent States: economic downturn and uncertain prospects

**The CIS region moves from sluggish growth to outright contraction**

Economic activity in the CIS area contracted sharply in 2015, as the region suffered a deterioration in the terms of trade, precarious access to external finance and high levels of uncertainty. Contracting output in the Russian Federation, the largest economy in the CIS,[1] had a depressing influence throughout the region; declines were also observed in other large economies, including Belarus and Ukraine. The aggregate GDP of the CIS and Georgia is estimated to have contracted by about 3.0 per cent in 2015, following an increase of 0.8 per cent in 2014. A return to growth is expected in 2016, but the recovery will be limited, with GDP increasing by about 0.7 per cent and 1.8 per cent in 2017.

**Domestic demand plummets**

The region has suffered from a combination of an adverse external environment and powerful domestic contractionary forces. Falling real wages, eroded by inflation, and worsened access to credit depressed household consumption. Investment suffered from poor economic prospects and high financing costs, as well as the diversion of retained earnings to more profitable financial assets. In the Russian Federation, investment contracted sharply, despite growing profits, which were mainly used to reduce corporate debt. Although net private capital outflows from the economy moderated in 2015, they may still surpass $70 billion (equivalent to 6 per cent of GDP). These capital outflows have been associated with a substantial reduction in external debt as the corporate sector repays loans instead of rolling them over. In Ukraine, the destruction of productive capacity due to the conflict in the East of the country and the precarious access to the Russian market led to a sharp fall of exports. However, with imports plummeting, net external demand partly offset the contraction of domestic demand—consumption, in particular. Public investment programmes boosted growth in Azerbaijan, Turkmenistan and Uzbekistan. A decline in remittances, which almost fell by half in dollar terms, and other spillover effects, including reduced exports and investment from the Russian Federation, largely offset the impact of lower energy prices in the region's small energy-importing countries. A number of these countries still managed to register decent growth rates in 2015; this may be explained by one-off factors, such as base-year effects or ample agricultural output, but also increased linkages with China.

---

[1]    Georgia's performance is discussed in the context of this group of countries for reasons of geographic proximity and similarities in economic structure.

The sharp deterioration in economic performance took its toll on the region's labour markets. The unemployment rate has marginally increased in the Russian Federation, despite the preference of cutting wages, rather than labour. Unemployment in Ukraine, which increased sharply throughout 2014, continued to climb higher. As a lagging indicator of economic activity, unemployment is expected to further increase in the CIS in 2016, before declining in 2017.

*Labour markets deteriorate*

Inflation rose throughout the region, driven by the sharp depreciation of national currencies. In Ukraine, higher gas prices added to headline inflation, which is expected to average about 50 per cent in 2015. Weak domestic demand partly offset the inflationary pressures that resulted from the depreciation, while price controls remained in place in some countries. As exchange rates are expected to stabilize somewhat in 2016, inflationary pressures should moderate; however, in some countries inflation will remain in double digits.

*Inflation accelerates in many economies*

Amid a more stable foreign-exchange environment, some CIS countries were able to start reversing the tightening of monetary policy that had been initiated in late 2014 or early 2015 in order to contain depreciation pressures. In the Russian Federation, the authorities started to ease monetary policy, but persistent fragility has mandated a gradual approach, following a series of rapid cuts earlier in the year. The policy rate was also cut in Ukraine. By contrast, the central banks in Georgia, Kazakhstan, and the Republic of Moldova tightened monetary policy in the second half of 2015 to mitigate the pressure on their currencies. Kazakhstan, in turn, switched to a free-floating exchange-rate regime. In many countries, currency interventions to reduce exchange-rate pressures have depleted foreign-exchange reserves.

*Monetary policy remains tight, despite some rate cuts*

The poor economic performance and falling oil prices have eroded fiscal revenues and reduced fiscal space. This has been partially offset by weaker exchange rates, since a significant part of fiscal revenues (related to the sale of oil and gas) is in dollars, while fiscal spending is largely in domestic currency. In addition, the unexpectedly strong increase in inflation has supported fiscal balances, as expenditure budgets have been fixed in nominal terms. In Ukraine, a temporary import surcharge was introduced to boost revenues. Energy-exporting countries used their oil funds to offset lost revenue, support the banking sector, and, in the case of Kazakhstan, finance stimulus measures. In the Russian Federation, these domestic resources also provided an alternative to external funding, although the authorities have sought to avoid further depletion. In Azerbaijan, expansionary fiscal policy has supported growth. By contrast, Belarus was forced to consolidate its public finances in the face of growing external constraints.

The economies of the region face a difficult external environment, which will heighten internal vulnerabilities. A persistent period of low commodity prices makes fiscal consolidation unavoidable. Low investment will constrain future growth and prevent progress towards much-needed economic diversification. In many countries, the persistent fragilities in the banking systems have been exacerbated by the weakening of exchange rates in highly dollarized financial systems. Geopolitical tensions continue to weigh on business sentiment. On the positive side, the Russian Federation is less exposed than other emerging markets to growing financial uncertainty, given the lack of access to international capital markets due to the sanctions. The establishment of the Eurasian Economic Union of Armenia, Belarus, Kazakhstan, Kyrgyzstan and the Russian Federation on the basis of the former Customs Union in January 2015 opens new possibilities for increased trade and investment in the region, although many aspects of the regional integration still have to be negotiated.

*Prospects are largely unfavourable*

Box IV.2

## Financial dollarization in the Commonwealth of Independent States

Financial dollarization is widespread among the Commonwealth of Independent States (CIS) economies, although with significant cross-country differences. The use of foreign currencies as a store of value was a result of very high inflation that followed the introduction of national currencies in the early years of transition. Even though the extreme turbulences that characterized this early period have now disappeared, the memory of past inflation has been reinforced by periodic bouts of macroeconomic instability across the region. This high inflation volatility has contributed to the persistence of financial dollarization, as confidence in national currencies remains fragile. Foreign-currency assets provide an alternative for savers in the absence of other instruments that provide a hedge against inflation. In the CIS, high levels of financial dollarization are often associated with lower financial sector development (figure IV.2.1).

Figure IV.2.1

## Foreign-currency deposits and total deposits in the CIS, as of end-2014

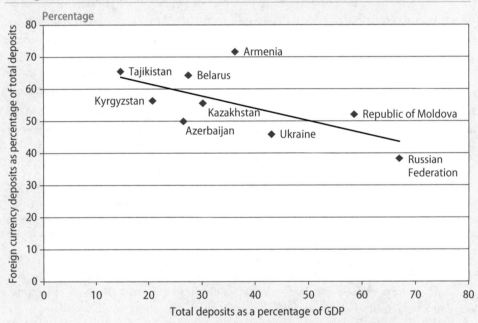

Source: National central
banks and IMF.

Further drivers of dollarization often include limited exchange-rate flexibility and a policy bias against depreciation, as they introduce asymmetric risks for holders of foreign assets. Expectations of further depreciation of the national currency can also be a factor promoting higher levels of financial dollarization. In Kazakhstan, for example, the currency devaluation in February 2014 was initially followed by a period of exchange-rate stability. However, given the dynamics of oil prices and the depreciation of the currencies of major trading partners in the region, there was a widespread belief that the tenge would weaken further.[a] As a result, the ratio of deposits in foreign currency to total deposits—which had remained roughly stable at about 30 per cent, up to the second half of 2013—started to pick up and increased to 53 per cent in March 2015. Nevertheless, in comparison with other Central Asian economies, Kazakhstan had made rapid progress in reducing financial dollarization since 2001 and, until the 2007-2008 crisis, had registered better macroeconomic performance. This phase of de-dollarization took place in a context of rapid financial development but with limited presence of foreign banks, which often promote the use of foreign currencies in their countries of operation.

Remittances inflows are also seen in the literature as contributing to financial dollarization in the banking sector. In some countries in Central Asia and the Caucasus, remittances are very large relative to

a This expectation was
confirmed after the
authorities let the exchange
rate float freely in
August 2015.

*(continued)*

Box IV.2 (*continued*)

GDP and have exhibited a generally increasing trend. In these countries, financial dollarization is particularly significant. In Tajikistan, for example, remittances represent almost half of GDP and the country also has the largest ratio of foreign-currency deposits to total deposits, at about 70 per cent (figure IV.2.2).

Figure IV.2.2
**Remittances and foreign-currency deposits in the CIS, as of end-2014**

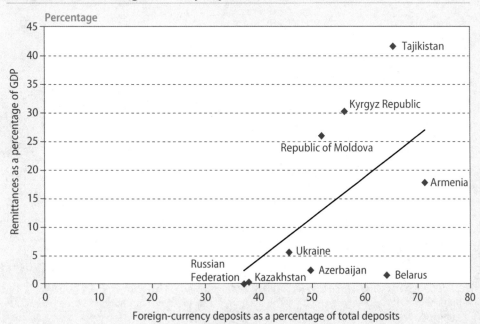

Source: National central banks, IMF and World Bank.
Note: Data for Kazakhstan are from 2013.

The banking sector also plays an important role in driving dollarization. For example, in countries where a significant part of deposits are held in foreign currencies and banks have often limited access to long-term funding in domestic currencies, banks seek to avoid currency mismatching by lending in foreign currencies. Therefore, a close correlation between deposit and loan dollarization can be observed (figure IV.2.3). The fact that banks charge higher rates on loans in local currency in order to offset the risk of depreciation also perpetuates financial dollarization.

National currencies in the CIS have experienced large depreciations since late 2014. The sharp fall of the Russian rouble and the weakening of commodity prices have prompted significant exchange-rate declines. As a result, loans denominated in foreign currencies have become more expensive in national currency terms. These loans are sometimes provided to borrowers who do not have foreign-currency earnings and, therefore, are likely to face increasing difficulties to service their debt, especially in the context of declining or slow growth in real earnings. Thus, currency depreciation might translate into a rise in non-performing loans, putting additional pressure on the banking system in the region. At the moment, such risks appear to be higher in Azerbaijan, Belarus, Kazakhstan and Ukraine.

Dollarization is an important policy concern since the use of foreign currency reduces the demand for national currency and, therefore, seigniorage revenue. Moreover, it has major implications for the conduct of monetary policy and financial stability. It restricts the efficiency of the monetary transmission mechanism by weakening the interest-rate pass-through from policy to market rates. In this context, exchange rates acquire more importance for monetary policy than interest rates. At the same time, the presence of large public and private foreign-currency liabilities leads to "fear of floating", as the impact of currency depreciation on the balance sheet can pose a threat to financial stability. It may also strengthen the effect of exchange-rate variations on inflation.

International experience, including that of the CIS countries, shows that financial dollarization can persist long after sustained declines in inflation. De-dollarization would require a monetary policy that

(*continued*)

Box IV.2 (*continued*)

Figure IV.2.3
**Shares of foreign-currency deposits and loans in the CIS, 2015**

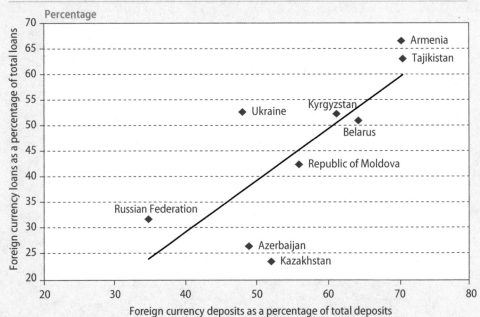

Source: National
central banks.
Note: Most data are from
June/July 2015.

ensures price stability, while allowing for some exchange-rate flexibility to discourage taking risks in foreign currencies. The development of deeper financial markets would also contribute to the increased use of national currencies. Prudential banking regulations to reduce the relative attraction of foreign-currency assets, such as differential reserves and provision requirements, can also be useful instruments, provided they are accompanied by supportive macro conditions. By contrast, outright administrative restrictions may have a damaging impact on policy credibility and entrench negative expectations regarding national currencies' values.

Source: UN/ECE.

## Developing economies

Aggregate growth of developing economies further slowed in the past year amid lower commodity prices, large capital outflows and increased financial market volatility. On average, GDP in developing countries grew by 3.8 per cent in 2015, down from 4.3 per cent in 2014 and only about half the rate recorded in the period 2004-07. The severe slowdown in developing countries since 2011 reflects both cyclical and structural factors, with potential growth estimated to be significantly lower than before the global financial crisis. In the near term, the external environment for developing countries is expected to remain challenging in the face of subdued import demand in developed economies and elevated global financial risks. In addition, many large developing countries (such as Brazil, China and South Africa) are grappling with structural economic challenges, including a sharp downturn in productivity growth. This implies that any growth recovery in the outlook period will likely be modest. In the baseline forecast, average developing-country growth is projected to strengthen to 4.3 per cent in 2016 and 4.8 per cent in 2017. Even as China's economy will likely continue to slow, East and South Asia will remain the world's most dynamic and fastest-growing regions. The gap with other regions is, however, expected to narrow as growth in Africa, Western Asia and Latin America is set to gradually recover.

## Africa: domestic demand drives accelerating growth

Economic growth in Africa has reached 3.7 per cent in 2015, about the same level as in the previous year (excluding Libya), underpinned by private consumption and investment. Government spending, in particular on infrastructure projects, has also been positively contributing to growth over the period. However, the external balance has negatively impacted growth in 2015 because of weak demand and volatile commodity prices, although this impact is expected to soften in 2016. With forecasted growth of 4.4 per cent, the prospects for Africa for 2016 look relatively favourable, despite the uncertainty in the global economy and the weakening of oil and commodity prices. The growth momentum is set to continue, underpinned by increasing domestic demand, coupled with an improving regional business environment, improving macroeconomic management, increasing public investment (especially in infrastructure), a buoyant services sector and increasing trade and investment ties with emerging economies.

East Africa maintained the highest growth rate in the region, at 6.2 per cent in 2015, with a projected increase to 6.8 per cent in 2016. Growth decreased relative to 2014 as a consequence of lower growth in Ethiopia. However, the political uncertainties and instabilities in Burundi and South Sudan and terrorism threats in Kenya and Somalia have weighed on the subregion's growth.

Growth in West Africa decreased to 4.4 per cent in 2015, based on a considerably lower growth rate in Nigeria, following a weaker oil sector and the uncertainty caused by the elections of March 2015. The consequences of the Ebola outbreak in the most-affected countries, namely Guinea, Liberia and Sierra Leone, also impacted their growth potential, although Guinea and Liberia returned to positive growth. West Africa's growth is projected to increase to 5.2 per cent and 5.3 per cent in 2016 and 2017, respectively, driven mainly by the improving economic performance of Nigeria, with its emphasis on the growing non-oil sectors.

The overall growth rate decreased slightly from 5.7 per cent in 2014 to 3.4 per cent in 2015 in the Central Africa subregion, despite improved performance in the mining sector. While most countries in the subregion maintained a relatively high growth path, security concerns in the Central African Republic and the decrease in oil production in Equatorial Guinea led to a decline in the subregion's GDP growth. The subregion is expected to experience a rise in its average growth rate to 4.3 per cent in 2016, mainly driven by investment in energy and infrastructure, strong performance of the service sector (notably in Cameroon and Chad), and an increase in oil production, for example, in Chad.

Growth in North Africa accelerated from 2.8 per cent to 3.6 per cent over the 2014-2015 period (excluding Libya), and is projected to increase further to 4.0 per cent in 2016. The positive developments have been helped by some improvements in political and economic stability in the subregion, and the subsequent increase in business confidence, especially in Egypt and Tunisia. The gradual recovery of export markets and improved security should support growth, especially through tourism. Algeria's oil production increased for the first time in eight years and is boosting growth together with the non-oil sectors. Mauritania continues to achieve the highest and steadiest growth in the region, supported by favourable macroeconomic and structural policies. This was mainly boosted by developments in the mining and construction sectors, as well as increased private consumption and investment. Ongoing political challenges in Libya continue to negatively impact both political and economic governance in the subregion.

Southern Africa's growth has remained flat at 2.5 per cent in 2014 and 2015, with an increase to 3.0 per cent and 3.3 per cent forecast over the next two years. The subregion's

East Africa is seeing strong growth thanks to FDI, infrastructure spending and growing domestic markets

A weaker oil sector pulled down growth in West Africa

North Africa benefitted from improved political and economic stability

South Africa's subdued growth pulled down Southern Africa's regional growth performance

low growth performance—relative to previous years and also other subregions—was driven by the relatively poor growth in the biggest economy, South Africa, where weak export demand and low commodity prices for its key raw materials, as well as electricity shortages, contributed to the subdued performance. In Angola, GDP growth remained strong despite low oil prices, as the Government embarks on investing in strategic non-oil sectors such as electricity, construction and technology. Mozambique and Zambia recorded the highest growth in the region, driven by large infrastructure projects and FDI in the mining sector, respectively.

**Inflation will moderate**

African inflation ticked up to 7.5 per cent in 2015, but is forecast to decrease to 6.7 per cent in 2016 and 6.3 per cent in 2017. Inflationary pressure was reduced by lower global oil prices and the continuing fall of food prices (estimated to be 14 per cent for 2015), while currency depreciations have increased the risk of imported inflation. Public spending in Nigeria in the lead-up to the elections also contributed to inflationary pressure in the subregion, together with the pressure on the naira caused by the lower oil prices. Inflation in West Africa is expected to remain at about 8.4 per cent in 2016 and 2017. In other subregions except North Africa, inflation rates increased in 2015 as well, driven by weather-related shocks, currency depreciations and the removal of subsidies.

**Fiscal deficits will improve owing to stabilizing oil prices and public expenditure adjustments**

The fiscal deficit of Africa increased from 5.1 per cent of GDP in 2014 to an estimated 5.6 per cent of GDP in 2015 (figure IV.4). The continued decline of oil prices and volatile commodity prices reduced fiscal revenue in most of the African countries, while high spending on infrastructure and higher spending in the lead-up to elections contributed to increased expenditure in some countries.

Figure IV.4
**Africa: average budget balance as a share of GDP by subregion, 2012–2016**

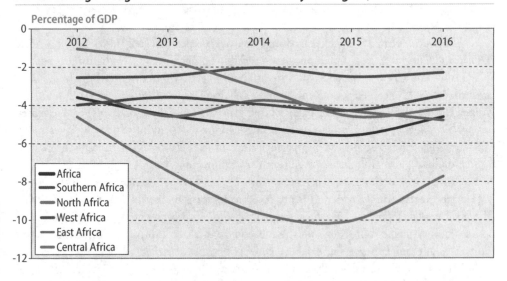

Source: UN/ECA, based on Economist Intelligence Unit. Note: Data were retrieved on 16 September 2015; data for 2015 and 2016 are forecast.

**Lower oil prices have put fiscal budgets under pressure**

The low oil prices have reduced public revenue in oil-exporting countries such as Algeria, Angola, Nigeria and Sudan. At the same time, increased spending for large public investments, continued subsidies for basic goods, in Morocco and Tunisia, for example, and election-related expenditure in Morocco have continued to exert pressure on public expenditure. In West Africa, the widening deficit was driven by the deterioration of fiscal balances mainly in Ghana and Nigeria. In Nigeria, the impact of low oil prices on fiscal balances is limited because of the use of buffers from oil-revenue savings and improved performance of non-oil sectors. In East Africa, the deficit deterioration is mainly a reflection of expansionary fiscal policies in Ethiopia, Kenya, Madagascar, Uganda and the United Republic of Tanzania. The deterioration of the fiscal balance was greatest in Central Africa, where the deficit widened from 3.1 per cent to an estimated 4.6 per cent, driven by expansionary fiscal policies, including infrastructure development in Cameroon, Chad and Equatorial Guinea, as well as election spending in Chad.

Africa's current-account deficit increased to 5.0 per cent of GDP in 2015, with all economic groupings and subregions reporting a current-account deficit. This was driven to a certain extent by the declining oil prices. Oil-exporting African countries recorded a deficit of 2.1 per cent of GDP in 2014, the first deficit since 2009. In 2015, the deficit increased to 5.1 per cent. For oil importers, the low oil prices led to a narrowing of the deficit. Among the subregions, the current-account deficit was the largest for Central Africa (8.1 per cent), followed by East Africa (7.4 per cent) and Southern Africa (5.7 per cent).

Lower oil prices led to a rise in Africa's current-account deficit

The expected improvement in the economic performance of the euro area will have a positive influence on current-account balances of African countries in 2016 and 2017. The depreciation of major currencies will also assist in promoting exports. However, the reliance of many African countries on imports, particularly capital goods, and the faster rate of growth of imports relative to exports may exacerbate external balances (box IV.3). At the same time, the slowdown in China's growth has also been a concern for African countries, given the increasing importance of the Chinese market. Africa's exports to China are still dominated by commodities, although manufacturing exports have increased in importance in the last five years (figure IV.5).

Exports to the euro area and currency depreciation will support Africa's current-account balance

**Figure IV.5**
**Africa's exports to China, 2000–2014**

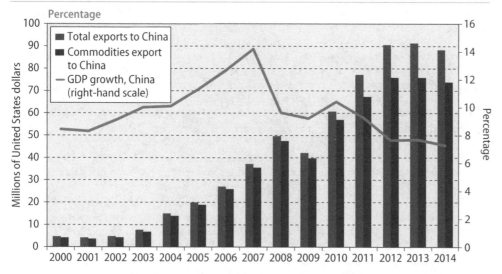

Source: UNCTADstat and UN/DESA.

The falling oil and commodity prices drew down the international reserves of African countries to an estimated 15.8 per cent of GDP in 2015, down from 17.1 per cent in 2014. The oil-price decline also impacted the net debt of Africa, which increased from 5.8 per cent in 2014 to an estimated 9.9 per cent of GDP in 2015, compared to 2.9 per cent in 2013. From 2014 to 2015, total gross debt for Africa increased from 22.9 per cent to about 25.7 per cent of GDP.

Lower oil and commodity prices also impacted international reserves and debt levels

## Box IV.3
## Africa's resource exports and product imports: the untapped potential of value-added production

Intermediate products accounted for 60 per cent of Africa's merchandise imports over the last decade and significantly contributed to African countries' growth (United Nations, Economic Commission for Africa, 2015). Over the same decade, intermediate exports have constituted the most dynamic component of Africa's exports, mainly driven by fuel and mineral exports.[a] Africa's exports grew from an average of $84 billion in 2000-2002 to $356 billion 10 years later. However, the region continues to account for only a minimal proportion of global trade (World Trade Organization and IDE-JETRO, 2011).

The lack of global competitiveness of Africa's manufacturing sectors and the extent of untapped potential of domestic value-added production limit the continent's participation in the global supply chain. For example, Africa accounted for $3.9 billion—that is, roughly 16 per cent of global cotton exports in 2012—but only about one tenth of this was cotton fabric. At the same time, the region imported $0.4 billion of cotton and $4 billion of cotton fabrics, suggesting that the continent was effectively trading raw cotton for cotton fabrics. Similarly, Nigeria exported $89.0 billion of crude oil but only $5.6 billion of refined oil products in 2012, while importing $5.5 billion in refined oil (United Nations, Economic Commission for Africa, 2015). Most African countries export the bulk of agricultural intermediates, but with little domestic processing and value addition. For instance, more than 75 per cent of the cocoa exported from West Africa is in the form of cocoa beans, the production of which requires far less value addition than cocoa paste, cocoa butter or chocolate. Overall, African economies import 88 per cent of their intermediates from the rest of the world, with minimal imports from the continent itself. Among intra-Africa imports, the field is dominated by a handful of players—Algeria, Egypt, Morocco, Nigeria, Tunisia and South Africa—which account for nearly 75 per cent of the total.

At the sectoral level, intermediate imports are concentrated in a few sectors such as manufacturing, agriculture, mining and quarrying, with manufacturing being the main driver of imported intermediate demand. Manufacturing intermediates represent more than two thirds of intra-African exports, while mining and quarrying constitute half of Africa's intermediate exports to the rest of the world. With Egypt, Ghana, Kenya, Nigeria, South Africa, the United Republic of Tanzania and Zambia recording gains in their exports of manufacturing inputs within Africa, there is evidence of enhanced forward linkages with manufacturing firms on the continent. However, the small size of Africa's trade in intermediates and the geographical pattern of such trade suggest that there are persistent structural weaknesses in these sectors.

While evidence points to some backward linkages in mining and quarrying (where 25 per cent of imported intermediates are sourced within Africa), the potential to establish regional value chains (RVCs) in the textiles or agriculture sectors is still largely untapped, as less than 10 per cent of intermediates are imported from the region. The extractive industries remain the main channel through which African economies are connected to downstream global value chains, and linkages to the regional market are weak (Organization for Economic Cooperation and Development, 2015g). Most African economies remain mired in the low end of value chains, supplying raw materials and other intermediates that embody very limited domestic value addition (United Nations, Economic Commission for Africa, 2013). This, in turn, fails to foster the establishment of forward linkages with the domestic economies, resulting in minimal contributions to employment generation and growth.

The lack of intermediate exports in the manufacturing sector mirrors the persistently low intra-industry trade in the region, and points to the low levels of African economies' integration into regional and global production networks. Most African countries continue to have poorly diversified structures of production and have experienced premature de-industrialization, which further curtails the scope for intra-industry trade.

African countries should thus develop and strengthen RVCs, as intra-African trade represents a promising avenue to support industrialization. The experiences of selected African countries suggest that an appropriate policy framework focused on enhancing industrialization could go a long way in fostering value-added production in downstream activities, even in extractive industries. For instance, Botswana has managed to foster the emergence of a viable diamond cutting and polishing cluster that employs several thousand workers. Similarly, small and medium-sized Mozambican enterprises have entered the aluminium value chain that is centred on the Mozal smelter.

Source: UN/ECA.
a Such as Algeria, Nigeria, Sudan and Zambia.

The weak recovery of the global economy continues to pose a challenge for Africa's economic performance through its impact on trade, investment and remittances. At the same time, however, solid performances by the most dynamic export markets for African countries—India and Africa itself—may buffer the impact on trade. Low oil prices continue to pose a challenge, especially for oil-exporting countries, although they have been generally beneficial for oil importers. The depreciation of major African currencies, while possibly beneficial for exports, puts pressure on monetary stability through imported inflation.

While FDI flows are expected to remain steady at about 3 per cent of GDP, monetary policy decisions by the Fed present a risk in the medium term. The low interest rates and therefore returns in both the United States and the European countries have increased investors' appetite for emerging markets. The likely rate increase by the Fed may divert investment flows from emerging markets back to developed countries, also negatively affecting the African economies. This presents a risk, particularly for those countries that have introduced sovereign bonds as an alternative source of finance, such as Gabon, Ghana and Zambia.

At the regional level, economic performance continues to be hampered by weather-related shocks. Droughts in East Africa in particular remain a challenge to the agricultural sector, which is still the main employer on the continent. As a consequence, poor harvests could also increase the risk of inflation through higher food prices in the drought- or flood-affected countries. Security in some African countries also remains an issue. Security concerns in Egypt and Tunisia have already had a negative impact on income from tourism. The continuing presence of Boko Haram in West Africa and political unrest in countries such as Burkina Faso and Burundi, and more recently Mali, can be a source of domestic disruption and instability, leading to a decrease in investment in these countries.

**Major risks and challenges for Africa include weaker growth in China and the euro area, commodity price levels and currency depreciation**

**Higher interest rates in the United States could divert investment flows from Africa**

**Weather-related shocks and security issues are further risks for Africa's growth performance**

## East Asia: despite a weaker-than-expected performance the region drives global growth

Given the subdued growth in most developed countries, domestic demand in East Asian economies continues to play an important role in driving growth. The tepid performance of the export sector is a key factor behind lower-than-expected GDP growth in 2015. With policy support, primarily from the fiscal side, GDP growth is projected to accelerate in 2016 in most of the region's major economies, while China continues on a slower growth path as it seeks to achieve more sustainable growth. In aggregate, East Asian economies are expected to grow by 5.6 per cent in 2016, similar to 2015, but down from an annual average of 6.3 per cent in 2012-2014. Excluding China, however, growth is expected to rebound to 4.1 per cent in 2016, from an estimated 3.4 per cent in 2015. Consumer price inflation is at a multi-year low for major economies in the region, with the most notable exception being Indonesia. As reflected in wider budget deficits, fiscal policy has generally become more expansionary, with scaled-up health and infrastructure spending and stimulus focused on jobs and small and medium-sized enterprises. Further monetary support is expected to remain limited owing to already-low policy rates and anticipated increases in the United States interest rates. Financial market and exchange-rate volatility increased in August 2015, amid concerns about China's outlook as well as the expectation of a United States interest-rate hike. The weakening of the region's currencies against the United States dollar poses risks for external debt (United Nations, Economic and Social Commission for Asia and the Pacific, 2016), and so far has done little to lift the region's exports. Capital outflows could lead to further volatility in asset markets, but bank capital and foreign-currency reserves in most economies seem adequate, based on Basel standards and import cover.[2]

China's economy is estimated to have grown by 6.8 per cent in 2015, down from 7.3 per cent in 2014. Growth is likely to have further moderated in the second half of the year owing to weaker exports and restrained investment as the country is working through excess inventories in the property market and overcapacity of heavy industries. Local government spending has also been constrained by fiscal drag resulting from the restrictions on bank lending to local government financing vehicles and reduced land sales revenue (even though revenue has shown signs of recovery in the second half of 2015). Consumer spending continues to expand, despite corrections in real estate and equity markets, but retail sales growth has slowed down compared to previous years. GDP growth is expected to ease further to 6.4 per cent in 2016. The Republic of Korea's economy is estimated to have grown by 2.6 per cent in 2015, down from 3.3 per cent in 2014, as net exports have declined significantly (figure IV.6). The decline in exports is closely linked to the slowdown of the Chinese economy given the Republic of Korea's high trade exposure to China. However, as consumer and business sentiment began to improve in the second half of 2015 and a $20 billion fiscal stimulus was announced in mid-2015, GDP growth is expected to improve to 3.0 per cent in 2016.

Figure IV.6

**East Asia: contributions of expenditure components to real GDP growth, January 2014–June 2015**

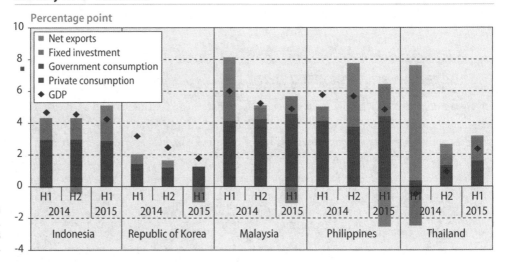

Growth estimates for 2015 have been revised downward from the previous forecasts for the majority of Association of Southeast Asian Nations (ASEAN) economies, with the notable exceptions of Myanmar and Viet Nam. Myanmar is projected to have grown by 8.4 per cent in 2015, driven by new investments, rapid credit growth and higher government spending. Viet Nam is expected to grow by 6.4 per cent in 2015 as consumer spending recovered and manufacturing exports remained strong. Similar levels of GDP growth are

---

2    For further discussion on reserve adequacy, see International Monetary Fund (2011) and Williams (2005).

foreseen for the two economies in 2016, as the aforementioned contributing factors should remain at play.

The Indonesian economy is estimated to have grown by 5.1 per cent in 2015, as commodity exports and investment remained subdued and consumer spending was hit by higher-than-expected inflation. Expected improvement in investment and lower inflation should lift GDP growth to 5.4 per cent in 2016. Thailand's economy is projected to have grown by 2.5 per cent in 2015, up from 0.9 per cent in 2014 when growth stalled amid political unrest. Prolonged weakness in exports held back growth even as government expenditures rebounded. Consumer spending is constrained by household debt and lower farm incomes due to drought. A fiscal stimulus announced in September 2015 and the upcoming large infrastructure projects are expected to improve Thailand's growth prospect.

Malaysia's economy is estimated to have grown by 4.5 per cent in 2015, down from 6 per cent in 2014, as exports fell, largely in the commodity sectors, and private investment growth slowed. Consumer spending held up well, despite softening after April 2015 when a new goods and services tax came into effect. A modest recovery in exports and ongoing investment aimed at upgrading industry and infrastructure should support stronger growth during the outlook period. The Philippines' economy—one of the better performers in ASEAN—is estimated to have grown by 5.8 per cent in 2015, as consumer spending and investment remained robust. Weak exports of goods are partially offset by exports of services, including business process outsourcing. Continued strong domestic demand and public spending that typically precedes elections should lift the Philippines' growth. Singapore is estimated to have grown by 2.3 per cent in 2015 as services and construction growth partly offset manufacturing contraction. Investment will pick up speed in 2016-2017 and play an elevated role in lifting Singapore's growth.

Outside of ASEAN, weak performance of the export sector has significantly slowed down the GDP growth rate of Taiwan Province of China to 1 per cent in 2015—one of the lowest in the region. While projected to grow at a higher rate of 2.3 per cent, output growth of the Hong Kong Special Administrative Region (SAR) of China has also been hit by weak export performance in 2015. A moderate export recovery during the forecast period, coupled with continued steady private consumption growth, is expected to moderately improve the growth outlook of both economies.

Among major economies, the official unemployment rate is generally low, in the range of 1 to 4 per cent, except in Indonesia and the Philippines where it stands near or above 6 per cent. The jobless rates for those aged 25 to 29 are much higher, ranging from 4.5 per cent in Thailand to 21.5 per cent in Indonesia. The share of unpaid family workers and own-account workers in total employment remains high, ranging from 21.3 per cent in the Republic of Korea to 61.5 per cent in Viet Nam, based on International Labour Organization estimates. Reflecting low wages and low productivity, two thirds of the employed in Indonesia and the Philippines earn below $4 a day. For East Asian economies to rebalance towards domestic demand (without relying too heavily on debt), it is important to improve labour's share in total income, which has declined or remains low in some economies (United Nations, Economic and Social Commission for Asia and the Pacific, 2016; and International Labour Organization, 2013).

**Official unemployment rate is generally low, but other employment-related concerns exist**

Consumer price inflation is expected to pick up to 2.2 per cent in 2016 from an estimated multi-year low of 1.6 per cent in 2015, in line with stronger economic activity in the majority of the region's economies and a modest rise in global oil prices. In 2015, economies such as Singapore, Taiwan Province of China and Thailand experienced mild headline deflation. Against the backdrop of low oil and commodity prices, inflation was below the

**Consumer price inflation is expected to pick up from the subdued levels in 2015**

Figure IV.7
**East Asia: selected vulnerability indicators**

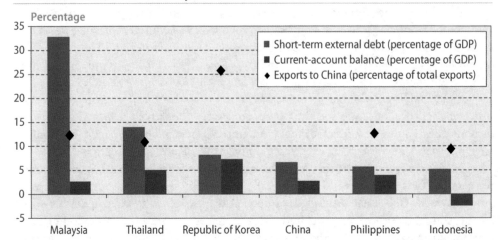

Source: UN/ESCAP, based on data from Trademap and CEIC database.
Note: Exports and current-account balance figures are based on data from 2014 Q3 to 2015 Q2. External debt figures are based on data as of end-2014.

central bank's target band in many major economies, with Indonesia being a notable exception. Core inflation declined in the Philippines, albeit from a high base, and in Thailand, in line with weak domestic demand, but was stable in China and the Republic of Korea. In contrast, inflation remained relatively high in Indonesia and accelerated in Malaysia, owing to the phase-out of fuel subsidies, sharp depreciations against the United States dollar, plus import restrictions in the former and a new consumption tax in the latter.

**Monetary policy has been accommodative, but further easing is likely to be limited**

Monetary policy has been generally accommodative, although real interest rates have returned to positive territory in all countries, owing to low inflation. In response to weakening domestic demand, the central banks of China, the Republic of Korea and Thailand lowered their policy rates more than once in the first half of 2015; in China and Thailand, policy rates are now at a record low of 1.5 per cent. China reduced reserve requirements and injected liquidity into the banking system through open-market operations and refinancing facilities to support liquidity, which has roughly offset the decline of foreign-exchange deposits, a major source of liquidity. After a hike in response to the fuel subsidy cut announcement, Indonesia's central bank returned its policy rate to 7.5 per cent, while loosening macroprudential measures to support lending for housing and car purchases. Central banks in Malaysia, the Philippines and Viet Nam kept their benchmark rates unchanged in 2015. Further monetary easing is expected to be limited due to anticipated increases in the United States interest rates, low policy rates, and high household debt and asset market speculations in some of the region's economies.

**Fiscal policies have generally been expansionary**

Fiscal policy stances have become more expansionary amid slowing economic growth. There is room to do even more as public debt levels are relatively low in a majority of the region's economies. Indonesia, the Republic of Korea and Thailand introduced stimulus packages or countercyclical measures in 2015. All major economies except Malaysia had wider budget deficits in 2015 compared to 2014, due to higher social and infrastructure spending, although the deficits also reflected weaker natural resource revenues and, in some cases, general taxation revenues. Both Indonesia and the Philippines increased their deficit targets in 2015 to accommodate higher infrastructure investment and social service spending, although budget disbursements were often delayed. In contrast, the fiscal deficit narrowed in Malaysia, in line with its target to balance the budget and lower debt by 2020.

Regardless of the fiscal stance, countries are reprioritizing expenditures, as seen in recent fuel subsidy reforms in Indonesia and Malaysia. Countries are also strengthening their tax revenues. Malaysia introduced a 6 per cent goods and services tax in April 2015. Thailand will introduce an inheritance tax in early 2016. China is introducing the value added tax (VAT) to more sectors—replacing the existing turnover tax—and plans to introduce a nationwide residential real estate tax.

East Asia's trade and current-account surpluses have narrowed since the global financial crisis that began in 2008. In 2015, exports remained weak, given the persistently moderate economic recovery in most developed countries and the continued slowdown in China—a top export destination. Net exports weighed on GDP growth in most of the region's bigger economies. Lower global oil prices have substantially reduced oil and gas revenues in Brunei, Indonesia, Malaysia and Papua New Guinea. Short-term external debt is particularly high in Malaysia, at 33 per cent of GDP as of end-2014 (figure IV.7). This poses risks, especially in the context of much narrower current-account surpluses and tighter global financing conditions. Larger capital outflows could lead to volatility in asset markets, but regional banks are well capitalized and foreign-currency reserves are adequate. In addition to the Chiang Mai multilateral swap arrangement of ASEAN+3 members,[3] East Asia has a number of bilateral swaps, which in the case of Indonesia and Malaysia are equivalent to about a third to nearly half of their own reserves (United Nations, Economic and Social Commission for Asia and the Pacific, 2015a).

> **Exports remained weak in 2015 and weighed on growth in most of the larger economies.**

Risks to the regional forecast remain largely on the downside. One key risk is the possible acceleration of the slowdown of the Chinese economy. Stabilizing China's growth would require the rebalancing of the economy towards consumption and managing the challenges associated with the rapidly rising private debt. From a longer-term perspective, the ageing population and the fact that China is now crossing the Lewis Turning Point—meaning that room for productivity gains through rural-urban migration is increasingly limited—will also pose considerable challenges. The Government's announcement of ending the one-child policy in October is a welcome step towards addressing the demographic challenge, but its effects will remain limited in the short and medium run. The direct impact of a sharper-than-expected slowdown in China on East Asia would be mainly felt through the trade and investment channels, given the close trade linkages and rising Chinese investment in the region. Another key risk is the possibility of excessive market reactions to the pending rate hike in the United States, which could result in further deprecations of East Asia's currencies, significant capital outflows, and tightening of the liquidity conditions in the region. However, since the market has already internalized some of the anticipated interest-rate differentials in 2016 and the rate rise is expected to be modest, the short-term impact of the rate hike is likely to be limited.

> **Further slowdown of China's economy poses downside risks**

## South Asia: growth expected to strengthen, driven by private consumption and investment

Economic growth in South Asia is projected to accelerate in 2016-2017, contingent upon steady progress on domestic policy reforms. South Asia's GDP is expected to grow by 6.7

---

3    The +3 members of the Association of Southeast Asian Nations (ASEAN) are China, Japan and the Republic of Korea.

## Box IV. 4
## The potential impact of monetary policy normalization in the United States on Asia and the Pacific

As the economy of the United States of America regains growth momentum and labour market indicators improve, market expectations of imminent yet gradual increases in the federal funds rate are almost universal; the only difference of opinion is related to their timing. In September 2015, the United States Federal Reserve estimated that the federal funds rate could rise from the current rate of near zero to 3.4 per cent by end-2018. This will put pressure on other economies to follow suit, although the magnitude of the rate increase in each economy will be determined by country-specific factors, such as macroeconomic fundamentals and economic growth prospects.

This box examines the potential impact of these likely changes in the monetary policy stance of the United States on developing Asia-Pacific economies. In the short term, the United States rate hike could lead to financial market volatility, including further downward pressure on currencies; in the longer term, it will result in higher borrowing costs, which could be particularly detrimental for small economies that rely heavily on foreign borrowings.

In recent years, a mismatch between actual and anticipated announcements regarding the direction of United States monetary policy has already affected global risk appetite and led to episodes of financial turmoil, resulting in large capital outflows, sharp corrections in equity prices and steep currency depreciations in many Asia-Pacific economies. In mid-2013, amid fears that the United States quantitative easing programme would be tapered earlier than expected, the Indian rupiah quickly lost 15 per cent against the dollar, and the currencies of Indonesia, Malaysia, the Philippines and Thailand weakened by 7-9 per cent. While increases in United States interest rates are widely anticipated, the pace remains uncertain and the actual announcement could still lead to financial market volatility in some of the region's economies. The global stock market sell-off in August 2015, driven largely by concerns over slower economic growth in China, illustrates how strongly investors sometimes react to developments that have been generally expected.

A more fundamental, longer-term effect of the United States monetary policy normalization is higher financing costs for developing economies. It is estimated that a one percentage point increase in domestic short-term interest rates over 2016, in response to United States interest-rate increases, could lower annual output growth in eight major Asia-Pacific economies by 0.3-0.7 percentage points.[a] As expected, there is a positive association between the size of the estimated impact and the domestic credit-to-GDP ratio. Economies that are more sensitive to higher borrowing costs, namely China, Hong Kong Special Administrative Region (SAR) of China, the Republic of Korea and Singapore all have credit-to-GDP ratios of at least 110 per cent.

While the estimated economic growth impact of higher financing costs in these major economies is notable, a more worrying case is the impact on smaller developing economies that are particularly vulnerable to higher interest rates. This includes economies where growth and financial stability could be negatively impacted by higher borrowing costs, while room for macroeconomic policy responses is limited.

Lao People's Democratic Republic, Mongolia and Papua New Guinea are the three Asia-Pacific countries that rely most heavily on foreign capital to finance their investment needs. During 2012-2014, these countries had large current-account deficits, ranging, on average, from 16-30 per cent of GDP.[b] In these economies, external debt stood at about 80-180 per cent of gross national income in 2013 and debt service payments were substantial. In Mongolia, debt service amounted to almost 30 per cent of goods and services exports and primary income in 2013. Since these economies exhibit low foreign-currency sovereign ratings, borrowing on a non-concessional basis would also incur higher costs amid tighter global financial liquidity. As credit default risks tend to rise with higher interest rates, a healthy banking sector is needed to maintain financial stability. However, in Lao People's Democratic Republic, direct exposure of banks to foreign-currency loans remains high (International Monetary Fund, 2015h). In Mongolia, a stress test has revealed that some banks have inadequate capital positions in the case of an economic shock (International Monetary Fund, 2015i). In both countries, banks' balance sheets have deteriorated recently after years of rapid credit growth.

(continued)

a This simulation is based on the Oxford Global Economic Model. The eight economies are China, Hong Kong SAR, India, Indonesia, the Philippines, the Republic of Korea, Singapore and Thailand. For more details, see ESCAP (2015b, box 2).

b Another country with a large current-account deficit during the same period is Bhutan (21 per cent of GDP), but this was largely due to funds from India to finance large-scale hydropower projects.

In terms of fiscal policy space, the three countries face different situations. According to a joint IMF-World Bank debt sustainability analysis, the risk of public debt distress in Mongolia is considered high, with key debt indicators staying above the relevant thresholds for the coming years. In Lao People's Democratic Republic, the risk of distress is still moderate, but has risen in recent years and the public debt profile is highly sensitive to currency depreciation. In contrast, Papua New Guinea appears to have a more comfortable fiscal position (International Monetary Fund, 2014b; 2015j). In the case of an adverse shock, such fiscal space can be used to implement countercyclical measures, such as temporary tax reductions for households and small businesses that face higher debt burdens.

Taken together, rising international interest rates in the coming years tend to affect economies such as Lao People's Democratic Republic and Mongolia more than others because of the high degree of exposure and the limited room for fiscal policy response. As both economies are commodity exporters, their near-term growth outlook is further constrained by lower global prices of primary commodities and sluggish import demand from China.

per cent in 2016, up from an estimated growth of 6.0 per cent in 2015.[4] The improved outlook is likely to be broad-based. In most economies, including Bangladesh, India, Pakistan and Sri Lanka, strong private consumption will continue to be the main driver of growth, offsetting relatively tight fiscal policies and subdued exports. Consumer spending will be supported by low commodity prices, moderate inflation, steady employment growth (especially in the service sector), and rising workers' remittances. Some country-specific factors, such as the lifting of international sanctions against the Islamic Republic of Iran and reconstruction spending in Nepal, are also expected to help growth during the outlook period. A significant downside risk for the region is deteriorating market confidence, should progress on policy reforms fall short of expectations. Given the limited room for expansionary fiscal policy responses, any adverse shock, such as lower-than-average monsoon rainfalls, could have a sizable negative impact on output growth.

South Asia's estimated growth of 6.0 per cent in 2015 is marginally lower than the 2014 growth of 6.4 per cent, but well above the average growth rate of 5.0 per cent recorded in 2011-2013. As in recent years, growth in 2015 was largely driven by domestic demand. Private consumption and investment were supported by relatively stable macroeconomic conditions and easier monetary policy in several countries, including India and Pakistan. Real exports, which account for a relatively small proportion of GDP in most countries, performed poorly amid subdued demand in major trading partners. India's economy, which accounts for over 70 per cent of the regional GDP, is projected to grow by 7.3 per cent in 2016 and 7.5 per cent in 2017, slightly up from an estimated 7.2 per cent in 2015. The macroeconomic environment in India has improved notably over the past two years, helped by the sharp decline in the prices of oil, metals and food. Consumer and investor confidence has risen even as the Government faces difficulties in implementing its wide-ranging reform agenda. In other economies such as Bangladesh, Pakistan and Sri Lanka, robust consumer spending, supported by lower energy prices and strong remittance inflows, continues to drive the expansion of service sectors, in particular domestic trade activities. In the Islamic Republic of Iran, the removal of international sanctions is expected to provide a boost to economic activity, with oil production and exports forecast to recover gradually. In Nepal, growth is projected to be supported by reconstruction efforts, following the devastating

**India's outlook is largely favourable, but reform challenges remain**

---

4    The regional averages for GDP growth and consumer price inflation are based on data for the following countries: Bangladesh, India, the Islamic Republic of Iran, Nepal, Pakistan and Sri Lanka.

earthquake in April 2015; however, the damage caused to critical infrastructure will continue to negatively impact economic activity in 2016. In Bhutan, economic growth is expected to strengthen following the construction of large-scale hydropower projects. Given the highly cyclical and volatile investment patterns in the hydropower sector, the authorities in Bhutan face the challenge of stimulating investment in the productive non-hydropower and non-construction sectors, while also improving the overall capital efficiency.

Available data point to generally stable labour markets in South Asia although high-frequency data is limited. Moreover, official data does not fully reflect labour market developments across the region. In India, official labour market surveys indicate significant employment gains in the industrial sector in late 2014 and early 2015, driven by strong performances in the textile and information technology sectors. In Sri Lanka, total employment expanded by 1.7 per cent in the first half of 2015 (year on year), while the unemployment rate remained relatively low at 4.5 per cent. During this period, average real wages rose by about 4 per cent, with even faster gains for agricultural workers. By contrast, in Bangladesh and Nepal, nominal wages are estimated to have increased at about the same rate as consumer prices, resulting in a stagnation of real wages. In the Islamic Republic of Iran, the unemployment rate has been in double digits for the past several years, standing at 10.8 per cent in mid-2015. For all countries with available data, unemployment rates were significantly higher among women than men. This is a concern given that the labour force participation rate is much lower among women. Given the high number of new labour market entrants each year, employment pressures will remain significant even as economic growth in South Asia gains further strength in the forecast period.

**Consumer price inflation has declined to its lowest level in a decade**

As a net oil-importing region, South Asia has seen reduced inflationary pressures owing to the sharp decline in international oil prices. Average consumer price inflation slowed from 8.2 per cent in 2014 to 6.2 per cent in 2015, the lowest level in more than a decade. All of the region's economies recorded a decline in inflation. Besides the sharp drop in international oil prices, the reduction in inflationary pressures can also be attributed to domestic factors such as robust harvests, some easing of supply-side bottlenecks, and decelerations in rural wage growth. The relative importance of these factors varies from country to country, as does the extent of the decline in inflation. In India, Pakistan and Sri Lanka, inflation rates have fallen significantly and upward price pressures are expected to remain limited in the short run. According to the forecasts, South Asia's average inflation rate in 2016 will be below the average GDP growth rate for the first time since 2006 (figure IV.8).

**Monetary policy has been loosened amid lower inflation**

Lower inflation has allowed for monetary policy easing in several economies. The policy interest rates have been cut by 50 to 300 basis points in India, Nepal, Pakistan and Sri Lanka in the first three quarters of 2015 as central banks aim to support credit growth and boost economic activity. However, interest rate cuts by the central banks have so far had limited impact on credit growth, as there has been little pass-through to either bank lending rates or lending conditions. For example, the Reserve Bank of India reduced the policy rate by 125 basis points between January and September 2015, but this translated into much smaller decreases in the base interest rate of the country's major banks, and commercial loan growth has not increased during the same period. Available data suggests stable bank asset quality, even as the level of non-performing loans has remained elevated in some countries, notably Pakistan. Going forward, monetary policy is projected to remain accommodative in most countries. The room for further easing is, however, constrained by an expected pickup in inflation and concerns that rate cuts could further weaken the domestic currencies and push up the external debt burden.

Figure IV.8
**South Asia: annual GDP growth and consumer price inflation rates, 2010–2017**

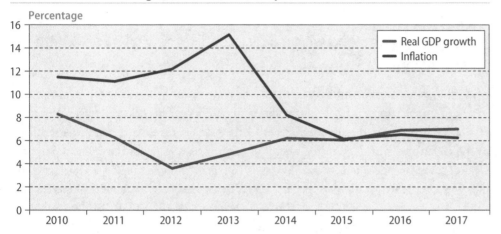

Source: UN/DESA.
Note: Figures for 2015 are
partially estimated; figures for
2016 and 2017 are forecast.

Fiscal deficits narrowed to about 3-5 per cent of GDP in most economies in 2015. This improvement reflects lower oil prices, stronger economic activity and rationalization of fuel subsidies in some economies. India abolished diesel subsidies, while Bangladesh, India, the Islamic Republic of Iran and Nepal reduced subsidies on fuel and/or electricity. These policy reforms should help to enhance the fiscal space in the region. Nonetheless, fiscal positions in most economies remain fundamentally weak owing to the small tax base, poor tax administration, and the large expenditures required for closing the infrastructure and energy gaps and maintaining internal security. Afghanistan and Bhutan continue to rely heavily on foreign aid inflows, which account for 70 and 30 per cent of total government spending, respectively. Looking ahead, fiscal deficits are expected to moderate gradually in most economies as a result of still low energy prices and stronger economic growth. Fiscal reforms to boost government revenues would support fiscal consolidation efforts, but such reforms have experienced delays in most economies amid strong public and political opposition.

**Fiscal deficits are declining owing to lower oil prices, robust growth and subsidy cuts**

Merchandise exports were generally weak owing to subdued demand in the major trading partners. Intraregional trade is relatively small. Most economies in the region saw their export revenues decline in 2015. In India, the dollar value of exports in the first three quarters of 2015 fell by 15 per cent from a year ago and was at the lowest level since 2010. In addition to sluggish external demand, this decline also reflects the sharp drop in the prices of fuel and other commodities and the strong appreciation of the dollar. Despite the weakness in exports, the trade deficits narrowed in most economies as import bills fell even more sharply. The performance of service exports, particularly tourism, was mixed. Growth in overseas visitors to India and Sri Lanka decelerated, while arrivals in Bhutan were more buoyant. Meanwhile, workers' remittances continued to increase in all countries where remittances account for a sizeable proportion of GDP, namely Bangladesh, Nepal, Pakistan and Sri Lanka. While remittance growth generally slowed, the weaker exchange rates in these economies (except Bangladesh) have supported household incomes in local currencies. In the wake of improved trade balances and steady remittance growth, the current-account balances in South Asia generally improved in 2015. For 2016-2017, a mild recovery in merchandise export growth is projected relative to the low base in 2015 as economic activity in some major destination markets, particularly the United States and Europe, picks up. Some

**Weakness in merchandise trade persists**

country-specific factors, such as the expected removal of international sanctions against the Islamic Republic of Iran, are also expected to support export growth.

## Western Asia: along with military conflicts, low oil prices weigh on regional GDP growth

In addition to the ongoing military conflicts, the main factor influencing the region's economies during the past year has been the slump in oil prices. This has created very different prospects for countries, depending on whether they are net oil exporters or importers. But for the region as a whole, given the weight of oil exporters in regional output, the overall effect of lower oil prices is negative. Average GDP growth in the region is thus expected to be weak, estimated at 2.0 per cent in 2015. A partial recovery in countries experiencing conflicts is expected to help GDP growth to accelerate to 2.4 per cent in 2016, even though this remains very weak when compared with GDP growth figures of the past 15 years. In 2017, oil-exporting economies are expected to benefit from a recovery in oil prices, leading to a regional GDP growth figure of 3.0 per cent (figure IV.9).

Given the expectations of low oil prices in the near future, growth prospects in oil-exporting countries will largely depend on non-oil economic activities. Despite low oil prices, a moderate domestic demand expansion is projected in some economies of the Cooperation Council for the Arab States of the Gulf (GCC), sustained by substantial fiscal spending on infrastructure. Particularly in Qatar and Saudi Arabia, where financial reserves are sufficiently large, fiscal spending continued to support GDP growth in 2015 and will, to some extent, do so in 2016. However, fiscal consolidation is expected in most countries, especial-

**Figure IV.9**
**GDP growth by economy groups in Western Asia, 2014–2017**

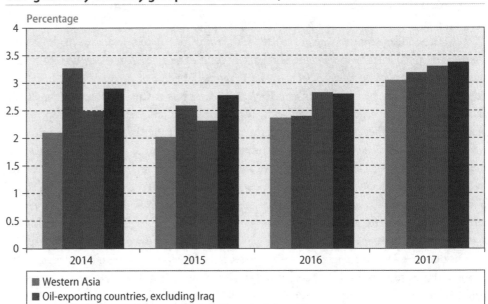

Source: UN/DESA.
Note: Growth rates for 2015 are partially estimated; rates for 2016 and 2017 are forecast.

Box IV.5

## The impact of the current oil-price shock on public finances for oil-exporting countries in Western Asia

Oil prices are of central importance to many Western Asian economies, as oil-exporting countries rely heavily on oil revenues to fund their budgets. The share of oil revenues in national budget revenues ranges from 31.9 per cent in Qatar to 91.5 per cent in Iraq.[a] As a share of gross domestic product (GDP), oil revenues range from 14.6 per cent in Qatar to 59 per cent in Kuwait.

Given the strong dependence on oil-export revenues, the current oil-price slump has severe implications. The consequent strain on Arab oil exporters' public finances can be assessed by comparing the Brent oil price of $43 per barrel (pb) (as of 16 November 2015) to the International Monetary Fund (IMF) 2015 projections of countries' fiscal break-even oil price: Kuwait, $49.1 pb; Qatar, $55.5 pb; United Arab Emirates, $72.6 pb; Oman, $94.7 pb; Saudi Arabia, $105.6 pb; and Bahrain, $107.0 pb (International Monetary Fund, 2015m). As a result of subdued oil prices, all these oil-exporting economies are expected to register fiscal deficits in 2015 (figure IV.5.1).

Figure IV.5.1

## Western Asia: budget balance for selected oil-exporting countries, 2012–2016

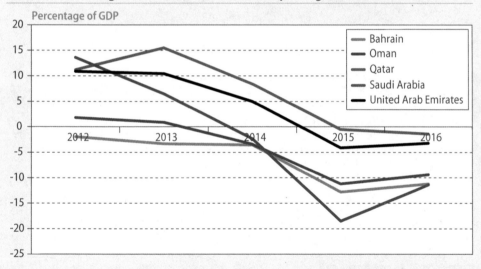

Source: Economist Intelligence Unit. Data for 2015 and 2016 are forecast.
Note: Budget balance is defined here as central government receipts minus central government outlays.

At the same time, oil subsidies are also relatively high in the region, amounting to approximately 8.6 per cent of the regional GDP (Sdralevich and others, 2014), compared with only 2 per cent at the global level. Although the phenomenon prevails in oil-importing countries as well, the GDP share of subsidies tends to be higher in oil-exporting countries. In terms of actual subsidy per capita, the five highest levels in 2013 were observed in countries of the Cooperation Council for the Arab States of the Gulf (GCC): Qatar $2,853; Kuwait, $2,721; United Arab Emirates, $2,378; Saudi Arabia, $2,155; and Bahrain, $1,888 (figure IV.5.2). The specific combination of subsidized products differs across countries, but they generally focus on food and oil products. The region's average fossil-fuel subsidization rates are also among the highest in the world, ranging from 53.3 per cent in Iraq to 78.5 per cent in Qatar.[b]

Against this backdrop, oil-exporting economies in Western Asia have different options, depending on their specific macroeconomic conditions. First, they may tap into their sovereign wealth funds (SWF). However, even though all oil-exporters have SWFs,[c] only Saudi Arabia has sufficient buffers ($660 billion) that would allow it to cover approximately 5.3 years of the projected 2015 fiscal deficit (International Monetary Fund, 2015n). Indeed, the country is exercising this option, as Saudi Arabia's SWF is projected to shrink by $94.4 billion in 2015.

(*continued*)

Box IV.5 (*continued*)

**Figure IV.5.2**

**Top 10 countries in the world with the highest fossil-fuel subsidy per capita, 2013**

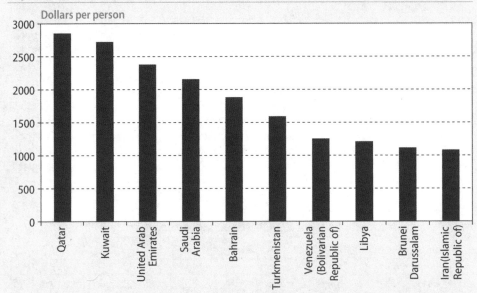

Source: International Energy Agency (2014b).

Source: UN/ESCWA.
a Latest IMF Article IV Consultations (International Monetary Fund, 2015k; 2015l).
b Average fossil-fuel subsidisation rate is defined as the average fossil-fuel subsidy as a share of the full cost of supply (International Energy Agency, 2014b).
c See Sovereign Wealth Funds Asset Map, available from http://www.swfinstitute.org/ sovereignwealthmap.html.

The second option is to issue debt, which is particularly appealing in the current context of ultra-low interest rates (and this applies to all countries, given that their currencies are pegged to the United States dollar). Furthermore, the current levels of debt in the region are generally low: with the exception of Iraq, which has a total debt-to-GDP ratio of 70 per cent, total debt in oil-exporting countries ranges from 1.2 per cent of GDP in Oman to 44 per cent in Bahrain. The debt option has been considered by Saudi Arabia, for instance, which has announced that it will issue $27 billion in bonds. Other countries such as Kuwait and the United Arab Emirates are also considering this option.

The third option is to reduce spending, which raises a number of vital questions. Countries can postpone large capital projects, similar to what Saudi Arabia is doing with Riyadh's metro system, or even delay payments to contractors. However, this option may not suffice and cuts might have to include current spending on some existing subsidies. For instance, Bahrain has reduced subsidies on common food products such as beef and chicken, while Oman is lowering subsidies on rice, flour, and sugar. Cutting subsidies is arguably the most viable option in the long term, but in the short term it can be politically challenging, as it may provoke adverse public reactions. For instance, in 2014, Yemen undertook reforms to cut fuel subsidies, only to be reversed months later owing to a spike in social unrests.

The traditional approach in oil-exporting countries has often been to direct their natural wealth towards their citizens in the form of granting benefits and privileges (e.g., facilitating job creation for their nationals, heavily subsidizing oil and food products, or massively investing public funds towards public goods). These privileges are now at risk, at least partly, adding to pressures on the socioeconomic models in the region. Therefore, countries will have to strike a delicate balance between the sustainability of public finances and sociopolitical stability.

ly in 2016 (box IV.5), as revenues plummet along with lower oil prices, leading to a slower economic expansion during the forecast period.

In the more diversified economies of the region, macroeconomic prospects are mixed, despite the positive effect of lower oil prices. In Turkey, GDP growth is estimated to have slowed down to 2.8 per cent in 2015 and the same rate is projected for 2016. The slowdown reflects a number of factors, including efforts to consolidate fiscal spending, limited monetary policy space, weaker domestic demand, currency volatility and capital outflows. In Israel, the economic growth estimate for 2015 has also been revised down, to 2.3 per cent, as exports declined in volume, while private demand has been held back by the recent surge in violence.

Conversely, economic prospects are expected to improve in Jordan and Lebanon during the forecast period, even though these economies will continue to be constrained by the conflict in the Syrian Arab Republic. In Jordan, large infrastructure projects already under way and expansionary monetary policies will stimulate domestic demand. In Lebanon, the tourism sector will continue to be an important economic driver, as long as the security situation does not deteriorate. These economies are also benefiting from positive spillover effects related to the dynamic non-oil sectors in GCC countries, where many national emigrants are employed and continue to send remittances and transfer capital, helping to sustain domestic demand.

Geopolitical turmoil, armed conflict and humanitarian crises remain a heavy burden for the economies of Iraq, the Syrian Arab Republic and Yemen. In particular, Iraq and the Syrian Arab Republic are engulfed in conflicts that have led to substantial destruction of their economic structures. The consequences on public finances (through increased spending), foreign direct investments and tourism are being felt across the region. In terms of social capital, the high cost of the conflicts has translated into large amounts of refugees fleeing to Europe.

The region will continue to register some of the highest unemployment rates among developing countries. Unemployment figures are not expected to improve during the forecast period, as extremely high structural unemployment, particularly among youth, and several armed conflicts will require longer-term solutions. In Turkey, for instance, the unemployment rate reached 10.2 per cent in the second quarter of 2015, almost a full percentage point higher than one year earlier. Considering current macroeconomic developments, including tighter monetary policy and the expected growth in the working-age population, unemployment is expected to increase in Turkey during the forecast period.

*The region will continue to register high unemployment rates, especially among youth*

Besides oil, the continued decline in commodity prices—particularly of food items—has eased inflationary pressures in the region, especially in Jordan and Lebanon. The main driver of inflation in GCC countries remains real estate assets. Inflation has also been contained in Iraq despite the armed conflict. Conversely, hyperinflation continued in the Syrian Arab Republic in 2015 as a direct consequence of the current foreign-exchange constraints. Yemen also saw high inflationary pressures as the armed conflict intensified. The inflation rate is now expected to reach about 22 per cent in 2015. In 2016, the upward shift in real estate prices in GCC countries is expected to taper off, moderately lowering consumer price inflation. Inflation in the Syrian Arab Republic and Yemen is expected to remain high, owing to foreign-exchange constraints and ongoing sociopolitical instability, which negatively affects supply chains.

*Inflationary pressures have eased in most countries*

Monetary policies in GCC countries have remained unchanged, as most countries have their currencies pegged to the United States dollar and their monetary policies thus mirror that of the Fed. The funding cost in terms of three-month interbank money market rates in GCC countries stayed at about 1.0 percent, although it started to rise slowly in the first half of 2015. Given that United States interest rates are projected to rise during the forecast period, the monetary stance in GCC countries is expected to change accordingly. Falling international commodity prices have created sizeable policy space for monetary easing in Jordan and Lebanon: the Central Bank of Jordan took monetary easing measures in February and July 2015, while Banque du Liban, the Lebanese central bank, has also used monetary stimulus measures to boost domestic demand. In Turkey, monetary policy is expected to tighten further during the forecast period, given relatively high inflation and the persistent depreciation of the Turkish lira (TRY). Between January and September 2015, the TRY lost more than 25 per cent against the dollar.

Limited fiscal space for countercyclical measures

In oil-exporting countries, fiscal revenues have plummeted as oil prices have dropped, leading to a process of fiscal readjustment, spending cuts and even reforms of subsidy policies. In parallel, fiscal consolidation in some countries has also entailed issuance of debt securities. For instance, Saudi Arabia issued in July 2015 its first sovereign bonds since 2007. Conversely, low oil prices have alleviated balance-of-payment and fiscal constraints in non-oil-exporting countries, notably Jordan, Lebanon and Turkey. Similarly, Israel has also reduced its fiscal deficit, helped both by higher public revenues and fiscal consolidation in 2015. However, revenue prospects remain generally weak for both oil-exporting and more diversified economies. For some countries, such as Jordan and Yemen, direct and indirect external assistance has become essential to maintaining their capital spending levels.

Many oil-exporting economies record current-account deficits

With the exception of Kuwait and Qatar, countries are estimated to register current-account deficits in 2015. Import levels in GCC countries are sustained by the growing non-oil sector, while exports from GCC countries have weakened, owing to lower oil prices. The current-account deficits of Iraq and Yemen are estimated to deteriorate significantly, owing to the continuing armed conflicts. The Syrian Arab Republic remains under severe foreign-exchange constraints, as the Syrian pound continued to depreciate sharply against the dollar. At the same time, the current-account deficits are estimated to edge down in Jordan and Lebanon, as their trade balances are improving and remittances continue to support the current account.

Downside risks include lower external demand for oil and higher capital outflows

There are downside risk factors to this outlook. The first is the expansion of conflicts beyond Iraq, the Syrian Arab Republic and Yemen. The breakdown of social capital due to the increasing displaced population, as well as the destruction of economic capital, are fundamental concerns regarding the long-term economic prospects. The second factor is an abrupt decline in demand for crude oil. Despite the low level of oil prices, global demand for oil has been increasing only slightly. Concerns are growing about China's economic slowdown, which could inhibit oil demand further. This would impact GCC countries' already weak fiscal positions, as well as business confidence in the region. The third factor is the effect of United States monetary tightening, which can take two interrelated forms: first, countries may suffer capital outflows as investors leave riskier markets in search of rising returns in the United States; second, as many countries have their currency pegged to the United States dollar, higher interest rates may hinder growth via lower investment.

## Latin America and the Caribbean: on a "two-track" growth path

After a decade of robust growth, economic activity has sharply decelerated

Latin America and the Caribbean entered into a period of economic difficulties amid domestic weaknesses and less supportive external conditions. After experiencing robust growth during the commodity boom period, with average regional growth above 4.0 per cent per annum between 2004 and 2013, the region has seen growth fall sharply to 1.0 per cent in 2014 and then a contraction of 0.5 per cent in 2015 (figure IV. 10). The challenging global context—including lower commodity prices and subdued global trade, the slowdown in China and the expected normalization of United States monetary policy—is affecting the region through different channels. As a result, several economies have experienced a deterioration of their terms of trade, with negative effects on their fiscal accounts, investment prospects and capital inflows. In the outlook period, economic activity in Latin America

Figure IV.10
**Latin America and the Caribbean: GDP growth rates, 2010–2016**

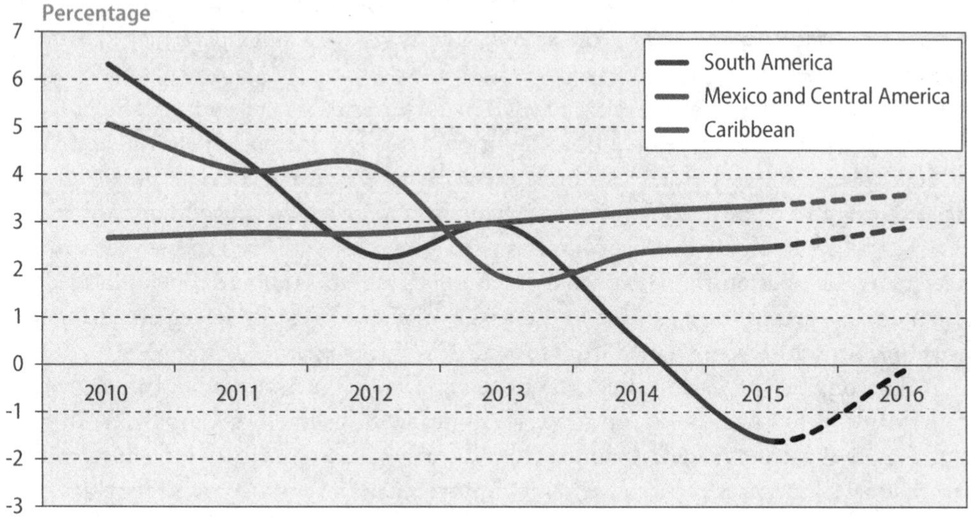

Source: UN/DESA.
Note: Growth rates for 2015 are partially estimated; rates for 2016 are forecast.

and the Caribbean is projected to expand by only 0.7 per cent in 2016; growth is forecast to accelerate to 2.7 per cent in 2017, but this recovery is subject to significant downside risks.

This aggregate picture encompasses divergent subregional situations. The economies of Mexico and Central America are projected to expand by 2.9 per cent in 2016, up from 2.5 per cent in 2015, benefiting from stronger domestic demand and the recovery in the United States. By contrast, after an estimated contraction of 1.6 per cent in 2015, South American economies are expected to contract more moderately—by 0.1 per cent in 2016—with some large economies facing considerable difficulties in narrowing the output gap. Meanwhile, the Caribbean economies are expected to expand by 3.6 per cent in 2016, slightly above 2015, benefiting from a strengthening of tourism activity.

Among the largest countries, GDP growth in Mexico is expected to accelerate from 2.3 per cent in 2015 to 2.7 per cent in 2016, owing to a recovery in investment demand and the strengthening of the United States. In South America, the Brazilian economy is expected to remain in recession, contracting by 0.8 per cent in 2016 amid continuing weakness in investment and challenging fiscal and monetary conditions. Argentina is expected to grow by 1.6 per cent in 2016, while facing strong pressures to implement a fiscal adjustment. Meanwhile, the economy of the Bolivarian Republic of Venezuela is expected to contract by 6.0 per cent in 2016, amid serious domestic imbalances and very high inflation. Smaller economies such as Costa Rica, the Dominican Republic, Guyana, Honduras, Nicaragua Panama and the Plurinational State of Bolivia are projected to continue to register relatively robust growth rates in 2016, above 4.0 per cent.

At the regional level, the weakening aggregate demand has been driven by the continuing fall in investment and, to a lesser degree, by the slowdown in private consumption. The contribution of gross capital formation to growth, which had been declining for several years, fell more sharply by the end of 2013. Regional gross fixed capital formation contracted by 1.9 per cent in 2014 and continued to decline in the first half of 2015. Efforts to stimulate public investment and private-public partnerships across the region in recent years have not succeeded in boosting private investment. The ongoing weak performance

**Investment demand continues to decline, especially in South American economies**

of investment is a serious concern because of its adverse impacts on the dynamics of the business cycle and on the medium- and long-term growth prospects in the region.

Labour markets gradually worsen across the region

The economic slowdown is gradually affecting labour markets across the region, particularly in South America. Since the second quarter of 2015, unemployment rates have started to increase visibly, amid lower job creation and decreasing employment rates. Hence, the regional unemployment rate is expected to increase from 6.0 per cent in 2014 to 6.6 per cent in 2015, and even further in 2016. This upward trend in unemployment will be driven by South American economies. For instance, in Brazil the rise in unemployment started to become visible by early 2015 and it has strengthened since then. In addition, real wages continue to rise modestly in most countries, which together with the expected increase in unemployment will constrain households' consumption in the near term. Preliminary data also point to a gradual deterioration in the quality of employment in the region, illustrated by an incipient shift from salaried work towards self-employment.

Fiscal policy space is increasingly constrained

The capacity of Latin American and Caribbean countries to stimulate aggregate domestic demand is contingent on the space available for countercyclical policies. In this regard, both fiscal and monetary authorities still seem to have some room for maneuvering, but external shocks have reduced the space. In particular, the fiscal accounts have deteriorated in 2015, owing to a sharp fall in revenues in several economies resulting from lower commodity prices. For instance, countries such as Brazil, Colombia, Ecuador and Mexico have implemented important adjustments in public budgets for 2015 and 2016. Meanwhile, tax revenues have shown signs of recovery in the wake of the reforms implemented by some countries in the last few years.

Importantly, the higher deficits have not led to an increase in the central government debt in Latin American economies—estimated at about 34 per cent of GDP—as financing conditions remain favourable. However, the public debt levels continue to differ greatly across countries. For instance, the public debt in Brazil is the highest in Latin America, close to 65 per cent of GDP, and it has continued to rise owing to the economic recession. At the other extreme, debt levels in Chile, Paraguay and Peru are only about 20 per cent of GDP. It is important to note, however, that debt in the non-financial public sector has increased strongly in some countries recently, especially among public sector firms.

The region is facing increasing monetary policy dilemmas

In terms of monetary policy, most economies in the region have adopted a countercyclical approach since 2014. For instance, countries such as Chile, Mexico and Peru significantly cut interest rates in order to stimulate economic activity. The most notable exception was Brazil, which continued to raise interest rates in an attempt to contain inflation pressures and capital outflows. Countries that use monetary aggregates as their main policy instrument in Central and South America experienced faster growth in their monetary base since the second half of 2014. In this context, domestic lending in the region continued to grow in 2015, albeit at lower rates than in previous years. However, in the near term, the region—particularly South American economies—will face increasingly complex dilemmas regarding their monetary stances. In particular, growth remains subdued, while inflation has visibly accelerated. In addition, expectations over the normalization of the monetary policy in the United States could increase financial volatility and further reduce capital inflows. For example, authorities in Chile, Colombia and Peru have already raised interest rates moderately in recent months.

Overall, the countercyclical monetary policy stance was facilitated by relatively low regional inflation. In Mexico and Central American countries, inflation remains stable and low. By contrast, inflation in South American economies has visibly accelerated, mainly because of the significant depreciation of domestic currencies in several economies. In Brazil, inflation remains relatively high and above the central bank's target, but is expected to slow down gradually in 2016. The extreme case is the Bolivarian Republic of Venezuela, where consumer price inflation is expected to rise above 150 per cent in 2016, aggravated by severe macroeconomic imbalances.

The regional economic slowdown, together with the expectation of an interest-rate hike in the United States, lower commodity prices and the sharp contraction of capital inflows, have led to a significant depreciation of domestic currencies in Brazil, Chile, Colombia and Mexico. Mirroring the reduction in capital inflows—including not only portfolio flows but also foreign direct investments, international reserves have started to decline. So far, the sharpest declines in international reserves have been observed in the Bolivarian Republic of Venezuela, Uruguay and Trinidad and Tobago.

**Several economies have seen a sharp depreciation of domestic currencies...**

In 2015, the value of exports fell for the third consecutive year, dropping by almost 14.0 per cent, owing to the lower commodity prices. In Mexico and Central American countries exports edged up, benefiting from the recovery in the United States. By contrast, South American commodity exporters have been seriously affected by the slowdown in China and the lower prices for minerals and metals. In the first six months of 2015, Colombian and Brazilian exports to China declined by more than 70 and 20 per cent, respectively. The region's trade balance has deteriorated further in 2015. Overall, the regional current-account deficit, which stood at 2.7 per cent of GDP in 2014, is expected to have increased to 3.0 per cent in 2015.

**...but the value of exports continues to decline**

The downside risks to the baseline scenario for the region are a sharper-than-expected slowdown in China and additional declines in commodity prices. An escalation of global financial turbulences involving a sharp increase in external financing costs could also affect the growth outlook for the region. Besides the short-term fluctuations, it seems that the

**The region is encountering significant difficulties in its attempts to continue improving socio-economic indicators**

Box IV.6

## Commodity price volatility and its impacts on Latin American and Caribbean economies

Since the 2000s, commodity prices have exhibited significant swings. After registering one of the most intense, long-lasting and broad-based booms in history in the first decade of the 2000s, commodity markets have subsequently declined sharply. The slump in prices is visible across all commodities (figure IV.6.1), but it has been felt with greater intensity in energy and metals and minerals, with accumulated declines of 52.6 and 46.5 per cent, respectively, between 2011 Q2 and 2015 Q3.

The sharp price declines are explained in part by economic fundamentals. The decline of growth in China has been a key factor. China's consumption accounts for roughly 11 per cent of global oil consumption, with one third for coal, two thirds for iron ore, and more than half for copper. Large changes in prices are required to adapt to changes in demand and supply in order to clear the market, due to the relatively small short-run supply and demand price elasticities of commodities, in particular for energy and metals.

Speculation is also an important factor behind commodity price movements. Commodities are playing an increasing role as financial assets, with prices responding to changes in expectations about future demand conditions, rather than to the actual supply and demand. The growing role of commodities as financial assets is reflected in the growth in activity on commodity future markets, including commodity derivatives. Between 1995 and 2012, the number of outstanding contracts on commodity exchanges increased from $36.6 million to $182 million for futures, and from $373.6 million to $2.1

*(continued)*

Box IV.6 (*continued*)

Figure IV.6.1

**Average quarterly growth of commodity indices, selected periods between 2000 Q1 and 2015 Q3**

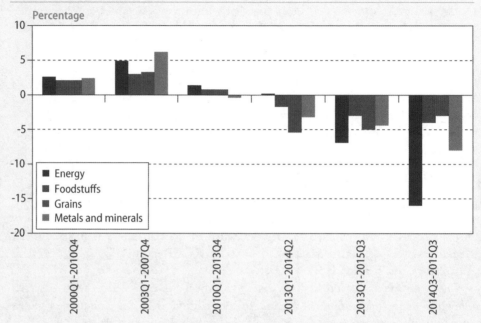

Source: UN/ECLAC, based on Pink Sheet Commodity Data, World Bank, 2015, available from http://www.worldbank.org/en/research/commodity-markets. Growth rates were computed using geometric averaging procedure.
Note: Data from 2015 Q3 refers to August 2015.

Figure IV.6.2

**Share of statistically significant correlations between commodity indices and equity indices (returns and volatilities), 1991–2000, 2001–2007 and 2010–2015**

Source: UN/ECLAC.
Note: The chart depicts the share of statistically significant monthly pairwise correlations between commodity indices and equity indices (returns and volatilities of these indices). The indices examined include different commodity indices (agriculture, energy, industrial metals, livestock, precious metals and non-energy), the Dow Jones AIG and Standard and Poor Commodity Indices (DJAIG, GSCI), and equity indices including the Dow Jones Industrial Average (DJIA) and Standard and Poor's 500 (S&P500).

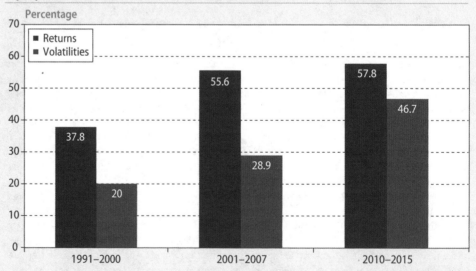

billion for derivatives. Similarly, between 1998 and 2014, the volume of over-the-counter commodity derivative contracts expanded from $4.3 billion to $2.2 trillion (notional amounts outstanding). Currently commodity derivatives represent less than 0.5 per cent of the total across all asset classes (Financial Conduct Authority, 2014). Commodities have also become more closely correlated with traditional financial assets such as equities. Available evidence indicates that the share of statistically significant monthly

(*continued*)

correlations between the returns and volatilities for different commodity indices and equity indices has increased since the 1990s (figure IV.6.2).[a]

Box IV.6 (*continued*)

The changes in commodity prices have important real and financial effects on Latin America and the Caribbean. Higher volatility in commodity prices can lead to greater uncertainty regarding world demand and supply conditions (both of commodities and of economic activity), a postponement of investment decisions, difficulties for firms in strategic planning, and disruptions and uncertainties in the implementation of fiscal budgets.

The recent commodity-price declines clearly benefit net-energy-importing countries such as those of Central America. At the same time, falling commodity prices are detrimental to commodity-exporting countries such as those of South America. In fact, commodities represent, on average, 71.4 per cent of total exports in South America. In addition, commodities are also a main source of government revenues. For mineral producing countries (e.g., Chile, Peru and the Plurinational State of Bolivia), the fiscal income generated by the production of minerals is equivalent on average to 2.0 per cent of gross domestic product (GDP) and 8.6 per cent of total revenues for the period 2010-2013. The contribution from hydrocarbon production is even greater, accounting during the same period for more than 10 per cent of GDP and 40 per cent of total revenues on average for Ecuador, Trinidad and Tobago, the Plurinational State of Bolivia and Venezuela (Bolivarian Republic of). In addition, the economic sectors that depend on commodities explain a large share of the output, foreign direct investment inflows, and also domestic investment.

Figure IV.6.3
**Latin America (seven countries): average annual rate of investment growth in real terms, 1991–2014**

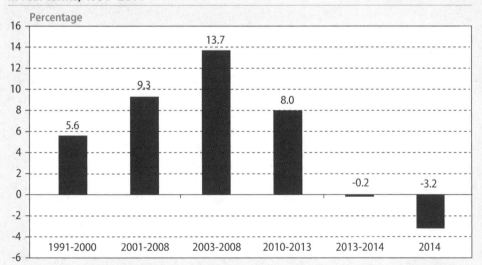

Source: UN/ECLAC, based on official quarterly data.
Note: The countries included are Argentina, Brazil, Chile, Colombia, Peru, Plurinational State of Bolivia and Venezuela (Bolivarian Republic of).

The decline and volatility of commodity prices have had a significant effect on the behaviour of investment, which shows a marked decline for most economies since 2011, and in some cases contractions since 2014. The data available for seven Latin American countries (Argentina, Brazil, Chile, Colombia, Peru, the Plurinational State of Bolivia and Venezuela (Bolivarian Republic of)) show that the unweighted average investment growth rate for this group of countries peaked at 13.7 per cent in the period 2003-2008. Since then, the investment growth rate has continuously declined with averages of 8.0 per cent, -0.2 per cent and -3.2 per cent for 2010-2013, 2013-2014, and 2014, respectively (figure IV.6.3).

The investment cycle is highly linked and synchronized with the GDP cycle. In fact, investment volatility reflects specific characteristics of the region's business cycle. The available empirical evidence suggests that the dynamic of the investment cycle has been unfavourable to sustained, inclusive medium- and long-term growth. Investment behaviour not only affects the speed and rate of capital accumulation but also has a direct bearing on productivity, which is an important determinant of long-term growth.

Source: UN/ECLAC.
a See Büyüksahin, Haigh and Robe (2010). The rate of return on the $j^{th}$ investable index in period t is equal to $r^j_t = 100 \text{Log}(P^j_t / P^j_{t-1})$, where $P^j_t$ is the value of the index at time t. The volatility of an index in period t is $(r^j_t - X)^2$, where X is the mean value of $r^j_t$ over the sample period.

# Statistical annex

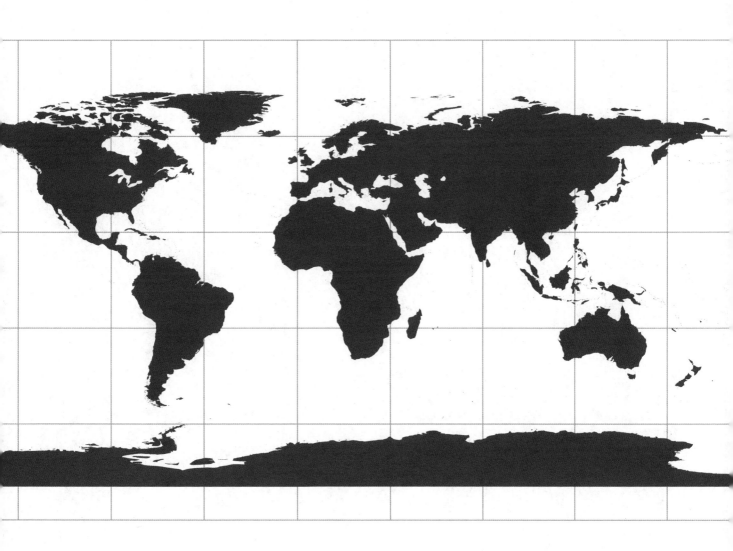

# Country classifications

## Data sources, country classifications and aggregation methodology

The statistical annex contains a set of data that the World Economic Situation and Prospects (WESP) employs to delineate trends in various dimensions of the world economy.

### Data sources

The annex was prepared by the Development Policy and Analysis Division (DPAD) of the Department of Economic and Social Affairs of the United Nations Secretariat (UN/DESA). It is based on information obtained from the Statistics Division and the Population Division of UN/DESA, as well as from the five United Nations regional commissions, the United Nations Conference on Trade and Development (UNCTAD), the United Nations World Tourism Organization (UNWTO), the International Monetary Fund (IMF), the World Bank, the Organization for Economic Cooperation and Development (OECD), and national and private sources. Estimates for the most recent years were made by DPAD in consultation with the regional commissions, UNCTAD, UNWTO and participants in Project LINK, an international collaborative research group for econometric modelling coordinated jointly by DPAD and the University of Toronto. Forecasts for 2016 and 2017 are primarily based on the World Economic Forecasting Model of DPAD, with support from Project LINK.

Data presented in WESP may differ from those published by other organizations for a series of reasons, including differences in timing, sample composition and aggregation methods. Historical data may differ from those in previous editions of WESP because of updating and changes in the availability of data for individual countries.

### Country classifications

For analytical purposes, WESP classifies all countries of the world into one of three broad categories: developed economies, economies in transition and developing economies. The composition of these groupings, specified in tables A, B and C, is intended to reflect basic economic country conditions. Several countries (in particular the economies in transition) have characteristics that could place them in more than one category; however, for purposes of analysis, the groupings have been made mutually exclusive. Within each broad category, some subgroups are defined based either on geographical location or on ad hoc criteria, such as the subgroup of "major developed economies", which is based on the membership of the

Group of Seven. Geographical regions for developing economies are as follows: Africa, East Asia, South Asia, Western Asia, and Latin America and the Caribbean.[1]

In parts of the analysis, a distinction is made between fuel exporters and fuel importers from among the economies in transition and the developing countries. An economy is classified as a fuel exporter if the share of fuel exports in its total merchandise exports is greater than 20 per cent and the level of fuel exports is at least 20 per cent higher than that of the country's fuel imports. This criterion is drawn from the share of fuel exports in the total value of world merchandise trade. Fuels include coal, oil and natural gas (table D).

For other parts of the analysis, countries have been classified by their level of development as measured by per capita gross national income (GNI). Accordingly, countries have been grouped as high-income, upper middle income, lower middle income and low-income (table E). To maintain compatibility with similar classifications used elsewhere, the threshold levels of GNI per capita are those established by the World Bank. Countries with less than $1,045 GNI per capita are classified as low-income countries, those with between $1,046 and $4,125 as lower middle income countries, those with between $4,126 and $12,735 as upper middle income countries, and those with incomes of more than $12,736 as high-income countries. GNI per capita in dollar terms is estimated using the World Bank Atlas method,[2] and the classification in table E is based on data for 2014.

The list of the least developed countries (LDCs) is decided upon by the United Nations Economic and Social Council and, ultimately, by the General Assembly, on the basis of recommendations made by the Committee for Development Policy. The basic criteria for inclusion require that certain thresholds be met with regard to per capita GNI, a human assets index and an economic vulnerability index.[3] As at 30 November 2015, there were 48 LDCs (table F).

WESP also makes reference to the group of heavily indebted poor countries (HIPCs), which are considered by the World Bank and IMF as part of their debt-relief initiative (the Enhanced HIPC Initiative).[4] In September 2015, there were 39 HIPCs (see table G).

## Aggregation methodology

Aggregate data are either sums or weighted averages of individual country data. Unless otherwise indicated, multi-year averages of growth rates are expressed as compound annual percentage rates of change. The convention followed is to omit the base year in a multi-year growth rate. For example, the 10-year average growth rate for the decade of the 2000s would be identified as the average annual growth rate for the period from 2001 to 2010.

WESP utilizes exchange-rate conversions of national data in order to aggregate output of individual countries into regional and global totals. The growth of output in each group of countries is calculated from the sum of gross domestic product (GDP) of individual countries measured at 2010 prices and exchange rates. Data for GDP in 2010 in national

---

1    Names and composition of geographical areas follow those specified in the statistical paper entitled "Standard country or area codes for statistical use" (ST/ESA/STAT/SER.M/49/Rev. 4).

2    See http://data.worldbank.org/about/country-classifications.

3    Handbook on the Least Developed Country Category: Inclusion, Graduation and Special Support Measures, 2nd ed. (United Nations publication, Sales No. E.15.II.A.1). Available from http://www.un.org/en/development/desa/policy/cdp/cdp_publications/2015cdphandbook.pdf.

4    IMF, Debt Relief Under the Heavily Indebted, Poor Countries (HIPC) Initiative. Available from http://www.imf.org/external/np/exr/facts/hipc.htm.

currencies were converted into dollars (with selected adjustments) and extended forwards and backwards in time using changes in real GDP for each country. This method supplies a reasonable set of aggregate growth rates for a period of about 15 years, centred on 2010.

The exchange-rate based method differs from the one mainly applied by the IMF and the World Bank for their estimates of world and regional economic growth, which is based on purchasing power parity (PPP) weights. Over the past two decades, the growth of world gross product (WGP) on the basis of the exchange-rate based approach has been below that based on PPP weights. This is because developing countries, in the aggregate, have seen significantly higher economic growth than the rest of the world in the 1990s and 2000s and the share in WGP of these countries is larger under PPP measurements than under market exchange rates.

Table A
**Developed economies**

| Europe | | Other countries | Major developed economies (G7) |
|---|---|---|---|
| **European Union** | **Other Europe** | | |
| EU-15 | Iceland | Australia | Canada |
|   Austria | Norway | Canada | Japan |
|   Belgium | Switzerland | Japan | France |
|   Denmark | | New Zealand | Germany |
|   Finland | | United States | Italy |
|   France | | | United Kingdom |
|   Germany | | | United States |
|   Greece | | | |
|   Ireland | | | |
|   Italy | | | |
|   Luxembourg | | | |
|   Netherlands | | | |
|   Portugal | | | |
|   Spain | | | |
|   Sweden | | | |
|   United Kingdom | | | |
| New EU member States | | | |
|   Bulgaria | | | |
|   Croatia | | | |
|   Cyprus | | | |
|   Czech Republic | | | |
|   Estonia | | | |
|   Hungary | | | |
|   Latvia | | | |
|   Lithuania | | | |
|   Malta | | | |
|   Poland | | | |
|   Romania | | | |
|   Slovakia | | | |
|   Slovenia | | | |

## Table B
### Economies in transition

| South-Eastern Europe | Commonwealth of Independent States and Georgia[a] | |
|---|---|---|
| Albania | Armenia | Republic of Moldova |
| Bosnia and Herzegovina | Azerbaijan | Russian Federation |
| Montenegro | Belarus | Tajikistan |
| Serbia | Georgia[a] | Turkmenistan |
| The former Yugoslav Republic of Macedonia | Kazakhstan | Ukraine |
| | Kyrgyzstan | Uzbekistan |

## Table C
### Developing economies by region[a]

| Africa | | Asia | Latin America and the Caribbean |
|---|---|---|---|
| **North Africa** | **Southern Africa** | **East Asia** | **Caribbean** |
| Algeria | Angola | Brunei Darussalam | Barbados |
| Egypt | Botswana | China | Cuba |
| Libya | Lesotho | Hong Kong SAR[b] | Dominican Republic |
| Mauritania | Malawi | Indonesia | Guyana |
| Morocco | Mauritius | Malaysia | Haiti |
| Sudan | Mozambique | Myanmar | Jamaica |
| Tunisia | Namibia | Papua New Guinea | Trinidad and Tobago |
| **Central Africa** | South Africa | Philippines | |
| | Zambia | Republic of Korea | **Mexico and Central America** |
| Cameroon | Zimbabwe | Singapore | Costa Rica |
| Central African Republic | | Taiwan Province of China | El Salvador |
| Chad | **West Africa** | Thailand | Guatemala |
| Congo | | Viet Nam | Honduras |
| Equatorial Guinea | Benin | | Mexico |
| Gabon | Burkina Faso | **South Asia** | Nicaragua |
| Sao Tome and Prinicipe | Cabo Verde | | Panama |
| | Côte d'Ivoire | Bangladesh | |
| **East Africa** | Gambia | India | **South America** |
| | Ghana | Iran (Islamic Republic of) | |
| Burundi | Guinea | Nepal | Argentina |
| Comoros | Guinea-Bissau | Pakistan | Bolivia (Plurinational State of) |
| Democratic Republic of the Congo | Liberia | Sri Lanka | Brazil |
| Djibouti | Mali | **Western Asia** | Chile |
| Eritrea | Niger | | Colombia |
| Ethiopia | Nigeria | Bahrain | Ecuador |
| Kenya | Senegal | Iraq | Paraguay |
| Madagascar | Sierra Leone | Israel | Peru |
| Rwanda | Togo | Jordan | Uruguay |
| Somalia | | Kuwait | Venezuela (Bolivarian Republic of) |
| Uganda | | Lebanon | |
| United Republic of Tanzania | | Oman | |
| | | Qatar | |
| | | Saudi Arabia | |
| | | Syrian Arab Republic | |
| | | Turkey | |
| | | United Arab Emirates | |
| | | Yemen | |

Table D
**Fuel-exporting countries**

| Economies in transition | Developing countries | | | | |
| --- | --- | --- | --- | --- | --- |
| | Latin America and the Caribbean | Africa | East Asia | South Asia | Western Asia |
| Azerbaijan | Bolivia (Plurinational State of) | Algeria | Brunei Darussalam | Iran (Islamic Republic of) | Bahrain |
| Kazakhstan | | Angola | Indonesia | | Iraq |
| Russian Federation | Colombia | Cameroon | Viet Nam | | Kuwait |
| Turkmenistan | Ecuador | Chad | | | Oman |
| Uzbekistan | Trinidad and Tobago | Congo | | | Qatar |
| | Venezuela (Bolivarian Republic of) | Côte d'Ivoire | | | Saudi Arabia |
| | | Egypt | | | United Arab Emirates |
| | | Equatorial Guinea | | | Yemen |
| | | Gabon | | | |
| | | Libya | | | |
| | | Nigeria | | | |
| | | Sudan | | | |

Table E

**Economies by per capita GNI in 2014[a]**

| High-income | | Upper middle income | | Lower middle income | |
|---|---|---|---|---|---|
| Argentina [b] | Lithuania | Albania | Jordan | Armenia | Mauritania |
| Australia | Luxembourg | Algeria | Kazakhstan | Bangladesh [b] | Morocco |
| Austria | Malta | Angola | Lebanon | Bolivia (Plurinational | Myanmar [b] |
| Bahrain | Netherlands | Azerbaijan | Libya | State of) | Nicaragua |
| Barbados | New Zealand | Belarus | Malaysia | Cameroon | Nigeria |
| Belgium | Norway | Bosnia and | Mauritius | Cabo Verde | Pakistan |
| Brunei | Oman | Herzegovina | Mexico | Congo | Papua New Guinea |
| Darussalam | Poland | Botswana | Montenegro | Côte d'Ivoire | Philippines |
| Canada | Portugal | Brazil | Namibia | Djibouti | Republic of Moldova |
| Chile | Qatar | Bulgaria | Panama | Egypt | São Tomé and |
| Croatia | Republic | China | Paraguay [b] | El Salvador | Principe |
| Cyprus | of Korea | Colombia | Peru | Georgia | Senegal |
| Czech | Russian Federation | Costa Rica | Romania | Ghana | Sri Lanka |
| Republic | Saudi Arabia | Cuba | Serbia | Guatemala | Sudan |
| Denmark | Singapore | Dominican | South Africa | Guyana | Syrian Arab Republic |
| Equatorial | Slovak | Republic | Thailand | Honduras | Tajikistan [b] |
| Guinea | Republic | Ecuador | The former | India | Ukraine |
| Estonia | Slovenia | Gabon | Yugoslav | Indonesia | Uzbekistan |
| Finland | Spain | Iran (Islamic | Republic of | Kenya [b] | Viet Nam |
| France | Sweden | Republic of) | Macedonia | Kyrgyz Republic[c] | Yemen |
| Germany | Switzerland | Iraq | Tunisia | Lesotho | Zambia |
| Greece | Taiwan Province | Jamaica | Turkey | | |
| Hong Kong | of China | | Turkmenistan | | |
| SAR [c] | Trinidad and | | | | |
| Hungary [b] | Tobago | | | | |
| Iceland | United Arab | | | | |
| Ireland | Emirates | | | | |
| Israel | United Kingdom | | | | |
| Italy | United States | | | | |
| Japan | Uruguay | | | | |
| Kuwait | Venezuela | | | | |
| Latvia | (Bolivarian | | | | |
| | Republic of) [b] | | | | |

| Low-income | |
|---|---|
| Benin | Liberia |
| Burkina Faso | Madagascar |
| Burundi | Malawi |
| Central African | Mali |
| Republic | Mozambique |
| Chad | Nepal |
| Comoros | Niger |
| Democratic Republic | Rwanda |
| of the Congo | Sierra Leone |
| Eritrea | Somalia |
| Ethiopia | Togo |
| Gambia | Uganda |
| Guinea | United Republic |
| Guinea-Bissau | of Tanzania |
| Haiti | Zimbabwe |

**a** Economies systematically monitored for the World Economic Situation and Prospects report and included in the United Nations' global economic forecast.

**b** Indicates the country has been shifted upward by one category from previous year's classification.

**c** Special Administrative Region of China.

## Table F
**Least developed countries** (*as of November 2015*)

| Africa | | East Asia | South Asia | Western Asia | Latin America and the Caribbean |
|---|---|---|---|---|---|
| Angola | Madagascar | Cambodia[a] | Afghanistan[a] | Yemen | Haiti |
| Benin | Malawi | Kiribati[a] | Bangladesh | | |
| Burkina Faso | Mali | Lao People's | Bhutan[a] | | |
| Burundi | Mauritania | Democratic | Nepal | | |
| Central African Republic | Mozambique | Republic[a] | | | |
| Chad | Niger | Myanmar | | | |
| Comoros | Rwanda | Solomon | | | |
| Democratic Republic of the Congo | Sao Tome and Principe | Islands[a] | | | |
| Djibouti | Senegal | Timor Leste[a] | | | |
| Equatorial Guinea | Sierra Leone | Tuvalu[a] | | | |
| Eritrea | Somalia | Vanuatu[a] | | | |
| Ethiopia | South Sudan[a] | | | | |
| Gambia | Sudan | | | | |
| Guinea | Togo | | | | |
| Guinea-Bissau | Uganda | | | | |
| Lesotho | United Republic of Tanzania | | | | |
| Liberia | Zambia | | | | |

a  Not included in the WESP discussion because of insufficient data.

## Table G
**Heavily indebted poor countries** (*as of September 2015*)

| Post-completion point HIPCs[a] | | Interim HIPCs[b] | Pre-decision point HIPCs[c] |
|---|---|---|---|
| Afghanistan | Honduras | Chad | Eritrea |
| Benin | Liberia | | Somalia |
| Bolivia | Madagascar | | Sudan |
| Burkina Faso | Malawi | | |
| Burundi | Mali | | |
| Cameroon | Mauritania | | |
| Central African Republic | Mozambique | | |
| Comoros | Nicaragua | | |
| Congo | Niger | | |
| Côte D'Ivoire | Rwanda | | |
| Democratic Republic of the Congo | São Tomé and Principe | | |
| Ethiopia | Senegal | | |
| Gambia | Sierra Leone | | |
| Ghana | Togo | | |
| Guinea | Uganda | | |
| Guinea-Bissau | United Republic of Tanzania | | |
| Guyana | Zambia | | |
| Haiti | | | |

a  Countries that have qualified for irrevocable debt relief under the HIPC Initiative.

b  Countries that have qualified for assistance under the HIPC Initiative (that is to say, have reached decision point), but have not yet reached completion point.

c  Countries that are potentially eligible and may wish to avail themselves of the HIPC Initiative or the Multilateral Debt Relief Initiative (MDRI).

Table H
**Small island developing States**

| United Nations members | | Non-UN members/Associate members of the Regional Commissions |
|---|---|---|
| Antigua and Barbuda | Marshall Islands | American Samoa |
| Bahamas | Mauritius | Anguilla |
| Bahrain | Nauru | Aruba |
| Barbados | Palau | Bermuda |
| Belize | Papua New Guinea | British Virgin Islands |
| Cabo Verde | Saint Kitts and Nevis | Cayman Islands |
| Comoros | Saint Lucia | Commonwealth of Northern Marianas |
| Cuba | Saint Vincent and the Grenadines | |
| Dominica | | Cook Islands |
| Dominican Republic | Samoa | Curaçao |
| Federated States of Micronesia | São Tomé and Príncipe | French Polynesia |
| | Seychelles | Guadeloupe |
| Fiji | Singapore | Guam |
| Grenada | Solomon Islands | Martinique |
| Guinea-Bissau | Suriname | Montserrat |
| Guyana | Timor-Leste | New Caledonia |
| Haiti | Tonga | Niue |
| Jamaica | Trinidad and Tobago | Puerto Rico |
| Kiribati | Tuvalu | Turks and Caicos Islands |
| Maldives | Vanuatu | U.S. Virgin Islands |

Table I
**Landlocked developing countries**

| Landlocked developing countries | | |
|---|---|---|
| Afghanistan | Kyrgystan | South Sudan |
| Armenia | Lao People's Democratic Republic | Swaziland |
| Azerbaijan | | Tajikistan |
| Bhutan | Lesotho | The former Yugoslav Republic of Macedonia |
| Bolivia (Plurinational State of) | Malawi | |
| Botswana | Mali | Turkmenistan |
| Burkina Faso | Mongolia | Uganda |
| Burundi | Nepal | Uzbekistan |
| Central African Republic | Niger | Zambia |
| Chad | Paraguay | Zimbabwe |
| Ethiopia | Republic of Moldova | |
| Kazakhstan | Rwanda | |

Table J
**International Organization for Standardization Country Codes**

| ISO Code | Country | ISO Code | Country | ISO Code | Country | ISO Code | Country |
|---|---|---|---|---|---|---|---|
| AFG | Afghanistan | DZA | Algeria | LBN | Lebanon | ROU | Romania |
| AGO | Angola | ECU | Ecuador | LBR | Liberia | RUS | Russian Federation |
| ALB | Albania | EGY | Egypt | LBY | Libya | RWA | Rwanda |
| AND | Andorra | ERI | Eritrea | LCA | Saint Lucia | SAU | Saudi Arabia |
| ARE | United Arab Emirates | ESP | Spain | LIE | Liechtenstein | SDN | Sudan |
| ARG | Argentina | EST | Estonia | LKA | Sri Lanka | SEN | Senegal |
| ARM | Armenia | ETH | Ethiopia | LSO | Lesotho | SGP | Singapore |
| ATG | Antigua and Barbuda | FIN | Finland | LTU | Lithuania | SLB | Solomon Islands |
| AUS | Australia | FJI | Fiji | LUX | Luxembourg | SLE | Sierra Leone |
| AUT | Austria | FRA | France | LVA | Latvia | SLV | El Salvador |
| AZE | Azerbaijan | FSM | Micronesia (Federated States of) | MAR | Morocco | SMR | San Marino |
| BDI | Burundi | | | MCO | Monaco | SOM | Somalia |
| BEL | Belgium | GAB | Gabon | MDA | Republic of Moldova | SRB | Serbia |
| BEN | Benin | GBR | United Kingdom of Great Britain and Northern Ireland | MDG | Madagascar | SSD | South Sudan |
| BFA | Burkina Faso | | | MDV | Maldives | STP | Sao Tome and Principe |
| BGD | Bangladesh | | | MEX | Mexico | | |
| BGR | Bulgaria | GEO | Georgia | MHL | Marshall Islands | SUR | Suriname |
| BHR | Bahrain | GHA | Ghana | MKD | The former Yugoslav Republic of Macedonia | SVK | Slovakia |
| BHS | Bahamas | GIN | Guinea | | | SVN | Slovenia |
| BIH | Bosnia and Herzegovina | GMB | Gambia | | | SWE | Sweden |
| | | GNB | Guinea Bissau | MLI | Mali | SWZ | Swaziland |
| BLR | Belarus | GNQ | Equatorial Guinea | MLT | Malta | SYC | Seychelles |
| BLZ | Belize | GRC | Greece | MMR | Myanmar | SYR | Syrian Arab Republic |
| BOL | Bolivia (Plurinational State of) | GRD | Grenada | MNE | Montenegro | TCD | Chad |
| | | GTM | Guatemala | MNG | Mongolia | TGO | Togo |
| BRA | Brazil | GUY | Guyana | MOZ | Mozambique | THA | Thailand |
| BRB | Barbados | HND | Honduras | MRT | Mauritania | TJK | Tajikistan |
| BRN | Brunei Darussalam | HRV | Croatia | MUS | Mauritius | TKM | Turkmenistan |
| BTN | Bhutan | HTI | Haiti | MWI | Malawi | TLS | Timor-Leste |
| BWA | Botswana | HUN | Hungary | MYS | Malaysia | TON | Tonga |
| CAF | Central African Republic | IDN | Indonesia | NAM | Namibia | TTO | Trinidad and Tobago |
| | | IND | India | NER | Niger | TUN | Tunisia |
| CAN | Canada | IRL | Ireland | NGA | Nigeria | TUR | Turkey |
| CHE | Switzerland | IRN | Iran (Islamic Republic of) | NIC | Nicaragua | TUV | Tuvalu |
| CHL | Chile | | | NLD | Netherlands | TZA | United Republic of Tanzania |
| CHN | China | IRQ | Iraq | NOR | Norway | | |
| CIV | Côte D'Ivoire | ISL | Iceland | NPL | Nepal | UGA | Uganda |
| CMR | Cameroon | ISR | Israel | NRU | Nauru | UKR | Ukraine |
| COD | Democratic Republic of the Congo | ITA | Italy | NZL | New Zealand | URY | Uruguay |
| | | JAM | Jamaica | OMN | Oman | USA | United States of America |
| COG | Congo | JOR | Jordan | PAK | Pakistan | | |
| COL | Colombia | JPN | Japan | PAN | Panama | UZB | Uzbekistan |
| COM | Comoros | KAZ | Kazakhstan | PER | Peru | VCT | Saint Vincent and the Grenadines |
| CPV | Cabo Verde | KEN | Kenya | PHL | Philippines | | |
| CRI | Costa Rica | KGZ | Kyrgyzstan | PLW | Palau | VEN | Venezuela (Bolivarian Republic of) |
| CUB | Cuba | KHM | Cambodia | PNG | Papua New Guinea | | |
| CYP | Cyprus | KIR | Kiribati | POL | Poland | VNM | Viet Nam |
| CZE | Czech Republic | KNA | Saint Kitts and Nevis | PRK | Democratic People's Republic of Korea | VUT | Vanuatu |
| DEU | Germany | KOR | Republic of Korea | | | WSM | Samoa |
| DJI | Djibouti | KWT | Kuwait | PRT | Portugal | YEM | Yemen |
| DMA | Dominica | LAO | Lao People's Democratic Republic | PRY | Paraguay | ZAF | South Africa |
| DNK | Denmark | | | QAT | Qatar | ZMB | Zambia |
| DOM | Dominican Republic | | | | | ZWE | Zimbabwe |

# Annex tables

Table A.1
## Developed economies: rates of growth of real GDP, 2007–2017

Annual percentage change

| | 2007-2014[a] | 2007 | 2008 | 2009 | 2010 | 2011 | 2012 | 2013 | 2014 | 2015[b] | 2016[c] | 2017[c] |
|---|---|---|---|---|---|---|---|---|---|---|---|---|
| Developed economies | 0.8 | 2.5 | 0.1 | -3.7 | 2.6 | 1.5 | 1.1 | 1.0 | 1.7 | 1.9 | 2.2 | 2.3 |
| United States | 1.1 | 1.8 | -0.3 | -2.8 | 2.5 | 1.6 | 2.2 | 1.5 | 2.4 | 2.4 | 2.6 | 2.8 |
| Canada | 1.6 | 2.0 | 1.2 | -2.7 | 3.4 | 3.0 | 1.9 | 2.0 | 2.4 | 1.2 | 2.2 | 2.9 |
| Japan | 0.4 | 2.2 | -1.0 | -5.5 | 4.7 | -0.5 | 1.7 | 1.6 | -0.1 | 0.5 | 1.3 | 0.6 |
| Australia | 2.8 | 4.5 | 2.5 | 1.6 | 2.3 | 2.6 | 3.7 | 2.0 | 2.7 | 2.3 | 2.5 | 2.2 |
| New Zealand | 1.9 | 3.7 | -0.8 | 0.5 | 2.0 | 1.4 | 2.9 | 2.5 | 3.3 | 2.5 | 2.4 | 2.5 |
| European Union | 0.5 | 3.1 | 0.5 | -4.4 | 2.1 | 1.8 | -0.5 | 0.2 | 1.4 | 1.9 | 2.1 | 2.2 |
| EU-15 | 0.4 | 2.9 | 0.2 | -4.4 | 2.1 | 1.7 | -0.6 | 0.1 | 1.2 | 1.8 | 2.0 | 2.1 |
| Austria | 0.9 | 3.6 | 1.5 | -3.8 | 1.9 | 2.8 | 0.8 | 0.3 | 0.4 | 0.7 | 1.7 | 1.8 |
| Belgium | 1.0 | 3.4 | 0.7 | -2.3 | 2.7 | 1.8 | 0.2 | 0.0 | 1.3 | 1.3 | 1.7 | 1.9 |
| Denmark | -0.2 | 0.8 | -0.7 | -5.1 | 1.6 | 1.2 | -0.1 | -0.2 | 1.3 | 1.7 | 2.2 | 2.3 |
| Finland | 0.0 | 5.2 | 0.7 | -8.3 | 3.0 | 2.6 | -1.4 | -1.1 | -0.4 | 0.1 | 1.2 | 1.4 |
| France | 0.6 | 2.4 | 0.2 | -2.9 | 2.0 | 2.1 | 0.2 | 0.7 | 0.2 | 1.2 | 1.5 | 1.5 |
| Germany | 1.1 | 3.3 | 1.1 | -5.6 | 4.1 | 3.7 | 0.4 | 0.3 | 1.6 | 1.8 | 2.1 | 2.3 |
| Greece | -3.3 | 3.3 | -0.3 | -4.3 | -5.5 | -9.1 | -7.3 | -3.2 | 0.7 | -2.4 | -1.2 | 2.8 |
| Ireland | 0.9 | 5.5 | -2.2 | -5.6 | 0.4 | 2.6 | 0.2 | 1.4 | 5.2 | 6.0 | 4.5 | 3.8 |
| Italy | -1.0 | 1.5 | -1.1 | -5.5 | 1.7 | 0.6 | -2.8 | -1.7 | -0.4 | 0.7 | 1.3 | 1.5 |
| Luxembourg | 2.2 | 8.4 | -0.8 | -5.4 | 5.7 | 2.6 | -0.8 | 4.3 | 4.1 | 3.1 | 3.6 | 2.5 |
| Netherlands | 0.5 | 3.7 | 1.7 | -3.8 | 1.4 | 1.7 | -1.1 | -0.5 | 1.0 | 2.0 | 2.4 | 2.1 |
| Portugal | -0.6 | 2.5 | 0.2 | -3.0 | 1.9 | -1.8 | -4.0 | -1.1 | 0.9 | 1.5 | 1.6 | 1.4 |
| Spain | -0.4 | 3.8 | 1.1 | -3.6 | 0.0 | -1.0 | -2.6 | -1.7 | 1.4 | 3.1 | 2.5 | 2.6 |
| Sweden | 1.2 | 3.4 | -0.6 | -5.2 | 6.0 | 2.7 | -0.3 | 1.2 | 2.3 | 2.7 | 2.6 | 2.1 |
| United Kingdom | 0.9 | 2.6 | -0.5 | -4.2 | 1.5 | 2.0 | 1.2 | 2.2 | 2.9 | 2.5 | 2.4 | 2.6 |
| New EU member States | 1.9 | 6.4 | 3.6 | -3.7 | 2.0 | 3.1 | 0.5 | 1.2 | 2.7 | 3.2 | 3.0 | 3.2 |
| Bulgaria | 1.7 | 7.7 | 5.6 | -4.2 | 0.1 | 1.6 | 0.2 | 1.3 | 1.5 | 1.9 | 2.4 | 3.6 |
| Croatia | -0.8 | 5.2 | 2.1 | -7.4 | -1.7 | -0.3 | -2.2 | -1.1 | -0.4 | 0.8 | 1.1 | 2.0 |
| Cyprus | -0.4 | 4.9 | 3.7 | -2.0 | 1.4 | 0.4 | -2.4 | -5.9 | -2.5 | 1.2 | 1.8 | 1.9 |
| Czech Republic | 1.0 | 5.5 | 2.7 | -4.8 | 2.3 | 2.0 | -0.9 | -0.5 | 2.0 | 4.0 | 2.5 | 2.9 |
| Estonia | 0.7 | 7.7 | -5.4 | -14.7 | 2.5 | 7.6 | 5.2 | 1.6 | 2.9 | 1.9 | 2.5 | 3.0 |
| Hungary | 0.1 | 0.4 | 0.8 | -6.6 | 0.7 | 1.8 | -1.7 | 1.9 | 3.7 | 2.7 | 2.1 | 2.3 |
| Latvia | 0.2 | 10.0 | -3.6 | -14.3 | -3.8 | 6.2 | 4.0 | 3.0 | 2.4 | 2.5 | 2.8 | 3.1 |
| Lithuania | 1.9 | 11.1 | 2.6 | -14.8 | 1.6 | 6.0 | 3.8 | 3.5 | 3.0 | 1.6 | 2.6 | 3.2 |
| Malta | 2.4 | 4.0 | 3.3 | -2.5 | 3.5 | 2.1 | 2.5 | 2.6 | 3.5 | 3.9 | 3.0 | 2.2 |
| Poland | 3.6 | 7.2 | 3.9 | 2.6 | 3.7 | 5.0 | 1.6 | 1.3 | 3.3 | 3.5 | 3.4 | 3.4 |
| Romania | 1.8 | 6.9 | 8.5 | -7.1 | -0.8 | 1.1 | 0.6 | 3.5 | 2.8 | 3.8 | 3.8 | 4.0 |
| Slovakia | 3.0 | 10.8 | 5.7 | -5.5 | 5.1 | 2.8 | 1.5 | 1.4 | 2.5 | 3.3 | 3.2 | 3.5 |
| Slovenia | 0.4 | 6.9 | 3.3 | -7.8 | 1.2 | 0.6 | -2.7 | -1.1 | 3.0 | 2.7 | 3.0 | 2.6 |
| Other Europe | 1.5 | 3.7 | 1.5 | -2.0 | 1.9 | 1.5 | 1.8 | 1.5 | 2.0 | 1.2 | 1.4 | 2.0 |
| Iceland | 1.4 | 9.5 | 1.5 | -4.7 | -3.6 | 2.0 | 1.2 | 3.9 | 1.8 | 5.0 | 4.0 | 3.7 |
| Norway | 1.1 | 2.9 | 0.4 | -1.6 | 0.6 | 1.0 | 2.7 | 1.0 | 2.2 | 1.4 | 1.2 | 2.2 |
| Switzerland | 1.7 | 4.1 | 2.3 | -2.1 | 3.0 | 1.8 | 1.1 | 1.8 | 1.9 | 0.9 | 1.4 | 1.8 |
| *Memorandum items* | | | | | | | | | | | | |
| North America | 1.2 | 1.8 | -0.2 | -2.8 | 2.6 | 1.7 | 2.2 | 1.5 | 2.4 | 2.3 | 2.5 | 2.8 |
| Western Europe | 0.5 | 3.1 | 0.6 | -4.3 | 2.1 | 1.7 | -0.3 | 0.3 | 1.4 | 1.8 | 2.0 | 2.2 |
| Asia and Oceania | 0.8 | 2.6 | -0.4 | -4.2 | 4.2 | 0.1 | 2.1 | 1.7 | 0.5 | 0.9 | 1.5 | 1.0 |
| Major developed economies | 0.8 | 2.1 | -0.2 | -3.8 | 2.9 | 1.5 | 1.4 | 1.2 | 1.6 | 1.8 | 2.1 | 2.2 |
| Euro area | 0.3 | 3.0 | 0.5 | -4.5 | 2.1 | 1.6 | -0.9 | -0.3 | 0.9 | 1.6 | 1.9 | 2.0 |

**Sources:** UN/DESA, based on data of the United Nations Statistics Division and individual national sources.

**Note:** Country groups are calculated as a weighted average of individual country growth rates of gross domestic product (GDP), where weights are based on GDP in 2010 prices and exchange rates.

a Average percentage change.

b Partly estimated.

c Baseline scenario forecasts, based in part on Project LINK and UN/DESA World Economic Forecasting Model.

Table A.2
**Economies in transition: rates of growth of real GDP, 2007–2017**

Annual percentage change

| | 2007–2014[a] | 2007 | 2008 | 2009 | 2010 | 2011 | 2012 | 2013 | 2014 | 2015[b] | 2016[c] | 2017[c] |
|---|---|---|---|---|---|---|---|---|---|---|---|---|
| **Economies in transition** | 2.8 | 8.8 | 5.3 | -6.6 | 4.8 | 4.5 | 3.3 | 2.1 | 0.9 | -2.8 | 0.8 | 1.9 |
| **South-Eastern Europe** | 1.8 | 6.2 | 5.8 | -2.0 | 1.5 | 1.7 | -0.6 | 2.4 | 0.2 | 2.1 | 2.6 | 3.0 |
| Albania | 3.5 | 5.9 | 7.5 | 3.4 | 3.7 | 2.5 | 1.6 | 1.4 | 2.1 | 3.0 | 3.2 | 3.8 |
| Bosnia and Herzegovina | 1.6 | 5.7 | 5.5 | -2.9 | 0.8 | 0.9 | -0.9 | 2.4 | 1.2 | 3.0 | 3.0 | 2.5 |
| Montenegro | 2.3 | 10.7 | 6.9 | -5.7 | 2.5 | 3.2 | -2.5 | 3.3 | 1.1 | 2.7 | 3.3 | 3.0 |
| Serbia | 1.2 | 5.9 | 5.4 | -3.1 | 0.6 | 1.4 | -1.0 | 2.6 | -1.8 | 1.0 | 1.9 | 3.0 |
| The former Yugoslav Republic of Macedonia | 2.9 | 6.5 | 5.5 | -0.4 | 3.4 | 2.3 | -0.5 | 2.7 | 3.8 | 3.2 | 3.6 | 2.5 |
| **Commonwealth of Independent States and Georgia[d]** | 2.8 | 8.9 | 5.3 | -6.8 | 4.9 | 4.7 | 3.4 | 2.0 | 0.9 | -3.0 | 0.7 | 1.8 |
| **Net fuel exporters** | 3.0 | 9.0 | 5.4 | -6.3 | 4.9 | 4.6 | 3.7 | 2.2 | 1.4 | -2.6 | 0.7 | 1.8 |
| Azerbaijan | 7.1 | 25.5 | 10.6 | 9.4 | 4.6 | -1.6 | 2.1 | 5.9 | 2.6 | 3.9 | 2.5 | 2.9 |
| Kazakhstan | 5.4 | 8.9 | 3.3 | 1.2 | 7.3 | 7.3 | 5.0 | 6.0 | 4.3 | 1.5 | 2.1 | 2.8 |
| Russian Federation | 2.4 | 8.5 | 5.2 | -7.8 | 4.5 | 4.3 | 3.4 | 1.3 | 0.6 | -3.8 | 0.0 | 1.2 |
| Turkmenistan | 10.9 | 11.1 | 14.7 | 6.1 | 9.2 | 14.7 | 11.1 | 10.2 | 10.3 | 9.0 | 10.5 | 9.9 |
| Uzbekistan | 8.5 | 9.5 | 9.4 | 8.1 | 8.5 | 8.3 | 8.2 | 8.0 | 8.1 | 8.0 | 7.0 | 6.9 |
| **Net fuel importers** | 1.4 | 8.6 | 4.4 | -10.4 | 5.0 | 5.5 | 1.3 | 1.2 | -2.8 | -6.1 | 0.7 | 2.4 |
| Armenia | 3.1 | 13.7 | 6.9 | -14.2 | 2.2 | 4.7 | 7.2 | 3.5 | 3.4 | 3.8 | 2.5 | 3.0 |
| Belarus | 4.5 | 8.6 | 10.2 | 0.2 | 7.7 | 5.5 | 1.7 | 1.0 | 1.6 | -3.8 | 0.0 | 2.0 |
| Georgia | 4.8 | 12.6 | 2.6 | -3.7 | 6.2 | 7.2 | 6.4 | 3.3 | 4.8 | 2.5 | 2.5 | 2.7 |
| Kyrgyzstan | 4.9 | 8.5 | 8.4 | 2.9 | -0.5 | 6.0 | -0.1 | 10.5 | 3.6 | 6.0 | 4.8 | 5.0 |
| Republic of Moldova | 3.9 | 3.0 | 7.8 | -6.0 | 7.1 | 6.8 | -0.7 | 9.4 | 4.4 | 2.8 | 2.8 | 3.0 |
| Tajikistan | 6.2 | 7.6 | 7.6 | 4.0 | 6.5 | 2.4 | 7.5 | 7.4 | 6.7 | 6.0 | 5.0 | 6.0 |
| Ukraine | -0.5 | 8.2 | 2.2 | -15.1 | 4.1 | 5.4 | 0.2 | 0.0 | -6.8 | -10.5 | 0.0 | 2.1 |

Sources:  UN/DESA, based on data of the United Nations Statistics Division and individual national sources.
Note:  Country groups are calculated as a weighted average of individual country growth rates of gross domestic product (GDP), where weights are based on GDP in 2010 prices and exchange rates.
**a** Average percentage change.
**b** Partly estimated.
**c** Baseline scenario forecasts, based in part on Project LINK and the UN/DESA World Economic Forecasting Model.
**d** Georgia officially left the Commonwealth of Independent States on 18 August 2009. However, its performance is discussed in the context of this group of countries for reasons of geographic proximity and similarities in economic structure.

Table A.3
**Developing economies: rates of growth of real GDP, 2007–2017**

Annual percentage change

| | 2007–2014[a] | 2007 | 2008 | 2009 | 2010 | 2011 | 2012 | 2013 | 2014 | 2015[b] | 2016[c] | 2017[c] |
|---|---|---|---|---|---|---|---|---|---|---|---|---|
| Developing countries[d] | 5.4 | 8.0 | 5.5 | 2.9 | 7.6 | 6.0 | 4.7 | 4.6 | 4.4 | 3.7 | 4.3 | 4.8 |
| Africa | 4.2 | 6.1 | 5.8 | 3.2 | 5.2 | 1.0 | 5.5 | 3.3 | 3.4 | 3.7 | 4.4 | 4.4 |
| North Africa | 2.8 | 5.4 | 6.5 | 3.5 | 4.5 | -5.7 | 7.3 | 1.1 | 0.7 | 3.5 | 4.1 | 4.1 |
| East Africa | 6.7 | 7.5 | 6.2 | 4.4 | 8.0 | 7.6 | 5.8 | 6.9 | 7.0 | 6.2 | 6.8 | 6.6 |
| Central Africa | 5.0 | 7.3 | 4.6 | 6.1 | 5.1 | 4.4 | 6.1 | 0.9 | 5.7 | 3.4 | 4.3 | 4.2 |
| West Africa | 5.9 | 5.8 | 6.3 | 6.0 | 7.2 | 4.9 | 5.0 | 5.7 | 6.1 | 4.4 | 5.2 | 5.3 |
| Southern Africa | 3.4 | 6.6 | 4.5 | 0.0 | 3.7 | 3.4 | 3.7 | 3.1 | 2.5 | 2.5 | 3.0 | 3.3 |
| Net fuel exporters | 4.3 | 6.6 | 6.8 | 4.6 | 5.7 | -1.9 | 6.8 | 2.7 | 3.4 | 3.9 | 4.6 | 4.6 |
| Net fuel importers | 4.0 | 5.4 | 4.5 | 1.5 | 4.7 | 4.7 | 4.0 | 4.1 | 3.4 | 3.5 | 4.1 | 4.3 |
| East and South Asia | 7.1 | 10.2 | 6.5 | 5.8 | 9.1 | 7.2 | 5.8 | 6.1 | 6.2 | 5.7 | 5.8 | 5.8 |
| East Asia | 7.4 | 10.7 | 7.0 | 5.8 | 9.4 | 7.4 | 6.3 | 6.4 | 6.1 | 5.6 | 5.6 | 5.6 |
| South Asia | 6.1 | 8.6 | 4.5 | 5.8 | 8.2 | 6.5 | 3.8 | 4.9 | 6.4 | 6.0 | 6.7 | 7.0 |
| Net fuel exporters | 4.6 | 7.0 | 4.7 | 3.8 | 6.0 | 5.6 | 2.5 | 2.9 | 4.5 | 3.9 | 5.4 | 5.7 |
| Net fuel importers | 7.4 | 10.7 | 6.7 | 6.1 | 9.5 | 7.4 | 6.2 | 6.4 | 6.4 | 5.9 | 5.9 | 5.8 |
| Western Asia | 3.3 | 4.5 | 4.1 | -1.0 | 5.8 | 6.4 | 2.5 | 2.0 | 2.6 | 2.0 | 2.4 | 3.0 |
| Net fuel exporters | 4.3 | 3.8 | 6.0 | -0.9 | 4.5 | 8.0 | 6.7 | 3.7 | 2.6 | 2.4 | 2.5 | 3.4 |
| Net fuel importers | 2.3 | 5.3 | 2.1 | -1.1 | 7.2 | 4.8 | -2.0 | 0.0 | 2.6 | 1.6 | 2.2 | 2.7 |
| Latin America and the Caribbean | 3.2 | 5.8 | 4.0 | -1.3 | 5.9 | 4.7 | 3.0 | 2.8 | 1.0 | -0.5 | 0.7 | 2.7 |
| South America | 3.6 | 6.6 | 4.8 | -0.3 | 6.4 | 5.0 | 2.7 | 3.1 | 0.5 | -1.6 | -0.1 | 2.4 |
| Mexico and Central America | 2.3 | 3.7 | 1.7 | -4.3 | 5.0 | 4.1 | 4.1 | 1.7 | 2.5 | 2.5 | 2.9 | 3.4 |
| Caribbean | 2.9 | 6.3 | 3.0 | -0.1 | 3.2 | 2.4 | 2.3 | 3.1 | 3.3 | 3.4 | 3.6 | 3.3 |
| Net fuel exporters | 3.2 | 7.3 | 4.7 | -1.1 | 1.0 | 5.3 | 4.9 | 3.1 | 0.3 | -2.3 | -1.2 | 2.3 |
| Net fuel importers | 3.2 | 5.6 | 3.8 | -1.3 | 6.9 | 4.6 | 2.7 | 2.7 | 1.2 | -0.2 | 1.1 | 2.7 |
| *Memorandum items:* | | | | | | | | | | | | |
| Least developed countries | 5.9 | 8.3 | 7.4 | 5.5 | 6.1 | 3.7 | 5.3 | 5.1 | 5.6 | 4.5 | 5.6 | 5.6 |
| Africa (excluding Libya) | 4.5 | 6.1 | 5.4 | 3.4 | 5.3 | 3.8 | 3.8 | 4.0 | 4.1 | 3.7 | 4.3 | 4.4 |
| North Africa (excluding Libya) | 3.6 | 5.0 | 5.1 | 3.5 | 4.2 | 2.5 | 2.9 | 2.8 | 2.7 | 3.7 | 4.0 | 4.0 |
| East Asia (excluding China) | 4.3 | 6.2 | 3.3 | 0.9 | 7.7 | 4.4 | 4.1 | 4.0 | 3.9 | 3.4 | 4.1 | 4.3 |
| South Asia (excluding India) | 3.5 | 6.6 | 3.2 | 2.7 | 5.0 | 4.6 | 0.2 | 1.4 | 4.5 | 3.3 | 5.3 | 5.6 |
| Western Asia (excluding Israel and Turkey) | 3.2 | 4.2 | 5.8 | 0.4 | 4.4 | 5.5 | 2.6 | 0.7 | 2.4 | 1.6 | 2.1 | 2.9 |
| Arab States[e] | 3.1 | 4.5 | 6.0 | 1.3 | 4.4 | 2.3 | 3.9 | 0.8 | 2.0 | 2.1 | 2.7 | 3.2 |
| Landlocked developing economies | 6.4 | 9.5 | 6.6 | 3.9 | 7.5 | 6.0 | 5.3 | 6.6 | 5.5 | 4.3 | 4.5 | 4.8 |
| Small island developing economies | 4.1 | 7.6 | 2.8 | -0.1 | 8.8 | 4.4 | 2.8 | 3.5 | 3.1 | 2.8 | 3.1 | 3.4 |
| Major developing economies | | | | | | | | | | | | |
| Argentina | 4.1 | 8.0 | 3.1 | 0.1 | 9.5 | 8.4 | 0.8 | 2.9 | 0.5 | 1.0 | 1.6 | 2.0 |
| Brazil | 3.3 | 6.0 | 5.0 | -0.2 | 7.6 | 3.9 | 1.8 | 2.7 | 0.1 | -2.8 | -0.8 | 2.3 |
| Chile | 3.8 | 5.2 | 3.3 | -1.0 | 5.8 | 5.8 | 5.5 | 4.2 | 1.9 | 2.0 | 2.4 | 3.0 |
| China | 9.4 | 14.2 | 9.6 | 9.2 | 10.6 | 9.5 | 7.7 | 7.7 | 7.3 | 6.8 | 6.4 | 6.2 |
| Colombia | 4.5 | 6.9 | 3.5 | 1.7 | 4.0 | 6.6 | 4.0 | 4.9 | 4.6 | 2.7 | 3.0 | 4.0 |
| Egypt | 4.0 | 7.1 | 7.2 | 4.7 | 5.1 | 1.9 | 2.2 | 2.1 | 2.2 | 4.2 | 4.4 | 4.2 |
| Hong Kong SAR[f] | 3.1 | 6.5 | 2.1 | -2.5 | 6.8 | 4.8 | 1.7 | 3.1 | 2.5 | 2.3 | 2.7 | 2.9 |
| India | 7.3 | 9.7 | 5.3 | 7.4 | 9.8 | 7.5 | 5.5 | 6.5 | 7.2 | 7.2 | 7.3 | 7.5 |
| Indonesia | 5.8 | 6.3 | 6.0 | 4.6 | 6.2 | 6.2 | 6.0 | 5.6 | 5.0 | 5.1 | 5.4 | 5.6 |

Table A.3
**Developing economies: rates of growth of real GDP, 2007–2017** (*continued*)

Annual percentage change

| | 2007–2014[a] | 2007 | 2008 | 2009 | 2010 | 2011 | 2012 | 2013 | 2014 | 2015[b] | 2016[c] | 2017[c] |
|---|---|---|---|---|---|---|---|---|---|---|---|---|
| Iran (Islamic Republic of) | 2.2 | 8.4 | 2.6 | 2.0 | 5.7 | 4.3 | -4.4 | -3.0 | 3.0 | 0.5 | 4.8 | 5.4 |
| Israel | 3.7 | 6.1 | 3.1 | 1.3 | 5.5 | 5.0 | 2.9 | 3.3 | 2.6 | 2.3 | 2.8 | 3.2 |
| Republic of Korea | 3.4 | 5.5 | 2.8 | 0.7 | 6.5 | 3.7 | 2.3 | 2.9 | 3.3 | 2.6 | 3.0 | 3.1 |
| Malaysia | 4.8 | 6.3 | 4.8 | -1.5 | 7.4 | 5.3 | 5.5 | 4.7 | 6.0 | 4.5 | 5.3 | 5.1 |
| Mexico | 2.0 | 3.2 | 1.4 | -4.7 | 5.2 | 3.9 | 4.0 | 1.4 | 2.2 | 2.3 | 2.7 | 3.3 |
| Nigeria | 6.0 | 6.5 | 6.3 | 6.9 | 7.8 | 4.9 | 4.3 | 5.4 | 6.3 | 4.3 | 5.1 | 5.3 |
| Pakistan | 3.4 | 3.2 | 2.3 | 2.2 | 2.2 | 3.1 | 4.0 | 4.9 | 5.4 | 5.1 | 5.0 | 5.0 |
| Peru | 5.9 | 8.5 | 9.1 | 1.0 | 8.5 | 6.5 | 6.0 | 5.8 | 2.4 | 2.5 | 3.5 | 4.0 |
| Philippines | 5.4 | 6.6 | 4.2 | 1.1 | 7.6 | 3.7 | 6.8 | 7.2 | 6.1 | 5.8 | 6.4 | 5.5 |
| Saudi Arabia | 4.0 | 1.8 | 6.3 | -2.1 | 4.8 | 10.0 | 5.4 | 2.7 | 3.5 | 3.4 | 2.0 | 3.1 |
| Singapore | 5.2 | 9.1 | 1.8 | -0.6 | 15.2 | 6.2 | 3.4 | 4.4 | 2.9 | 2.3 | 2.9 | 3.5 |
| South Africa | 2.4 | 5.4 | 3.2 | -1.5 | 3.0 | 3.2 | 2.2 | 2.2 | 1.5 | 1.8 | 2.2 | 2.6 |
| Taiwan Province of China | 3.5 | 6.5 | 0.7 | -1.6 | 10.6 | 3.8 | 2.1 | 2.2 | 3.9 | 1.0 | 2.4 | 3.5 |
| Thailand | 3.2 | 5.4 | 1.7 | -0.7 | 7.5 | 0.8 | 7.3 | 2.8 | 0.9 | 2.5 | 3.7 | 3.9 |
| Turkey | 3.4 | 4.7 | 0.7 | -4.8 | 9.2 | 8.8 | 2.1 | 4.2 | 2.9 | 2.8 | 2.8 | 3.4 |
| Venezuela (Bolivarian Republic of) | 2.0 | 8.8 | 5.3 | -3.2 | -1.5 | 4.2 | 5.6 | 1.3 | -4.0 | -7.5 | -6.0 | 0.5 |

Sources: UN/DESA, based on data of the United Nations Statistics Division and individual national sources.

Note: Country groups are calculated as a weighted average of individual country growth rates of gross domestic product (GDP), where weights are based on GDP in 2010 prices and exchange rates.

a  Average percentage change.

b  Partly estimated.

c  Baseline scenario forecasts, based in part on Project LINK and the UN/DESA World Economic Forecasting Model.

d  Covering countries that account for 98 per cent of the population of all developing countries.

e  Currently includes data for Algeria, Bahrain, Comoros, Djibouti, Egypt, Iraq, Jordan, Kuwait, Lebanon, Libya, Mauritania, Morocco, Oman, Qatar, Saudi Arabia, Somalia, Sudan, Syrian Arab Republic, Tunisia, United Arab Emirates and Yemen.

f  Special Administrative Region of China.

Table A.4
**Developed economies: consumer price inflation, 2007–2017**

Annual percentage change[a]

| | 2007 | 2008 | 2009 | 2010 | 2011 | 2012 | 2013 | 2014 | 2015[b] | 2016[c] | 2017[c] |
|---|---|---|---|---|---|---|---|---|---|---|---|
| Developed economies | 2.1 | 3.3 | 0.1 | 1.5 | 2.6 | 1.9 | 1.3 | 1.2 | 0.3 | 1.2 | 1.9 |
| United States | 2.9 | 3.8 | -0.4 | 1.6 | 3.2 | 2.1 | 1.5 | 1.3 | 0.2 | 1.6 | 2.3 |
| Canada | 2.1 | 2.4 | 0.3 | 1.8 | 2.9 | 1.5 | 0.9 | 1.9 | 1.2 | 1.7 | 2.0 |
| Japan | 0.1 | 1.4 | -1.3 | -0.7 | -0.3 | 0.0 | 0.4 | 2.7 | 0.7 | 0.5 | 1.1 |
| Australia | 2.3 | 4.4 | 1.8 | 2.9 | 3.3 | 1.8 | 2.5 | 2.5 | 1.7 | 1.8 | 1.9 |
| New Zealand | 2.4 | 4.0 | 2.1 | 2.3 | 4.0 | 1.1 | 1.1 | 1.2 | 0.7 | 1.3 | 1.9 |
| European Union | 2.3 | 3.5 | 0.8 | 1.9 | 3.0 | 2.6 | 1.5 | 0.6 | 0.1 | 1.0 | 1.7 |
| EU-15 | 2.1 | 3.3 | 0.6 | 1.9 | 2.9 | 2.5 | 1.5 | 0.6 | 0.2 | 1.0 | 1.7 |
| Austria | 2.2 | 3.2 | 0.4 | 1.7 | 3.6 | 2.6 | 2.1 | 1.5 | 0.8 | 1.4 | 2.0 |
| Belgium | 1.8 | 4.5 | 0.0 | 2.3 | 3.4 | 2.6 | 1.2 | 0.5 | 0.2 | 1.2 | 1.9 |
| Denmark | 1.7 | 3.6 | 1.1 | 2.2 | 2.7 | 2.4 | 0.5 | 0.3 | 0.4 | 1.4 | 1.9 |
| Finland | 1.6 | 3.9 | 1.6 | 1.7 | 3.3 | 3.2 | 2.2 | 1.2 | -0.1 | 0.7 | 1.5 |
| France | 1.6 | 3.2 | 0.1 | 1.7 | 2.3 | 2.2 | 1.0 | 0.6 | 0.1 | 0.6 | 1.5 |
| Germany | 2.3 | 2.8 | 0.2 | 1.2 | 2.5 | 2.1 | 1.6 | 0.8 | 0.4 | 1.1 | 1.8 |
| Greece | 3.0 | 4.2 | 1.3 | 4.7 | 3.1 | 1.0 | -0.9 | -1.4 | -0.8 | 0.2 | 0.8 |
| Ireland | 2.9 | 3.1 | -1.7 | -1.6 | 1.2 | 1.9 | 0.5 | 0.3 | 0.1 | 1.0 | 1.5 |
| Italy | 2.0 | 3.5 | 0.8 | 1.6 | 2.9 | 3.3 | 1.3 | 0.2 | 0.1 | 0.9 | 1.6 |
| Luxembourg | 2.3 | 3.4 | 0.4 | 2.3 | 3.4 | 2.7 | 1.7 | 0.6 | 0.2 | 0.8 | 1.4 |
| Netherlands | 1.6 | 2.2 | 1.0 | 0.9 | 2.5 | 2.8 | 2.6 | 0.3 | 0.5 | 1.1 | 1.7 |
| Portugal | 2.4 | 2.7 | -0.9 | 1.4 | 3.6 | 2.8 | 0.4 | -0.2 | 0.6 | 1.9 | 2.5 |
| Spain | 2.8 | 4.1 | -0.2 | 2.0 | 3.1 | 2.4 | 1.5 | -0.2 | -0.3 | 1.0 | 1.8 |
| Sweden | 1.7 | 3.4 | 1.9 | 1.9 | 1.4 | 0.9 | 0.5 | 0.2 | 0.1 | 1.0 | 1.5 |
| United Kingdom | 2.3 | 3.6 | 2.2 | 3.3 | 4.5 | 2.8 | 2.6 | 1.5 | 0.0 | 1.0 | 1.8 |
| New EU member States | 3.9 | 6.0 | 3.1 | 2.7 | 3.8 | 3.7 | 1.5 | 0.2 | -0.2 | 1.1 | 2.1 |
| Bulgaria | 8.4 | 12.3 | 2.8 | 2.4 | 4.2 | 3.0 | 0.9 | -1.4 | 0.0 | 1.5 | 2.8 |
| Croatia | 2.9 | 6.1 | 2.4 | 1.0 | 2.3 | 3.4 | 2.2 | -0.3 | -0.2 | 1.1 | 2.3 |
| Cyprus | 2.4 | 4.7 | 0.4 | 2.4 | 3.3 | 2.4 | -0.4 | -1.4 | -2.2 | 0.3 | 2.4 |
| Czech Republic | 3.0 | 6.3 | 0.6 | 1.2 | 2.1 | 3.5 | 1.4 | 0.4 | 0.6 | 1.5 | 2.0 |
| Estonia | 6.7 | 10.6 | 0.2 | 2.7 | 5.1 | 4.2 | 3.3 | 0.5 | 0.0 | 1.8 | 2.5 |
| Hungary | 7.9 | 6.0 | 4.0 | 4.7 | 3.9 | 5.7 | 1.7 | 0.0 | 0.0 | 1.5 | 2.9 |
| Latvia | 10.1 | 15.4 | 3.5 | -1.1 | 4.4 | 2.3 | 0.0 | 0.6 | 0.4 | 1.9 | 2.1 |
| Lithuania | 5.7 | 10.9 | 4.4 | 1.3 | 4.1 | 3.1 | 1.0 | 0.1 | -1.2 | 1.3 | 2.0 |
| Malta | 1.3 | 4.3 | 2.1 | 1.5 | 2.7 | 2.4 | 1.4 | 0.3 | 1.2 | 1.4 | 1.7 |
| Poland | 2.6 | 4.2 | 4.0 | 2.7 | 3.9 | 3.7 | 0.8 | 0.1 | -0.5 | 1.2 | 2.0 |
| Romania | 4.8 | 7.8 | 5.6 | 6.1 | 5.8 | 3.3 | 4.0 | 1.1 | -0.5 | -0.2 | 1.5 |
| Slovakia | 1.9 | 3.9 | 0.9 | 0.7 | 4.1 | 3.7 | 1.5 | -0.1 | -0.2 | 0.9 | 1.9 |
| Slovenia | 3.8 | 5.5 | 0.9 | 2.1 | 2.1 | 2.8 | 1.9 | 0.4 | -0.2 | 1.0 | 1.4 |
| Other Europe | 0.8 | 2.9 | 0.7 | 1.4 | 0.6 | -0.2 | 0.9 | 0.8 | 0.3 | 1.0 | 1.6 |
| Iceland | 5.0 | 12.7 | 12.0 | 5.4 | 4.0 | 5.2 | 3.9 | 2.1 | 0.0 | 1.5 | 1.6 |
| Norway | 0.7 | 3.4 | 2.3 | 2.3 | 1.3 | 0.4 | 2.0 | 1.9 | 2.0 | 2.0 | 2.0 |
| Switzerland | 0.8 | 2.3 | -0.7 | 0.6 | 0.1 | -0.7 | 0.1 | 0.0 | -1.0 | 0.2 | 1.3 |
| *Memorandum items* | | | | | | | | | | | |
| North America | 2.8 | 3.7 | -0.3 | 1.7 | 3.1 | 2.0 | 1.4 | 1.4 | 0.3 | 1.6 | 2.3 |
| Western Europe | 2.2 | 3.5 | 0.8 | 1.9 | 2.8 | 2.4 | 1.5 | 0.6 | 0.1 | 1.0 | 1.7 |
| Asia and Oceania | 0.5 | 2.0 | -0.7 | 0.0 | 0.5 | 0.3 | 0.8 | 2.7 | 0.9 | 0.8 | 1.3 |
| Major developed economies | 2.1 | 3.1 | -0.1 | 1.3 | 2.5 | 1.8 | 1.3 | 1.4 | 0.3 | 1.2 | 1.9 |
| Euro area | 2.1 | 3.3 | 0.3 | 1.6 | 2.7 | 2.5 | 1.4 | 0.4 | 0.2 | 0.9 | 1.7 |

**Sources:** UN/DESA, based on OECD, Main Economic Indicators; Eurostat; and individual national sources.

a Data for country groups are weighted averages, where weights for each year are based on 2010 GDP in United States dollars.

b Partly estimated.

c Baseline scenario forecasts, based in part on Project LINK and the UN/DESA World Economic Forecasting Model.

Table A.5
**Economies in transition: consumer price inflation, 2007–2017**

Annual percentage change[a]

| | 2007 | 2008 | 2009 | 2010 | 2011 | 2012 | 2013 | 2014 | 2015[b] | 2016[c] | 2017[c] |
|---|---|---|---|---|---|---|---|---|---|---|---|
| **Economies in Transition** | 9.4 | 15.0 | 10.9 | 6.9 | 9.6 | 6.2 | 6.4 | 7.8 | 16.1 | 10.5 | 7.1 |
| **South-Eastern Europe** | 4.3 | 9.4 | 4.3 | 4.1 | 7.2 | 4.8 | 4.4 | 1.0 | 1.1 | 2.2 | 2.5 |
| Albania | 2.9 | 3.4 | 2.3 | 3.6 | 3.5 | 2.0 | 1.9 | 1.6 | 2.0 | 2.5 | 2.5 |
| Bosnia and Herzegovina | 1.5 | 7.4 | -0.4 | 2.2 | 3.7 | 2.1 | -0.1 | -0.9 | -0.8 | 1.5 | 1.5 |
| Montenegro | 3.4 | 9.0 | 3.6 | 0.7 | 3.1 | 3.6 | 2.2 | -0.7 | 1.0 | 1.5 | 2.4 |
| Serbia | 6.4 | 12.4 | 8.1 | 6.1 | 11.1 | 7.3 | 7.7 | 2.1 | 2.0 | 2.7 | 3.0 |
| The former Yugoslav Republic of Macedonia | 2.3 | 8.3 | -0.7 | 1.5 | 3.9 | 3.3 | 2.8 | -0.3 | 0.0 | 1.2 | 2.0 |
| **Commonwealth of Independent States and Georgia[d]** | 9.6 | 15.2 | 11.2 | 7.1 | 9.7 | 6.2 | 6.4 | 8.1 | 16.7 | 10.8 | 7.3 |
| **Net fuel exporters** | 9.5 | 14.5 | 10.9 | 6.9 | 8.4 | 5.1 | 6.7 | 7.5 | 14.5 | 9.9 | 6.8 |
| Azerbaijan | 16.6 | 20.8 | 1.6 | 5.7 | 7.9 | 1.0 | 2.4 | 1.4 | 5.0 | 3.5 | 3.5 |
| Kazakhstan | 10.8 | 17.2 | 7.3 | 7.1 | 8.3 | 5.1 | 5.8 | 6.7 | 5.8 | 6.5 | 4.5 |
| Russian Federation | 9.1 | 14.0 | 11.7 | 6.8 | 8.4 | 5.1 | 6.8 | 7.8 | 15.9 | 10.5 | 7.1 |
| Turkmenistan | 6.3 | 14.5 | -2.7 | 4.5 | 5.3 | 5.3 | 6.8 | 6.0 | 6.0 | 6.3 | 5.9 |
| Uzbekistan | 12.3 | 12.7 | 14.1 | 9.4 | 12.8 | 12.1 | 11.2 | 8.4 | 11.0 | 9.9 | 8.0 |
| **Net fuel importers** | 11.2 | 20.8 | 13.1 | 8.7 | 19.2 | 15.0 | 4.8 | 12.4 | 33.9 | 17.6 | 11.1 |
| Armenia | 4.4 | 9.0 | 3.4 | 8.2 | 7.7 | 2.6 | 5.8 | 3.0 | 5.4 | 4.8 | 2.9 |
| Belarus | 8.4 | 14.8 | 13.0 | 7.7 | 53.2 | 59.2 | 18.3 | 18.1 | 16.0 | 14.0 | 11.0 |
| Georgia | 9.2 | 10.0 | 1.7 | 7.1 | 8.5 | -0.9 | -0.5 | 3.1 | 5.8 | 5.1 | 3.0 |
| Kyrgyzstan | 10.2 | 24.5 | 6.9 | 8.0 | 16.5 | 2.7 | 6.6 | 7.5 | 6.5 | 6.0 | 4.5 |
| Republic of Moldova | 12.1 | 12.9 | -0.1 | 7.4 | 7.6 | 4.6 | 4.6 | 5.1 | 8.6 | 8.0 | 4.8 |
| Tajikistan | 13.2 | 20.4 | 6.4 | 6.5 | 12.4 | 5.8 | 5.0 | 6.1 | 6.5 | 6.5 | 5.1 |
| Ukraine | 12.8 | 25.2 | 15.9 | 9.4 | 8.0 | 0.6 | -0.3 | 12.2 | 48.6 | 22.2 | 13.2 |

**Source:** UN/DESA, based on data of the Economic Commission for Europe.

a  Data for country groups are weighted averages, where weights for each year are based on 2010 GDP in United States dollars.

b  Partly estimated.

c  Baseline scenario forecasts, based in part on Project LINK and the UN/DESA World Economic Forecasting Model.

d  Georgia officially left the Commonwealth of Independent States on 18 August 2009. However, its performance is discussed in the context of this group of countries for reasons of geographic proximity and similarities in economic structure.

Table A.6
**Developing economies: consumer price inflation, 2007–2017**

Annual percentage change[a]

| | 2007 | 2008 | 2009 | 2010 | 2011 | 2012 | 2013 | 2014 | 2015[b] | 2016[c] | 2017[c] |
|---|---|---|---|---|---|---|---|---|---|---|---|
| Developing countries by region | 5.7 | 8.4 | 4.1 | 5.6 | 6.6 | 5.8 | 6.9 | 6.7 | 7.7 | 8.3 | 6.0 |
| Africa | 6.5 | 11.6 | 8.3 | 7.6 | 8.7 | 9.1 | 7.2 | 7.0 | 7.5 | 6.7 | 6.3 |
| North Africa | 6.0 | 10.7 | 7.0 | 6.8 | 8.3 | 9.3 | 8.3 | 8.5 | 8.3 | 6.9 | 5.8 |
| East Africa | 11.2 | 21.9 | 9.4 | 6.0 | 17.3 | 13.3 | 5.9 | 5.3 | 5.9 | 6.0 | 5.7 |
| Central Africa | 1.2 | 6.6 | 4.4 | 2.8 | 2.3 | 5.0 | 3.0 | 2.5 | 2.8 | 3.1 | 3.0 |
| West Africa | 5.5 | 11.4 | 10.4 | 11.6 | 9.7 | 10.6 | 7.7 | 7.5 | 8.6 | 8.4 | 8.3 |
| Southern Africa | 7.4 | 10.6 | 8.4 | 6.1 | 6.6 | 6.7 | 6.5 | 5.9 | 6.6 | 5.7 | 5.6 |
| Net fuel exporters | 6.3 | 11.6 | 9.5 | 10.0 | 10.0 | 10.8 | 8.6 | 8.6 | 9.2 | 8.0 | 7.2 |
| Net fuel importers | 6.7 | 11.5 | 6.9 | 4.5 | 7.0 | 6.8 | 5.5 | 5.0 | 5.3 | 5.1 | 5.1 |
| East and South Asia | 5.2 | 7.5 | 2.5 | 5.0 | 6.3 | 4.6 | 5.3 | 3.5 | 2.5 | 3.1 | 3.3 |
| East Asia | 4.3 | 6.2 | 0.3 | 3.3 | 5.1 | 2.7 | 2.8 | 2.3 | 1.6 | 2.2 | 2.6 |
| South Asia | 8.6 | 12.5 | 11.1 | 11.5 | 11.1 | 12.2 | 15.1 | 8.2 | 6.2 | 6.5 | 6.3 |
| Net fuel exporters | 10.1 | 16.3 | 7.6 | 7.1 | 11.6 | 12.2 | 17.1 | 9.7 | 8.3 | 7.1 | 6.7 |
| Net fuel importers | 4.6 | 6.5 | 1.9 | 4.7 | 5.7 | 3.8 | 3.9 | 2.8 | 1.8 | 2.6 | 3.0 |
| Western Asia | 7.9 | 10.5 | 3.5 | 4.8 | 4.9 | 7.8 | 12.0 | 11.7 | 7.8 | 7.5 | 6.2 |
| Net fuel exporters | 9.7 | 10.4 | 2.4 | 3.2 | 4.4 | 2.9 | 2.8 | 2.8 | 3.0 | 2.9 | 3.3 |
| Net fuel importers | 6.1 | 10.5 | 4.8 | 6.5 | 5.5 | 12.9 | 21.5 | 20.9 | 12.6 | 12.2 | 9.2 |
| Latin America and the Caribbean | 5.6 | 8.4 | 6.5 | 6.7 | 7.3 | 6.5 | 8.1 | 11.7 | 20.1 | 21.4 | 12.2 |
| South America | 6.0 | 9.0 | 6.9 | 7.5 | 8.5 | 7.2 | 9.6 | 14.3 | 26.1 | 27.5 | 15.1 |
| Mexico and Central America | 4.3 | 5.9 | 5.1 | 4.1 | 3.7 | 4.1 | 3.8 | 4.0 | 2.6 | 3.8 | 3.9 |
| Caribbean | 7.1 | 12.6 | 3.8 | 7.9 | 7.6 | 5.5 | 5.4 | 4.3 | 3.1 | 4.1 | 4.2 |
| Net fuel exporters | 12.0 | 19.1 | 15.7 | 15.5 | 15.0 | 12.4 | 21.5 | 35.6 | 89.6 | 99.2 | 46.8 |
| Net fuel importers | 4.5 | 6.4 | 4.7 | 5.1 | 5.9 | 5.4 | 5.7 | 7.3 | 7.4 | 7.2 | 5.9 |
| *Memorandum items* | | | | | | | | | | | |
| Least developed countries | 10.7 | 14.2 | 7.7 | 8.9 | 12.1 | 11.7 | 9.9 | 9.5 | 9.1 | 7.6 | 7.1 |
| East Asia (excluding China) | 3.6 | 6.6 | 2.1 | 3.3 | 4.5 | 3.0 | 2.9 | 2.8 | 1.9 | 2.6 | 3.1 |
| South Asia (excluding India) | 13.3 | 21.1 | 11.6 | 10.5 | 15.8 | 18.1 | 23.9 | 12.1 | 8.8 | 8.5 | 8.0 |
| Western Asia (excluding Israel and Turkey) | 8.6 | 11.3 | 2.4 | 3.5 | 4.4 | 8.2 | 15.6 | 14.6 | 9.1 | 8.6 | 7.3 |
| Arab States[d] | 7.8 | 11.1 | 3.7 | 4.4 | 5.6 | 8.5 | 13.4 | 12.8 | 8.9 | 8.1 | 6.9 |
| Landlocked developing economies | 9.7 | 16.5 | 6.5 | 6.1 | 9.8 | 7.1 | 5.9 | 5.9 | 5.9 | 6.0 | 5.1 |
| Small island developing economies | 3.5 | 7.8 | 1.7 | 4.0 | 5.3 | 4.5 | 3.1 | 1.9 | 0.7 | 2.1 | 2.8 |
| Major developing economies | | | | | | | | | | | |
| Argentina | 8.9 | 8.5 | 6.2 | 10.5 | 9.8 | 10.0 | 10.6 | 23.9 | 16.5 | 21.6 | 18.0 |
| Brazil | 3.6 | 5.7 | 4.8 | 5.0 | 6.6 | 5.4 | 6.2 | 6.3 | 8.8 | 6.6 | 4.9 |
| Chile | 4.4 | 8.7 | 0.4 | 1.4 | 3.3 | 3.0 | 1.8 | 4.4 | 4.4 | 4.4 | 3.2 |
| China | 4.8 | 6.0 | -0.7 | 3.3 | 5.5 | 2.6 | 2.7 | 2.0 | 1.4 | 2.0 | 2.3 |
| Colombia | 5.5 | 7.0 | 4.2 | 2.3 | 3.4 | 3.2 | 2.0 | 2.9 | 4.3 | 3.9 | 3.7 |
| Egypt | 9.3 | 18.3 | 11.8 | 11.3 | 10.1 | 7.1 | 9.4 | 10.1 | 11.0 | 8.9 | 7.0 |
| Hong Kong SAR[e] | 2.0 | 4.3 | 0.6 | 2.3 | 5.3 | 4.1 | 4.4 | 4.4 | 3.0 | 3.2 | 3.0 |
| India | 6.4 | 8.4 | 10.9 | 12.0 | 8.9 | 9.3 | 10.9 | 6.3 | 4.9 | 5.6 | 5.4 |
| Indonesia | 6.4 | 10.2 | 4.4 | 5.2 | 5.4 | 4.3 | 6.4 | 6.4 | 6.7 | 5.0 | 4.8 |
| Iran (Islamic Republic of) | 17.2 | 25.6 | 13.5 | 10.1 | 20.6 | 27.4 | 39.3 | 17.2 | 13.4 | 11.8 | 10.5 |

Table A.6
**Developing economies: consumer price inflation, 2007–2017** (*continued*)

Annual percentage change[a]

| | 2007 | 2008 | 2009 | 2010 | 2011 | 2012 | 2013 | 2014 | 2015[b] | 2016[c] | 2017[c] |
|---|---|---|---|---|---|---|---|---|---|---|---|
| Israel | 0.5 | 4.6 | 3.3 | 2.7 | 3.5 | 1.7 | 1.6 | 0.5 | -0.5 | 0.8 | 1.4 |
| Republic of Korea | 2.5 | 4.7 | 2.8 | 2.9 | 4.0 | 2.2 | 1.3 | 1.3 | 0.7 | 1.8 | 2.3 |
| Malaysia | 2.0 | 5.4 | 0.6 | 1.7 | 3.2 | 1.7 | 2.1 | 3.1 | 2.2 | 3.4 | 2.7 |
| Mexico | 4.0 | 5.1 | 5.3 | 4.2 | 3.4 | 4.1 | 3.8 | 4.0 | 2.7 | 3.8 | 3.9 |
| Nigeria | 5.4 | 11.6 | 11.5 | 13.7 | 10.8 | 12.2 | 8.5 | 8.1 | 9.6 | 9.3 | 9.2 |
| Pakistan | 7.6 | 20.3 | 13.6 | 13.9 | 11.9 | 9.7 | 7.7 | 7.2 | 2.9 | 4.5 | 5.3 |
| Peru | 1.8 | 5.8 | 2.9 | 1.5 | 3.4 | 3.7 | 2.8 | 3.2 | 3.6 | 3.5 | 3.1 |
| Philippines | 2.9 | 8.3 | 4.2 | 3.8 | 4.6 | 3.2 | 3.0 | 4.1 | 1.8 | 2.8 | 3.5 |
| Saudi Arabia | 4.1 | 10.0 | 5.0 | 5.4 | 5.8 | 2.9 | 3.5 | 2.7 | 2.2 | 2.8 | 3.5 |
| Singapore | 2.1 | 6.5 | 0.6 | 2.8 | 5.3 | 4.5 | 2.4 | 1.0 | -0.4 | 1.3 | 2.3 |
| South Africa | 6.1 | 10.1 | 7.3 | 4.1 | 5.0 | 5.8 | 5.8 | 5.3 | 5.9 | 5.4 | 5.4 |
| Taiwan Province of China | 1.4 | 1.7 | -1.0 | 1.1 | 1.1 | 1.1 | 0.6 | 0.3 | -0.6 | 0.3 | 1.8 |
| Thailand | 2.2 | 5.5 | -0.8 | 3.3 | 3.8 | 3.0 | 2.2 | 1.9 | -0.8 | 1.2 | 2.8 |
| Turkey | 8.8 | 10.4 | 6.3 | 8.6 | 6.5 | 8.9 | 7.5 | 8.9 | 7.4 | 7.2 | 5.4 |
| Venezuela (Bolivarian Republic of) | 18.7 | 30.4 | 27.1 | 28.2 | 26.1 | 21.1 | 40.6 | 68.1 | 175.5 | 195.1 | 89.8 |

Source: UN/DESA, based on IMF, International Financial Statistics.
a Data for country groups are weighted averages, where weights are based on GDP in 2010 prices and exchange rates.
b Partly estimated.
c Baseline scenario forecasts, based in part on Project LINK and the UN/DESA World Economic Forecasting Model.
d Currently includes data for Algeria, Bahrain, Comoros, Djibouti, Egypt, Iraq, Jordan, Kuwait, Lebanon, Libya, Mauritania, Morocco, Oman, Qatar, Saudi Arabia, Somalia, Sudan, Syrian Arab Republic, Tunisia, United Arab Emirates and Yemen.
e Special Administrative Region of China.

Table A.7
**Developed economies: unemployment rates,[a,b] 2007–2017**

Percentage of labour force

| | 2007 | 2008 | 2009 | 2010 | 2011 | 2012 | 2013 | 2014 | 2015[c] | 2016[d] | 2017[d] |
|---|---|---|---|---|---|---|---|---|---|---|---|
| **Developed economies** | 5.8 | 6.1 | 8.4 | 8.8 | 8.5 | 8.6 | 8.5 | 7.8 | 7.2 | 7.0 | 6.7 |
| United States | 4.6 | 5.8 | 9.3 | 9.6 | 9.0 | 8.1 | 7.4 | 6.2 | 5.3 | 5.2 | 5.1 |
| Canada | 6.1 | 6.1 | 8.4 | 8.1 | 7.5 | 7.3 | 7.1 | 6.9 | 6.8 | 6.6 | 6.5 |
| Japan | 3.8 | 4.0 | 5.1 | 5.1 | 4.6 | 4.4 | 4.0 | 3.6 | 3.4 | 3.3 | 3.3 |
| Australia | 4.4 | 4.2 | 5.6 | 5.2 | 5.1 | 5.2 | 5.7 | 6.1 | 6.2 | 6.3 | 6.3 |
| New Zealand | 3.7 | 4.2 | 6.1 | 6.6 | 6.5 | 6.9 | 6.2 | 5.8 | 6.3 | 6.2 | 6.1 |
| **European Union** | 7.2 | 7.0 | 9.0 | 9.6 | 9.7 | 10.5 | 10.9 | 10.2 | 9.6 | 9.2 | 8.9 |
| **EU-15** | 7.1 | 7.2 | 9.1 | 9.6 | 9.6 | 10.6 | 11.1 | 10.5 | 10.0 | 9.6 | 9.2 |
| Austria | 4.9 | 4.1 | 5.3 | 4.8 | 4.6 | 4.9 | 5.4 | 5.6 | 5.8 | 5.8 | 5.7 |
| Belgium | 7.5 | 7.0 | 7.9 | 8.3 | 7.2 | 7.6 | 8.5 | 8.5 | 8.5 | 8.3 | 8.0 |
| Denmark | 3.8 | 3.5 | 6.0 | 7.5 | 7.6 | 7.5 | 7.0 | 6.6 | 6.2 | 6.0 | 5.8 |
| Finland | 6.9 | 6.4 | 8.2 | 8.4 | 7.8 | 7.7 | 8.2 | 8.7 | 9.6 | 9.5 | 9.4 |
| France | 8.0 | 7.4 | 9.1 | 9.3 | 9.2 | 9.8 | 10.3 | 10.3 | 10.6 | 10.2 | 10.0 |
| Germany | 8.5 | 7.4 | 7.6 | 7.0 | 5.8 | 5.4 | 5.2 | 5.0 | 4.7 | 4.5 | 4.5 |
| Greece | 8.4 | 7.8 | 9.6 | 12.8 | 17.9 | 24.5 | 27.5 | 26.6 | 26.0 | 27.0 | 23.1 |
| Ireland | 4.7 | 6.4 | 12.0 | 13.9 | 14.7 | 14.7 | 13.1 | 11.3 | 9.5 | 8.4 | 8.1 |
| Italy | 6.1 | 6.7 | 7.8 | 8.4 | 8.4 | 10.6 | 12.1 | 12.7 | 12.3 | 11.8 | 11.4 |
| Luxembourg | 4.2 | 5.4 | 5.1 | 4.2 | 5.0 | 5.2 | 6.0 | 6.3 | 5.7 | 5.2 | 5.2 |
| Netherlands | 4.2 | 3.7 | 4.4 | 5.0 | 5.0 | 5.8 | 7.2 | 7.4 | 6.9 | 6.7 | 6.5 |
| Portugal | 9.1 | 8.8 | 10.7 | 12.0 | 12.9 | 15.8 | 16.4 | 14.1 | 12.3 | 11.8 | 11.5 |
| Spain | 8.2 | 11.3 | 17.9 | 19.9 | 21.4 | 24.8 | 26.1 | 24.5 | 22.1 | 20.5 | 19.8 |
| Sweden | 6.1 | 6.2 | 8.3 | 8.6 | 7.8 | 8.0 | 8.0 | 7.9 | 7.6 | 7.2 | 7.1 |
| United Kingdom | 5.3 | 5.6 | 7.6 | 7.8 | 8.1 | 7.9 | 7.6 | 6.1 | 5.6 | 5.5 | 5.4 |
| **New EU member States** | 7.7 | 6.5 | 8.4 | 9.9 | 9.8 | 10.0 | 10.1 | 8.7 | 8.2 | 7.9 | 7.5 |
| Bulgaria | 6.9 | 5.6 | 6.8 | 10.2 | 11.3 | 12.3 | 13.0 | 11.4 | 10.6 | 9.6 | 9.1 |
| Croatia | 9.6 | 8.4 | 9.1 | 11.8 | 13.4 | 15.8 | 17.3 | 17.3 | 16.4 | 16.0 | 15.2 |
| Cyprus | 3.8 | 3.6 | 5.4 | 6.3 | 8.0 | 11.8 | 15.9 | 16.1 | 16.9 | 17.1 | 16.2 |
| Czech Republic | 5.3 | 4.4 | 6.7 | 7.3 | 6.7 | 7.0 | 7.0 | 6.1 | 5.8 | 5.4 | 5.1 |
| Estonia | 4.6 | 5.5 | 13.6 | 16.7 | 12.4 | 10.0 | 8.6 | 7.4 | 7.1 | 6.5 | 6.2 |
| Hungary | 7.4 | 7.8 | 10.0 | 11.2 | 11.1 | 11.0 | 10.1 | 7.7 | 6.8 | 6.5 | 6.1 |
| Latvia | 6.0 | 7.4 | 17.1 | 18.7 | 16.2 | 15.0 | 11.9 | 10.8 | 10.1 | 9.7 | 9.2 |
| Lithuania | 4.3 | 5.7 | 13.7 | 17.8 | 15.3 | 13.2 | 11.8 | 11.3 | 10.4 | 9.9 | 9.5 |
| Malta | 6.3 | 5.7 | 6.7 | 6.6 | 6.4 | 6.3 | 6.4 | 5.9 | 5.3 | 5.3 | 5.2 |
| Poland | 9.6 | 7.0 | 8.1 | 9.7 | 9.7 | 10.1 | 10.3 | 9.0 | 8.2 | 8.0 | 7.8 |
| Romania | 6.4 | 5.6 | 6.5 | 7.0 | 7.2 | 6.8 | 7.1 | 6.8 | 6.2 | 6.0 | 5.6 |
| Slovakia | 11.2 | 9.6 | 12.1 | 14.5 | 13.7 | 14.0 | 14.2 | 13.2 | 11.2 | 10.4 | 10.0 |
| Slovenia | 4.9 | 4.4 | 5.9 | 7.3 | 8.2 | 8.9 | 10.1 | 9.7 | 8.9 | 8.2 | 7.8 |
| **Other Europe** | 3.2 | 3.1 | 4.0 | 4.2 | 3.8 | 3.8 | 4.0 | 4.1 | 4.3 | 4.3 | 4.1 |
| Iceland[e] | 2.2 | 3.2 | 7.1 | 7.5 | 6.9 | 5.8 | 5.2 | 4.6 | 4.0 | 4.1 | 4.2 |
| Norway | 2.5 | 2.6 | 3.2 | 3.6 | 3.3 | 3.2 | 3.5 | 3.5 | 4.4 | 4.6 | 4.2 |
| Switzerland | 3.6 | 3.3 | 4.3 | 4.5 | 4.0 | 4.1 | 4.3 | 4.4 | 4.2 | 4.1 | 4.0 |
| *Memorandum items* | | | | | | | | | | | |
| Major developed economies | 5.4 | 5.8 | 8.0 | 8.2 | 7.7 | 7.4 | 7.1 | 6.4 | 5.9 | 5.7 | 5.6 |
| Euro area | 7.5 | 7.6 | 9.6 | 10.2 | 10.2 | 11.4 | 12.0 | 11.6 | 11.1 | 10.6 | 10.2 |

Source: UN/DESA, based on data of the OECD and Eurostat.

a  Unemployment data are standardized by the OECD and Eurostat for comparability among countries and over time, in conformity with the definitions of the International Labour Organization (see OECD, Standardized Unemployment Rates: Sources and Methods (Paris, 1985)).

b  Data for country groups are weighted averages, where labour force is used for weights.

c  Partly estimated.

d  Baseline scenario forecasts, based in part on Project LINK and the UN/DESA World Economic Forecasting Model.

e  Not standardized.

Table A.8
**Economies in transition and developing economies: unemployment rates,[a] 2006–2015**

Percentage of labour force

| | 2006 | 2007 | 2008 | 2009 | 2010 | 2011 | 2012 | 2013 | 2014 | 2015[b] |
|---|---|---|---|---|---|---|---|---|---|---|
| **South-Eastern Europe** | | | | | | | | | | |
| Albania | 13.8 | 13.4 | 13.1 | 13.8 | 14.0 | 14.0 | 13.4 | 15.9 | 17.5 | 16.9 |
| Bosnia and Herzegovina | 31.1 | 29.0 | 23.4 | 24.1 | 27.2 | 27.6 | 28.0 | 27.5 | 27.5 | .. |
| Montenegro | 29.6 | 19.4 | 16.8 | 19.1 | 19.7 | 19.7 | 19.7 | 19.5 | 18.0 | 17.5 |
| Serbia | 20.9 | 18.1 | 13.6 | 16.1 | 19.2 | 23.0 | 23.9 | 22.1 | 19.4 | 18.8 |
| The former Yugoslav Republic of Macedonia | 36.0 | 34.9 | 33.8 | 32.2 | 32.1 | 31.4 | 31.0 | 29.0 | 28.0 | 27.1 |
| **Commonwealth of Independent States and Georgia[c]** | | | | | | | | | | |
| Armenia | 27.8 | 28.7 | 16.4 | 18.7 | 19.0 | 18.4 | 17.3 | 16.2 | 17.6 | .. |
| Azerbaijan | 6.8 | 6.5 | 6.0 | 5.9 | 5.6 | 5.4 | 5.2 | 5.0 | 4.9 | .. |
| Belarus[d] | 1.1 | 1.0 | 0.8 | 0.9 | 0.7 | 0.6 | 0.5 | 0.5 | 0.5 | .. |
| Georgia[c] | 13.6 | 13.3 | 16.5 | 16.9 | 16.3 | 15.1 | 15.0 | 14.6 | .. | .. |
| Kazakhstan | 7.8 | 7.3 | 6.6 | 6.6 | 5.8 | 5.4 | 5.3 | 5.2 | 5.0 | .. |
| Kyrgyzstan | 8.3 | 8.2 | 8.2 | 8.4 | 8.6 | 8.5 | 8.4 | 8.3 | 8.0 | .. |
| Republic of Moldova | 7.6 | 5.1 | 4.0 | 6.4 | 7.4 | 6.7 | 5.6 | 5.1 | 3.9 | 4.5 |
| Russian Federation | 7.0 | 6.0 | 6.2 | 8.2 | 7.3 | 6.5 | 5.5 | 5.5 | 5.2 | 5.4 |
| Tajikistan[d] | 2.3 | 2.5 | 2.1 | 2.1 | 2.2 | 2.1 | 2.6 | 2.5 | 2.5 | .. |
| Turkmenistan[d] | .. | 3.6 | 2.5 | 2.2 | 2.0 | 2.3 | 2.1 | 2.0 | 2.0 | .. |
| Ukraine | 7.4 | 6.6 | 6.4 | 8.8 | 8.2 | 8.0 | 7.6 | 7.3 | 9.3 | 9.6 |
| Uzbekistan[d] | 0.3 | 0.2 | 0.2 | 0.2 | 0.2 | 0.2 | 0.2 | 0.2 | 0.2 | .. |
| **Africa** | | | | | | | | | | |
| Algeria | 12.3 | 13.8 | 11.3 | 10.2 | 10.0 | 10.0 | 11.0 | 9.8 | 9.8 | .. |
| Botswana | 17.6 | 20.2 | .. | .. | 17.8 | 19.9 | .. | 20.0 | .. | .. |
| Egypt | 10.7 | 8.9 | 8.7 | 9.4 | 9.0 | 12.0 | 12.7 | 13.2 | 13.0 | .. |
| Mauritius | 9.1 | 8.5 | 7.2 | 7.3 | 7.8 | 7.9 | 8.0 | 8.0 | 7.8 | 8.1 |
| Morocco | 9.7 | 9.8 | 9.5 | 9.0 | 8.9 | 8.4 | 8.7 | 9.1 | 9.5 | .. |
| South Africa | 25.5 | 23.3 | 22.5 | 23.7 | 24.9 | 24.8 | 24.9 | 24.7 | 25.1 | 25.6 |
| Tunisia | 12.5 | 12.4 | 12.4 | 13.3 | 13.0 | 18.6 | 17.4 | 15.8 | 15.1 | 15.2 |
| **Developing America** | | | | | | | | | | |
| Argentina[e] | 10.2 | 8.5 | 7.9 | 8.7 | 7.8 | 7.2 | 7.2 | 7.1 | 7.3 | 6.5 |
| Barbados | 8.7 | 7.4 | 8.1 | 10.0 | 10.7 | 11.2 | 11.6 | 11.6 | 12.3 | 11.8 |
| Bolivia[e] (Plurinational State of) | 8.0 | 7.7 | 6.7 | 7.9 | 6.1 | 5.8 | .. | .. | .. | .. |
| Brazil[f] | 10.0 | 9.3 | 7.9 | 8.1 | 6.7 | 6.0 | 5.5 | 5.4 | 4.8 | 6.8 |
| Chile | 7.8 | 7.1 | 7.8 | 9.7 | 8.3 | 7.2 | 6.5 | 6.0 | 6.3 | 6.3 |
| Colombia | 12.0 | 11.2 | 11.3 | 12.0 | 11.8 | 10.8 | 10.4 | 9.6 | 9.1 | 9.2 |
| Costa Rica | 6.0 | 4.8 | 4.8 | 8.5 | 7.1 | 7.7 | 7.8 | 9.2 | 9.7 | 9.6 |
| Dominican Republic | 16.2 | 15.6 | 14.1 | 14.9 | 14.3 | 14.6 | 14.7 | 15.0 | 14.5 | .. |
| Ecuador[g] | 8.1 | 7.3 | 6.9 | 8.5 | 7.6 | 6.0 | 4.9 | 4.7 | 5.7 | .. |
| El Salvador | 5.7 | 5.8 | 5.5 | 7.3 | 7.0 | 6.6 | 6.2 | .. | .. | .. |
| Guatemala | .. | .. | .. | .. | 3.7 | 4.1 | 2.9 | 3.2 | 2.9 | .. |
| Honduras | 4.6 | 3.9 | 4.2 | 4.9 | 6.4 | 6.8 | 5.6 | 3.6 | .. | .. |
| Jamaica | 10.3 | 9.8 | 10.6 | 11.4 | 12.4 | 12.6 | 13.9 | 15.3 | 13.8 | 13.5 |
| Mexico | 4.6 | 4.8 | 4.9 | 6.6 | 6.4 | 6.0 | 4.9 | 4.9 | 4.8 | 4.4 |
| Nicaragua[h] | 5.2 | 5.9 | 6.1 | 8.2 | 7.8 | 5.9 | 5.9 | 5.7 | 6.8 | .. |

## Table A.8
## Economies in transition and developing economies: unemployment rates,[a] 2006–2015 *(continued)*

Percentage of labour force

| | 2006 | 2007 | 2008 | 2009 | 2010 | 2011 | 2012 | 2013 | 2014 | 2015[b] |
|---|---|---|---|---|---|---|---|---|---|---|
| Panama | 10.4 | 7.8 | 6.5 | 7.9 | 7.7 | 5.4 | 4.8 | 5.1 | 3.1 | 3.8 |
| Paraguay[f] | 8.9 | 7.2 | 7.4 | 8.2 | 7.2 | 7.1 | 8.0 | 8.1 | 8.0 | 7.0 |
| Peru[i] | 7.1 | 6.7 | 6.7 | 6.1 | 5.7 | 5.6 | 5.0 | 4.7 | 4.9 | 5.3 |
| Trinidad and Tobago | 6.2 | 5.5 | 4.6 | 5.3 | 5.9 | 5.1 | 5.2 | 3.8 | .. | 3.7 |
| Uruguay[e] | 10.8 | 9.4 | 8.0 | 7.7 | 7.2 | 6.3 | 6.5 | 6.5 | 6.6 | 7.4 |
| Venezuela (Bolivarian Republic of) | 10.6 | 8.4 | 7.3 | 7.9 | 8.7 | 8.3 | 8.1 | 8.1 | 7.0 | .. |
| **Developing Asia** | | | | | | | | | | |
| China | 4.1 | 4.0 | 4.2 | 4.3 | 4.1 | 4.1 | 4.1 | 4.1 | 4.1 | 4.0 |
| Hong Kong SAR[j] | 4.8 | 4.0 | 3.5 | 5.3 | 4.3 | 3.4 | 3.3 | 3.4 | 3.3 | 3.3 |
| India[k] | .. | .. | .. | .. | .. | 3.8 | 4.7 | 4.9 | .. | .. |
| Indonesia | 10.4 | 9.4 | 8.4 | 8.0 | 7.3 | 6.7 | 6.2 | 6.0 | 5.8 | 6.0 |
| Iran (Islamic Republic of) | 11.3 | 10.6 | 10.5 | 12.0 | 13.5 | 12.3 | 12.1 | 10.4 | 10.8 | .. |
| Israel | 8.4 | 7.3 | 6.1 | 7.6 | 6.6 | 5.6 | 6.9 | 6.2 | 5.9 | 5.2 |
| Jordan | 14.0 | 13.1 | 12.7 | 12.9 | 12.5 | 12.9 | 12.2 | 12.6 | 11.9 | 12.8 |
| Korea, Republic of | 3.5 | 3.3 | 3.2 | 3.7 | 3.7 | 3.4 | 3.2 | 3.1 | 3.5 | 3.7 |
| Malaysia | 3.3 | 3.2 | 3.3 | 3.7 | 3.3 | 3.1 | 3.0 | 3.1 | 2.9 | 3.1 |
| Pakistan | 6.1 | 5.1 | 5.0 | 5.2 | 5.3 | 5.7 | .. | 6.0 | .. | .. |
| Philippines[l] | 7.9 | 7.3 | 7.4 | 7.5 | 7.3 | 7.0 | 7.0 | 7.1 | 7.1 | 6.5 |
| Saudi Arabia | 6.3 | 6.1 | 6.3 | 6.3 | 6.2 | 5.9 | 5.6 | 5.6 | 5.8 | .. |
| Singapore | 2.7 | 2.1 | 2.2 | 3.0 | 2.2 | 2.0 | 2.0 | 1.9 | 2.0 | 2.0 |
| Sri Lanka[m] | 6.5 | 6.0 | 5.2 | 5.7 | 4.9 | 4.0 | 3.9 | 4.3 | 4.2 | 4.6 |
| Taiwan Province of China | 3.9 | 3.9 | 4.1 | 5.9 | 5.2 | 4.4 | 4.2 | 4.2 | 4.0 | 3.8 |
| Thailand | 1.5 | 1.4 | 1.4 | 1.5 | 1.1 | 0.7 | 0.7 | 0.7 | 0.8 | 0.9 |
| Turkey[n] | 9.0 | 9.2 | 10.0 | 13.1 | 11.1 | 9.1 | 8.4 | 9.0 | 9.9 | 10.2 |
| Viet Nam[e] | 4.8 | 4.6 | 4.7 | 4.6 | 4.3 | 3.6 | 3.2 | 3.6 | 3.6 | .. |

**Sources:** UN/DESA, based on data of the Economic Commission for Europe (ECE); ILO LABORSTAT database and KILM 9th edition; Economic Commission for Latin America and the Caribbean (ECLAC); and national sources.

**a** As a percentage of labour force. Reflects national definitions and coverage. Not comparable across economies.

**b** Partly estimated.

**c** Georgia officially left the Commonwealth of Independent States on 18 August 2009. However, its performance is discussed in the context of this group of countries for reasons of geographic proximity and similarities in economic structure.

**d** End-of-period registered unemployment data (as a percentage of labour force).

**e** Urban areas.

**f** Six main cities.

**g** Covers Quito, Guayaquil and Cuenca.

**h** Break in series; new methodlogy starting in 2010.

**i** Metropolitan Lima.

**j** Special Administrative Region of China.

**k** Data for fiscal year 2011/12, 2012/13 and 2013/14, respectively.

**l** Partly adopts the ILO definition; that is to say, it does not include one ILO criterion, namely, "currently available for work".

**m** Excluding Northern and Eastern provinces.

**n** Data based on a new methodology starting from February 2014 onward.

Table A.9
**Major developed economies: quarterly indicators of growth, unemployment and inflation, 2013–2015**

Percentage

| | 2013 | | | | 2014 | | | | 2015 | | |
|---|---|---|---|---|---|---|---|---|---|---|---|
| | I | II | III | IV | I | II | III | IV | I | II | III |
| **Growth of gross domestic product**[a] (*percentage change in seasonally adjusted data from preceding quarter*) | | | | | | | | | | | |
| Canada | 4.1 | 1.8 | 2.8 | 4.0 | 0.5 | 3.7 | 2.1 | 3.4 | -0.7 | -0.3 | 2.3 |
| France | 0.6 | 3.1 | -0.4 | 0.7 | -0.6 | -0.5 | 1.0 | 0.5 | 2.9 | 0.2 | 1.4 |
| Germany | -1.1 | 3.7 | 1.5 | 1.3 | 2.9 | -0.2 | 0.8 | 2.5 | 1.4 | 1.8 | 1.3 |
| Italy | -3.3 | -0.7 | 0.2 | -0.2 | -0.5 | -0.8 | -0.3 | -0.2 | 1.7 | 1.1 | 0.8 |
| Japan | 5.5 | 2.3 | 2.5 | -0.9 | 4.7 | -7.7 | -1.1 | 1.2 | 4.6 | -0.7 | -0.8 |
| United Kingdom | 2.7 | 2.4 | 3.8 | 2.6 | 2.5 | 3.8 | 2.6 | 3.0 | 1.5 | 2.6 | 1.9 |
| United States | 1.9 | 1.1 | 3.0 | 3.8 | -0.9 | 4.6 | 4.3 | 2.1 | 0.6 | 3.9 | 2.1 |
| Major developed economies[b] | 1.9 | 1.7 | 2.4 | 2.2 | 0.8 | 1.1 | 2.2 | 1.8 | 1.6 | 2.2 | 1.4 |
| Euro area | -1.0 | 1.6 | 0.9 | 0.9 | 0.8 | 0.3 | 1.0 | 1.6 | 2.1 | 1.4 | 1.2 |
| **Unemployment rate**[c] (*percentage of total labour force*) | | | | | | | | | | | |
| Canada | 7.1 | 7.1 | 7.1 | 7.1 | 7.0 | 7.0 | 7.0 | 6.7 | 6.7 | 6.8 | 7.0 |
| France | 10.3 | 10.4 | 10.3 | 10.1 | 10.2 | 10.2 | 10.3 | 10.5 | 10.4 | 10.4 | 10.7 |
| Germany | 5.3 | 5.3 | 5.2 | 5.1 | 5.1 | 5.0 | 5.0 | 4.9 | 4.8 | 4.7 | 4.5 |
| Italy | 11.9 | 12.1 | 12.2 | 12.4 | 12.7 | 12.5 | 12.7 | 12.8 | 12.3 | 12.4 | 11.9 |
| Japan | 4.2 | 4.0 | 4.0 | 3.9 | 3.6 | 3.6 | 3.6 | 3.5 | 3.5 | 3.3 | 3.4 |
| United Kingdom | 7.8 | 7.7 | 7.6 | 7.1 | 6.7 | 6.3 | 5.9 | 5.6 | 5.5 | 5.6 | .. |
| United States | 7.7 | 7.5 | 7.2 | 7.0 | 6.6 | 6.2 | 6.1 | 5.7 | 5.6 | 5.4 | 5.2 |
| Major developed economies[d] | 7.3 | 7.2 | 7.0 | 6.8 | 6.6 | 6.4 | 6.3 | 6.1 | 6.0 | 5.9 | .. |
| Euro area | 12.0 | 12.1 | 12.0 | 11.9 | 11.8 | 11.6 | 11.5 | 11.5 | 11.2 | 11.0 | 10.9 |
| **Change in consumer prices** (*percentage change from one year ago*) | | | | | | | | | | | |
| Canada | 0.9 | 0.8 | 1.2 | 0.9 | 1.4 | 2.2 | 2.1 | 1.9 | 1.1 | 0.9 | 1.2 |
| France | 1.2 | 0.9 | 1.1 | 0.8 | 0.9 | 0.8 | 0.5 | 0.3 | -0.2 | 0.3 | 0.1 |
| Germany | 1.8 | 1.5 | 1.7 | 1.3 | 1.0 | 0.9 | 0.8 | 0.4 | -0.1 | 0.4 | 0.0 |
| Italy | 2.1 | 1.3 | 1.1 | 0.7 | 0.5 | 0.4 | -0.1 | 0.1 | -0.1 | 0.1 | 0.3 |
| Japan | -0.6 | -0.3 | 0.9 | 1.4 | 1.5 | 3.6 | 3.4 | 2.5 | 2.3 | 0.5 | 0.2 |
| United Kingdom | 2.8 | 2.7 | 2.7 | 2.1 | 1.8 | 1.7 | 1.5 | 0.9 | 0.1 | 0.0 | 0.0 |
| United States | 1.7 | 1.4 | 1.5 | 1.2 | 1.4 | 2.1 | 1.8 | 1.2 | -0.1 | 0.0 | 0.1 |
| Major developed economies[b] | 1.3 | 1.1 | 1.4 | 1.3 | 1.3 | 2.0 | 1.7 | 1.2 | 0.4 | 0.2 | 0.1 |
| Euro area | 1.9 | 1.4 | 1.3 | 0.8 | 0.6 | 0.6 | 0.4 | 0.2 | -0.3 | 0.2 | 0.1 |

Source: UN/DESA, based on Eurostat, OECD and national sources.

a Expressed as an annualized rate.

b Calculated as a weighted average, where weights are based on 2010 GDP in United States dollars.

c Seasonally adjusted data as standardized by OECD.

d Calculated as a weighted average, where weights are based on labour force.

Table A.10
**Selected economies in transition: quarterly indicators of growth and inflation, 2013–2015**

Percentage

| | 2013 | | | | 2014 | | | | 2015 | | |
|---|---|---|---|---|---|---|---|---|---|---|---|
| | I | II | III | IV | I | II | III | IV | I | II | III |
| **Rates of growth of gross domestic product[a]** | | | | | | | | | | | |
| Armenia | 7.3 | 0.9 | 1.7 | 5.1 | 2.9 | 2.0 | 5.5 | 2.7 | 2.5 | 5.1 | .. |
| Azerbaijan[b] | 3.1 | 5.0 | 5.4 | 5.8 | 2.5 | 2.1 | 2.5 | 2.8 | 5.3 | 5.7 | 3.7 |
| Belarus | 4.0 | -0.5 | 0.8 | 0.0 | 0.9 | 1.6 | 2.1 | 1.5 | -2.1 | -4.5 | .. |
| Bosnia and Herzegovina | 2.3 | 1.8 | 3.2 | 2.3 | 2.6 | -0.5 | 0.1 | 2.3 | 2.3 | 4.4 | .. |
| Georgia | 2.4 | 1.5 | 1.4 | 7.1 | 7.2 | 4.9 | 5.6 | 1.7 | 3.3 | 2.5 | .. |
| Kazakhstan[b] | 4.7 | 5.1 | 5.7 | 5.9 | 3.8 | 3.9 | 4.1 | 4.3 | 2.3 | 1.7 | .. |
| Kyrgyzstan[b] | 7.6 | 7.9 | 9.2 | 13.1 | 5.6 | 4.1 | 3.0 | 3.6 | 7.0 | 7.3 | 6.3 |
| Republic of Moldova | 3.8 | 6.5 | 13.5 | 11.9 | 3.7 | 4.3 | 5.8 | 4.2 | 4.8 | 2.5 | .. |
| Russian Federation | 0.7 | 1.2 | 1.3 | 2.1 | 0.6 | 0.7 | 0.9 | 0.4 | -2.2 | -4.6 | -4.1 |
| The former Yugoslav Republic of Macedonia | 1.9 | 2.1 | 2.5 | 4.1 | 3.3 | 4.7 | 4.3 | 2.7 | 3.2 | 2.6 | .. |
| Ukraine | -1.3 | -1.2 | -1.2 | 3.4 | -1.2 | -4.5 | -5.4 | -14.8 | -17.2 | -14.6 | .. |
| **Change in consumer prices[a]** | | | | | | | | | | | |
| Armenia | 3.0 | 5.2 | 8.7 | 6.4 | 4.6 | 3.3 | 0.9 | 3.1 | 5.1 | 5.1 | 3.7 |
| Azerbaijan | 1.2 | 2.8 | 3.0 | 2.8 | 2.1 | 1.7 | 1.5 | 1.5 | 1.7 | 3.3 | 3.7 |
| Belarus | 22.6 | 19.4 | 16.0 | 15.9 | 15.7 | 19.0 | 20.5 | 18.0 | 16.8 | 14.0 | 12.0 |
| Bosnia and Herzegovina | 0.8 | 0.4 | 0.0 | -1.0 | -1.6 | -1.4 | -0.5 | -0.1 | -0.5 | -0.5 | .. |
| Georgia | -1.9 | -0.5 | -0.6 | 1.0 | 3.3 | 2.6 | 3.7 | 2.7 | 1.8 | 3.5 | 5.1 |
| Kazakhstan | 6.8 | 6.1 | 5.7 | 4.8 | 5.4 | 6.8 | 7.0 | 7.5 | 6.8 | 4.2 | 4.1 |
| Kyrgyzstan | 7.8 | 7.8 | 6.7 | 4.3 | 4.7 | 8.0 | 7.6 | 9.8 | 10.4 | 6.1 | 5.7 |
| Republic of Moldova | 4.4 | 5.2 | 4.0 | 4.9 | 5.4 | 5.2 | 5.1 | 4.8 | 6.1 | 8.0 | 11.1 |
| Russian Federation | 7.1 | 7.2 | 6.4 | 6.4 | 6.4 | 7.5 | 7.7 | 9.6 | 16.2 | 15.8 | 15.7 |
| The former Yugoslav Republic of Macedonia | 3.5 | 3.6 | 2.8 | 1.3 | 0.6 | -1.0 | -0.4 | -0.4 | -0.9 | 0.3 | -0.2 |
| Ukraine | -0.5 | -0.4 | -0.3 | 0.2 | 1.7 | 9.9 | 14.8 | 22.2 | 36.5 | 58.9 | 50.3 |

Source:  UN/DESA, based on data of the Economic Commission for Europe, European Bank for Reconstruction and Development and national sources.
a  Percentage change from the corresponding period of the preceding year.
b  Data reflect growth rate of cumulative GDP from the beginning of the year.

Table A.11
**Major developing economies: quarterly indicators of growth, unemployment and inflation, 2013–2015**

Percentage

| | 2013 | | | | 2014 | | | | 2015 | | |
|---|---|---|---|---|---|---|---|---|---|---|---|
| | I | II | III | IV | I | II | III | IV | I | II | III |
| **Rates of growth of gross domestic product[a]** | | | | | | | | | | | |
| Argentina | 1.3 | 5.2 | 3.3 | 1.7 | 0.8 | 0.7 | -0.2 | 0.5 | 2.1 | 2.3 | .. |
| Brazil | 2.6 | 3.9 | 2.4 | 2.1 | 2.7 | -1.2 | -0.6 | -0.2 | -2.0 | -3.0 | -4.5 |
| Chile | 5.4 | 4.0 | 4.8 | 2.8 | 2.7 | 2.1 | 1.0 | 1.8 | 2.5 | 1.9 | 2.2 |
| China | 7.8 | 7.5 | 7.9 | 7.6 | 7.3 | 7.4 | 7.2 | 7.2 | 7.0 | 7.0 | 6.9 |
| Colombia | 2.9 | 4.7 | 6.1 | 6.0 | 6.5 | 4.2 | 4.2 | 3.4 | 2.8 | 3.0 | .. |
| Ecuador | 3.3 | 4.0 | 5.2 | 5.7 | 4.7 | 4.2 | 3.3 | 2.6 | 3.2 | 1.0 | .. |
| Hong Kong SAR[b] | 3.4 | 3.1 | 3.1 | 2.8 | 2.7 | 2.0 | 2.9 | 2.4 | 2.4 | 2.8 | 2.3 |
| India | 4.7 | 7.0 | 7.5 | 6.4 | 6.7 | 6.7 | 8.4 | 6.6 | 7.5 | 7.0 | 7.4 |
| Indonesia | 6.0 | 5.7 | 5.6 | 5.7 | 5.2 | 5.1 | 5.0 | 5.0 | 4.7 | 4.7 | 4.7 |
| Israel | 2.3 | 5.3 | 2.1 | 3.8 | 3.9 | 1.4 | 2.4 | 2.6 | 2.9 | 1.8 | 2.4 |
| Republic of Korea | 2.1 | 2.7 | 3.2 | 3.5 | 3.9 | 3.4 | 3.3 | 2.7 | 2.5 | 2.2 | 2.6 |
| Malaysia | 4.2 | 4.5 | 5.0 | 5.1 | 6.3 | 6.5 | 5.6 | 5.7 | 5.6 | 4.9 | 4.7 |
| Mexico | 1.0 | 1.7 | 1.6 | 1.1 | 2.3 | 1.8 | 2.2 | 2.6 | 2.5 | 2.3 | 2.6 |
| Philippines | 7.5 | 7.9 | 6.1 | 6.1 | 5.6 | 6.7 | 5.5 | 6.6 | 5.0 | 5.8 | 6.0 |
| Singapore | 0.3 | 4.2 | 5.0 | 4.9 | 4.8 | 2.4 | 2.8 | 2.1 | 2.7 | 2.0 | 1.9 |
| South Africa | 1.8 | 2.2 | 1.8 | 2.9 | 1.9 | 1.3 | 1.6 | 1.4 | 2.2 | 1.3 | 1.0 |
| Taiwan Province of China | 1.5 | 2.5 | 1.5 | 3.3 | 3.7 | 4.2 | 4.3 | 3.6 | 4.0 | 0.6 | -0.6 |
| Thailand | 5.0 | 2.2 | 3.3 | 1.3 | -0.7 | 0.8 | 1.0 | 2.2 | 3.1 | 2.7 | 2.8 |
| Turkey | 3.1 | 4.6 | 4.2 | 4.5 | 5.1 | 2.4 | 1.8 | 2.7 | 2.5 | 3.8 | .. |
| Venezuela (Bolivarian Republic of) | 0.8 | 2.6 | 1.1 | 1.0 | -4.8 | -4.9 | -2.3 | .. | .. | .. | .. |
| **Unemployment rate[c]** | | | | | | | | | | | |
| Argentina | 7.9 | 7.2 | 6.8 | 6.4 | 7.1 | 7.5 | 7.5 | 6.9 | 7.1 | 6.6 | 5.9 |
| Brazil | 5.6 | 5.9 | 5.4 | 4.7 | 5.0 | 4.9 | 4.9 | 4.6 | 5.8 | 6.7 | 7.6 |
| Chile | 6.2 | 6.2 | 5.7 | 5.7 | 6.5 | 6.5 | 6.6 | 6.0 | 6.1 | 6.5 | 6.4 |
| Colombia | 11.4 | 9.6 | 9.4 | 8.2 | 10.5 | 9.0 | 8.8 | 8.1 | 9.8 | 8.9 | 9.0 |
| Ecuador | 4.6 | 4.9 | 4.6 | 4.2 | 4.9 | 4.7 | 3.9 | 3.8 | 3.8 | 4.5 | 4.2 |
| Hong Kong SAR[b] | 3.5 | 3.4 | 3.5 | 3.1 | 3.1 | 3.3 | 3.5 | 3.1 | 3.2 | 3.3 | 3.5 |
| Israel | 6.7 | 6.7 | 5.9 | 5.7 | 5.9 | 6.1 | 6.2 | 5.6 | 5.4 | 5.1 | 5.2 |
| Republic of Korea | 3.6 | 3.1 | 3.0 | 2.8 | 4.0 | 3.7 | 3.3 | 3.2 | 4.1 | 3.8 | 3.4 |
| Malaysia | 3.1 | 3.0 | 3.1 | 3.2 | 3.1 | 2.7 | 2.7 | 2.8 | 3.1 | 3.1 | 3.2 |
| Mexico | 4.9 | 5.0 | 5.2 | 4.6 | 4.8 | 4.9 | 5.3 | 4.4 | 4.2 | 4.4 | 4.6 |
| Philippines | 7.1 | 7.5 | 7.3 | 6.5 | 7.5 | 7.0 | 6.7 | 6.0 | 6.6 | 6.4 | 6.5 |
| Singapore | 1.9 | 2.0 | 1.8 | 1.9 | 2.0 | 2.0 | 1.9 | 1.9 | 1.8 | 2.0 | 2.0 |
| South Africa | 25.0 | 25.3 | 24.5 | 24.1 | 25.2 | 25.5 | 25.4 | 24.3 | 26.4 | 25.0 | 25.5 |
| Taiwan Province of China | 4.2 | 4.1 | 4.3 | 4.2 | 4.0 | 3.9 | 4.0 | 3.9 | 3.7 | 3.7 | 3.9 |
| Thailand | 0.7 | 0.7 | 0.7 | 0.8 | 0.9 | 1.0 | 0.8 | 0.7 | 1.0 | 0.9 | 0.9 |
| Turkey[d] | 10.4 | 9.0 | 9.7 | 9.9 | 9.2 | 9.6 | 10.5 | 10.5 | 10.2 | 10.2 | .. |
| Uruguay | 6.8 | 6.6 | 6.3 | 6.3 | 6.7 | 6.8 | 6.2 | 6.7 | 7.0 | 7.6 | 7.6 |
| Venezuela (Bolivarian Republic of) | 8.2 | 7.8 | 7.9 | 7.0 | 8.4 | 7.2 | .. | .. | .. | .. | .. |

Table A.11
**Major developing economies: quarterly indicators of growth, unemployment and inflation, 2013–2015** (*continued*)

Percentage

| | 2013 | | | | 2014 | | | | 2015 | | |
|---|---|---|---|---|---|---|---|---|---|---|---|
| | I | II | III | IV | I | II | III | IV | I | II | III |
| **Change in consumer prices**[a] | | | | | | | | | | | |
| Argentina[e] | .. | .. | .. | .. | 10.0 | 15.0 | 19.8 | 22.7 | 18.4 | 15.4 | 14.7 |
| Brazil | 6.4 | 6.6 | 6.1 | 5.8 | 5.8 | 6.4 | 6.6 | 6.5 | 7.7 | 8.5 | 9.5 |
| Chile | 1.5 | 1.3 | 2.1 | 2.3 | 3.2 | 4.5 | 4.7 | 5.3 | 4.4 | 4.2 | 4.7 |
| China | 2.4 | 2.4 | 2.8 | 2.9 | 2.3 | 2.2 | 2.0 | 1.5 | 1.2 | 1.4 | 1.7 |
| Colombia | 1.9 | 2.1 | 2.3 | 1.8 | 2.3 | 2.8 | 2.9 | 3.5 | 4.2 | 4.5 | 4.9 |
| Ecuador | 3.6 | 2.9 | 2.1 | 2.3 | 2.9 | 3.4 | 4.2 | 3.8 | 3.8 | 4.6 | 4.1 |
| Hong Kong SAR[b] | 3.7 | 4.0 | 5.3 | 4.3 | 4.1 | 3.7 | 4.8 | 5.1 | 4.4 | 3.0 | 2.3 |
| India[f] | 10.7 | 9.5 | 9.7 | 10.4 | 8.2 | 7.8 | 6.7 | 4.1 | 5.3 | 5.1 | 3.9 |
| Indonesia | 5.3 | 5.6 | 8.6 | 8.4 | 7.8 | 7.1 | 4.4 | 6.5 | 6.5 | 7.1 | 7.1 |
| Israel | 1.4 | 1.2 | 1.6 | 1.9 | 1.3 | 0.8 | 0.0 | -0.2 | -0.8 | -0.4 | -0.4 |
| Republic of Korea | 1.6 | 1.2 | 1.4 | 1.1 | 1.1 | 1.6 | 1.4 | 1.0 | 0.6 | 0.5 | 0.7 |
| Malaysia | 1.5 | 1.8 | 2.2 | 3.0 | 3.4 | 3.3 | 3.0 | 2.8 | 0.7 | 2.2 | 3.0 |
| Mexico | 3.7 | 4.5 | 3.4 | 3.7 | 4.2 | 3.6 | 4.1 | 4.2 | 3.1 | 2.9 | 2.6 |
| Philippines | 3.2 | 2.7 | 2.4 | 3.4 | 4.1 | 4.3 | 4.7 | 3.6 | 2.4 | 1.7 | 0.6 |
| Singapore | 4.0 | 1.6 | 1.9 | 2.0 | 1.0 | 2.2 | 1.0 | -0.4 | -0.3 | -0.4 | -0.6 |
| South Africa | 5.7 | 5.7 | 6.2 | 5.4 | 5.9 | 6.5 | 6.2 | 5.7 | 4.1 | 4.6 | 4.7 |
| Taiwan Province of China | 1.8 | 0.8 | 0.0 | 0.6 | 0.8 | 1.6 | 1.5 | 0.8 | -0.6 | -0.7 | -0.3 |
| Thailand | 3.1 | 2.3 | 1.7 | 1.7 | 2.0 | 2.5 | 2.0 | 1.1 | -0.5 | -1.1 | -1.1 |
| Turkey | 7.2 | 7.0 | 8.3 | 7.5 | 8.0 | 9.4 | 9.2 | 8.8 | 7.5 | 7.7 | 7.3 |
| Venezuela (Bolivarian Republic of) | 23.4 | 34.8 | 45.8 | 56.2 | 57.7 | 60.9 | 63.2 | 65.4 | .. | .. | .. |

Sources:  IMF, International Financial Statistics, and national sources.
a  Percentage change from the corresponding quarter of the previous year.
b  Special Administrative Region of China.
c  Reflects national definitions and coverage. Not comparable across economies.
d  Data based on new methodology starting from February 2014 onward.
e  In December 2013, Argentina launched a new national consumer price index.  The numbers reported correspond to the accumulated variation of the index since that date.  No matching data for the period before December 2013 were released.
f  Data based on new statistics available from 2014 onward.

Table A.12
**Major developed economies: financial indicators, 2006–2015**

Percentage

| | 2006 | 2007 | 2008 | 2009 | 2010 | 2011 | 2012 | 2013 | 2014 | 2015[a] |
|---|---|---|---|---|---|---|---|---|---|---|
| **Short-term interest rates[b]** | | | | | | | | | | |
| Canada | 4.2 | 4.6 | 3.3 | 0.7 | 0.8 | 1.2 | 1.2 | 1.2 | 1.2 | 0.8 |
| France[c] | 3.1 | 4.3 | 4.6 | 1.2 | 0.8 | 1.4 | 0.6 | 0.2 | 0.2 | 0.0 |
| Germany[c] | 3.1 | 4.3 | 4.6 | 1.2 | 0.8 | 1.4 | 0.6 | 0.2 | 0.2 | 0.0 |
| Italy[c] | 3.1 | 4.3 | 4.6 | 1.2 | 0.8 | 1.4 | 0.6 | 0.2 | 0.2 | 0.0 |
| Japan | 0.3 | 0.7 | 0.8 | 0.6 | 0.4 | 0.3 | 0.3 | 0.2 | 0.2 | 0.2 |
| United Kingdom | 4.8 | 6.0 | 5.5 | 1.2 | 0.7 | 0.9 | 0.8 | 0.5 | 0.5 | 0.5 |
| United States | 5.2 | 5.3 | 3.0 | 0.6 | 0.3 | 0.3 | 0.3 | 0.2 | 0.1 | 0.2 |
| **Long-term interest rates[d]** | | | | | | | | | | |
| Canada | 4.2 | 4.3 | 3.6 | 3.2 | 3.2 | 2.8 | 1.9 | 2.3 | 2.2 | 1.5 |
| France | 3.8 | 4.3 | 4.2 | 3.6 | 3.1 | 3.3 | 2.5 | 2.2 | 1.7 | 0.9 |
| Germany | 3.8 | 4.2 | 4.0 | 3.2 | 2.7 | 2.6 | 1.5 | 1.6 | 1.2 | 0.5 |
| Italy | 4.0 | 4.5 | 4.7 | 4.3 | 4.0 | 5.4 | 5.5 | 4.3 | 2.9 | 1.7 |
| Japan | 1.7 | 1.7 | 1.5 | 1.3 | 1.1 | 1.1 | 0.8 | 0.7 | 0.5 | 0.4 |
| United Kingdom | 4.5 | 5.0 | 4.6 | 3.6 | 3.6 | 3.1 | 1.9 | 2.4 | 2.6 | 1.9 |
| United States | 4.8 | 4.6 | 3.7 | 3.3 | 3.2 | 2.8 | 1.8 | 2.4 | 2.5 | 2.1 |
| **General government financial balances[e]** | | | | | | | | | | |
| Canada | 1.8 | 1.5 | -0.3 | -4.5 | -4.9 | -3.7 | -3.1 | -2.7 | -1.6 | -1.9 |
| France | -2.3 | -2.5 | -3.2 | -7.2 | -6.8 | -5.1 | -4.8 | -4.1 | -3.9 | -3.8 |
| Germany | -1.7 | 0.2 | -0.2 | -3.2 | -4.2 | -1.0 | -0.1 | -0.1 | 0.3 | 0.9 |
| Italy | -3.6 | -1.5 | -2.7 | -5.3 | -4.2 | -3.5 | -3.0 | -2.9 | -3.0 | -2.6 |
| Japan | -1.3 | -2.1 | -1.9 | -8.8 | -8.3 | -8.8 | -8.7 | -8.5 | -7.7 | -6.7 |
| United Kingdom | -2.9 | -3.0 | -5.1 | -10.8 | -9.7 | -7.7 | -8.3 | -5.7 | -5.7 | -3.9 |
| United States | -3.1 | -3.7 | -7.2 | -12.8 | -12.2 | -10.8 | -9.0 | -5.5 | -5.1 | -4.5 |

**Sources:** UN/DESA, based on OECD, Economic Outlook; OECD, Main Economic Indicators.

a Average for the first nine months for short- and long-term interest rates.

b Three-month Interbank or money market rate.

c Three-month Euro Interbank Offered Rate (EURIBOR).

d Yield on 10-year government bonds.

e Surplus (+) or deficit (-) as a percentage of nominal GDP. Estimates for 2015.

Table A.13
**Selected economies: real effective exchange rates, broad measurement,[a, b] 2006–2015**

| | 2006 | 2007 | 2008 | 2009 | 2010 | 2011 | 2012 | 2013 | 2014 | 2015[c] |
|---|---|---|---|---|---|---|---|---|---|---|
| **Developed economies** | | | | | | | | | | |
| Australia | 87.8 | 93.0 | 90.5 | 87.7 | 100.0 | 106.7 | 108.1 | 102.5 | 97.7 | 82.4 |
| Bulgaria | 86.4 | 91.4 | 99.1 | 103.5 | 100.0 | 101.7 | 100.1 | 100.7 | 100.1 | 89.2 |
| Canada | 96.7 | 99.5 | 96.3 | 91.9 | 100.0 | 101.2 | 100.7 | 96.9 | 91.2 | 77.7 |
| Croatia | 97.4 | 98.3 | 102.5 | 103.6 | 100.0 | 97.4 | 95.0 | 95.9 | 95.1 | 85.1 |
| Czech Republic | 87.9 | 90.9 | 104.5 | 100.1 | 100.0 | 101.7 | 97.5 | 95.7 | 90.4 | 80.7 |
| Denmark | 100.3 | 100.8 | 102.0 | 104.7 | 100.0 | 99.2 | 96.4 | 97.1 | 98.0 | 87.0 |
| Euro area | 104.6 | 106.8 | 108.3 | 109.1 | 100.0 | 99.2 | 94.2 | 97.3 | 97.8 | 82.5 |
| Hungary | 92.0 | 102.8 | 105.8 | 99.6 | 100.0 | 99.5 | 96.6 | 95.6 | 92.0 | 81.4 |
| Japan | 90.2 | 82.4 | 88.4 | 99.5 | 100.0 | 101.1 | 99.6 | 79.3 | 74.6 | 64.2 |
| New Zealand | 99.4 | 106.6 | 98.7 | 91.8 | 100.0 | 104.0 | 106.7 | 109.3 | 112.5 | 96.3 |
| Norway | 99.8 | 100.0 | 99.3 | 96.4 | 100.0 | 100.4 | 99.5 | 98.0 | 93.3 | 78.8 |
| Poland | 99.8 | 103.6 | 113.3 | 95.6 | 100.0 | 98.0 | 94.9 | 95.5 | 96.0 | 84.5 |
| Romania | 104.5 | 113.1 | 106.7 | 99.0 | 100.0 | 102.4 | 96.2 | 100.7 | 101.6 | 90.4 |
| Sweden | 106.0 | 107.3 | 104.6 | 94.6 | 100.0 | 105.2 | 104.5 | 105.6 | 100.0 | 85.7 |
| Switzerland | 93.2 | 89.2 | 92.6 | 96.2 | 100.0 | 109.3 | 105.0 | 103.2 | 104.3 | 101.5 |
| United Kingdom | 126.1 | 127.9 | 110.8 | 99.9 | 100.0 | 100.3 | 104.1 | 102.6 | 109.6 | 104.4 |
| United States | 111.0 | 105.7 | 100.8 | 104.7 | 100.0 | 94.9 | 96.9 | 96.9 | 98.9 | 98.7 |
| **Economies in transition** | | | | | | | | | | |
| Russian Federation | 89.0 | 93.9 | 99.7 | 92.4 | 100.0 | 103.6 | 104.4 | 106.3 | 97.1 | 74.2 |
| **Developing economies** | | | | | | | | | | |
| Argentina | 79.7 | 82.7 | 92.2 | 93.4 | 100.0 | 106.0 | 122.9 | 127.3 | 119.7 | 153.2 |
| Brazil | 81.4 | 87.1 | 89.8 | 88.8 | 100.0 | 103.2 | 92.2 | 86.6 | 84.3 | 66.2 |
| Chile | 101.3 | 99.0 | 99.1 | 94.9 | 100.0 | 100.3 | 102.1 | 100.4 | 90.5 | 82.0 |
| China | 86.9 | 89.8 | 97.2 | 101.3 | 100.0 | 102.1 | 108.0 | 114.7 | 117.2 | 116.4 |
| Colombia | 82.6 | 91.8 | 94.5 | 90.3 | 100.0 | 98.5 | 103.9 | 99.6 | 94.9 | 73.8 |
| Ecuador | 104.2 | 97.1 | 95.2 | 101.3 | 100.0 | 97.1 | 100.3 | 101.4 | 104.8 | 106.5 |
| Egypt | 72.5 | 73.5 | 82.4 | 94.6 | 100.0 | 97.0 | 102.8 | 97.0 | 104.2 | 105.4 |
| Hong Kong SAR[d] | 114.2 | 107.6 | 101.0 | 103.1 | 100.0 | 96.1 | 98.3 | 100.7 | 104.5 | 102.0 |
| India | 83.7 | 90.3 | 85.5 | 87.9 | 100.0 | 100.2 | 95.5 | 94.4 | 96.1 | 94.5 |
| Indonesia | 94.9 | 93.9 | 89.4 | 88.7 | 100.0 | 100.2 | 96.8 | 93.6 | 87.7 | 81.7 |
| Israel | 88.0 | 88.5 | 98.1 | 95.7 | 100.0 | 100.3 | 95.4 | 101.3 | 102.4 | 93.6 |
| Republic of Korea | 132.0 | 129.9 | 104.9 | 92.7 | 100.0 | 99.8 | 99.3 | 103.5 | 109.3 | 100.9 |
| Kuwait | 93.7 | 93.3 | 100.6 | 100.0 | 100.0 | 100.6 | 104.0 | 104.4 | 106.8 | 102.5 |
| Malaysia | 96.3 | 98.1 | 98.1 | 95.0 | 100.0 | 99.8 | 99.5 | 99.4 | 98.9 | 84.9 |
| Mexico | 111.2 | 109.1 | 105.9 | 93.1 | 100.0 | 99.0 | 96.1 | 101.5 | 100.6 | 84.6 |
| Morocco | 104.0 | 102.8 | 102.9 | 104.6 | 100.0 | 97.2 | 95.0 | 96.3 | 96.7 | 88.5 |
| Nigeria | 94.7 | 93.3 | 101.3 | 92.3 | 100.0 | 99.7 | 109.6 | 116.0 | 120.0 | 106.4 |
| Pakistan | 103.8 | 102.3 | 97.1 | 96.6 | 100.0 | 102.0 | 103.2 | 100.7 | 107.6 | 106.5 |
| Peru | 94.3 | 92.4 | 95.4 | 97.7 | 100.0 | 97.9 | 105.2 | 103.8 | 101.6 | 93.0 |

Table A.13

**Selected economies: real effective exchange rates, broad measurement,[a, b] 2006–2015** (continued)

| | 2006 | 2007 | 2008 | 2009 | 2010 | 2011 | 2012 | 2013 | 2014 | 2015[c] |
|---|---|---|---|---|---|---|---|---|---|---|
| **Developing economies** (continued) | | | | | | | | | | |
| Philippines | 88.1 | 95.4 | 98.2 | 96.6 | 100.0 | 100.3 | 105.2 | 108.9 | 108.8 | 105.9 |
| Saudi Arabia | 94.2 | 90.5 | 91.7 | 99.6 | 100.0 | 97.8 | 100.5 | 103.0 | 105.4 | 105.3 |
| Singapore | 92.0 | 92.4 | 97.0 | 97.0 | 100.0 | 105.2 | 110.0 | 112.0 | 111.7 | 101.1 |
| South Africa | 99.2 | 92.6 | 80.3 | 87.1 | 100.0 | 97.8 | 91.7 | 81.3 | 76.2 | 69.6 |
| Taiwan Province of China | 112.9 | 106.4 | 104.3 | 99.5 | 100.0 | 99.9 | 99.8 | 99.9 | 98.8 | 91.8 |
| Thailand | 92.9 | 105.1 | 98.7 | 94.9 | 100.0 | 98.9 | 99.3 | 104.6 | 101.3 | 94.9 |
| Turkey | 89.2 | 96.4 | 97.1 | 91.3 | 100.0 | 88.4 | 91.4 | 90.3 | 85.6 | 77.2 |
| Venezuela (Bolivarian Republic of) | 90.8 | 99.6 | 120.6 | 159.5 | 100.0 | 116.5 | 139.9 | 134.4 | 202.7 | 301.6 |

Source:  JPMorgan Chase.

**a**  Year 2010=100.

**b**  Indices based on a "broad" measure currency basket of 46 currencies (including the euro). The real effective exchange rate, which adjusts the nominal index for relative price changes, gauges the effect on international price competitiveness of the country's manufactures owing to currency changes and inflation differentials. A rise in the index implies a fall in competitiveness and vice versa. The relative price changes are based on indices most closely measuring the prices of domestically produced finished manufactured goods, excluding food and energy, at the first stage of manufacturing. The weights for currency indices are derived from 2000 bilateral trade patterns of the corresponding countries.

**c**  Average for the first ten months.

**d**  Special Administrative Region of China.

Table A.14
**Indices of prices of primary commodities, 2006–2015**

Index: Year 2000=100

| | Non-fuel commodities | | | | | Combined index | | | | |
| | Food | Tropical beverages | Vegetable oilseeds and oils | Agricultural raw materials | Minerals and metals | Dollar | SDR | Manufactured export prices | Real prices of non-fuel commodities[a] | Crude petroleum[b] |
|---|---|---|---|---|---|---|---|---|---|---|
| 2006 | 151 | 134 | 148 | 147 | 278 | 183 | 164 | 125 | 146 | 221.3 |
| 2007 | 164 | 148 | 226 | 164 | 313 | 207 | 178 | 135 | 153 | 250.4 |
| 2008 | 234 | 178 | 298 | 198 | 332 | 256 | 213 | 142 | 180 | 342.2 |
| 2009 | 220 | 181 | 213 | 163 | 232 | 213 | 182 | 134 | 159 | 221.2 |
| 2010 | 230 | 213 | 262 | 226 | 327 | 256 | 222 | 136 | 188 | 280.6 |
| 2011 | 265 | 270 | 333 | 289 | 375 | 302 | 253 | 150 | 201 | 389.3 |
| 2012 | 270 | 212 | 307 | 223 | 322 | 277 | 239 | 146 | 190 | 396.6 |
| 2013 | 255 | 174 | 269 | 206 | 306 | 258 | 225 | 149 | 173 | 383.6 |
| 2014 | 240 | 214 | 253 | 186 | 280 | 243 | 211 | 148 | 164 | 348.9 |
| **2012** | | | | | | | | | | |
| I | 257 | 232 | 316 | 246 | 342 | 280 | 241 | 147 | 191 | 425.4 |
| II | 264 | 208 | 318 | 229 | 323 | 275 | 238 | 143 | 192 | 386.8 |
| III | 285 | 211 | 318 | 205 | 306 | 278 | 242 | 143 | 194 | 386.2 |
| IV | 276 | 198 | 277 | 211 | 319 | 274 | 236 | 146 | 188 | 388.6 |
| **2013** | | | | | | | | | | |
| I | 266 | 186 | 280 | 216 | 332 | 273 | 237 | 152 | 180 | 396.7 |
| II | 260 | 176 | 262 | 202 | 297 | 259 | 228 | 150 | 173 | 365.6 |
| III | 251 | 169 | 258 | 202 | 296 | 252 | 220 | 148 | 170 | 387.4 |
| IV | 243 | 164 | 274 | 203 | 297 | 250 | 215 | 151 | 165 | 385.7 |
| **2014** | | | | | | | | | | |
| I | 244 | 198 | 279 | 198 | 289 | 249 | 214 | 151 | 165 | 379.6 |
| II | 245 | 220 | 270 | 191 | 281 | 248 | 212 | 150 | 165 | 383.6 |
| III | 238 | 220 | 237 | 181 | 285 | 242 | 210 | 149 | 162 | 365.2 |
| IV | 233 | 219 | 227 | 172 | 265 | 232 | 209 | 143 | 162 | 265.8 |
| **2015** | | | | | | | | | | |
| I | 218 | 201 | 215 | 164 | 235 | 214 | 201 | 133 | 161 | 182.3 |
| II | 204 | 196 | 210 | 166 | 236 | 207 | 196 | 132 | 157 | 217.0 |
| III | 200 | 197 | 194 | 160 | 209 | 196 | 185 | .. | .. | 174.5 |

Sources: UNCTAD, Monthly Commodity Price Bulletin; United Nations, Monthly Bulletin of Statistics; and data from the Organization of the Petroleum Exporting Countries (OPEC) website, available from http://www.opec.org.

a Combined index of non-fuel commodity prices in dollars, deflated by manufactured export price index.

b The new OPEC reference basket, introduced on 16 June 2005, currently has 12 crudes.

Table A.15
**World oil supply and demand, 2007–2016**

| | 2007 | 2008 | 2009 | 2010 | 2011 | 2012 | 2013 | 2014 | 2015[a] | 2016[b] |
|---|---|---|---|---|---|---|---|---|---|---|
| **World oil supply[c, d]** *(millions of barrels per day)* | 84.6 | 84.7 | 83.9 | 85.6 | 86.9 | 89.0 | 89.3 | 91.5 | 93.6 | 94.3 |
| Developed economies | 15.9 | 15.5 | 15.7 | 15.9 | 16.1 | 17.0 | 18.1 | 20.1 | 21.0 | 20.8 |
| Economies in transition | 13.0 | 12.9 | 13.4 | 13.7 | 13.7 | 13.7 | 13.9 | 14.0 | 14.1 | 13.9 |
| Developing economies | 53.7 | 54.3 | 52.8 | 53.8 | 55.0 | 56.2 | 55.1 | 55.2 | 56.3 | 57.3 |
| OPEC[e] | 35.0 | 35.6 | 34.2 | 34.7 | 35.8 | 37.5 | 36.6 | 36.6 | 37.7 | 38.9 |
| Non-OPEC | 18.7 | 18.7 | 18.6 | 19.1 | 19.2 | 18.7 | 18.5 | 18.6 | 18.6 | 18.3 |
| Processing gains[f] | 2.0 | 2.0 | 2.0 | 2.1 | 2.1 | 2.1 | 2.2 | 2.2 | 2.2 | 2.3 |
| Global biofuels[g] | 1.1 | 1.4 | 1.6 | 1.8 | 1.9 | 1.9 | 2.0 | 2.2 | 2.3 | 2.4 |
| **World total demand[h]** | 87.1 | 86.7 | 85.5 | 88.5 | 89.5 | 90.7 | 91.9 | 92.7 | 94.5 | 95.5 |
| **Oil prices** *(dollars per barrel)* | | | | | | | | | | |
| OPEC basket[i] | 69.1 | 94.5 | 61.1 | 77.5 | 107.5 | 109.5 | 105.9 | 96.3 | 53.3 | .. |
| Brent oil | 72.7 | 97.6 | 61.9 | 79.6 | 110.9 | 112.0 | 108.9 | 98.9 | 53.0 | 51.0 |

**Sources:** UN/DESA, International Energy Agency; U.S. Energy Information Administration; and OPEC.
a Partly estimated.
b Baseline scenario forecasts.
c Including global biofuels, crude oil, condensates, natural gas liquids (NGLs), oil from non-conventional sources and other sources of supply.
d Totals may not add up because of rounding.
e Includes Angola as of January 2007 and Ecuador as of December 2007.
f Net volume gains and losses in the refining process (excluding net gain/loss in the economies in transition and China) and marine transportation losses.
g Global biofuels comprise all world biofuel production including fuel ethanol from Brazil and the United States.
h Including deliveries from refineries/primary stocks and marine bunkers, and refinery fuel and non-conventional oils.
i The new OPEC reference basket, introduced on 16 June 2005, currently has 12 crudes.

Table A.16
**World trade:[a] changes in value and volume of exports and imports, by major country group, 2007–2017**

Annual percentage change

| | 2007 | 2008 | 2009 | 2010 | 2011 | 2012 | 2013 | 2014[b] | 2015[c] | 2016[c] | 2017[c] |
|---|---|---|---|---|---|---|---|---|---|---|---|
| **Dollar value of exports** | | | | | | | | | | | |
| World | 16.3 | 14.2 | -19.6 | 19.6 | 18.1 | 1.3 | 2.7 | 1.3 | -6.7 | 3.1 | 7.4 |
| **Developed economies** | **15.6** | **11.0** | **-19.6** | **14.1** | **15.4** | **-1.5** | **3.2** | **2.4** | **-3.6** | **4.5** | **6.3** |
| North America | 11.5 | 9.6 | -16.7 | 17.4 | 14.3 | 3.7 | 2.4 | 3.1 | -0.4 | 4.0 | 6.1 |
| EU plus other Europe | 17.6 | 11.0 | -19.9 | 10.7 | 16.4 | -3.0 | 5.1 | 2.4 | -4.0 | 5.0 | 6.7 |
| Developed Asia | 11.2 | 13.9 | -23.3 | 31.3 | 11.6 | -2.5 | -6.8 | 0.9 | -8.5 | 2.4 | 3.6 |
| **Economies in transition** | **21.0** | **32.9** | **-32.4** | **27.8** | **30.8** | **3.3** | **-0.6** | **-8.9** | **-36.3** | **-6.9** | **13.4** |
| South-Eastern Europe | 19.5 | 22.3 | -18.7 | 13.7 | 21.6 | -6.6 | 16.2 | 5.1 | -9.4 | 4.4 | 5.1 |
| Commonwealth of Independent States and Georgia | 21.1 | 33.3 | -32.9 | 28.4 | 31.2 | 3.7 | -1.1 | -9.5 | -37.6 | -7.6 | 14.0 |
| **Developing economies** | **16.9** | **17.7** | **-18.2** | **27.5** | **20.7** | **4.8** | **2.4** | **0.9** | **-8.3** | **1.8** | **8.6** |
| Latin America and the Caribbean | 12.9 | 15.2 | -20.5 | 31.0 | 17.9 | 1.4 | 0.0 | 0.0 | -9.0 | 2.4 | 7.1 |
| Africa | 12.0 | 29.4 | -27.3 | 27.3 | 16.3 | 7.2 | -9.0 | -4.1 | -21.3 | 0.4 | 12.4 |
| East Asia | 18.3 | 14.0 | -15.1 | 28.4 | 18.3 | 4.6 | 4.0 | 3.0 | -3.3 | 2.3 | 7.4 |
| South Asia | 24.1 | 15.7 | -6.1 | 25.9 | 24.8 | -0.8 | 6.9 | -3.1 | -10.7 | 3.6 | 11.3 |
| Western Asia | 15.9 | 29.4 | -26.4 | 20.8 | 34.9 | 9.9 | 2.1 | -2.1 | -20.1 | -1.4 | 12.4 |
| **Dollar value of imports** | | | | | | | | | | | |
| World | 16.1 | 14.6 | -20.0 | 19.2 | 18.4 | 1.1 | 2.5 | 1.0 | -6.8 | 3.5 | 8.2 |
| **Developed economies** | **13.7** | **11.5** | **-21.9** | **14.5** | **16.2** | **-1.9** | **1.6** | **2.2** | **-5.3** | **4.5** | **8.0** |
| North America | 6.6 | 7.6 | -22.0 | 19.7 | 13.6 | 3.0 | 0.1 | 2.9 | -3.3 | 5.5 | 7.6 |
| EU plus other Europe | 17.4 | 11.9 | -21.5 | 11.1 | 16.2 | -5.1 | 3.5 | 2.1 | -5.3 | 4.7 | 8.3 |
| Developed Asia | 10.6 | 20.5 | -24.8 | 24.1 | 23.1 | 5.5 | -5.4 | 1.0 | -10.7 | 0.2 | 6.6 |
| **Economies in transition** | **34.0** | **30.0** | **-30.2** | **22.2** | **28.2** | **8.1** | **3.4** | **-10.2** | **-22.5** | **-3.6** | **9.2** |
| South-Eastern Europe | 30.4 | 27.0 | -27.0 | 2.3 | 19.9 | -6.7 | 5.2 | 3.1 | -8.7 | 5.6 | 9.0 |
| Commonwealth of Independent States and Georgia | 34.4 | 30.3 | -30.5 | 24.1 | 28.8 | 9.2 | 3.3 | -11.1 | -23.5 | -4.4 | 9.2 |
| **Developing economies** | **19.5** | **19.2** | **-15.2** | **27.0** | **21.0** | **5.0** | **3.8** | **0.4** | **-7.6** | **2.5** | **8.6** |
| Latin America and the Caribbean | 19.3 | 20.8 | -20.2 | 28.4 | 19.7 | 5.6 | 4.7 | -1.9 | -10.2 | 2.4 | 8.3 |
| Africa | 28.1 | 26.3 | -9.8 | 11.8 | 15.4 | 4.1 | 2.6 | 1.8 | -5.5 | 3.0 | 8.2 |
| East Asia | 15.7 | 16.9 | -15.8 | 32.8 | 21.7 | 4.8 | 3.7 | 0.6 | -8.1 | 3.3 | 8.9 |
| South Asia | 25.8 | 19.8 | -2.7 | 22.6 | 24.7 | 4.4 | 0.1 | -2.9 | -11.2 | -1.3 | 10.2 |
| Western Asia | 28.9 | 22.3 | -17.7 | 15.2 | 20.7 | 6.5 | 6.6 | 3.7 | -1.3 | 1.3 | 6.9 |
| **Volume of exports** | | | | | | | | | | | |
| World | 7.4 | 2.9 | -9.8 | 12.0 | 6.4 | 3.0 | 3.2 | 3.6 | 2.7 | 4.0 | 4.5 |
| **Developed economies** | **6.7** | **2.0** | **-11.8** | **11.4** | **5.6** | **2.4** | **2.7** | **3.8** | **3.8** | **4.2** | **4.9** |
| North America | 7.2 | 3.3 | -9.7 | 10.8 | 6.4 | 3.3 | 2.6 | 3.8 | 2.7 | 3.0 | 3.5 |
| EU plus other Europe | 6.4 | 1.6 | -11.6 | 10.5 | 6.3 | 2.2 | 2.8 | 3.2 | 4.4 | 4.7 | 5.5 |
| Developed Asia | 7.4 | 1.8 | -17.8 | 18.9 | -0.2 | 1.4 | 2.4 | 7.8 | 2.6 | 3.5 | 3.7 |
| **Economies in transition** | **7.2** | **1.6** | **-6.7** | **6.8** | **2.9** | **1.2** | **2.7** | **-1.1** | **-2.7** | **0.2** | **1.7** |
| South-Eastern Europe | 2.4 | 5.4 | -6.7 | 15.7 | 7.6 | 0.2 | 12.9 | 5.5 | 6.1 | 5.6 | 5.5 |
| Commonwealth of Independent States and Georgia | 7.4 | 1.5 | -6.7 | 6.4 | 2.7 | 1.3 | 2.3 | -1.4 | -3.1 | -0.1 | 1.5 |

Table A.16

**World trade[a]: changes in value and volume of exports and imports, by major country group, 2007–2017** (*continued*)

Annual percentage change

| | 2007 | 2008 | 2009 | 2010 | 2011 | 2012 | 2013 | 2014[b] | 2015[c] | 2016[c] | 2017[c] |
|---|---|---|---|---|---|---|---|---|---|---|---|
| **Developing economies** | 8.5 | 4.4 | -7.1 | 13.3 | 7.9 | 4.0 | 3.9 | 3.8 | 1.7 | 4.1 | 4.3 |
| Latin America and the Caribbean | 3.5 | 0.8 | -9.3 | 8.5 | 6.7 | 2.5 | 1.0 | 1.8 | 2.8 | 3.8 | 4.7 |
| Africa | 3.2 | 8.2 | -14.5 | 10.1 | 1.3 | 3.7 | -6.2 | 2.6 | 4.5 | 4.8 | 4.2 |
| East Asia | 12.1 | 4.6 | -6.4 | 17.1 | 7.7 | 3.7 | 6.3 | 4.5 | 0.0 | 3.4 | 4.1 |
| South Asia | 6.3 | 7.9 | 0.8 | 12.3 | 13.1 | 3.4 | 6.0 | 2.1 | -1.3 | 5.0 | 5.7 |
| Western Asia | 5.1 | 3.6 | -6.3 | 6.0 | 11.4 | 7.4 | 1.3 | 4.1 | 7.9 | 6.9 | 4.3 |
| **Volume of imports** | | | | | | | | | | | |
| World | 8.1 | 2.9 | -10.9 | 13.0 | 7.0 | 2.8 | 3.0 | 2.9 | 2.6 | 4.0 | 4.9 |
| **Developed economies** | 5.3 | 0.4 | -12.1 | 10.8 | 5.0 | 1.0 | 1.8 | 3.8 | 4.6 | 4.5 | 4.7 |
| North America | 3.0 | -2.0 | -13.5 | 12.9 | 5.5 | 2.5 | 1.1 | 3.5 | 4.7 | 4.6 | 4.1 |
| EU plus other Europe | 6.4 | 1.2 | -11.2 | 9.7 | 4.4 | -0.4 | 2.0 | 3.8 | 5.2 | 5.0 | 5.3 |
| Developed Asia | 4.6 | 2.5 | -14.1 | 12.0 | 7.1 | 5.4 | 2.0 | 5.2 | 1.1 | 1.3 | 2.6 |
| **Economies in transition** | 22.8 | 11.8 | -26.6 | 16.7 | 16.4 | 8.4 | 2.6 | -8.0 | -14.2 | -2.7 | 6.4 |
| South-Eastern Europe | 12.7 | 10.5 | -16.1 | 3.5 | 6.1 | 0.8 | 4.3 | 4.4 | 4.5 | 5.7 | 5.9 |
| Commonwealth of Independent States and Georgia | 23.7 | 11.9 | -27.4 | 18.0 | 17.2 | 9.0 | 2.5 | -8.9 | -15.6 | -3.5 | 6.5 |
| **Developing economies** | 12.3 | 6.6 | -7.4 | 16.4 | 9.3 | 5.0 | 4.9 | 2.6 | 1.1 | 3.8 | 5.1 |
| Latin America and the Caribbean | 13.2 | 8.5 | -14.8 | 21.2 | 11.6 | 4.4 | 2.4 | 0.5 | -0.3 | 3.2 | 5.3 |
| Africa | 17.8 | 8.8 | -5.7 | 7.5 | 1.5 | 6.8 | 3.9 | 3.5 | 3.5 | 4.2 | 5.0 |
| East Asia | 10.0 | 4.4 | -5.7 | 19.3 | 8.4 | 4.4 | 6.6 | 3.3 | 1.0 | 3.9 | 5.3 |
| South Asia | 9.3 | 13.7 | 1.6 | 10.1 | 14.9 | 5.6 | -1.6 | -1.6 | -1.7 | 4.1 | 5.3 |
| Western Asia | 19.6 | 8.1 | -12.4 | 9.2 | 11.7 | 6.7 | 5.9 | 4.7 | 4.0 | 3.5 | 4.2 |

Source: UN/DESA.

**a** Includes goods and non-factor services.

**b** Partly estimated.

**c** Baseline scenario forecasts, based in part on Project LINK.

Table A.17
**Balance of payments on current accounts, by country or country group, summary table, 2006–2014**

Billions of dollars

| | 2006 | 2007 | 2008 | 2009 | 2010 | 2011 | 2012 | 2013 | 2014 |
|---|---|---|---|---|---|---|---|---|---|
| Developed economies | -573.6 | -556.9 | -765.2 | -250.8 | -181.9 | -223.4 | -190.2 | -11.4 | -44.6 |
| Japan | 174.5 | 212.1 | 142.6 | 145.2 | 221.0 | 129.8 | 59.7 | 40.7 | 24.4 |
| United States | -806.7 | -718.6 | -690.8 | -384.0 | -442.0 | -460.4 | -449.7 | -376.8 | -389.5 |
| Europe[a] | 93.7 | 10.9 | -157.0 | 76.0 | 143.7 | 203.6 | 333.2 | 436.6 | 408.3 |
| EU-15 | 41.6 | 20.8 | -123.0 | 34.1 | 60.4 | 136.5 | 229.5 | 305.6 | 308.1 |
| New EU member States | -63.9 | -107.3 | -118.9 | -41.3 | -48.8 | -47.0 | -27.7 | 1.4 | 1.2 |
| Economies in transition[b] | 88.5 | 53.8 | 89.7 | 35.3 | 63.2 | 99.4 | 58.9 | 12.2 | 50.1 |
| South-Eastern Europe | -5.4 | -11.6 | -18.6 | -7.5 | -6.0 | -8.5 | -8.5 | -6.0 | -6.6 |
| Commonwealth of Independent States[c] | 95.1 | 67.3 | 111.0 | 43.9 | 70.4 | 109.8 | 69.3 | 19.1 | 58.3 |
| Developing economies | 708.6 | 777.8 | 785.3 | 390.2 | 412.7 | 479.6 | 501.3 | 394.3 | 361.9 |
| Net fuel exporters | 393.4 | 344.3 | 437.8 | 75.6 | 221.1 | 493.2 | 479.3 | 379.5 | 196.6 |
| Net fuel importers | 315.2 | 433.5 | 347.4 | 314.6 | 191.6 | -13.6 | 22.0 | 14.8 | 165.3 |
| Latin America and the Caribbean | 48.3 | 8.0 | -37.2 | -28.3 | -93.8 | -100.3 | -135.7 | -170.5 | -172.3 |
| Net fuel exporters | 33.9 | 18.5 | 37.9 | 0.3 | 3.5 | 17.4 | 2.3 | -5.0 | -7.6 |
| Net fuel importers | 14.5 | -10.6 | -75.1 | -28.6 | -97.3 | -117.7 | -138.0 | -165.4 | -164.7 |
| Africa | 91.8 | 78.3 | 70.0 | -30.3 | 11.1 | 0.6 | -11.1 | -43.7 | -96.8 |
| Net fuel exporters | 108.1 | 103.6 | 112.4 | 3.5 | 39.7 | 46.5 | 54.0 | 22.9 | -35.1 |
| Net fuel importers | -16.3 | -25.3 | -42.4 | -33.8 | -28.5 | -45.9 | -65.2 | -66.6 | -61.7 |
| Western Asia | 188.2 | 148.7 | 224.6 | 41.5 | 95.1 | 283.0 | 348.8 | 279.1 | 187.5 |
| Net fuel exporters | 215.7 | 184.0 | 268.4 | 53.4 | 143.5 | 360.9 | 409.0 | 351.2 | 235.6 |
| Net fuel importers | -27.5 | -35.3 | -43.7 | -11.9 | -48.4 | -77.9 | -60.2 | -72.0 | -48.2 |
| East and South Asia | 380.3 | 542.9 | 527.8 | 407.4 | 400.2 | 296.4 | 299.3 | 329.3 | 443.5 |
| Net fuel exporters | 35.7 | 38.3 | 19.2 | 18.4 | 34.4 | 68.5 | 13.9 | 10.5 | 3.7 |
| Net fuel importers | 344.6 | 504.6 | 508.7 | 388.9 | 365.8 | 227.9 | 285.4 | 318.9 | 439.8 |
| World residual[d] | 223.5 | 274.7 | 109.7 | 174.7 | 294.0 | 355.6 | 370.0 | 395.1 | 367.4 |

Sources:   International Monetary Fund (IMF), World Economic Outlook, October 2015.
Note: IMF-WEO has adopted the sixth edition of the Balance of Payments Manual (BPM6).
a  Europe consists of the EU-15, the new EU member States and Iceland, Norway and Switzerland.
b  Includes Georgia.
c  Excludes Georgia, which left the Commonwealth of Independent States on 18 August 2009.
d  Statistical discrepancy.

Table A.18
**Balance of payments on current accounts, by country or country group, 2006–2014**

Billions of dollars

| | 2006 | 2007 | 2008 | 2009 | 2010 | 2011 | 2012 | 2013 | 2014 |
|---|---|---|---|---|---|---|---|---|---|
| **Developed economies** | | | | | | | | | |
| Trade balance | -724.1 | -705.2 | -817.1 | -398.8 | -489.9 | -675.6 | -632.4 | -488.0 | -506.2 |
| Services, net | 225.0 | 311.4 | 316.5 | 289.3 | 324.0 | 414.6 | 413.4 | 471.8 | 510.5 |
| Primary income | 203.4 | 168.3 | 99.6 | 217.9 | 353.6 | 423.4 | 412.8 | 407.9 | 362.7 |
| Secondary income | -278.0 | -331.4 | -364.3 | -359.3 | -369.6 | -385.8 | -383.9 | -403.0 | -411.5 |
| Current-account balance | -573.6 | -556.9 | -765.2 | -250.8 | -181.9 | -223.4 | -190.2 | -11.4 | -44.6 |
| **Japan** | | | | | | | | | |
| Trade balance | 94.9 | 120.9 | 55.6 | 57.8 | 108.5 | -4.5 | -53.9 | -90.0 | -99.3 |
| Services, net | -32.0 | -37.0 | -38.0 | -34.9 | -30.3 | -35.0 | -47.8 | -35.7 | -29.2 |
| Primary income | 122.3 | 139.8 | 138.1 | 134.6 | 155.1 | 183.1 | 175.6 | 176.4 | 171.9 |
| Secondary income | -10.7 | -11.5 | -13.1 | -12.3 | -12.4 | -13.8 | -14.2 | -10.0 | -19.0 |
| Current-account balance | 174.5 | 212.1 | 142.6 | 145.2 | 221.0 | 129.8 | 59.7 | 40.7 | 24.4 |
| **United States** | | | | | | | | | |
| Trade balance | -837.3 | -821.2 | -832.5 | -509.7 | -648.7 | -740.6 | -741.2 | -702.6 | -741.5 |
| Services, net | 75.6 | 115.8 | 123.8 | 125.9 | 154.0 | 192.0 | 204.4 | 224.2 | 233.1 |
| Primary income | 43.3 | 100.6 | 146.1 | 123.6 | 177.7 | 221.0 | 212.2 | 224.5 | 238.0 |
| Secondary income | -88.3 | -113.9 | -128.2 | -123.8 | -125.0 | -132.7 | -125.1 | -122.9 | -119.2 |
| Current-account balance | -806.7 | -718.6 | -690.8 | -384.0 | -442.0 | -460.4 | -449.7 | -376.8 | -389.5 |
| **Europe[a]** | | | | | | | | | |
| Trade balance | -8.8 | -24.5 | -71.7 | 63.1 | 46.3 | 43.9 | 184.1 | 306.0 | 328.1 |
| Services, net | 186.4 | 243.5 | 249.7 | 213.2 | 225.0 | 288.3 | 291.4 | 319.3 | 335.3 |
| Primary income | 93.2 | -3.9 | -112.2 | 19.9 | 99.8 | 105.4 | 96.3 | 77.1 | 14.4 |
| Secondary income | -177.1 | -204.1 | -222.7 | -220.3 | -227.4 | -233.9 | -238.6 | -265.7 | -269.6 |
| Current-account balance | 93.7 | 10.9 | -157.0 | 76.0 | 143.7 | 203.6 | 333.2 | 436.6 | 408.3 |
| **EU-15** | | | | | | | | | |
| Trade balance | -5.4 | 0.7 | -51.2 | 47.0 | 7.7 | -3.2 | 107.2 | 205.2 | 239.3 |
| Services, net | 130.1 | 174.2 | 171.7 | 151.5 | 163.6 | 220.7 | 225.2 | 248.0 | 260.7 |
| Primary income | 92.4 | 48.3 | -27.6 | 47.4 | 109.3 | 144.4 | 124.4 | 103.5 | 54.4 |
| Secondary income | -175.5 | -202.5 | -215.8 | -211.8 | -220.1 | -225.4 | -227.4 | -251.1 | -246.4 |
| Current-account balance | 41.6 | 20.8 | -123.0 | 34.1 | 60.4 | 136.5 | 229.5 | 305.6 | 308.1 |
| **New EU member States** | | | | | | | | | |
| Trade balance | -71.7 | -101.2 | -125.8 | -43.9 | -45.3 | -49.4 | -32.6 | -10.9 | -12.7 |
| Services, net | 31.7 | 39.9 | 44.7 | 35.6 | 36.2 | 44.7 | 45.6 | 52.6 | 57.3 |
| Primary income | -31.8 | -54.1 | -44.3 | -37.8 | -47.1 | -49.8 | -45.0 | -46.3 | -46.7 |
| Secondary income | 8.0 | 8.2 | 6.5 | 4.8 | 7.4 | 7.5 | 4.3 | 5.9 | 3.3 |
| Current-account balance | -63.9 | -107.3 | -118.9 | -41.3 | -48.8 | -47.0 | -27.7 | 1.4 | 1.2 |
| **Economies in transition[b]** | | | | | | | | | |
| Trade balance | 133.5 | 113.9 | 176.3 | 105.1 | 155.3 | 221.9 | 205.5 | 184.5 | 205.0 |
| Services, net | -15.6 | -23.7 | -27.9 | -24.0 | -31.2 | -36.7 | -52.8 | -65.3 | -67.1 |
| Primary income | -41.9 | -48.3 | -72.4 | -59.1 | -74.5 | -100.5 | -106.1 | -116.8 | -98.0 |
| Secondary income | 12.6 | 11.8 | 13.6 | 13.4 | 13.6 | 14.7 | 12.3 | 9.7 | 10.1 |
| Current-account balance | 88.5 | 53.8 | 89.7 | 35.3 | 63.2 | 99.4 | 58.9 | 12.2 | 50.1 |

Table A.18
**Balance of payments on current accounts, by country or country group, 2006–2014** (*continued*)

Billions of dollars

| | 2006 | 2007 | 2008 | 2009 | 2010 | 2011 | 2012 | 2013 | 2014 |
|---|---|---|---|---|---|---|---|---|---|
| **Economies in transition[b]** (*continued*) | | | | | | | | | |
| **South-Eastern Europe** | | | | | | | | | |
| Trade balance | -15.5 | -22.7 | -29.8 | -19.8 | -17.5 | -20.8 | -19.4 | -17.0 | -18.1 |
| Services, net | 1.3 | 2.0 | 2.3 | 2.3 | 2.4 | 3.1 | 2.8 | 3.0 | 3.6 |
| Primary income | 0.1 | -0.5 | -0.8 | -0.4 | -1.0 | -1.2 | -1.6 | -1.9 | -2.1 |
| Secondary income | 8.8 | 9.7 | 9.7 | 10.4 | 10.1 | 10.4 | 9.7 | 9.9 | 10.0 |
| Current-account balance | -5.4 | -11.6 | -18.6 | -7.5 | -6.0 | -8.5 | -8.5 | -6.0 | -6.6 |
| **Commonwealth of Independent States[c]** | | | | | | | | | |
| Trade balance | 151.0 | 139.5 | 209.9 | 127.3 | 175.5 | 246.2 | 229.1 | 205.0 | 227.3 |
| Services, net | -17.1 | -25.9 | -30.2 | -26.7 | -34.2 | -40.5 | -56.7 | -69.7 | -72.0 |
| Primary income | -42.2 | -47.8 | -71.5 | -58.7 | -73.3 | -98.9 | -104.4 | -114.6 | -95.7 |
| Secondary income | 3.3 | 1.4 | 2.9 | 2.0 | 2.4 | 2.9 | 1.2 | -1.6 | -1.3 |
| Current-account balance | 95.1 | 67.3 | 111.0 | 43.9 | 70.4 | 109.8 | 69.3 | 19.1 | 58.3 |
| **Developing economies** | | | | | | | | | |
| Trade balance | 802.5 | 855.6 | 918.4 | 577.6 | 720.0 | 883.5 | 932.1 | 951.7 | 909.4 |
| Services, net | -125.7 | -141.7 | -186.5 | -183.7 | -207.3 | -241.6 | -272.9 | -309.4 | -365.3 |
| Primary income | -155.1 | -149.2 | -182.2 | -210.7 | -318.9 | -382.6 | -354.4 | -426.4 | -353.9 |
| Secondary income | 186.9 | 213.1 | 235.5 | 206.9 | 219.0 | 220.4 | 196.5 | 178.4 | 171.7 |
| Current-account balance | 708.6 | 777.8 | 785.3 | 390.2 | 412.7 | 479.6 | 501.3 | 394.3 | 361.9 |
| **Net fuel exporters** | | | | | | | | | |
| Trade balance | 517.8 | 521.0 | 707.1 | 341.1 | 540.6 | 877.6 | 889.0 | 819.0 | 652.4 |
| Services, net | -114.6 | -157.7 | -209.7 | -192.7 | -209.1 | -242.1 | -258.5 | -270.2 | -305.5 |
| Primary income | -23.8 | -25.4 | -64.2 | -64.7 | -97.2 | -121.3 | -123.1 | -125.1 | -110.5 |
| Secondary income | 14.0 | 6.4 | 4.6 | -8.1 | -13.4 | -21.0 | -28.2 | -44.2 | -40.3 |
| Current-account balance | 393.4 | 344.3 | 437.8 | 75.6 | 221.0 | 493.2 | 479.3 | 379.5 | 196.1 |
| **Net fuel importers** | | | | | | | | | |
| Trade balance | 284.7 | 334.7 | 211.3 | 236.5 | 179.3 | 5.9 | 43.2 | 132.7 | 257.0 |
| Services, net | -11.1 | 16.1 | 23.3 | 9.0 | 1.8 | 0.4 | -14.5 | -39.2 | -59.8 |
| Primary income | -131.2 | -123.9 | -118.0 | -145.9 | -221.8 | -261.3 | -231.3 | -301.3 | -243.3 |
| Secondary income | 172.9 | 206.6 | 230.9 | 215.0 | 232.3 | 241.3 | 224.6 | 222.6 | 212.1 |
| Current-account balance | 315.2 | 433.5 | 347.5 | 314.6 | 191.7 | -13.6 | 22.0 | 14.8 | 165.9 |
| **Latin America and the Caribbean** | | | | | | | | | |
| Trade balance | 99.3 | 69.5 | 40.7 | 51.0 | 48.4 | 71.2 | 43.5 | 11.8 | -3.8 |
| Services, net | -17.3 | -24.9 | -32.4 | -33.9 | -49.9 | -65.2 | -70.6 | -74.5 | -74.4 |
| Primary income | -97.5 | -103.4 | -112.5 | -102.9 | -153.7 | -169.5 | -170.6 | -169.7 | -159.3 |
| Secondary income | 63.9 | 66.8 | 67.0 | 57.4 | 61.5 | 63.2 | 62.0 | 62.0 | 65.1 |
| Current-account balance | 48.3 | 8.0 | -37.2 | -28.3 | -93.8 | -100.3 | -135.7 | -170.5 | -172.3 |
| **Africa** | | | | | | | | | |
| Trade balance | 92.6 | 95.6 | 109.4 | -0.8 | 54.7 | 60.0 | 48.8 | 14.7 | -58.8 |
| Services, net | -16.1 | -27.9 | -47.2 | -42.2 | -45.0 | -54.2 | -52.0 | -48.5 | -53.8 |
| Primary income | -33.9 | -46.5 | -57.5 | -47.6 | -65.3 | -78.0 | -83.2 | -87.0 | -78.5 |

Table A.18
**Balance of payments on current accounts, by country or country group, 2006–2014** (*continued*)

Billions of dollars

| | 2006 | 2007 | 2008 | 2009 | 2010 | 2011 | 2012 | 2013 | 2014 |
|---|---|---|---|---|---|---|---|---|---|
| **Africa** (*continued*) | | | | | | | | | |
| Secondary income | 49.3 | 57.1 | 65.3 | 60.3 | 66.8 | 72.7 | 75.3 | 77.1 | 94.4 |
| Current-account balance | 91.8 | 78.3 | 70.0 | -30.3 | 11.1 | 0.6 | -11.1 | -43.7 | -96.8 |
| **Western Asia** | | | | | | | | | |
| Trade balance | 232.3 | 217.6 | 347.1 | 170.2 | 253.4 | 466.6 | 546.8 | 499.4 | 438.3 |
| Services, net | -45.0 | -65.3 | -85.8 | -75.9 | -89.6 | -106.3 | -115.0 | -125.4 | -153.5 |
| Primary income | 16.3 | 23.3 | -5.6 | -12.4 | -19.0 | -16.9 | -11.9 | -9.4 | -3.1 |
| Secondary income | -15.4 | -26.9 | -31.1 | -40.3 | -49.8 | -60.3 | -71.2 | -85.6 | -94.2 |
| Current-account balance | 188.2 | 148.7 | 224.6 | 41.5 | 95.1 | 283.0 | 348.8 | 279.1 | 187.5 |
| **East Asia** | | | | | | | | | |
| Trade balance | 430.4 | 544.8 | 537.9 | 479.7 | 481.5 | 442.6 | 496.4 | 575.4 | 696.0 |
| Services, net | -65.2 | -48.7 | -57.0 | -52.8 | -52.6 | -67.2 | -87.0 | -121.9 | -147.1 |
| Primary income | -28.7 | -13.5 | 5.4 | -33.6 | -58.1 | -97.7 | -62.1 | -130.5 | -81.2 |
| Secondary income | 38.4 | 51.0 | 62.9 | 49.1 | 55.0 | 43.3 | 23.5 | 14.7 | -6.1 |
| Current-account balance | 374.8 | 533.7 | 549.2 | 442.3 | 425.8 | 321.1 | 370.8 | 337.8 | 461.7 |
| **South Asia** | | | | | | | | | |
| Trade balance | -52.0 | -71.8 | -116.6 | -122.5 | -118.0 | -157.0 | -203.4 | -149.7 | -162.3 |
| Services, net | 18.0 | 25.1 | 35.9 | 21.2 | 29.7 | 51.3 | 51.7 | 60.9 | 63.4 |
| Primary income | -11.3 | -9.2 | -12.0 | -14.1 | -22.8 | -20.5 | -26.7 | -29.7 | -31.7 |
| Secondary income | 50.8 | 65.0 | 71.4 | 80.5 | 85.4 | 101.5 | 106.9 | 110.2 | 112.5 |
| Current-account balance | 5.5 | 9.2 | -21.3 | -35.0 | -25.6 | -24.7 | -71.5 | -8.4 | -18.1 |
| **World residual**[d] | | | | | | | | | |
| Trade balance | 211.9 | 264.4 | 277.6 | 283.9 | 385.4 | 429.8 | 505.2 | 648.2 | 608.1 |
| Services, net | 83.7 | 145.9 | 102.2 | 81.6 | 85.5 | 136.3 | 87.7 | 97.1 | 78.1 |
| Primary income | 6.4 | -29.2 | -154.9 | -51.9 | -39.9 | -59.7 | -47.7 | -135.2 | -89.1 |
| Secondary income | -78.5 | -106.5 | -115.2 | -139.0 | -137.0 | -150.7 | -175.1 | -215.0 | -229.7 |
| Current-account balance | 223.5 | 274.7 | 109.7 | 174.7 | 294.0 | 355.6 | 370.0 | 395.1 | 367.4 |

Sources:  International Monetary Fund (IMF), World Economic Outlook, October 2015.
Note:  IMF-WEO has adopted the sixth edition of the Balance of Payments Manual (BPM6).
a  Europe consists of EU-15, new EU member States plus Iceland, Norway and Switzerland.
b  Includes Georgia.
c  Excludes Georgia, which left the Commonwealth of Independent States on 18 August 2009.
d  Statistical discrepancy.

Table A.19
Net ODA from major sources, by type, 1993–2014

| Donor group or country | Growth rate of ODA (2013 prices and exchange rates) | | | | | ODA as a percentage of GNI | Total ODA (millions of dollars) | Percentage distribution of ODA by type, 2014 | | | |
|---|---|---|---|---|---|---|---|---|---|---|---|
| | | | | | | | | Bilateral | Multilateral | | |
| | 1993-2003 | 2003-2011 | 2012 | 2013 | 2014 | 2014 | 2014 | Total | Total (United Nations & Other) | United Nations | Other |
| Total DAC countries | 0.1 | 5.1 | -3.7 | 5.7 | -0.3 | .. | 135172 | 69.2 | 30.8 | 4.9 | 25.9 |
| Total EU | 0.3 | 5.0 | -6.9 | 6.0 | 1.6 | .. | 73895 | 60.7 | 39.3 | 5.1 | 34.2 |
| Austria | 9.6 | 3.1 | 6.0 | 1.0 | -3.8 | 0.26 | 1144 | 48.8 | 51.2 | 1.8 | 49.4 |
| Belgium | 4.2 | 4.3 | -12.6 | -5.2 | 3.3 | 0.45 | 2385 | 59.4 | 40.6 | 6.1 | 34.5 |
| Denmark | 2.5 | 0.3 | -3.2 | 3.8 | 1.8 | 0.86 | 3003 | 71.0 | 29.0 | 13.1 | 16.0 |
| Finland | -2.2 | 8.0 | -1.1 | 2.9 | 12.5 | 0.60 | 1635 | 57.4 | 42.6 | 14.4 | 28.2 |
| France[a] | -2.8 | 4.8 | -1.2 | -9.4 | -9.2 | 0.36 | 10371 | 60.7 | 39.3 | 2.1 | 37.2 |
| Germany | -1.6 | 5.4 | -2.2 | 4.3 | 12.0 | 0.41 | 16249 | 70.2 | 29.8 | 2.4 | 27.4 |
| Greece | .. | 0.9 | -16.6 | -27.7 | 6.3 | 0.11 | 248 | 18.6 | 81.4 | 6.1 | 75.3 |
| Ireland | 15.9 | 6.1 | -5.5 | 0.3 | -4.5 | 0.39 | 809 | 64.6 | 35.4 | 11.4 | 23.9 |
| Italy | -4.2 | 0.2 | -32.6 | 19.6 | -2.9 | 0.16 | 3342 | 22.3 | 77.7 | 5.9 | 71.8 |
| Luxembourg | 13.8 | 4.7 | 2.0 | 2.8 | -2.0 | 1.06 | 423 | 71.0 | 29.0 | 12.8 | 16.2 |
| Netherlands | 2.4 | 1.9 | -7.0 | -5.7 | 1.6 | 0.64 | 5573 | 72.3 | 27.7 | 8.1 | 19.7 |
| Portugal | 1.3 | 2.6 | -10.9 | -20.4 | -14.9 | 0.19 | 419 | 57.2 | 42.8 | 2.3 | 40.5 |
| Spain | 3.6 | 7.6 | -47.3 | 12.1 | -20.3 | 0.14 | 1893 | 26.1 | 73.9 | 3.4 | 70.6 |
| Sweden | 1.4 | 6.1 | -3.4 | 5.9 | 11.0 | 1.10 | 6223 | 70.3 | 29.7 | 9.9 | 19.7 |
| United Kingdom | 4.0 | 8.5 | -0.1 | 28.2 | 1.2 | 0.71 | 19387 | 57.5 | 42.5 | 4.4 | 38.1 |
| Australia | 0.6 | 6.8 | 8.3 | -4.8 | -7.2 | 0.27 | 4203 | 92.5 | 7.5 | 3.5 | 4.0 |
| Canada | -2.6 | 5.3 | 3.0 | -10.9 | -10.7 | 0.24 | 4196 | 77.1 | 22.9 | 4.5 | 18.5 |
| Japan | -1.5 | -1.5 | -1.1 | 34.4 | -15.3 | 0.19 | 9188 | 64.7 | 35.3 | 6.4 | 28.9 |
| New Zealand | 2.6 | 5.2 | 3.9 | -2.0 | 6.8 | 0.27 | 502 | 80.2 | 19.8 | 8.8 | 11.0 |
| Norway | 2.4 | 3.7 | 0.9 | 15.4 | -4.3 | 0.99 | 5024 | 75.6 | 24.4 | 11.1 | 13.2 |
| Switzerland | 1.0 | 5.0 | 5.8 | 3.9 | 9.2 | 0.49 | 3548 | 79.1 | 20.9 | 6.8 | 14.1 |
| United States | 0.2 | 7.9 | -2.8 | 0.6 | 3.0 | 0.19 | 32729 | 83.1 | 16.9 | 2.8 | 14.1 |

Source: UN/DESA, based on OECD/DAC online database, available from http://www.oecd-ilibrary.org/statistics.

a  Excluding flows from France to the Overseas Departments, namely Guadeloupe, French Guiana, Martinique and Réunion.

Table A.20
**Total net ODA flows from OECD Development Assistance Committee countries, by type, 2005–2014**

| | Net disbursements at current prices and exchange rates (billions of dollars) | | | | | | | | | |
|---|---|---|---|---|---|---|---|---|---|---|
| | 2005 | 2006 | 2007 | 2008 | 2009 | 2010 | 2011 | 2012 | 2013 | 2014 |
| **Official Development Assistance** | 108.3 | 105.4 | 104.9 | 122.8 | 120.6 | 128.4 | 134.7 | 126.9 | 134.9 | 135.2 |
| **Bilateral official development assistance** | 83.1 | 77.5 | 73.7 | 87.1 | 83.9 | 90.6 | 94.5 | 88.4 | 93.5 | 93.5 |
| *in the form of:* | | | | | | | | | | |
| Technical cooperation | 20.8 | 22.4 | 15.1 | 17.3 | 17.6 | 18.6 | 17.7 | 18.2 | 16.9 | .. |
| Humanitarian aid | 7.2 | 6.8 | 6.5 | 8.8 | 8.6 | 9.3 | 9.7 | 8.5 | 10.5 | 12.9 |
| Debt forgiveness | 26.2 | 18.9 | 9.7 | 11.1 | 2.0 | 4.2 | 6.3 | 3.3 | 6.1 | .. |
| Bilateral loans | -0.8 | -2.4 | -2.2 | -1.1 | 2.5 | 3.8 | 1.9 | 2.6 | 1.4 | .. |
| **Contributions to multilateral institutions**[a] | 25.2 | 27.9 | 31.2 | 35.7 | 36.6 | 37.8 | 40.2 | 38.5 | 41.3 | 41.6 |
| *of which are:* | | | | | | | | | | |
| UN agencies | 5.5 | 5.3 | 5.9 | 5.9 | 6.2 | 6.5 | 6.5 | 6.6 | 6.9 | 6.6 |
| EU institutions | 9.4 | 10.1 | 12.0 | 13.5 | 14.2 | 13.6 | 13.7 | 12.0 | 12.8 | 13.0 |
| World Bank | 5.3 | 7.2 | 6.2 | 8.6 | 7.6 | 9.1 | 10.2 | 8.6 | 9.3 | 10.0 |
| Regional development banks | 2.2 | 2.5 | 2.4 | 3.2 | 3.1 | 3.2 | 4.1 | 3.9 | 3.9 | 4.0 |
| Others | 2.7 | 2.7 | 4.7 | 4.4 | 5.4 | 5.7 | 5.8 | 7.5 | 8.4 | .. |
| *Memorandum item* | | | | | | | | | | |
| Bilateral ODA to least developed countries | 15.9 | 17.4 | 19.7 | 23.5 | 24.3 | 28.2 | 30.7 | 27.4 | 30.1 | .. |

Source: UN/DESA, based on OECD/DAC online database, available from http://www.oecd.org/dac/stats/idsonline.
a Grants and capital subscriptions. Does not include concessional lending to multilateral agencies.

Table A.21

## Commitments and net flows of financial resources, by selected multilateral institutions, 2005–2014

Billions of dollars

| | 2005 | 2006 | 2007 | 2008 | 2009 | 2010 | 2011 | 2012 | 2013 | 2014 |
|---|---|---|---|---|---|---|---|---|---|---|
| Resource commitments[a] | 71.7 | 64.7 | 74.5 | 135.2 | 193.7 | 245.4 | 163.8 | 189.8 | 130.8 | 185.0 |
| Financial institutions, excluding International Monetary Fund (IMF) | 51.4 | 55.7 | 66.6 | 76.1 | 114.5 | 119.6 | 106.8 | 96.5 | 98.8 | 99.2 |
| Regional development banks[b] | 23.7 | 23.8 | 31.9 | 36.7 | 55.1 | 46.2 | 46.9 | 43.0 | 45.8 | 41.1 |
| World Bank Group[c] | 27.7 | 31.9 | 34.7 | 39.4 | 59.4 | 73.4 | 59.9 | 53.5 | 53.0 | 58.1 |
| International Bank for Reconstruction and Development | 13.6 | 14.2 | 12.8 | 13.5 | 32.9 | 44.2 | 26.7 | 20.6 | 15.2 | 18.6 |
| International Development Association | 8.7 | 9.5 | 11.9 | 11.2 | 14.0 | 14.6 | 16.3 | 14.8 | 16.3 | 22.2 |
| International Financial Corporation | 5.4 | 8.2 | 10.0 | 14.6 | 12.4 | 14.6 | 16.9 | 18.2 | 21.4 | 17.3 |
| International Fund for Agricultural Development | 0.7 | 0.7 | 0.6 | 0.6 | 0.7 | 0.8 | 1.0 | 1.0 | 0.8 | 0.7 |
| International Monetary Fund | 12.6 | 1.0 | 2.0 | 48.7 | 68.2 | 114.1 | 45.7 | 82.5 | 19.6 | 72.7 |
| United Nations operational agencies[d] | 7.7 | 8.3 | 6.3 | 10.5 | 11.0 | 11.6 | 11.3 | 10.8 | 12.4 | 13.1 |
| Net flows | -38.8 | -24.7 | -4.4 | 43.4 | 54.6 | 64.6 | 78.7 | 35.1 | 8.8 | -5.1 |
| Financial institutions, excluding IMF | 1.6 | 6.3 | 13.6 | 24.5 | 22.6 | 27.2 | 38.0 | 26.3 | 22.2 | 25.0 |
| Regional development banks[b] | -1.5 | 3.2 | 6.2 | 21.4 | 15.7 | 9.9 | 10.5 | 8.6 | 5.7 | 11.2 |
| World Bank Group[c] | 3.1 | 3.1 | 7.4 | 3.1 | 6.9 | 17.2 | 27.6 | 17.7 | 16.5 | 13.8 |
| International Bank for Reconstruction and Development | -2.9 | -5.1 | -1.8 | -6.2 | -2.1 | 8.3 | 17.2 | 8.0 | 7.8 | 6.4 |
| International Development Association | 5.4 | 7.3 | 7.2 | 6.8 | 7.0 | 7.0 | 9.1 | 7.8 | 7.0 | 7.4 |
| International Financial Corporation | 0.6 | 0.9 | 1.9 | 2.4 | 2.1 | 1.9 | 1.2 | 1.9 | 1.6 | 0.1 |
| International Fund for Agricultural Development | 0.2 | 0.2 | 0.2 | 0.2 | 0.2 | 0.2 | 0.3 | 0.3 | 0.2 | 0.2 |
| International Monetary Fund | -40.4 | -31.0 | -18.0 | 18.9 | 32.0 | 37.4 | 40.7 | 8.9 | -13.4 | -30.1 |

Sources:  Annual reports of the relevant multilateral institutions, various issues.

a  Loans, grants, technical assistance and equity participation, as appropriate; all data are on a calendar-year basis.

b  African Development Bank (AfDB), Asian Development Bank (ADB), Caribbean Development Bank (CDB), European Bank for Reconstruction and Development (EBRD), Inter-American Development Bank (IaDB) and the International Fund for Agricultural Development (IFAD).

c  Data is for fiscal year.

d  United Nations Development Programme (UNDP), United Nations Population Fund (UNFPA), United Nations Children's Fund (UNICEF), and the World Food Programme (WFP).

# Bibliography

Acharya, Viral, and others (2015). Corporate debt in emerging economies: A threat to financial stability? Brookings Institution, Committee for International Policy Reform. Washington, D.C.: Brookings Institution and Centre for International Governance Innovation.

African Union Commission and United Nations Economic Commission for Africa (2015). Report of the High Level Panel on Illicit Financial Flows from Africa. Available from http://www.uneca.org/sites/default/files/PublicationFiles/iff_main_report_26feb_en.pdf.

Agenor, Pierre-Richard (2003). Benefits and costs of international financial integration: theory and facts. *The World Economy*, vol. 26, Issue 8, pp. 1089–1118 (August).

Ahmed, Swarnali, Maximiliano Appendino and Michele Ruta (2015). Depreciations without exports? Global value chains and the exchange rate elasticity of exports. Policy Research Working Paper, No. 7390. Washington, D.C.: World Bank, Trade and Competitiveness Global Practice Group.

Alexopoulos, Michelle, and Jon Cohen (2009). Uncertain times, uncertain measures. University of Toronto Working Paper, No. 352 (February). Department of Economics.

Ayala, Diana, Milan Nedeljkovic and Christian Saborowski (2015). What slice of the pie? The corporate bond market boom in emerging economies. IMF Working Paper, WP/15/148. Washington, D.C.: International Monetary Fund. July.

Bank for International Settlements (2015). International banking statistics at end-June 2015. BIS statistical releases. 21 October.

Bekaert, Geert, Campbell R. Harvey and Christian Lundblad (2006). Growth volatility and financial liberalization. *Journal of International Money and Finance*, vol. 25, Issue 3 (April), pp. 370–403.

Bernanke, Ben (1983). Irreversibility, uncertainty and cyclical investment. *Quarterly Journal of Economics*, vol. 97, No. 1 (February), pp. 85–106.

Blas, Javier (2015). Hedge fund losses from commodity slump sparking investor exodus. *Bloomberg Business*. 6 August. Available from http://www.bloomberg.com/news/articles/2015-08-06/hedge-fund-losses-from-commodity-slump-sparking-investor-exodus.

Bloom, Nicholas (2009). The impact of uncertainty shocks. *Econometrica*, vol. 77, No. 3 (May), pp. 623–685.

Bloom, Nicholas, Stephen Bond and John Van Reenen (2007). Uncertainty and investment dynamics. *Review of Economic Studies*, vol. 74, No. 2, pp. 391–415.

Bloom, Nicholas, Max Floetotto, and Nir Jaimovich (2007). Really uncertain business cycles. Mimeo. Stanford University.

Bloom, Nicholas, and others (2012). Really uncertain business cycles. NBER Working Paper, No. 18245. Cambridge, Massachusetts: National Bureau of Economic Research, July. Available from http://www.nber.org/papers/w18245.

Bourguignon, François (2003). The growth elasticity of poverty reduction: explaining heterogeneity across countries and time periods. In *Inequality and Growth: Theory and Policy Implications*, T. Eicher and S. Turnovsky, eds. Cambridge, Massachusetts: The MIT Press.

BP Global (2015). BP Statistical Review of World Energy, 64th ed. June 2015.

Brei, Michael, and Alfredo Schclarek (2013). Public bank lending in times of crisis. *Journal of Financial Stability*, vol. 9, Issue 4 (December), pp. 820–830.

Bruno, Valentina, and Hyun Song Shin (2015). Global dollar credit and carry trades: a firm-level analysis. BIS Working Paper, No. 510. August. Basel: Bank for International Settlements.

Büyükşahin, Bahattin, Michael S. Haigh and Michel A. Robe (2010). Commodities and Equities: Ever a 'Market of One'? Journal of Alternative Investments, vol. 12, No. 3 (Winter), pp. 75–95.

Cecchetti, Stephen G., and Enisse Kharroubi (2012). Reassessing the impact of finance on growth. BIS Working Paper, No. 381. Basel: Bank for International Settlements.

Christiaensen, Luc, Punam Chuhan-Pole and Aly Sanoh (2013). Africa's growth, poverty and inequality nexus—Fostering shared prosperity. Washington, D.C.: World Bank.

Claessens, Stijn, and Swati R. Ghosh (2013). Capital flow volatility and systemic risk in emerging markets: the policy toolkit. In *Dealing with the Challenges of Macro Financial Linkages in Emerging Markets*, Otaviano Canuto and Swati Ghosh, eds. Washington, D.C.: World Bank Publications.

Constâncio, Vítor (2015). Divergent monetary policies and the world economy. Keynote address. Hong Kong. 15 October.

Cottarelli, Carlo, and Laura Jaramillo (2012). Walking hand in hand: fiscal policy and growth in advanced economies. IMF Working Paper WP/12/137. May. Washington, D.C.: International Monetary Fund Available from https://www.imf.org/external/pubs/ft/wp/2012/wp12137.pdf.

Dasgupta, Dipak, Marc Uzan and Dominic Wilson, eds. (2001). *Capital Flows Without Crisis? Reconciling Capital Mobility and Economic Stability*. Abingdon and New York: Routledge.

De Paula, Luis Fernando R., and Antonio José Alves, Jr. (2000). External financial fragility and the 1998-1999 Brazilian currency crisis. *Journal of Post Keynesian Economics*, vol. 22, No. 4 (Summer), pp. 589–617.

Deutsche Bank (2015). Crossing the chasm. Deutsche Bank Markets Research. 27 February. Available from https://www.db.com/cr/en/docs/solar_report_full_length.pdf.

Development Initiatives (forthcoming). Aid for domestic resource mobilisation. United Kingdom.

Dobbs, Richard, and others (2015). Debt and (not much) deleveraging. February. McKinsey Global Institute, McKinsey & Company.

Easterly, William, Roumeen Islam and Joseph E. Stiglitz (2001). Shaken and stirred: explaining growth volatility. In *Annual World Bank Conference on Development Economics 2000*, Boris Pleskovic and Nicholas Stern, eds. Washington, D.C.: World Bank.

European Commission (2015). Autumn 2015 Forecast. Directorate General for Economic and Financial Affairs (DG ECFIN). Available from http://ec.europa.eu/economy_finance/eu/forecasts/2015_autumn_forecast_en.htm.

Feldstein, Martin, and Charles Horioka (1980). Domestic saving and international capital flows, *The Economic Journal*, vol. 90, No. 358 (June), pp. 314–329.

Financial Conduct Authority (2014). Commodity Markets Update. February. Available from https://www.fca.org.uk/static/documents/commodity-market-update-1402.pdf.

Financial Stability Board (2012). Identifying the effects of regulatory reforms on emerging market and developing economies: a review of potential unintended consequences. 19 June. Available from http://www.financialstabilityboard.org/wp-content/uploads/r_120619e.pdf.

Financial Stability Board (2014). Update on financial regulatory factors affecting the supply of long-term investment finance. Report to G20 Finance Ministers and Central Bank Governors. September.

Food and Agriculture Organization of the United Nations (2015). *The State of Food Insecurity in the World*. Rome.

Foster, Lucia, John Haltiwanger and C.J. Krizan (2000). Aggregate productivity growth: lessons from microeconomic evidence. In *New Developments in Productivity Analysis*, Charles R. Hulten, Edwin R. Dean and Michael J. Harper, eds. University of Chicago Press.

Foster, Lucia, John Haltiwanger and C.J. Krizan (2006). Market selection, reallocation and restructuring in the U.S. retail: trade Sector in the 1990s. *Review of Economics and Statistics*, vol. 88, No. 4 (November), pp. 748–758.

Frankel, Jeffrey A. (2010). Are bilateral remittances countercyclical? HKS Faculty Research Working Paper Series, No. RWP10-037. Cambridge, Massachusetts: Harvard University, John F. Kennedy School of Government.

Frey, Carl Benedikt (2015). The end of economic growth? How the digital economy could lead to secular stagnation. *Scientific American*, vol. 312, Issue 1.

Furceri, Davide, and Prakash Loungani (2013). Who let the GINI out? *Finance & Development*, vol. 50, No. 4 (December), pp. 25–27

Gitlin, Richard, and Brett House (2015). Just enough, just in time: improving sovereign debt restructuring for creditors, debtors and citizens. CIGI Special Report. 15 July. Ontario, Canada: Centre for International Governance Innovation.

Giuliano, Paola, and Marta Ruiz-Arranz (2009). Remittances, financial development and growth. *Journal of Development Economics*, vol. 90, Issue 1 (September), pp. 144–152.

Goossens, Ehren (2015). Cheap oil unlikely to slow growth of renewables, Citigroup says. *Bloomberg Business*. 30 March.

Gordon, Robert J. (2012). Is U.S. economic growth over? Faltering innovation confronts the six headwinds. NBER Working Paper, No. 18315. Cambridge, Massachusetts: National Bureau of Economic Research. August.

Griffith-Jones, Stephany, and José Antonio Ocampo (2010). Sovereign Wealth Funds: A Developing Country Perspective. Brussels: Foundation for European Progressive Studies. Available from http://www.jean-jaures.org/content/download/14006/134854/file/1005_SovereignWealthFunds_SGJ_JAO.pdf.

Group of Twenty (G20) (2015). G20 action plan to optimise the balance sheets of multilateral development banks.

Hoekman, Bernard (2015). Trade and growth – end of an era? In *The Global Trade Slowdown: A New Normal?* B. Hoekman, ed. London: Centre for Economic Policy Research Press.

Independent Commission for the Reform of International Corporate Taxation (2015). Declaration of the Independent Commission for the Reform of International Corporate Taxation. June. Available from http://www.icrict.org/declaration/.

Institute for International Finance (2015). EM equity and FX selloff: Crisis? Capital Markets Monitor. September.

Inter-American Development Bank (2014). Global recovery and monetary normalization: escaping a chronicle foretold? Latin American and the Caribbean Macroeconomic Report. March. Washington, D.C.

International Chamber of Commerce (2015). *ICC Global Survey on Trade Finance 2015: Rethinking Trade & Finance.* Paris. September.

International Energy Agency (2014a). *$CO_2$ Emissions from Fuel Combustions Highlights 2014.* Paris: Organization for Economic Cooperation and Development/International Energy Agency.

International Energy Agency (2014b). Fossil Fuel Subsidy Database. Available from http://www.worldenergyoutlook.org/resources/energysubsidies/fossilfuelsubsidydatabase/.

International Energy Agency (2015). *World Energy Outlook Special Report 2015: Energy and Climate Change.* Paris: Organization for Economic Cooperation and Development/International Energy Agency.

International Labour Organization (2013). *Global Wage Report 2012/13: Wages and equitable growth.* Geneva: International Labour Office.

International Monetary Fund (2006). *World Economic Outlook: Globalization and Inflation.* Washington, D.C. April.

International Monetary Fund (2010). Reserve accumulation and international monetary stability. IMF Policy Paper. 13 April. Available from https://www.imf.org/external/pp/longres.aspx?id=4456

International Monetary Fund (2011). Assessing reserve adequacy. 14 February. Available from https://www.imf.org/external/np/pp/eng/2011/021411b.pdf.

International Monetary Fund (2012). The liberalization and management of capital flows: an institutional view. 14 November. Available from http://www.imf.org/external/pp/longres.aspx?id=4720.

International Monetary Fund (2014a). 2014 Spillover Report. IMF Multilateral Policy Issues Report. 29 July. Washington, D.C.

International Monetary Fund (2014b). Papua New Guinea. 2014 Article IV Consultation. IMF Country Report No.14/325. Washington, D.C. Available from http://www.imf.org/external/pubs/ft/scr/2014/cr14325.pdf.

International Monetary Fund (2015a). *World Economic Outlook: Adjusting to Lower Commodity Prices.* Washington, D.C. October.

International Monetary Fund (2015b). *Regional Economic Outlook Update: Middle East and Central Asia.* Statistical appendix. Washington, D.C. May.

International Monetary Fund (2015c). Zambia. IMF Country Report No. 15/152. Washington, D.C. Available from https://www.imf.org/external/pubs/ft/scr/2015/cr15152.pdf.

International Monetary Fund (2015d). The role of the IMF in supporting the implementation of the post-2015 Development Agenda. 17 August. Available from http://siteresources.worldbank.org/DEVCOMMINT/Documentation/23689846/DC2015-0005(E)RoleofIMF.pdf

International Monetary Fund (2015e). *Global Financial Stability Report 2015—Vulnerabilities, Legacies, and Policy Challenges: Risks Rotating to Emerging Markets.* October. Washington, D.C.

International Monetary Fund (2015f). IMF supports reforms for more orderly sovereign debt restructurings. IMF Survey. 6 October. Available from http://www.imf.org/external/pubs/ft/survey/so/2014/NEW100614A.htm.

International Monetary Fund (2015g). Progress report on inclusion of enhanced contractual provisions in international bond contracts. 17 September. Available from http://www.imf.org/external/np/pp/eng/2015/091715.pdf.

International Monetary Fund (2015h). Lao People's Democratic Republic. 2014 Article IV Consultation. IMF Country Report No.15/45. Washington, D.C. Available from https://www.imf.org/external/pubs/ft/scr/2015/cr1545.pdf.

International Monetary Fund (2015i). Mongolia. 2014 Article IV Consultation. IMF Country Report No.15/109. Washington, D.C. Available from https://www.imf.org/external/pubs/ft/scr/2015/cr15109.pdf.

International Monetary Fund (2015j). Papua New Guinea. 2015 Article IV Consultation. IMF Country Report No.15/318. Washington, D.C. Available from http://www.imf.org/external/pubs/ft/scr/2015/cr15318.pdf.

International Monetary Fund (2015k). Iraq. 2015 Article IV Consultation. IMF Country Report No.15/325. Washington, D.C. Available from http://www.imf.org/external/pubs/ft/scr/2015/cr15235.pdf.

International Monetary Fund (2015l). Qatar. 2015 Article IV Consultation. IMF Country Report No.15/86. Washington, D.C. Available from http://www.imf.org/external/pubs/ft/scr/2015/cr1586.pdf.

International Monetary Fund (2015m). *Regional Economic Outlook: Middle East and Central Asia.* Washington, D.C. October.

International Monetary Fund (2015n). Saudi Arabia. 2015 Article IV Consultation. IMF Country Report No.15/251. Washington, D.C. Available from https://www.imf.org/external/pubs/ft/scr/2015/cr15251.pdf.

Kanbur, Ravi (2004). Growth, Inequality and Poverty: Some Hard Questions. Commentary prepared for the State of the World Conference, Princeton Institute for International and Regional Studies, Princeton University, 13-14 February.

Kar, Dev, and Joseph Spanjers (2015). Illicit Financial Flows from Developing Countries: 2004-2013. Washington, D.C.: Global Financial Integrity. December. Available from http://www.gfintegrity.org/wp-content/uploads/2015/12/IFF-Update_2015-Final.pdf.

Keynes, John Maynard (1936). *The General Theory of Employment, Interest, and Money.* London, United Kingdom: Palgrave Macmillan.

Kharas, Homi, Annalisa Prizzon and Andrew Rogerson (2014). Financing the post-2015 Sustainable Development Goals: a rough roadmap. London: Overseas Development Institute. Available from http://www.odi.org/sites/odi.org.uk/files/odi-assets/publications-opinion-files/9374.pdf.

Knotek, Edward S., and Shujaat Khan (2011). How do households respond to uncertainty shocks? *Economic Review*, Second Quarter, pp. 63–92. Federal Reserve Bank of Kansas City.

Kose, M. Ayhan, Eswar S. Prasad and Marco E. Terrones (2005). Growth and volatility in an era of globalization. IMF Staff Papers, vol. 52, Special Issue. Washington, D.C.: International Monetary Fund.

Krugman, Paul (2009). Finance myth busting, third world edition. Weblog, 9 November. Available from http://krugman.blogs.nytimes.com/2009/11/09/finance-mythbusting-third-world-edition/.

Lane, Philip R., and Gian Maria Milesi-Ferretti (2007). The external wealth of nations mark II: revised and extended estimates of foreign assets and liabilities, 1970–2004. *Journal of International Economics*, vol. 73, Issue 2 (November), pp. 223–250.

Leigh, Daniel, and others (2015). Exchange rates still matter for trade. VOX, 30 October. Available from http://www.voxeu.org/article/exchange-rates-still-matter-trade.

Levine, Ross (2005). Finance and growth: theory and evidence. In *Handbook of Economic Growth*, vol. 1A, Philippe Aghion and Steven N. Durlauf, eds. Amsterdam: North-Holland Elsevier.

Loayza, Norman V., Claudio Raddatz (2006). The composition of growth matters for poverty alleviation. World Bank Policy Research Working Paper, No. 4077. Washington, D.C.: World Bank. December.

Lloyd's (2014). Catastrophe modelling and climate change. London.

Martin, Matthew (2015). Private and blended development cooperation: assessing their effectiveness and impact for achieving the SDGs. 2016 Development Cooperation Forum Policy Brief, No. 7. July.

Mayda, Anna Maria (2010). International migration: a panel data analysis of the determinants of bilateral flows. *Journal of Population Economics*, vol. 23, Issue 4, pp. 1249–1274.

Mirabile, Mariana, Julia Benn and Cécile Sangaré (2013). Guarantees for development. OECD Development Cooperation Working Papers, No. 11. Available from http://dx.doi.org/10.1787/5k407lx5b8f8-en.

Mohapatra, Sanket, George Joseph and Dilip Ratha (2009). Remittances and natural disasters: Ex-post response and contribution to ex-ante preparedness. Policy Research Working Paper, No. 4972. Washington, D.C: World Bank.

Muchhala, Bhumika, ed. (2007). *Ten Years After: Revisiting the Asian Financial Crisis*. Washington, D.C.: Woodrow Wilson International Center for Scholars, Asia Program. Available from https://www.wilsoncenter.org/sites/default/files/Asia_TenYearsAfter_rpt.pdf.

Murina, Marina, and Alessandro Nicita (2014). Trading with conditions: the effect of sanitary and phytosanitary measures on lower income countries' agricultural exports. Policy Issues in International Trade and Commodities Research Study Series, No. 68. Geneva: United Nations Conference on Trade and Development.

Narayan, Paresh K., Seema Narayan and Sagarika Mishra (2011). Do remittances induce inflation? Fresh evidence from developing countries. *Southern Economic Journal*, vol. 77, No. 4 (July), pp. 914–933.

National Oceanic and Atmospheric Administration (2015). Climate Monitoring Monthly Available from www.noaa.gov (accessed on 10 October).

Ollivaud, Patrice, Elena Rusticelli and Cyrille Schwellnus (2015). The changing role of the exchange rate for macroeconomic adjustment. OECD Economics Department Working Papers, No. 1190. Paris: Organization for Economic Cooperation and Development. March.

Organization for Economic Cooperation and Development (2015a). *OECD Employment Outlook 2015*. Paris.

Organization for Economic Cooperation and Development (2015b). Climate finance in 2013-14 and the USD 100 billion goal. In collaboration with Climate Policy Initiative (CPI).

Organization for Economic Cooperation and Development (2015c). Measuring and monitoring BEPS, Action 11 - 2015 Final Report. OECD/G20 Base Erosion and Profit Shifting Project. Paris.

Organization for Economic Cooperation and Development (2015d). Developing a multilateral instrument to modify bilateral tax treaties. Action 15: 2014 Deliverable. OECD/G20 Base Erosion and Profit Shifting Project. Paris.

Organization for Economic Cooperation and Development (2015e). Work underway for the development of the BEPS Multilateral Instrument. 28 May. Available from http://www.oecd.org/tax/treaties/work-underway-for-the-development-of-the-beps-multilateral-instrument.htm.

Organization for Economic Cooperation and Development (2015f). Development aid stable in 2014 but flows to poorest countries still falling. 8 April. Paris.

Organization for Economic Cooperation and Development (2015g). Developing countries' participation in global value chains—implications for trade and trade-related policies. 30 January. TAD/TC/WP(2014)12/FINAL.

Orozco, Manuel, and Julia Yansura (2015). Remittances and financial inclusion: opportunities for Central America. Inter-American Dialogues. Available from http://www.thedialogue.org/wp-content/uploads/2015/06/RemitFinancialInclusion_FINAL_223.pdf.

Polterovich, Victor, and Vladimir Popov (2004). Accumulation of foreign exchange reserves and long term economic growth. In *Slavic Eurasia's Integration into the World Economy*, Tabata Shinichiro and Iwashita Akihiro, eds. Sapporo, Japan: Slavic Research Center, Hokkaido University.

Quiroga, Javiera (2015). Chile's economic outlook takes turn for worse, Valdes says. *Bloomberg Business*. 6 July. Available from http://www.bloomberg.com/news/articles/2015-07-06/chile-s-economic-outlook-takes-a-turn-for-the-worse-valdes-says.

Ramey, Garey, and Valerie A. Ramey (1995). Cross-country evidence on the link between volatility and growth. *American Economic Review*, vol. 85, No. 5, pp. 1138–1151.

Roy, Ripon, and Md. Moklesur Rahman (2014). An empirical analysis of remittance-inflation relationship in Bangladesh: post-floating exchange rate scenario. MPRA Paper, No. 55190 (April). Munich Personal RePEc Archive. Available from http://mpra.ub.uni-muenchen.de/55190/.

Sahay, Ratna, and others (2015). Rethinking financial deepening: stability and growth in emerging markets. IMF Staff Discussion Note, No. SDN/15/08. May.

Schumacher, Julian, Christoph Trebesch and Henrik Enderlein (2014). Sovereign defaults in court: the rise of creditor litigation. May.

Sdralevich, Carlo, and others (2014). Subsidy reform in the Middle East and North Africa: Recent progress and challenges ahead. Washington, D.C: International Monetary Fund.

Solow, Robert M. (1956). A contribution to the theory of economic growth. *Quarterly Journal of Economics*, vol. 70, No. 1 (February), pp. 65–94.

Spencer, David (2014). Transfer pricing: formulary apportionment is not a panacea, Part 6. *Journal of International Taxation*. September.

Spratt, Stephen, and Lily Ryan-Collins (2012). Development finance institutions and infrastructure: a systematic review of evidence for development additionality. Report commissioned by the Private Infrastructure Development Group, Surrey, United Kingdom.

Standard & Poor's Rating Services (2013). Inside credit: shadow banking looks set to capture a larger share of project financing in 2013. April.

Stiglitz, Joseph E., and others (2006). *Stability with Growth: Macroeconomics, Stabilization, and Development*. New York: Oxford University Press.

Strawson, Tim, and Guto Ifan (2014). Aid for domestic resource mobilisation: how much is there? Development Initiatives Briefing. February. United Kingdom.

Summers, Lawrence H. (2014). U.S. economic prospects: secular stagnation, hysteresis, and the zero lower bound. *Business Economics*, vol. 49, No. 2 (February).

Thirlwall, Anthony Philip (2011). Balance of payments constrained growth models: history and overview, *PSL Quarterly Review*, vol. 64. No. 259, pp. 307–351.

UN System Task Team on the Post-2015 UN Development Agenda (2013). Challenges in raising private sector resources for financing sustainable development. Chapter 3 in UNTT Working Group on Sustainable Development Financing. Available from https://sustainabledevelopment.un.org/content/documents/2106Chapter%203-challenges%20in%20raising%20private%20sector%20resources.pdf.

United Nations (1990). *World Economic Survey 1990: Current Trends and Policies in the World Economy*. Sales No. E.90.II.C.1.

United Nations (2013). *World Economic Situation and Prospects 2013*. Sales No. E.13.II.C.2.

United Nations (2015a). World economic situation and prospects as of mid-2015. May. E/2015/73.

United Nations (2015b). *World Economic Situation and Prospects 2015*. Sales No. E.15. II.C.2.

United Nations (2015c). *Millennium Development Goals Report 2015*. Sales No. E.15.I.7.

United Nations (2015d). *MDG Gap Task Force Report 2015: Taking Stock of the Global Partnership for Development*. Sales No. E.15.I.5.

United Nations, Economic and Social Commission for Asia and the Pacific (2015a). Report of the Working Group on Enhancing Financial Cooperation. Forthcoming.

United Nations, Economic and Social Commission for Asia and the Pacific (2015b). *2014 Year-end Update: Economic and Social Survey of Asia and the Pacific*. Bangkok.

United Nations, Economic and Social Commission for Asia and the Pacific (2016). *Economic and Social Survey of Asia and the Pacific*. Forthcoming.

United Nations, Economic Commission for Africa (2013). *Economic Report on Africa 2013: Making the Most of Africa's Commodities: Industrializing for Growth, Jobs and Economic Transformation*. Addis Ababa.

United Nations, Economic Commission for Africa (2015). *Economic Report on Africa 2015: Industrializing through Trade*. Addis Ababa.

United Nations, General Assembly (2015a). Transforming our world: the 2030 Agenda for Sustainable Development. Resolution 70/1 adopted by the General Assembly on 25 September 2015.

United Nations, General Assembly (2015b). Report of the Secretary-General on International trade and development. A/70/277. 4 August.

United Nations, General Assembly (2015c). Basic principles on sovereign debt restructuring processes. Resolution 69/319 adopted by the General Assembly on 10 September 2015.

United Nations Conference on Trade and Development (2013). *World Investment Report 2013—Global Value Chains: Investment and Trade for Development*. Sales No. E.13.II.D.5.

United Nations Conference on Trade and Development (2014). *Trade and Development Report 2014: Global Governance and Policy Space for Development*. Sales No. E.14.II.D.4.

United Nations Conference on Trade and Development (2015a). Note by the UNCTAD secretariat on evolution of the international trading system and its trends from a development perspective. TD/B/62/2. 10 July.

United Nations Conference on Trade and Development (2015b). Briefing note on current status of WTO negotiations. 25 August.

United Nations Conference on Trade and Development (2015c). *World Investment Report 2015: Reforming International Investment Governance*. Sales No. E.15.II.D.5.

United Nations Conference on Trade and Development (2015d). *Trade and Development Report 2015: Making the International Financial Architecture Work for Development*. Sales No. E.15.II.D.4.

United Nations Conference on Trade and Development (forthcoming). Trans-Pacific Partnership Agreement: Possible implications for third countries. UNCTAD Policy Brief.

United Nations Environment Programme (2015). *Global Trends in Renewable Energy Investment*. Prepared by Frankfurt School – UNEP Centre and Bloomberg New Energy Finance.

United Nations Framework Convention on Climate Change (2015a). Synthesis report on the aggregate effect of the intended nationally determined contributions. 30 October. FCCC/CP/2015/7.

United Nations Framework Convention on Climate Change (2015b). Global response to climate change keeps door open to 2 degree C temperature limit. Press release, 30 October. Available from http://newsroom.unfccc.int/unfccc-newsroom/indc-synthesis-report-press-release/.

United Nations World Tourism Organization (2015a). *UNWTO Tourism Highlights*. Madrid. Available from http://mkt.unwto.org/highlights.

United Nations World Tourism Organization (2015b). *UNWTO World Tourism Barometer*. Madrid. Available from http://mkt.unwto.org/barometer.

United Nations World Tourism Organization and International Labour Organization (2011). Economic crisis, international tourism decline and its impact on the poor: an analysis of the effects of the global economic crisis and on the employment of poor and vulnerable groups in the tourism sector. New York: United Nations Global Pulse.

United Nations World Tourism Organization and UN Women (2011). *Global Report on Women in Tourism 2010*. Madrid and New York.

Vanzetti, David (2015a). The impact of trade and trade agreements on employment in developing countries. Geneva: United Nations Conference on Trade and Development.

Vanzetti, David (2015b). ACP agricultural trade and the WTO negotiations. Geneva: United Nations Conference on Trade and Development.

Williams, Marion V. (2005). Foreign exchange reserves – how much is enough? Twentieth Adlith Brown Memorial Lecture delivered by Dr. Marion V. Williams, Governor of the Central Bank of Barbados, at the Central Bank of the Bahamas, Nassau, 2 November. Available from http://www.bis.org/review/r060123c.pdf.

World Bank (2015a). World Bank Quarterly External Debt Statistics. Available from http://go.worldbank.org/6V603CE490.

World Bank (2015b). *World Development Indicators 2015*. Washington, D.C.

World Bank (2015c). Migration and Development Brief, No. 24 (13 April). Available from http://siteresources.worldbank.org/INTPROSPECTS/Resources/334934-1288990760745/MigrationandDevelopmentBrief24.pdf.

World Bank (2015d). International financial institutions announce $400 Billion to achieve Sustainable Development Goals. 10 July. Available from http://www.worldbank.org/en/news/press-release/2015/07/10/international-financial-institutions-400-billion-sustainable-development-goals.

World Bank (2015e). 2015 Shareholding Review: Report to Governors. 28 September. DC2015-007. Available from http://siteresources.worldbank.org/DEVCOMMINT/Documentation/23689867/DC2015-0007(E)Shareholding.pdf.

World Bank and Ecofys (2015). *State and Trends of Carbon Pricing 2015*. Washington, D.C.

World Economic Forum (2014). Infrastructure Investment Policy Blueprint. February. Available from http://www3.weforum.org/docs/WEF_II_InfrastructureInvestmentPolicyBlueprint_Report_2014.pdf.

World Trade Organization (2015a). Report on G-20 trade measures (mid-October 2014 to mid-May 2015). 15 June.

World Trade Organization (2015b). Falling import demand, lower commodity prices push down trade growth prospects. Press release PRESS/752. 30 September. Available from https://www.wto.org/english/news_e/pres15_e/pr752_e.htm.

World Trade Organization and IDE-JETRO (2011). Trade patterns and global value chains in East Asia: from trade in goods to trade in tasks. Geneva.

Yang, Dean (2008). International migration, remittances and household investment: evidence from Philippine migrants' exchange rate shocks. The Economic Journal, vol. 118, No. 528 (April), pp. 591–630.